The Framework of the Story of Jesus

The Framework of the Story of Jesus

*Literary-Critical Investigations
of the Earliest Jesus Tradition*

Karl Ludwig Schmidt

TRANSLATED AND EDITED BY

Byron R. McCane

CASCADE *Books* · Eugene, Oregon

THE FRAMEWORK OF THE STORY OF JESUS
Literary-Critical Investigations of the Earliest Jesus Tradition

Copyright © 2021 Byron R. McCane. All rights reserved. Except for brief quotations in critical publications or reviews, no part of this book may be reproduced in any manner without prior written permission from the publisher. Write: Permissions, Wipf and Stock Publishers, 199 W. 8th Ave., Suite 3, Eugene, OR 97401.

Cascade Books
An Imprint of Wipf and Stock Publishers
199 W. 8th Ave., Suite 3
Eugene, OR 97401

www.wipfandstock.com

PAPERBACK ISBN: 978-1-5326-7557-7
HARDCOVER ISBN: 978-1-5326-7558-4
EBOOK ISBN: 978-1-5326-7559-1

Cataloguing-in-Publication data:

Names: Schmidt, Karl Ludwig, 1891–1956, author. | McCane, Byron R., translator and editor.

Title: The framework of the story of Jesus : literary-critical investigations of the earliest Jesus tradition / Karl Ludwig Schmidt ; translated and edited by Byron R. McCane.

Note: [German ed.: *Der Rahmen der Geschichte Jesu*, 1919].

Description: Eugene, OR: Cascade Books, 2021. | Includes bibliographical references and index.

Identifiers: ISBN 978-1-5326-7557-7 (paperback). | ISBN 978-1-5326-7558-4 (hardcover). | ISBN 978-1-5326-7559-1 (ebook).

Subjects: LCSH: Bible—Gospels—Criticism, interpretation, etc. | Jesus Christ—Biography—Sources. | Jesus Christ—Sources.

Classification: BT297 S34 2021 (print). | BT297 (ebook).

04/09/21

Contents

Abbreviations | xi

Introduction: Karl Ludwig Schmidt, Der Rahmen der Geschichte Jesu, *Form Criticism, and Gospel Genre*—Byron R. McCane | xiii

Preface | xxi

Intoduction: The Problem of the Framework of the Story of Jesus: Historical and Methodological Issues | 1

1. John the Baptist and Jesus (Mark 1:1–13par.) | 16
   John the Baptist (Mark 1:1–8; Matt 3:1–12; Luke 3:1–20) | 16
   The Baptism of Jesus (Mark 1:9–11; Matt 3:13–17; Luke 3:21–22) | 23
   The Age of Jesus (Luke 3:23) | 25
   The Temptation (Mark 1:12–13; Matt 4:1–11; Luke 4:1–13) | 26

2. Jesus' Activity in Galilee (Mark 1:14–45par.) | 28
   Jesus' Entry into Galilee (Mark 1:14–16; Matt 4:12–17; Luke 4:14–15) | 28
   Jesus' Inaugural Sermon in Nazareth (Luke 4:16–30) | 32
   The Calling of the First Disciples (Mark 1:16–20; Matt 4:18–22; Luke 5:1–11) | 36
   Excursus: Luke's Configuration of the Outline of the Story of Jesus | 38
   In the Synagogue at Capernaum (Mark 1:21–28; Luke 4:31–37) | 41
   The Healing of Peter's Mother-in-Law (Mark 1:29–31; Matt 8:14–15; Luke 4:38–39) | 47
   Healings in the Evening at Peter's House (Mark 1:32–34; Matt 8:16–17; Luke 4:40–41) | 48

Jesus Escapes into Solitude (Mark 1:35–38; Luke 4:42–53) | 49

Jesus' Preaching Tour in Galilee (Mark 1:39; Matt 4:23–25; Luke 4:44) | 51

The Healing of a Leper (Mark 1:40–45; Matt 8:1–4; Luke 5:12–16) | 54

> *Excursus:* The Complex of Mark 1:14–45 | 57
>
> *Excursus:* The Complex of Mark 1:14–45 in Matthew: Jesus' First Acts in Galilee | 59
>
>> Jesus' Teaching: The Sermon on the Mount (Matt 5–7) | 60
>>
>> Jesus' Deeds: The Centurion from Capernaum (Matt 8:5–13; Luke 7:1–10) | 60
>
> *Excursus:* The Complex of Mark 1:14–45 in Luke | 66
>
> *Excursus:* Literary and Historical Evaluation of Mark 1:14–45par | 66

3. Jesus' Conflicts with the Leaders of the People (Mark 2:1—3:6 par.) | 69

The Healing of a Paralytic (Mark 2:1–12; Matt 9:1–8; Luke 5:17–26) | 69

The Call of Levi and Dinner with the Tax Collectors (Mark 2:13–17; Matt 9:9–13; Luke 5:27–32) | 72

The Question about Fasting (Mark 2:18–22; Matt 9:14–17; Luke 5:33–39) | 77

Plucking Grain on the Sabbath (Mark 2:23–28; Matt 12:1–8; Luke 6:1–5) | 79

The Healing of the Withered Hand (Mark 3:1–6; Matt 12:9–14; Luke 6:6–11) | 88

Conclusion: Mark 2:1—3:6par | 92

4. Jesus and the People (Mark 3:7—6:13par.) | 94

Crowds and Healings (Mark 3:7–12; Matt 12:15–21; Luke 6:17–19) | 94

The Call of the Twelve Apostles (Mark 3:13–19; Matt 10:1–42; Luke 6:12–16) | 98

> *Excursus:* A Lukan Insertion (Luke 6:20—8:3) | 102
>
>> The Sermon on the Plain (Luke 6:20–49) | 102
>>
>> The Young Man from Nain (Luke 7:11–17) | 103
>>
>> John the Baptist's Question and Jesus' Testimony (Luke 7:18–35; Matt 11:2–19) | 105

> The Sinful Woman in Simon's House (Luke 7:36–50) | 107
>
> Controversy Stories (Mark 3:20–35; Matt 12:22–50; Luke 11:14–31; 8:19–21) | 109

Parables of Jesus (Mark 4:1–34; Matt 13:1–52; Luke 8:4–18) | 116

Three Stories on and around the Sea of Galilee (Mark 4:35—5:43 par.) | 124

> The Storm at Sea (Mark 4:35–41; Matt 8:23–27; Luke 8:22–25) | 124
>
> The Gerasene Demoniac (Mark 5:1–20; Matt 8:28–34; Luke 8:26–39) | 127
>
> Jairus' Daughter and the Hemorrhaging Woman (Mark 5:21–43; Matt 9:18–26; Luke 8:40–56) | 132
>
> *Excursus:* The Special Connection of the Three Stories: The Itinerary and Arrangement of Mark 4:35—5:43par. | 137

Jesus' Rejection in Nazareth (Mark 6:1–6; Matt 13:53–58) | 139

The Sending out of the Disciples (Mark 6:7–13; Matt 10:1–42; Luke 9:1–6; 10:1–12) | 148

> *Excursus:* Matthew 9:35—10:42: A Transitional Piece in the Matthean Outline | 155
>
> *Excursus:* The Complex Mark 3:7—6:13 and Its Rearrangement by Matthew and Luke | 156

5. Jesus outside of Galilee in Gentile Territory (Mark 6:14—8:26par.) | 158

Herod's Judgment upon Jesus (Mark 6:14–16; Matt 14:1–2; Luke 9:7–9) | 158

The Death of John the Baptist (Mark 6:17–29; Matt 14:3–12) | 161

Mark 6:30 | 164

> *Excursus:* The Itinerary of Mark 6:31—8:26 | 166

Jesus, Disciples, and the People (Mark 6:31–33; Matt 14:13; Luke 9:10–11a) | 171

The Feeding of the Five Thousand (Mark 6:34–44; Matt 14:14–21; Luke 9:11b [10]–17); The Feeding of the Four Thousand (Mark 8:1–10; Matt 15:32–39) | 175

Jesus Walks on the Sea (Mark 6:45–52; Matt 14:22–33) | 178

Jesus' Activity in the Area of Gennesaret (Mark 6:53–56; Matt 14:34–36) | 179

Controversies over Hand-washing, Purity, and Impurity
(Mark 7:1–23; Matt 15:1–20) | 180

The Canaanite Woman (Mark 7:24–30; Matt 15:21–28) | 182

The Healing of a Deaf and Dumb Man (Mark 7:31–37);
The Healing of Several Sick People (Matt 15:29–31) | 184

The Pharisees Seek a Sign (Mark 8:11–12; Matt 16:1–4; Luke 11:29;
11:16; 12:54–56) | 186

A Conversation about Leaven (Mark 8:13–21; Matt 16:5–12;
Luke 12:1) | 187

The Blind Man of Bethsaida (Mark 8:22–26) | 189

Excursus: The Complex Mark 6:14—8:26: The Question of
the Arrangement and Settings for the Activity of Jesus | 191

Excursus: Special Perspectives for the Problem of the Location
of Jesus' Activities: Woes over Galilean Towns (Matt 11:20–24;
Luke 10:13–15) | 193

Excursus: Allegorical Place Names? | 194

Excursus: The Complex Mark 6:14—8:26 in Matthew | 196

Excursus: The Complex Mark 6:14—8:26 in Luke: Critique of
Arrangement and Content | 197

6. Jesus and His Disciples, The Approaching Passion
(Mark 8:27—10:45par.) | 199

Peter's Confession at Caesarea Philippi (Mark 8:27–30;
Matt 16:13–23; Luke 9:18–22) | 199

Three Predictions of Jesus' Suffering (Mark 8:31–31: Matt 16:21; Luke
9:22; Mark 9:30–32; Matt 17:22–23; Luke 9:43b–45; Mark 10:32–34;
Matt 20:17–19; Luke 18:31–34) | 201

Satan and Peter (Mark 8:32b–33; Matt 16:22–23) | 203

Sayings about the Sufferings of Disciples (Mark 8:34—9:1;
Matt 16:24–28; Luke 9:23–27) | 204

Jesus' Transfiguration (Mark 9:2–8; Matt 17:1–8; Luke 9:28–36) | 205

Conversation on the Way Down from the Mount of Transfiguration
(Mark 9:9–13; Matt 17:9–13) | 208

The Healing of an Epileptic Boy (Mark 9:14–29; Matt 17:14–21;
Luke 9:37–43a) | 209

The Disciples Argue over Status (Mark 9:33–37; Matt 18:1–5;
Luke 9:46–48) | 211

The Temple Tax (Matt 17:24–27) | 214

Further Sayings with the Disciples (Mark 9:38–50;
Matt 18:6–35 et al; Luke 9:49 et al.) | 215

Marriage and Divorce (Mark 10:1–12; Matt 19:1–12) | 219

The Blessing of Children (Mark 10:13–16; Matt 19:13–15;
Luke 18:15–17) | 222

On the Danger of Riches (Mark 10:17–31; Matt 19:16–30;
Luke 18:18–30) | 222

Jesus and the Sons of Zebedee (Mark 10:35–45; Matt 20:20–28) | 225

Excursus: Summary: Mark 8:27—10:45 and Matt 16:13–20, 28 | 220

7. Luke's Travel Narrative (Luke 9:51—19:27) | 228

Introductory Issues | 228

General Characteristics | 228

Overview of the Parts of the Framework | 229

The Textual History of the Framing Pieces | 236

Pericope Introductions Adopted by Luke | 238

Pericope Introductions Formed and Reformed by Luke:
Chronological and Topographical | 240

Two Jericho Stories: Luke 18:35–43par; 19:1–10 | 244

Two Notes from the Journey to Jerusalem: Luke 9:53; 13:33 | 245

The Good Samaritan (Luke 9:51, 52–55) | 245

Excursus: Literary and Historical Evaluation of the Lukan
Travel Narrative | 249

Excursus: A Perspective on the Question about the Length
and Location of the Ministry of Jesus | 250

The Prophecy over Jerusalem | 250

8. Jesus' Final Activity in Jerusalem (Mark 10:46—13:37 par) | 253

Introduction | 253
    The Topography and Chronology of the Section | 253
    The Text History of the Framing Pieces | 254
Omissions | 256
Insertions | 256
Rearrangements | 260
    Excursus: Remodeling of Mark's Pericope Introductions by Matthew and Luke | 262
    Excursus: The Relationship between Framing and Content in Markan Pericopes | 265
    Excursus: Literary and Historical Evaluation of Mark 10:46—13:37 and Parallels | 278
    Excursus: Perspectives on the Question of the Length of Jesus' Ministry: Jesus' Earlier Visits to Jerusalem | 279

9. Jesus' Suffering and Death: Mark 14–15 (= Matt 26–27 = Luke 22–23) | 281
    The General Character of the Passion Narrative: The Logical Topography and Chronology | 281
    Some Seams and Gaps in the Passion Narrative | 283

10. The Pre-histories | 286
    The Matthean Pre-History | 286
    The Lukan Pre-History | 287
    Summary: Matthew 1–2 and Luke 1–2 | 291
    The Prologue: Luke 1:1–4 | 292

Conclusion: The Framework of the Story of Jesus in Mark, Matthew, and Luke | 294

Bibliography | 295
Authors Index | 301
Subject Index | 305

Abbreviations

Sigla for Biblical Codexes, Manuscripts, and Versions

ℵ	Codex Sinaiticus
ℵ*	Codex Sinaiticus, original scribe
33	minuscule 33 (formerly Codex Colbertinus 2844)
Γ	Codex Tischendorfianus IV
Δ	Codex Sangallensis
Λ	Codex Tischendorfianus III
X	Codex Monacensis
A	Codex Alexandrinus
B	Codex Vaticanus
C	Codex Ephremi
D	Codex Bezae (Cambrigiensis)
E	Codex Basiliensis
F	Codex Boreelianus
G	Codex Wolfii
L	Codex Regius

aeth	Ethiopic
arm	Armenian
cop	Coptic
Epiph	Epiphanius
go	Gothic

gr	various Greek mss.
Iren	Irenaeus
it	Itala (Old Latin mss.)
lat	Latin
LXX	Septuagint
Mss.	manuscripts
pesh	Peshitta
ς	Stephanus, Textus Receptus
syr	Syriac
syr^{cur}	Syriac Curetonian Gospels
syr^{sin}	Syriac Sinaitic palimpsest ms.
Tert	Tertullian
vg	Vulgate

Journals and Series

BibSt	Biblische Studien
BZ	Biblische Zeitschrift
BZAW	Beihefte zur Zeitschrift für die alttestamentliche Wissenschaft
FRLANT	Forschungen zur Religion und Literatur des Alten und Neuen Testament
HNT	Handkommentar zum Neuen Testament
KNT	Kommentar zum Neuen Testament
ThRu	Theologische Rundschau
TLZ	Theologische Literatur Zeitung
TQ	Theologischen Quartalschrift
TUGAL	Texte und Untersuchungen zur Geschichte der altchristlichen Literatur
ZDPV	Zeitschrift des deutschen Palästina-Vereins
ZKT	Zeitschrift für katholische Theologie
ZNW	Zeitschrift für die neutestamentliche Wissenschaft
ZWT	Zeitschrift für wissenschaftliche Theologie

Introduction

Karl Ludwig Schmidt, Der Rahmen der Geschichte Jesu, Form Criticism, and Gospel Genre

Schmidt's Life and Career

KARL LUDWIG SCHMIDT CAME into the world on February 5, 1891, the first-born child of working-class parents in Frankfurt, Germany.[1] During his childhood years, there was no reason to suspect that this son of a shoemaker and a farmer's daughter would one day rise to the highest levels of German scholarship, taking his place among the most influential voices in New Testament studies during the twentieth century. On the contrary, the early signs all indicated that this eldest son of Anton Friedrich Schmidt and Johanette Dorothea Schmidt (née Schwanz) would follow in his father's footsteps, learning a trade and leading a quiet life. Yet young Karl Ludwig's academic performance in the local *Volksschule* was of such high quality that, despite his family's modest circumstances, he was offered admission to the prestigious Lessing Gymnasium in Frankfurt. There he finished first in his class every year, excelling in Latin, Greek, and ancient history. Based upon this strong record, the Gymnasium faculty arranged for him to be admitted to university studies at Marburg, where he attended advanced seminars in ancient history and philology, and for the first time also in theology. From Marburg, Schmidt went on to Berlin, at that time the leading theological faculty in the country, where he studied with Adolf von Harnack and Adolf Deissmann. After receiving his doctorate in 1913 with a dissertation on the

---

1. The biographical section of this essay was substantially assisted by Prof. Dr. Andreas Mühling, professor of history at Trier and the author of the best biography of K. L. Schmidt: *Karl Ludwig Schmidt: "Und Wissenschaft ist Leben"*, Arbeiten zur Kirchengeschichte 66 (Berlin: de Gruyter, 1997). Prof. Mühling kindly responded to several important questions, and his understanding of Schmidt's life and work was consistently of value in the work of translation.

problem of the unity of the Gospel of John, Schmidt became *Assistent* to Deissmann, who would remain his most significant influence and mentor. In 1918 Schmidt's *Habilitationsschrift* was submitted to the faculty and published the following year under the title, *Der Rahmen der Geschichte Jesu: Literarkritische Untersuchungen zur Ältesten Jesusüberlieferung*. It was dedicated to Deissmann "with grateful respect."

In Berlin Karl Ludwig Schmidt made the acquaintance of Ursula von Wegnern, the daughter of a government minister whose family line could be traced back to Martin Luther. In view of her family's social and political standing, Fraulein von Wegnern and Herr Doktor Schmidt made an unlikely couple, but a couple they certainly were, and it was during this time in the social orbit of the family von Wegnern that Schmidt's social and political horizons were significantly broadened. His outlook came increasingly into harmony with the broad current of German liberalism, and he identified as a Social Democrat, becoming an active proponent of progressive public policy. A wedding was planned for 1915, but the outbreak the First World War forced an indefinite postponement.

Drafted into the German army on February 15, 1915, Schmidt underwent basic training and was inducted into an infantry battalion as a rifleman. Deissmann later claimed that Schmidt had volunteered for military service, but Schmidt's son Martin has specifically denied that claim. In his role as a rifleman, Schmidt saw combat action on September 13, 1915, during a march along the River Styr in today's Republic of Belarus. The unit had stopped for a short rest, when suddenly and without warning they came under heavy artillery bombardment. Corporal Schmidt, who had become absorbed in the reading of a theological article, did not take cover immediately and was struck by shrapnel in his right hand and in the right side of his head. These wounds were serious, and Schmidt spent the next nine months in a military hospital. Much of the work on *Der Rahmen* was done during these months of healing and recuperation, as he lay in his hospital bed and wrote out the manuscript longhand, using only his left hand. The consequences of Schmidt's war wounds would prove to be long-lasting, and complications and side-effects would plague him for the rest of his life. Never again would he be able to write clearly with his right hand, for example, and chronic headaches would gradually develop into a severe health problem. For his military service, Schmidt was awarded the *Eiserne Kreuz 2te Klasse* (Iron Cross, 2nd class) but no one in his family or circle of friends could recall ever seeing him wear the medal in public.

After his release from the hospital, Schmidt's military service had come to its end, and he returned to his position on the faculty at Berlin, where his academic career quickly resumed its steep upward trajectory.

Over the next ten years he would hold faculty posts at Berlin, Giessen, and Jena, developing along the way both scholarly and personal relationships with many of the most influential theological leaders in Germany at that time, including Paul Tillich, Albert Schweitzer, and Karl Barth. In 1923 he published his Habilitationsschrift under the title of *Die Stellung der Evangelien in der allgemeinen Literaturgeschichte* (The Place of the Gospels in the General History of Literature), an extended essay demonstrating on literary grounds that the New Testament Gospels belong to a genre of oral literature designated by Schmidt as *Kleinliteratur*. With this term Schmidt labeled a genre of literature that was, like the Gospels, the written form of an earlier oral tradition. Scholarly response to the book was positive, and on the combined strength of *Der Rahmen* and *Die Stellung*, Karl Ludwig Schmidt took his place alongside Martin Dibelius and Rudolf Bultmann in a scholarly triumvirate of *Formgeschichte*, at that time the most influential method in German New Testament studies. Today these two books comprise the body of work for which Schmidt is most widely known.

During this period in his career, and especially in his new role as founder and editor of the journal *Theologische Blätter*, Schmidt emerged as an influential voice in both academic and popular discussion across a wide range of public issues in theology and ethics. As a member of the Social Democratic Party (SPD), he was active in political discussions related to the struggling Weimar republic. On the home front, he and Ursula had three children—two sons and a daughter—and his steadily rising salary afforded them an increasingly comfortable lifestyle. In 1929, at the age of thirty-eight, Schmidt was appointed to the chair in New Testament studies at Bonn, at that time widely regarded as the premiere theological faculty in the country.

For Karl Ludwig Schmidt and his family, life was good; indeed, it was very good. Yet two dark clouds were gathering out on the edge of the horizon. The first of these was a rising level of concern among New Testament scholars in Germany about the sharp edge of Karl Ludwig Schmidt's tongue and pen. In his role as editor of *Theologische Blätter*, Schmidt now occupied an academic pulpit of considerable prominence, from which he could and did express himself on a wide range of issues in ongoing theological discussion. Significant concerns were beginning to arise about the manner in which Schmidt was giving voice to his opinions and judgments, especially his pointed criticisms of other scholars. Years later, at Schmidt's funeral, Oscar Cullmann would eulogize him as "a fighter," and that was (as is fitting for a eulogy) putting the matter nicely. In a similar vein, Karl Barth once said that Karl Ludwig Schmidt was his superior "in both erudition and combativeness." The evidence indicates that Schmidt did indeed mean what he said, as throughout his career he consistently regarded frank and spirited exchange as essential to substantial academic debate. Yet many of his remarks could be (and were) taken *ad hominem*. Perhaps his working-class background was playing a long-term role here, as Schmidt never seems to have quite mastered the full range of verbal sophistications and rhetorical elegances that were customary at the highest levels of German academic and social discourse during that era.

The other cloud on the horizon was the rising influence in Germany of the National Socialist Democratic Workers Party. After the elections of 1930, from which the Nazis emerged as the second-most powerful party in the government, Schmidt began to give public expression to a rigorous and principled theological critique of the Nazi movement. The force of his critique consistently was directed against the Nazis' social and economic policies, and most of all against what he regarded as their unhealthy combination of nationalism and socialism. In brief, Schmidt regarded Nazism as too much nationalism and not enough socialism. In a letter to Martin Buber he wrote: "This 'German,' this 'nationalist' government embarrasses me both as a German and as a Protestant Christian." He especially criticized the Nazi policy of requiring professors of theology to function independently of ecclesiastical authorities, for he regarded an independent theological faculty as an oxymoron, since theology was part and parcel of the teaching ministry of the church.

By January of 1933, Karl Ludwig Schmidt had staked out a position of public opposition to Nazism on a broad array of issues and on both political and theological grounds. On January 14, 1933, a Sabbath day, he appeared in Stuttgart for a *Zwiegespräch* (dialogue) with Martin Buber, and in the course of that conversation, which took place in a synagogue, Schmidt strongly affirmed the lasting place of Judaism in the history of salvation. Today the views he expressed that evening would be regarded as mildly supersessionist, but in Stuttgart, Germany, during January of 1933, it was an act of moral principle and political courage to participate constructively in a public dialogue with the local Jewish community in their synagogue on Shabbat. Only two weeks later Adolf Hitler came to power, and from that point on, Schmidt found himself increasingly under pressure. He continued to take practical steps against National Socialism—he was elected to the city council in Bonn for the SPD—but academic, ecclesiastical, and political sympathizers with the Nazis repeatedly blocked his efforts. When a National Socialist was elected president of the faculty, the situation became acute. Few of his colleagues rallied to his defense; perhaps Schmidt's sharp pen was coming back to haunt him. A personal low point came when he saw a Nazi flag hanging from the window of the apartment of his *Assistent*, Ernst Fuchs. On November 4, 1933, he left Bonn to participate in a theological conference in Switzerland, and he did not return. Karl Ludwig Schmidt never lived in Germany again.

The financial consequences of exile in Switzerland were immediate and severe, as Schmidt went without income for most of 1933 and 1934. With the help of Karl Barth, he was eventually able to secure a position as the pastor of a Lutheran church, where his salary was less than one-third of what he had been earning in Bonn. His bank accounts remained in Germany, where he had no access to them, and more than once he had to make ends meet by selling books from his personal library. Finally, in the summer of 1935, after almost two years in Switzerland, Schmidt secured a position on the faculty of New Testament at Basel, making it possible for him to bring his family to join him. Yet even this positive development did not fully restore his fortunes. Shortly after her arrival, his wife Ursula began to develop health problems, for which she was hospitalized for several weeks during 1936. At the same time, the ongoing effects of Schmidt's war wounds were now producing chronic severe headaches. In a vain search for relief, he turned to increasingly strong medications, with predictable results. By 1940 Karl Ludwig Schmidt was addicted to narcotics.

When the Second World War came to its end, Schmidt hoped to return to Germany and to reassume his previous academic status and activities. In particular, he looked forward to participating in the writing of a new reference encyclopedia, *Theologische Wörterbuch des Neuen Testaments*. He confided to friends that he hoped to be named to the position of editor of *TWNT*, and thus it came as an especially bitter disappointment when that position was awarded instead to Gerhard Kittel, a former Nazi party member and supporter of the Third Reich. This particular professional setback appears to have affected Schmidt especially deeply, as in its aftermath an air of increasing despondence began to settle over his correspondence. On the personal side, his marriage suffered: he and Ursula became increasingly distant, and although they never divorced, they did come to live in separate apartments. His long-running battle with chronic pain was not going well, and over time his general health began to decline. In 1952, while teaching a graduate seminar, he suffered a stroke. The following year he resigned his position on the faculty, and on January 10, 1956, Karl Ludwig Schmidt died in a hospital in Basel. He was sixty-five years old.

The career of Karl Ludwig Schmidt unfolded during the rise of one of history's most virulent forms of anti-Semitism, and for this reason it is important to observe that Schmidt was among the earliest and most outspoken German academic opponents of Nazism. He consistently criticized as naive those who believed that a political and theological dialogue with National Socialism might be possible. On one occasion, he derided Paul Althaus, whose Nazi sympathies were well-known, as a *psychikos anthropos*. There was, Schmidt maintained, a higher vision of humankind that transcended nation and race. Recalling his own combat experience, Schmidt wrote to

Althaus: "As I lay seriously wounded in a field hospital in Russia, being cared for by Russian prisoners, more than once the thought went through my head: 'Let's shoot a few of them first, and then we can make nice.' Now, thank God, I have come to a different point of view: there is a community that unites us in spite of the human affiliations that may stand between us."

By 1933, Schmidt was publically defending the rights of Jews. He wrote to Rudolf Bultmann that a church that turns its back on Jews has ceased to be the church. In his *Zwiegespräch* with Martin Buber, he took a public stance of support for Jews that was stronger than most Christian scholars in Germany at that time. Throughout the 1930s and 40s he maintained close relationships with leading Jewish scholars, among them Hans Jonas, and in 1942 Schmidt was writing about a day when the Nazis would be gone, and when Jews in Europe would be treated as human beings.

Yet the same person who took these courageous and principled stands, for which he was forced to flee from his homeland, is also known to have made occasional anti-Semitic remarks. His personal correspondence from those years includes occasional statements that suggest that he shared the view that Jewishness was a biological characteristic, and an inferior one at that. Perhaps this fact can help to explain why, although he vigorously opposed Nazism, there is no evidence that he was ever involved in practical efforts to protect Jews from the Third Reich. There can be no doubt that Karl Ludwig Schmidt was a man of moral courage and principle, willing to act upon those convictions in substantial and specific ways, to the point that the Nazis hounded him out of Germany. At the same time, however, the prevailing norms of German society, culture, and politics also situated him within a broad social and cultural framework of anti-Semitism. In this regard there are thought-provoking similarities between Schmidt and some American abolitionists of the ante-bellum era, who were passionately opposed to slavery, yet could not quite conceive of African Americans as their political, social, legal, and economic equals.

Der Rahmen der Geschichte Jesu

In the German university system, the *Habilitationsschrift* is an original work of scholarship submitted to the faculty after the dissertation, certifying that a young scholar has attained the level of competence necessary for teaching independently and for supervising doctoral dissertations. With its careful and thorough application of the form-critical method to the Synoptic gospels, *Der Rahmen der Geschichte Jesu* firmly established Schmidt as not only a competent teacher but also as a scholar at the cutting edge of New Testament research. Reception of the book was strongly positive. The thesis of the work is stated in the opening paragraph of the Foreword: "The oldest

Jesus tradition is a 'pericope' tradition, i.e., a tradition of individual scenes and sayings that were handed down within the community, usually without any firm chronological or topographical markings. Much of what appears to be chronological or topographical is only a framework that was added later to the individual pictures." More than three hundred and twenty pages later, that thesis is repeated in the concluding sentence: "But on the whole there is no chronological outline for the story of Jesus, only individual stories and pericopes placed into a framework."

Der Rahmen is thus a work of both literary and historical criticism, employing form-critical analysis in order to generate historical insights into the origins and background of the stories in the Synoptic Gospels. To that end, *Der Rahmen* follows a consistent pattern: proceeding through the sequence of pericopes as they appear in Mark, Schmidt starts with John the Baptist (Mark 1:1–13 par.) and concludes with Jesus' suffering and death (Mark 14–15). Periodic digressions interrupt this sequence, such as Luke's travel narrative (Luke 9:51—19:27), which is introduced between Mark 10:45 and 10:46; and the birth narratives of Matthew and Luke ("The Prehistories"). Yet the center of gravity in *Der Rahmen* is devoted to detailed analyses of gospel pericopes. In each case, Schmidt follows a consistent method, beginning with textual criticism. He evaluates significant variants, comparing and contrasting Mark's text with the parallel passages in Matthew and Luke. Form-critical observations follow, and in this part of the analysis Schmidt consistently centers upon the transitional links at the opening and closing of each pericope. These links, he argues, were added to the pericopes, so as to create not only the appearance of connections between the individual stories but also that they took place in a temporal sequence. In this way, the connecting links create a "framework" (*Rahmen*) for the story of Jesus. The crux of Schmidt's argument is that these framing pieces do not belong to the stories themselves, and that they give the stories the appearance of a chronological progression that did not inhere in the oral tradition. On the contrary, in the oral tradition that preceded the composition of the Gospels, the stories of Jesus circulated independently, without chronology or sequence. Schmidt recognizes that some pericopes—e.g., the Passion Narrative at the end of Mark—do unfold in a temporal sequence, but he regards these sequences as the exception rather than the rule. Throughout most of Mark, as Schmidt puts it, "only the ruined rubble of an itinerary" remains. Outside of the passion narrative, the historical location and sequence of most of the events narrated in the pericopes are irretrievably lost. The framework of the story of Jesus was a creation of the evangelists.

Alongside the works of Bultmann and Dibelius, *Der Rahmen der Geschichte Jesu* helped to establish the form-critical paradigm that prevailed in gospel scholarship until the late twentieth century. During those years under the influence of form criticism, many questions were regarded as well-settled, most notable among them, the question of gospel genre. As Schmidt argued in *The Place of the Gospels in the General History of Literature*, the Gospels were oral tradition written down. Yet over the course of time, renewed interest in these questions was reawakened during the closing decades of the twentieth century.

In 1986, Charles Talbert published *What Is a Gospel? The Genre of the Canonical Gospels*. Based upon careful observation and logical argument, Talbert challenged the prevailing consensus that as oral tradition, the Gospels do not belong to the genre of ancient biography. While Talbert's argument met with an immediate and sharp rebuke from David Aune, "The Problem of the Gospels: A Critique of Charles Talbert's *What Is a Gospel?*," other opinions were more favorable, notably Philip Shuler's, *A Genre for the Gospels: The Biographical Character of Matthew*. In 1992, Richard Burridge's *What Are the Gospels? A Comparison with Greco-Roman Biography* laid out a full-length case for the view that the Gospels do belong in the genre of ancient biography. The question has been open ever since, and yet, despite many good efforts to address these questions, the ongoing absence of a consensus is evident in commentaries published over the past twenty years. With regard to the Gospel of Mark, for example, some commentators (e.g., Craig S. Keener, R. T. France, Robert H. Stein) take the view that the Gospels are examples of ancient biography. Adopting the opposite position, i.e., that the Gospels are not ancient biographies, are François Bovon, Adela Yarbro Collins, Ulrich Luz, and Joel Marcus. At present, it does not appear that this question is approaching any resolution. The recent appearance of social memory theory in some circles of gospel studies seems likely to generate additional differences of opinion with regard to matters of tradition, history, and genre.

In view of these developments, the availability of an English translation of *Der Rahmen der Geschichte Jesu* is a scholarly *desideratum*. Deeper and wider acquaintance with this book will surely have a positive influence on the quality of ongoing scholarly discussion about the literary characteristics of the Gospels, along with the methods of interpretation that are most appropriate to those literary features. Certainly it is my hope that this translation will enable a wider array of NT scholars to engage seriously and constructively with the argument laid out in this longstanding classic in our field.

Byron R. McCane

Centre College

Preface

THIS STUDY FINDS ITS origin in a much-discussed problem of historical Jesus research: in what locations and for what length of time did Jesus' public ministry take place? The difficulty of determining the course of the story of Jesus derives less from the fact that the various topographical and chronological details in the Gospels can scarcely be reconciled with each other, as from the fact that these details are of such a nature as to prompt us to ask whether they contain any real topography or chronology at all. The historical problem is complicated, in other words, because it is at bottom a literary problem. Only after literary criticism has done its work will historians be able to make use of the outline of the story of Jesus as given by the Gospels. This book will show that questions about the value of the topographical and chronological details in the Gospels must be answered with a resounding negative. Only every now and then can the time or place of this or that event be determined, usually on the basis of a few incidental details, local color, or internal characteristics of that particular individual narrative. The significance of this study thus lies in literary criticism, for only there can we hope to comprehend the origin and peculiarity of the Gospels. The oldest Jesus tradition is a "pericope-tradition," i.e., a tradition of individual scenes and sayings that were handed down within a community, for the most part without any firm chronological or topographical markings. Much of what appears to be chronological or topographical is only a framework that was added later to the individual snapshots. Within the literary tradition, and still later when they were assembled into collections, the introductions to the pericopes, which often had no connection with what preceded or followed, took on the appearance of chronological and topographical indicators. Yet in most cases the "framework" character of these accessories still shows right through. Of course this basic methodological principle, which forced itself upon me during my analysis of the Synoptics and which does not generally apply to the passion narrative, should not be pressed too far.

It should not be asserted that the oldest Jesus tradition has no topography or chronology at all. The matter is not quite so simple. There are some details which always had a genuine chronological or topographical character, and these details can be signs of close connections within a complex of individual stories. On the whole, however, only the ruins and rubble of an itinerary remain. The fact that the introductions to the narratives display a remarkable variety, and that they have moved without regard to the proper sequence of events in the individual stories, points yet again to the "framework" character of this tradition. The earliest narrators and tradents of the stories of Jesus paid hardly any attention to these connections; instead, they were totally intent upon the vivid singularity of the pericope as it was used in worship. If the origin of Christianity is the life of a cult—and in recent years this discovery has been increasingly accepted—then it is clear that the origins of primitive Christian literature must be understood as rising from that cult as well. To my mind we cannot emphasize too much the significance of the primitive Christian cult, the practice of worship, for the development of Gospel literature. The earliest Jesus tradition was certainly cultic, and thereby also vivid and trans-historical.

The history of exegesis shows how little influence such assertions have had upon literary and historical criticism, and thus how much credit ought to go to positive efforts in this area. During antiquity and the Middle Ages ecclesiastical scholars offered a wide range of estimates about the length of Jesus' public activity. Recent Catholic scholarship has produced a voluminous (and disputatious) literature, but unfortunately the relationship between their discoveries about the treatment of the Gospels in early church lectionaries and the harmonizing that went on within that setting has generally not been well understood. Yet there are still some good ideas about literary criticism of the earliest Jesus tradition in the work of several recent Catholic exegetes. In early Protestant theology, by contrast, our topic was thoroughly overwhelmed by the influence of the doctrine of inspiration. Recent studies on the theological and philological side have taken the form of a subset of the Johannine-Synoptic problem: which outline is historical, the Synoptic or the Johannine? In this debate genuine literary observations often carry less weight than the overall position that has already been adopted with regard to the historicity of the Gospel of John versus the Synoptics. Advocates for the Johannine chronology misunderstand the literary distinctiveness of the Fourth Gospel, and exponents of the Markan hypothesis consistently overvalue the outline of the story of Jesus in Mark. This overestimation of the Markan (and thereby the synoptic) outline continues in recent critical analyses of the earliest Jesus tradition, with symptomatic examples in the works of J. Weiss, Wellhausen, Wendling, and Wrede (sceptic about Mark, champion of Ur-Mark!), as well as Merx and Spitta (preference for Luke!). It generally comes down to an either-or question of John vs. the Synoptics, and often in such discussions the literary and historical questions are not clearly distinguished. It is quite striking that astute exegetes should arrive at solutions so diametrically opposed to each other. The significance of this book lies, it seems to me, in the fact that my studies of the complex of differences among the Synoptics, and between John and the Synoptics, will either succeed in establishing an entirely new outlook, or will fail utterly and thus end up making no difference at all.

At this point reference may be made to Albert Schweitzer, who in his history of Life-of-Jesus research (the 2nd edition of his *von Reimarus zu Wrede*, 1913) also engaged with scholarly overestimation of Mark. Schweitzer rightly emphasized that the outline of the story of Jesus in the Gospel of Mark is illogical and unpsychological: there is no development of Jesus as a youth, nor is there any practical description, or psychological motivation, or connection between events. Exegetes, especially advocates of the Markan hypothesis, read all of that into the Second Gospel. On this point the only exception is Wrede, the advocate for "thoroughgoing skepticism" whose book "released the Markan hypothesis from its agonies." Schweitzer summarized his own overall conclusion very dramatically: "The material with which it has hitherto been usual to solder the sections together into a life of Jesus will not stand the temperature test. Exposed to the cold air of skepticism it cracks; when the furnace of eschatology is heated to a certain point the solderings melt. Formerly it was possible to book through-tickets at the supplementary-psychological-knowledge office which enabled those traveling in the interests of Life-of-Jesus research to use express trains, thus avoiding the inconvenience of having to stop at every little station, change, and run the risk of missing their connection. That ticket office is now closed. There is a station at the end of each section of the narrative, and the connections are not guaranteed."[1] With these words Schweitzer introduces what he regards as the only right answer to the peculiarity of the Gospel of Mark, namely, a thoroughly eschatological understanding of the story of Jesus. "Is it not the only conceivable view that the conduct of one who looked forward to His Messianic 'Parousia' in the near future should be determined, not by the natural course of events, but by that expectation? The chaotic confusion of the narratives ought to have suggested that events had been thrown into confusion by the volcanic force of an incalculable personality, not by some

---

1. Albert Schweitzer, *The Quest of the Historical Jesus*, trans. W. Montgomery (New York: Macmillan, 1966) 333.

kind of carelessness or freak of the tradition."[2] The shimmering simplicity of Schweitzer's assertion is seductive, yet it is insufficient and will ultimately lead us in the wrong direction. The complicated relationships that are evident in the framework of the story of Jesus do not submit to such an easy answer. Schweitzer seeks to solve the riddle of why Jesus left Galilee with the following considerations: Jesus' behavior in the preceding period was not entirely comprehensible to begin with; he had a distaste for publicity, because the aim of his preaching was not yet specified; as a result the reports of Jesus' wanderings came to have an odd restlessness and purposelessness. Here Schweitzer sees the problem correctly, but his explanation of it comes up short. For even if Jesus did not withdraw from Galilee, there would still be an "odd restlessness and purposelessness" about his movements. That restlessness lies, however, not in Jesus' own behavior but in the distinctive way in which the reports were handed down. We may have to reckon with a kind of reciprocal action here: the aimless conduct of the historical Jesus may have strengthened the aimless and careless transmission of the reports, which (as a pericope-tradition) put no stock in psychology and chronology. By rejecting Schweitzer's solution, however, I do not wish to imply anything negative about his statement regarding the thoroughly eschatological character of Jesus' activity. The debate over that question is most assuredly not closed. Yet I would like to lodge one protest, and it is this: we cannot succeed if we disregard studies of the individual pericopes and begin instead to develop literary, stylistic, and textual conceptions on the basis of some predetermined thesis, as if to heal by means of an off-the-shelf remedy.

The method I have employed here is a product of this conviction. The center of gravity has to be located squarely in studies of individual pericopes. After an introductory section, the question of the framework of the story of Jesus is situated more closely in its historical and essential aspects. The discussion of the larger sections, into which the Gospel of Mark breaks down, takes place in various ways: since we are dealing with individual pericopes, these are discussed in sequence according to their setting; but when there is an itinerary in a complex of stories, that is investigated first. Occasional reference will be made to parallel passages in Matthew and Luke, so that the investigations do take on a synoptic character. Certainly it is a sound principle to read each evangelist individually as much as possible, as Wendling has done in his study of the Gospel of Mark, but it would be absurd to exclude Matthew and Luke completely from the study of Mark, since these two evangelists were the first interpreters of Mark. That kind of valuable material cannot be overlooked. The same goes for the textual history. The profusion of readings which occur in the introductions and conclusions to the pericopes (i.e., in the framework of the story of Jesus) provides us with a

---

2. Schweitzer, *Quest*, 351.

reliable guide for interpretation. Thus it is not only a matter of dealing with later variants, which have value only as ancient and interesting explanatory glosses; rather it is a matter of dealing with distinctive forms of the text, in all their particularity and originality. Later use of the pericopes, as we encounter it in the history of the text, may have resurrected some readings which had belonged to the original text, in so far as it was influenced by use of the pericopes within the development of the gospel tradition.

Habent sua fata libelli,[3] which the world around us cannot affect, until a book actually sees the light of day. This topic first suggested itself to me during the New Testament seminars which I conducted as an assistant in the New Testament Seminar in Berlin during the last semester before the World War. After being wounded in the War, I was able to begin the individual analyses, but the work was slowed down by a stay in sick bay and in a reserve battalion. In 1917 the study was submitted to the theological faculty in Berlin as my *Habilitationsschrift*. More than nine months have elapsed since it went to press, and in that time a new comprehensive investigation by Vinzenz Hartl, a Roman Catholic, has appeared, "The Hypothesis of a Year-Long Ministry of Jesus Critically Examined," Neutestamentliche Abhandlungen, M. Meinertz, ed. Vol. 8, Nrs. 1–3 (1917). Hartl principally seeks to oppose Belser, but he stays away from the accusations of heresy which Catholic scholars so often throw at each other. He offers some good methodological observations. We also have Procksh to thank for a very instructive essay, "Jesus' Circle of Activity at the Sea of Galilee" in the 1918 *Palästinajahrbuch*. The essay is based upon careful consideration of both archaeology and literature, and illuminates the topics discussed below on pp. 133ff and 161ff. That my study has been able to appear at all during this period of time owes much to the generosity of the von Cuny Stiftung of Berlin. Heartfelt thanks are also owed to my friend Prof. Lic. Dr. O. Eissfeldt and cand. theol. G. Bertram, for their unflagging assistance with proofreading, and to my wife, who also helped me prepare the index.

Karl Ludwig Schmidt
Wernburg in Thüringen, March 1919

---

3. (Translator's Note): The Latin is a quotation from Terence, *De Litteris, de Syllabis, de Metris*, 1286. The full text reads: *pro captu lectoris habent sua fata libelli*, which means "Depending upon the capability of the reader, books have their destiny." Here Schmidt quotes only the second half of the line, applying it to the long and arduous process that preceded the publication of *Der Rahmen der Geschichte Jesu*. For details of that process, including his "stay in sick bay" after he was injured during an artillery bombardment, see the biographical essay in this volume.

Introduction
The Problem of the Framework of the Story of Jesus

Historical and Methodological Issues

UPON WHAT STAGE—OR RATHER, upon what stages—did the public ministry of Jesus play out, and how long did that ministry last? Questions about the topography and chronology of the story of Jesus are inseparable from each other and mutually condition each other, and although they have been vigorously debated since the days of Christian antiquity, they are still largely unanswered. Every conceivable solution has been offered: Jesus' ministry lasted for one year, two years, three years or longer. The question of location is closely correlated: except for the final days in Jerusalem, Jesus carried out his public activity only in Galilee (one year), or he spent much of his time in Jerusalem and southern Palestine (two years or more). The difficulty of this problem stems from the differing outlines of the story of Jesus in John and the Synoptics. The Synoptics mention only one Passover—and thus leave room for a ministry of one year at the most—while John, with its various feasts and pilgrimages to Jerusalem, allows for at least two years and perhaps three. The theory of an even longer ministry of Jesus, at least as it was advocated in the early church, builds on some rather unconventional data. It owes its existence to two passages in the Gospel of John (2:20: "it took forty-six years to build this temple"; and 8:57: "you are not yet fifty years old"), as well as to the kind of offbeat speculations that surface in the *Kerygma Petri*,[1] in the so-called *Second Book of Jehu*,[2] and in Irenaeus.[3]

Except for these idiosyncratic traditions, according to which we can reckon with a forty- or fifty-year-old Jesus who began his ministry at

---

1. Von Dobschütz, *Das Kerygma Petri*, 136ff.

2. Schmidt, *Gnostiche Schirften*, 196: "Jesus, however, had compassion upon his disciples, because they . . . had followed him for twelve years." Cf. also Resch, "Mitteilung eines apokryphen Jesuswortes, in dem von dem 12. Jahre nach der ἀνάλημψις des Herrn die Rede ist."

3. Irenaeus, *Adv. haer.* II.22.5 (Migne *PG* VII, 785–86).

about age thirty, scholars in the early church generally argued over one, two, or three years, and the real battle was between one and three. Oddly enough, in this early Christian controversy the Gospel chronology was never subjected to careful scrutiny; it was simply presumed that certain details (which by our lights actually say nothing about chronology) had to be interpreted as hidden evidence for the length of Jesus' ministry. The starting point for advocates of the one-year theory, for example, was the saying in Luke 4:19 about ἐνιαυτὸ κυρίου δέκτος, "the acceptable year of the Lord." This verse was seen as clandestine proof for a one-year ministry of Jesus. Apparently it was on the basis of this phrase, which was taken as an assertion about astronomy, that many gnostic groups conceived of the public activity of Jesus within a framework of one year. The root of this idea is anchored in gnostic speculations about the role of the number twelve in the life of Jesus (especially the selection of the twelve apostles). On this basis they inferred that twelve months = one year, and that the thirty aeons were related to the thirty-year life of the Lord.[4] Even prominent representatives of the great church were not totally free from this kind of allegorical artistry. Clement of Alexandria, a leading proponent of the one-year theory, based his argument on Luke 4:29 (ἐνιαυτὸν μόνον) and interpreted the 360 bells on the high priest's ephod as a representation of the year-long preaching of Christ.[5] Origen, who declared that "Jesus taught for a year and a few months,"[6] also delighted in this kind of allegorization, as for example when he interpreted the thirty pieces of silver given to Judas as a symbol for the thirty years of Jesus' life. In the West, Tertullian and Hippolytus were the leading voices, and their outlook held sway throughout almost all of western Christianity. Advocates for the three-year theory, on the other hand, attempted to deflect the force of the ἐνιαυτός quotation. No one did more in this regard than Irenaeus, who introduced a counter-argument based on the sequence of feasts in the Gospel of John. What Irenaeus began, i.e., the triumph of the Johannine chronology, Eusebius finished. He summarized the length of Jesus' ministry this way: τριέτης χρόνος; χρόνος τριῶν ἥμισυ ἐτῶν; μέχρι δὲ τῆς ἀρχῆς τοῦ Καϊάφα παραμείναντος οὐδ' ὅλος ὁ μεταξὺ τετραέτης παρίσταται χρόνος.[7] This statement from Eusebius, the founder of church history, was determinative for the East, and eventually for the West as well, particularly after Jerome translated Eusebius' *Chronicle* into Latin in the year 380. The Johannine chronology, which works out to three years

---

4. Irenaeus, *Adv. haer* I.1.3 (Migne PG VII, 449–50).
5. Clement of Alexandria, *Strom.* V.6 (Migne PG IX, 63–64).
6. Origen, *de Princ.* IV.5 (Migne PG XI, 349).
7. Eusebius, *Demonstr. Evangelica* VIII.2.108 (Migne PG XXII, 595ff).

(or at least two), was accepted right down the line. Even in the earlier period, when the one-year theory had held sway, the Johannine sequence of festivals had always made a strong impression, influencing Origen, whom we have already cited as a proponent of the one-year view. On the basis of his comprehensive study of John he seems to have changed his mind and abandoned his earlier position.[8]

In this controversy, described here only in broad strokes,[9] one assumption is unquestioned: there is no chronological contradiction between John and the Synoptics. The exact manner in which advocates of the one-year theory manage to reconcile themselves to the Johannine outline is not especially important. Either the contradictions are ignored, or an effort is made to fit the Johannine account into one year. Origen appears to have done this when he maintained that the feast in John 5:1 was not a Passover. Those who adopt the Johannine chronology manage to fit the Synoptics into it. Only the "Alogoi" asserted that there was a contradiction between the Gospels, because for them the sequence of festivals in John contradicted the Synoptics, a fact that they used as the basis for their rejection of the fourth gospel.[10] The degree of certainty in the assertions and conclusions in this debate is striking. Only a few participants exercise the kind of restraint we find in Augustine, who said that (as we know from the Gospels) the Lord was baptized at about the age of thirty years. How many more years he may have lived thereafter can perhaps be detected *textu ipso actionum*, but it is better to work by inference from a comparison of the Gospel with secular history, in order to avoid questions and mistakes.[11]

The Middle Ages and later periods added no new momentum to the discussion, but in the last two decades an extensive controversy has arisen within the literature of Catholic scholarship. It was kicked off in 1898 with J. van Bebber's *Zur Chronologie des Lebens Jesu: Eine exegetische Studie*. This book, along with several supplemental and controversial essays, sought to revive the one-year theory.[12] Van Bebber quickly found a spirited advocate

---

8. This set of circumstances explains why Origen is sometimes described by modern Catholic scholars as holding the one-year theory, and sometimes as holding the three-year theory. Other early church leaders also appear to have changed their minds.

9. This brief introductory sketch cites only those figures whose writings most clearly show the problem in the early church. In the literature produced by Catholic controversies on the subject, these things are dealt with more specifically, but probably not quite fully and completely.

10. Cf. Zahn, *Geschichte des neutestamentlichen Kanons*, 1021.

11. Augustine, *de Doctr. Christiana* II.28 (Migne *PL* XXXIV, 55).

12. Cf. van Bebber, "Zur Frage nach der Dauer"; and van Bebber, "Zur neuesten Datierung des Karfreitags."

in the learned exegete J. Belser, who had at first spoken out against van Bebber, but then (until his death a short time ago) argued for a one-year ministry of Jesus with great acumen in numerous studies and commentaries. He defended this view against the most common objections, first in an essay on the hypothesis of a one-year ministry in *Biblische Zeitschrift* (1903), and then in further studies, most of which were printed in the *Theologische Quartalschrift* (1907, 1911, 1913, 1914, and 1916). His paper on the problem of the Gospels (1913) is especially comprehensive. Belser's thesis quickly attracted attention and provoked a great deal of opposition from his colleagues. After E. Nagl objected to it in *Biblische Zeitschrift* (1904) 373ff, the Catholic theological faculty of Munich made "The Length of the Public Ministry of Jesus" the theme for the essay competition of the academic year 1904/05. Three contributors appeared in print: Fendt[13] argued for one year, Zellinger[14] for two years, and Homanner[15] for three. Since Belser had not fallen silent, and indeed now had found an ally in Fendt, the strongest polemic was directed against the two of them. C. Mommert, a good scholar of Palestine, wrote an unusually harsh study, *Zur Chronologie des Lebens Jesu*, in 1909. J. M. Pfättisch took his side in 1911 with *Die Dauer der Lehrtätigkeit Jesu nach dem Ev. des hl. Johannes*, as did the French Jesuit scholar F. Prat in 1912 with "La date de la passion et de la durée de la vie publique de Jésus Christ."[16] Other French scholars expressed their opinions as well. The Jesuit J. B. Nisius discussed the various works in a rather calm, substantial, and long essay, "Zur Kontroverse über die Dauer der öffentlichen Wirksamkeit Jesu," which appeared in *Zeitschrift für katholische Theologie* (1913) 457–503. P. Dausch, who had already produced "Bedenken gegen die Hypothese von der bloss einjährigen öffentliche Wirksamkeit Jesu" (*BZ* [1906] 49–60), now offered a new study of the question that was in the main an argument against Belser and Nisius (*BZ* 12 [1914] 158ff). The most recent summation was provided by M. Meinertz in the 2nd (1916, pp. 19ff) and 3rd (1917, pp. 236ff) volumes of *BZ*, titled "Methodisches und Sachliches über die Dauer der öffentlichen Wirksamkeit Jesu." In addition to this discussion, there is also another conversation about specific problems, especially those having to do with the early church. In *BZ* (1905), H. Klug wrote on the length of the public ministry of Jesus according to Daniel and Luke, and F. Schubert analyzed Tertullian's view of the year of Jesus' baptism. In 1906 all of the following essays appeared: F. Schubert, "Das Zeugnis des Irenaeus"; J. van

---

13. Fendt, *Die Dauer*.
14. Zellinger, *Die Dauer*.
15. Homanner, *Die Dauer*.
16. Prat, "La date de la passion."

Bebber, "Zur Berechnung der 70 Wochen Daniels"; H. Klug, "Das Osterfest nach Jo 6,4"; P. Heinisch, "Clement von Alexandria und die einjährige Lehrtätigkeit des Herrn."

Even a cursory reading of this literature will show that we are dealing here with a problem of the first order for Catholic biblical scholarship. Belser never tires of pointing out the great significance of the problem: it would be an important advance if—*contra* the opinions of the critics—it could be shown that there is harmony among the Gospels with regard to the length of Jesus' ministry. In his most recent article, "Abriss des Lebens Jesu: Von der Taufe bis zum Tod" (1916), Belser believes that he is "acting as secretary in the interest of an important and difficult question." Fendt writes almost with resignation on the first page of his book: "If we ask those who are in a position to know about the length of the public ministry of Jesus, we receive contradictory answers. Humankind gathers from the fields of that incarnate life sheaves with kernels of pure gold, but how long the official public period lasted is disputed. And that has been the case not only in the twentieth century, but also in the nineteenth and eighteenth and all the way back to the time when gray-haired old men who had known the departed disciples could still tell stories about the miracles they themselves had seen during the days of Jesus." The fervor on both sides is commensurate with how high they imagine the stakes to be. Belser wrote angrily in the *Tübinger Theologischen Quartalschrift* of 1911 (p. 625): "The one-year theory, recently attacked by Pfättisch and condemned as 'unscientific' in the exegetical lecture hall at Munich, will come back to triumph over Pfättisch, over Homanner, Zellinger, and their masters. Resistance is futile." Mommert, by contrast, whose support for the three-year theory is quite spirited, has turned not against Belser but the lesser lights van Bebber and Fendt. In his book he describes the one-year theory as a "fable produced by ancient heretics and then dragged along." On page 9 he dismisses Fendt's critical observations as "tasteless and stale suppositions that any decent person would prefer not to touch." On page 26 he asserts that van Bebber makes up for what he lacks in real knowledge with "high-browed audacity and fancy vocabulary." He calls down upon his opponents the promise of the Lord: "The gates of hell will not prevail against it." Homanner expresses himself somewhat more mildly on page 88 (footnote 2) in his book about Fendt (whose intelligent study may have been, in my judgment, more deserving of the prize than Zellinger's was): "Infected by the rationalistic ideas of a Loisy or Harnack, he rejects all the chronological material in the Gospels and treats it as simply the higgledy-piggledy of the Jesus tradition." To a disinterested observer this argument may look like a tempest in a teapot. But if we look closer and survey not only (as I have done here) the various journal articles but also examine their proposals, we will find that we are in fact dealing with a difficult and contested issue. And in this regard Catholic scholarship is a model of how individual scholars do not have to work side by side and ignore each other, but can have regard for each other.

For the moment the three-year theory is the more powerful: the chronology of feasts in the Gospel of John (and the outline that goes with it) is determinative, and individual stories from the Synoptics are then worked in. Defenders of the one-year theory (few as they are) do not reject the Johannine account, but rather set out to connect it with the Synoptics or to prove that the fourth evangelist actually describes a one-year ministry of Jesus. To that end it is necessary, along with some pretty complicated treatments of place-and-time designations in the Gospel of John, to delete τε πάσχα from John 6:4 and to interpret the phrase ἑορτὴ Ἰουδαίων as referring to the Feast of Tabernacles. We can see that the premises shared by all the proponents of modern Catholic scholarship rest on the same foundation as the ancient Christian tradition. In keeping with Catholicism's principled commitment to the importance of tradition, the church fathers are adduced as star witnesses. On the whole, however, current scholars have managed to extricate themselves from the chronological games of the ancients and are now occupying themselves instead with detailed exegesis of specific data from John and the Synoptics. The basic method is harmonization. In order to put together a potentially comprehensive sketch of the activity of the Lord, statements that are scattered throughout the Gospels must be collected and arranged in the proper sequence. Modern critical scholars will object to that kind of method, rejecting it at the outset, because all harmonizations are destructive, for they treat all the material equally. Such a method precludes a truly literary evaluation of the individual Gospels, which is in fact what is most necessary. Yet there is still much to be learned from the work of the Catholic scholars; there are positive contributions of genuine value here. That is due to the following circumstance: since Catholic harmonizers largely seek to compare John with the Synoptics (or, more often, the Synoptics with John), they often subject the Gospels to a first-rate pure literary criticism. Nagl, for example, who regards the Gospel of John as an authentic continuous report, wrote the following judgment of the Synoptics on page 494 of *Katholik* (1900): "The gaps which have been detected cannot have any special significance, because the evangelists were not pursuing a purely historical agenda, and in any event they betray an awareness of the gaps in their reports. What else are general phrases like Luke 4:15; Mark 1:39; Luke 8:1; and 9:6 (cf. Matt 4:23 and 9:35) supposed to indicate? Luke appears to intentionally organize his narrative around stopgap measures like these." With these words this Catholic scholar has appraised the character of the framework of the story of Jesus, at least with regard to the Synoptics, more correctly than most Protestant scholars do. He evaluates the properties of the Synoptics' (especially Luke's) collected reports and sequential connections quite rightly, and he expresses himself in good style. When Zellinger, another defender of the Johannine chronology, asserts that the Synoptics allow the presupposition that the ministry of Jesus lasted several years, but that they have merely described a single year, this too must be regarded as sound literary judgment. But these scholars, who offer such good observations on the Synoptics, generally let us down when it comes to characterizing the Gospel of John. We do find well-founded statements about the fourth gospel in the work of Fendt, who defends the one-year theory. He occupies a very unusual position within the world of Catholic scholarship, and he has been strongly resisted by his co-religionists, and we can see why. Not only is he "infected by Loisy and Harnack," but he has also formulated some substantial literary judgments of those two scholars, both of whom clung very closely to the Synoptic outline. In a special section of his article under the interesting heading, "Investigation of the Value of the Chronological Principle in the Composition of the Gospels" (129ff), he offers a number of excellent observations with regard to the framework of the Gospel of John and the Synoptics. The following sentence shows the clarity of his literary insight: "With regard to the sayings of the Lord . . . the Synoptics exhibit the character of a careful, primitive systematic representation, and the same conclusion is justified about their arrangement of events" (135). Or: "None of the Synoptics can be privileged simply because the broad outline of a historical course of events can be better maintained in one than in the others" (ibid.). Luke's καθεξῆς offers no support for the view that he actually achieved his goal of writing a coherent sequence of events. The chronological framework, in other words, may be only partially successful. Sayings and events may be compiled from the same material: ministry of Jesus *before* the imprisonment of the Baptist! Material that belongs in that time period is readily at hand, "because even an event that appears (on the basis of other internal considerations) to have taken place after the imprisonment of John, may actually go back to the beginning of the Synoptic account" (137). According to Fendt, the evangelists display a great deal of freedom in the matter of chronology. He also gives a very good answer to the question of John and the Synoptics when he writes that a chronology of the Synoptics cannot be fetched from the outline of John.

More recent Catholic scholarship has unfortunately lost its grip on the valuable critical achievements of its own greatest thinkers. Earlier I remarked that Augustine did an about-face on the question of the chronology of Jesus. He wrote a remarkable book, *de Consensu Evangelistarum*, in which he offered some interesting thoughts about the outline of the story of Jesus.[17] On his view, the evangelists intended to arrange events by means of *anticipatio* and/or *recapitulatio*:

> If therefore one incident is narrated after another one, that does not necessarily mean they happened in that order ... No human being, no matter how accurate or reliable his memory may be, has the ability to recall events in a specific sequence. For we remember some things sooner than others, depending on how they come back to us, not on how we want them to come back to us. Thus it is highly likely that each evangelist believed he had to relate the sequence of events just as God brought it back to his memory. But this applies only to those cases where it makes no difference to the standing and truthfulness of the Gospels whether the order was one way or the other. (*de Consensu Evangelistarum* 2.21.51)

In this vein, Augustine speaks of an *ordo rerum gestarum* and an *ordo recordationis*, paying close attention to the transitions and introductions to individual pericopes, with their chronological details. In 2.22.53 he discusses Mark 1:35 ("when evening had come") and asserts that it was not necessarily the evening of the same day. He remarks that Luke 7:1 does not explicitly state that Christ went straight to Capernaum after the end of his sermon. In Luke 10:1 the expression "after these things" (μετὰ δὲ ταῦτα) does not make explicit just what setting we should imagine, and Matt 12:9 does not indicate how long it may have been before Jesus came into their synagogue. Certainly Augustine is working here as a harmonizer, since he wants to fill in the gaps in the respective narratives from the other Gospels. But he consistently demonstrates the right feel for the project. Subsequent Catholic exegetes have completely lost that feel, and in so doing they have become even more papist than the Pope. But Augustine's outlook did exercise a powerful influence for a while. Zacharias of Chrysopolis, who wrote the first medieval harmony of the Gospels, was not too far off when he said: "Very often the Gospels summarize; very often they anticipate." Throughout the late Middle Ages the idea that none of the evangelists had written in chronological order was dominant. Johannes Gerson (d. 1429), for example, wrote: "According to Jerome, Mark is not comprised of the actual order of events, but an order based on Levitical priorities, and Luke is similar in many respects" (on p. 139, Vogels says of Gerson, "He cannot escape from the bonds that Augustine put on the harmony of the Gospels"). Gerson's remarks on the pericope of the healing of the lepers (Mark 1:40ff; Matt 8:1ff;

---

17. Vogels, *St Augustins Schrift de Consensu Evangelistarum*.

Luke 5:12ff) are especially instructive: "It is collected from several sources, because the evangelists did not always follow the actual order of events. Instead they used the rule of anticipation and recollection." Bishop Cornelius Jansen (d. 1576) asserted that the narratives of the first three evangelists clearly show a lack of concern for the sequence of events in the deeds of Christ; rather they wrote in random order (*miscellanea quaedam scripsisse*). Thus Bishop Jansen selected individual pieces from the Synoptics and fit them together, without touching the Gospel of John.

As has already been noted, the Catholic Church has backed away from these harmonizers. An instructive essay by Christian Pesch, a Jesuit, clearly points out this fact.[18] Yet when it comes to the question of chronology, Pesch stops short of the Protestant view, as he says on p. 454: "Among the Protestants an exaggerated concept of inspiration led early on to the hypothesis that everything which is narrated in the Gospels must have happened exactly as it is narrated, and in the same sequence, right down to the last jot and tittle. Every saying must have been spoken word-for-word as it is reported: no anticipation, no recapitulation can be allowed, not even that the reproduction of Jesus' words was basically correct." The chief representative of the exegesis that Pesch so rightly criticizes was Andreas Osiander, who (like Gerson) spoke of a *confusio evangeliorum* and described his own work of 1537 in the following way:

> A harmony of the four Gospels, in which the Gospel histories of the four evangelists are woven together into one, so that not one word is omitted, nothing foreign is introduced, the order is undisturbed, and nothing is out of place: everything is made clear with symbols and markers, so that you can understand at a glance what is distinctive about each evangelist, as well as what they all have in common.

One of Osiander's students, Karl Molinaeus, went further than his teacher when he maintained that the narratives about plucking ears of grain and about the healing of a withered hand in Luke and Matthew are not the same. In the wake of Augustine, harmonizers tacitly assumed that the Gospels are completely without order, treating the Gospels (as one nineteenth-century Catholic scholar aptly put it) as a kind of curio cabinet that could be rearranged, or as a quarry from which choice material could be mined. Much of this was, in my judgment, extremely naive; but on the whole the harmonizers had a better feel for the Gospels than their Protestant opponents, and much better than their modern adversaries in their own Church, who

---

18. Pesch, "Über Evangelienharmonien," 225–41.

want to give a straight-from-the-shoulder answer based on a one- or two- or three-year ministry of Jesus.

Recent Protestant scholarship, by contrast, presents a completely different picture. As on the Catholic side, there has been an abundance of research into the absolute chronology of the story of Jesus. Scholars have been busily occupied in particular with questions about the date of Jesus' birth and death, based on highly complicated astronomical calculations. A book by F. Westberg, *Die biblische Chronologie nach Flavius Josephus and das Todesjahr Jesu* (1910) is a recent example. The results of this study turn out to be highly uncertain, and they do not advance our knowledge of the length of Jesus' ministry. Turning away, then, from the highly problematic idea of an absolute chronology, scholars have instead examined the chronological framework of the evangelists itself. Here a recent short article by J. Boehmer is noteworthy.[19] Hans Windisch has also undertaken a very energetic engagement with this problem.[20] He poses the question of the relationship of the narrative to the chronological framework, and he clearly states the literary and historical problem: "How much of it is the evangelists' own construction based on the course of Jesus' ministry, and how much can we, through careful examination, extract from their accounts?" After the designations of time in the individual stories are carefully added up, the length of Jesus' ministry turns out to be roughly 4-1/2 months in Mark, a little less than five months in Matthew, and 4-1/4 months in Luke. Thus the Synoptics describe a story that could have played out in four to six months, but that, based on its vague calendrical details, must have actually lasted more than a year (note especially the plucking of grain on the Sabbath, which had to take place between Easter and Pentecost). The Johannine narrative, by contrast, could have unfolded in as little as two months, except for the fact that the sequence of festivals would have to stretch out over a period of two years. The strain in this chronology would be relieved if the order of chapters five and six was reversed, and if the date of the festival in 6:4 was deleted. These "slight but well-grounded critical operations" would produce a one-year ministry in the Gospel of John. The Synoptics and John are put together as follows: "The main features of the combination consist of limiting the Galilean activity to the summer months, which is supported by John and can easily be maintained in the Synoptics, and at the same time stretching out the Jerusalem ministry through the fall, winter, and spring (indicated by John and hinted at by the Synoptics)." While this effort on Windisch's part is highly original with regard to the details,

---

19. Boehmer, "Die chronologische," 121–47.
20. Windisch, "Die Dauer," 141–42.

the manner in which he compares John and the Synoptics (cf. esp. how he strikes the place reference in 6:4!) is strongly reminiscent of Catholic scholarship, particularly the work of Belser. It is commendable that for once the individual indicators of time in the Gospels are characterized as if they make up a continuous report, without regard to long-held opinions about them, but the most important question is whether the Gospels really support such an analysis of the time indicators. At the end of the day, after Windisch has worked out all the time indicators—both those we have to infer and those made explicit by the narrator—his analysis still boils down to harmonization, albeit very artful harmonization. In addition it must be objected that specific features of the Gospels rule out any chronological determination *a priori*, as it were. The introductory phrases, which often include statements about time, and the summary statements, which suggest that Jesus was active on a grand scale, are in my opinion a long way from chronological calculations. It will not work for us to read the Gospels as if they are a continuous and contemporaneous report and then collect the time indicators; on the contrary, the form of these indicators of time must first be examined, before they can be evaluated. What is needed is a thorough literary criticism of the chronological and topographical details that make up the framework of the story of Jesus.

Has this goal been successfully achieved (or even accurately understood) in recent scholarship? It can be said that Protestant scholars have not been particularly excited about the question of the length of Jesus' ministry. On the Catholic side all four Gospels have been treated equally, so that all the particular differences between the Gospels have been continually debated, but on the Protestant side our question has been regarded as a subset of the so-called "Johannine problem," with which it stands or falls. Put differently, a Protestant scholar who argues against the three-year theory will not try to overturn the individual pieces of that theory as they arise from the Gospel of John; instead the entire edifice of that Gospel will be attacked until the whole thing collapses. At this point there appears to be a broad agreement with the method used by Catholic exegetes. Scholars like H. J. Holtzmann, who deny any historical value to the Gospel of John, make no use at all of the chronology contained therein. Thus there is general acceptance of the idea that the Synoptics depict the ministry of Jesus as slightly more than one year long, while John has it as two or three years long, and "the question about the length of the public ministry of Jesus forces Protestant scholars to decide whether to adopt the Johannine or the Synoptic chronology."[21] The more scholars dispute the historical value of John, the more highly

---

21. So Windisch in "Leben und Lehre Jesu," 177.

they esteem the Synoptics. Th. Keim, for example, completely sets aside the Johannine account as unhistorical and plots the course of Jesus' story along the lines of the Synoptics, whose apparently historical outline seems to speak for a one-year ministry of Jesus (Jesus is active only in Galilee, right up to the trip to Jerusalem for the Passover).[22] It remains only to support this Synoptic outline with a little psychology, and then to elucidate its development. Keim, whose account of Jesus' development was very influential, realized in this way that the Gospel of Matthew is the oldest gospel document.[23] Confidence in the Synoptic tradition and its basic outline grew stronger as the Markan Hypothesis marched to victory thanks to the efforts of H. J. Holtzmann and J. Weiss. Even before Keim, Holtzmann had offered a highly influential picture of the life of Jesus based on the hypothesis of an "Ur-Mark."[24] Holtzmann was convinced that the outline of Mark rested on solid historical foundations. He went into the development of Jesus in great detail, believing that he could identify in the Gospel of Mark seven "stages in the public life of Jesus" in Galilee. In subsequent years there were some corrections to Holtzmann's presentation, but on the whole the course of Jesus' life as he laid it out remained determinative: the outline of the Gospel of John is historically worthless, but the Synoptic (i.e., the Markan) outline is of very high value. In his book *Jesus*, published in 1913, W. Heitmüller described the situation by saying that "we have to fall in line with the Gospel of Mark," since the journeys to Jerusalem in John are obviously schematic, while the Synoptics give the general impression of a story no longer than one year in duration.[25] Heitmüller fairly expressed the *communis opinio* among scholars, aside from those who still regarded the Gospel of John as a reliable historical source. Certainly we have since abandoned Holtzmann's confidence that the outline of the story of Jesus can be traced out right down to the last detail, but on the whole a one-year ministry of Jesus is now regarded as an assured result of scholarship.

In addition to the developments that I have sketched out briefly here, there was also an ongoing reappraisal of whether Mark was in fact such a highly valuable source document. The Markan Hypothesis was expanded into the Two-Source Hypothesis (i.e., Matthew and Luke had another source in addition to Mark, namely the so-called "Q" sayings collection).

---

22. Keim, *Die Geschichte Jesu von Nazara*.

23. Loofs, *Wer war Jesus Christus?*, said that the first sketch of "a liberal portrait of Jesus" appeared in Keim's 1861 inaugural address at Zurich, where these ideas were first set forth.

24. Holtzmann, *Die synoptischen Evangelien*.

25. Heitmüller, *Jesus*. Wernle's newest book on Jesus does not discuss these chronological issues.

Repeated attempts were made to account for the differences between Mark on the one hand and Matthew and Luke on the other. Conceptions of an "Ur-Mark," of varying lengths, tried to clarify the Synoptic problem more precisely. But a thorough examination of Mark itself, without reference to either of its companions, shows just how weak these connections are in most respects. J. Weiss took a close look at the structure and chronology of Mark in his groundbreaking study *Das älteste Evangelium* (1903), and had to arrive at rather negative conclusions. J. Wellhausen followed with his own highly stimulating study, but in the end shed light only on a few individual passages. His opinions had a strong influence on more recent exegetes such as E. Klostermann and A. Loisy. Scepticism about the historical value of the Markan outline began to make its presence felt. At this point the astute studies of Mark by E. Wendling (*Urmarkus* in 1905, then *Enstehung des Markusevangelium* in 1908) are of value. More than other scholars, Wendling sees the joints and seams and insertions in the Gospel of Mark as we now have it, and he tries to "recover the oldest data about the life of Jesus." These studies have seriously undermined confidence in Mark. Criticism has nearly reached the point of drawing the conclusion that there may be nothing of historical value about the ministry of Jesus or its length in either the Synoptics or Mark, i.e. in the best evidence we have.[26] In a completely different way F. Spitta mounted an energetic attack against the overestimation of Mark in a series of studies that was collected in his great work, *Die synoptische Grundschrift in ihrer Überlieferung durch das Lukasevangelium* (1912). He completely does away with the usual Synoptic outline, finding the basis for the Synoptics in Luke, with Jesus carrying out his ministry essentially in and around Judea. A whole series of Galilean incidents were transposed into Judea. The result is something most peculiar: a tradition that is related to, but independent of, the Gospel of John. Spitta, in other words, consigned the Markan and Two-Source Hypotheses to history.

While the wider theological and philological public remained untouched by these new assertions (and remains so to this day), experts immediately recognized that the Synoptic problem had in fact not been solved. J. Weiss wrote in his paper on the Synoptic Gospels in *Theologische Rundschau* (1913): "I simply cannot say that my opinion is as certain as I would like for it to be."[27] "Spitta's book demonstrates all over again that the Synoptic problem is ultimately insoluble: we make do with a kind of Synoptic eclecticism, using sources on a case by case basis as they seem to us to be either primary or

---

26. Cf. Haupt, *Wörte Jesu und Gemeindeüberlieferung,"* vol. 3.
27. J. Weiss, "Synoptische Evangelien," 183.

secondary."[28] This point of view is correct. When we ask about the historical facts in the original tradition, definite results can be achieved only on a case-by-case basis. But there is no reason to surrender to total scepticism. "The Two-Source Hypothesis can be regarded as an assured result of scholarship, or at any rate as the most useful of the hypotheses proposed so far,"[29] and Spitta's work is not sufficient to overturn it. Yet Spitta does deserve credit, for his studies have had symptomatic importance: a struggle against the conventional overestimation of the Gospel of Mark needed to be carried out, and still does. That Gospel simply does not contain the real historical outline of the story of Jesus. Even scholars like J. Weiss and Wellhausen, who get so much right with regard to the uniqueness of Mark, are still too much under the spell of the conventional overestimation of Mark as a good historical source. Wendling, whose program is so different, is not entirely free from the spell, for he trains his criticism on the connections in Mark but then wants to construct a new outline for the story of Jesus from that very same Gospel. He asserts that this new outline is in reality a *dis*-connected report. Spitta rightly demonstrated that Luke and John are in many respects historically sterile, but from these historical considerations he formulated a literary conclusion that cannot be sustained.[30] Historical and literary methods have been mixed up with each other too often. Advocates of the Markan hypothesis make the right literary observation, i.e., that Mark is the oldest Gospel, but then draw the wrong historical conclusion, i.e., that Mark has greater historical value than the other Gospels. Others (like Spitta) make the right historical observation, i.e., that Mark has no historical value, but they draw the wrong literary conclusion, i.e., that it is not the oldest Gospel. The present investigation will show that Mark does indeed contain the oldest outline of the story of Jesus, but that this outline is every bit as schematic as that of the Gospel of John. Further, this study will clarify the form of that schematization. Matthew and Luke, the oldest interpreters of Mark, sometimes altered the outline, just as the manuscript tradition was improved upon in many details. It does not follow from the fact that the outline of the Gospel of Mark is historically worthless that the outline of John is better, or that circumstantial evidence for Mark can be found therein. It is instead a matter of clarifying the earliest framework of the story of Jesus as it appears in the second Gospel, and this can only be done through literary critical studies of the individual stories, paying particular attention to

---

28. Ibid., 194. So also W. Bousset, "Review of W. Heintze, *Der Klemensroman und seine Greichischen Quelle*" (1914) TLZ 19 (1915), 295–297.

29. Loofs, *Wer war Jesus Christus?*, 65.

30. Cf. Dibelius, "Herodes und Pilatus," 116: "But thereby we fall into the familiar theological mistake of drawing historical conclusions from literary judgments."

the Synoptic problem and text criticism.[31] Perhaps a thorough study of this kind will elucidate the Synoptic problem especially well, and the problem of the original text may find a distinctive solution as well.

---

31. Wendling's work did not consider these two factors (the Synoptic problem and text criticism). Wendling thus obscures our view of some facts.

1

John the Baptist and Jesus

(Mark 1:1–13 par.)

John the Baptist
(Mark 1:1–8; Matt 3:1–12; Luke 3:1–20)

THE FIRST PERICOPE THAT comprises a self-contained unit in the Gospel of Mark is the account of the baptizing and preaching activity of John the Baptist in 1:1–8. Verses 4–8 make up the actual report, while vv. 1–3 (especially vv. 2–3) contain a characterization of what will follow and a theolegoumenon that speaks comprehensively of the εὐαγγέλιον Ἰησοῦ Χριστοῦ. The text also notes the significance and basis of John's baptismal activity, which was vouched for by the word of the prophet. A simple narrative report thus stands side-by-side with a reflective comment. Between v. 3 and v. 4 lies a literary seam that is evident in the change of style in vv. 4–8. A mere glance at later narratives in the Gospel of Mark will suffice to show that vv. 1–3 never belonged to this pericope. These introductory verses look like a piece of literary work, of a kind that cannot have been contained in the oral narratives of the story of Jesus as they were passed from person to person. It originated with the evangelist, who brought the separate stories together into a unified whole. The original narrative began with the words, καὶ ἐγένετο Ἰωάννης . . . ἐν τῷ ἐρήμῳ. Comparable introductory phrases occur in 1:9; 1:16; 1:21; 1:40, and elsewhere. The evangelist deleted the καί, either to preface vv. 1–3 or perhaps because v. 2 already supplied an explanation for v. 1 or vv. 4ff. Both are grammatically possible. If vv. 1–3 belong together grammatically, then these verses are an explanatory heading to vv. 4–8. If v. 1 stands alone, then it is a heading for vv. 2–8, or perhaps for the Gospel as a whole. Whatever the case may be, this first narrative that Mark made use of in his Gospel began with the words καὶ ἐγένετο.

It may seem surprising to assert that the first pericope began with the word καί. In their earliest stages, however, the narratives of the story of Jesus circulated by word of mouth. When Christians gathered together, they told each other stories about the words and deeds of their Lord, one person alternating with another, and each one supplementing the other. The Jewish Bible was the sacred text in their worshiping community, and their recollections of the sayings of Jesus also played a prominent role. We cannot be completely certain, but we should not underestimate just how vibrant such sayings and narratives about the story of Jesus were in the circles of storytellers in the cultic community. In order to bring the earliest period of the gospel tradition into view, we will have to make use of hypotheses that do not lead to infallible conclusions, but that nevertheless help us perceive and understand the historical situation correctly. In the free movement of oral tradition, one story about Jesus would have followed another. When one story ended, the next would begin with "and it happened that . . ." In this way complexes of several stories arose that were separated from each other by a simple καί. καί and its Aramaic correlate became a kind of caesura-word, and a rather primitive caesura at that. It is possible that such complexes were even written down for use in the worship service, so that several stories could be read in sequence. But one story, or one pericope, would still have been recited at a time. Thus καί remained, just as we today begin the Sunday Gospel reading in our churches with the word "and." Through it all the individual stories were passed on orally from person to person, with καί being retained. Ultimately it came down to the Gospel writer, who collected the individual stories and tried to create connections between them. Most of the time Mark left the word καί in place, but Matthew and Luke usually tried to give the scenes a greater internal cohesiveness. The purpose of this book, in fact, is to clarify the nature of that "literary" work.

In this case καί had to drop out, on account of the grammatical construction in the preceding vv. 1–3. Accordingly we now turn our attention to vv. 4–8: ἐγένετο Ἰωάννης ὁ βαπτίζων ἐν τῷ ἐρήμῳ κηρύσσων βάπτισμα . . .

> The manuscripts vary widely here. In my judgment the following readings are comprehensible as derivatives of our text: a) ἐγένετο Ἰωάννης ὁ βαπτίζων καὶ κηρύσσων (Sinaiticus, Westcott-Hort); and b) ἐγένετο Ἰωάννης (without ὁ) βαπτίζων καὶ κηρύσσων (A, D . . . it vg). Obviously ὁ βαπτίζων is not a title, since ὁ βαπτιστής had become established. Help came from one of two directions: either the two participles were joined by καί, or ὁ was stricken and then καί had to be inserted.

Here is the sense: John the Baptist appeared, preaching in the desert. John is mentioned without any sort of preparation, as if he is already known to the reader. There are no indicators of time, an absence that is highly significant, for in this narrative we encounter the bedrock of the ancient tradition, which by its very nature was handed down by people (initiates, who knew the events and the characters) who had no interest at all in any kind of biographical detail. Only after an authorial point of view had been adopted would this become an issue, and at that point the details were filled in. Among the canonical gospels only Luke provides information about the era, the year, and the family background of John the Baptist (Luke 3:1-2). A parallel fragment from the Gospel of the Ebionites is even more literary, handed down by Epiphanius. After a very precise designation of the time, it goes on: ἦλθεν (τις) Ἰωάννης (ὀνόματι) βαπτίζων βάπτισμα μετανοίας ἐν τῇ Ἰορδάνῃ ποταμῷ. ὃς ἐλέγετο εἶναι ἐκ γένους Ἀαρὼν τοῦ ἱερέως, παῖς Ζαχαρίου καὶ Ἐλισάβετ. The personal description and introduction is quite appropriate, as any reader with half an interest in biography would have expected, but in a tradition that was still completely esoteric, such factors carried no weight, and Mark has preserved that tradition intact.

John carries out his activity in the wilderness. There is no indication of the geographical location. Matthew adds τῆς Ἰουδαίας (Matt 3:1). Since the text only states that John chose an uncultivated environment, i.e., a desert, it would of course be a mistake to take τῆς as signifying a specific location. One might suppose, however, that the first narrator of this story did have a particular desert in mind. An explanation of the location may not have been necessary, since the desert in question was nearby, and he was addressing people who were its neighbors. In that case we would have to think of a Jerusalem tradition; but first we must read further in the text.

Καὶ ἐξεπορεύετο πρὸς αὐτὸν πᾶσα ἡ Ἰουδαία χώρα καὶ οἱ Ἱεροσολυμεῖται πάντες καὶ ἐβαπτίζοντο ὑπ' αὐτοῦ ἐν τῷ Ἰορδάνῃ ποταμῷ (v. 5). The subjects are hyperbolic and should not be pressed. 1:28 and 1:33 offer similar turns of phrase. The text also informs the reader that John was preaching and baptizing where the Jordan flows. The connection between v. 4 and v. 5 clearly indicates that the preaching and baptizing occur in the same place, so the Jordan is to be found in the desert. But therein lies a geographical difficulty. Often an attempt is made to overcome this difficulty by thinking of the "desert" named here as the Jordan Valley, which Josephus at one point refers to as ἐρημία. We should think instead of an actual desert, wasteland, or wilderness. The depiction of John's lifestyle in v. 6 brings that home. In addition, it is noteworthy that according to v. 12, Jesus goes out into the wilderness and is baptized there. No matter how we may analyze the material, it always results in a certain lack of geographical specificity. The evangelist appears not to have had any specific location in mind. Obviously such things made no difference to him, just as he also had no interest in chronology. Two reports intersect in this text: a) a narrative about a preacher in the wilderness, and b) a narrative about baptism in the Jordan. The older report—the one that is historical—says that John was baptizing in the area of the Jordan. We do not know the exact location, but if people from Jerusalem were among those being baptized, then the lower Jordan Valley is the most likely place. This historical inference is supported by the passage from Gospel of the Ebionites that I cited a moment ago, which appears to know nothing about John being in the desert. Nor does the fourth evangelist (John 1:19ff; 1:28) say anything about a desert. It appears doubtful that the desert motif goes back to any specific ancient source. On closer examination it becomes clear that the remarks about the desert (ἐν τῇ ἐρήμῳ in v. 4, and the description of the Baptist's lifestyle in v. 6) arise from the prophetic citation in vv. 2–3. The evangelist placed this citation at the very beginning and introduced this train of thought into the narrative. This hypothesis is confirmed by the ease with which these insertions can be dropped out. All of the geographical characteristics in this story fall away. As we suspected at the beginning, the one who brought the desert motif into the narrative was not thinking of any specific desert; instead, he had in mind a rather vague but grand picture of desert solitude, upon which he placed particular emphasis.

The parallel pericope in the Gospel of Matthew (3:1–6) is identical in content and form: (1) ἐν ταῖς ἡμέραις ἐκείναις παραγίνεται Ἰωάννης ὁ βαπτιστὴς κηρύσσων ἐν τῇ ἐρήμῳ τῆς Ἰουδαίας ... (5) τότε ἐξεπορεύετο πρὸς αὐτὸν Ἱεροσόλυμα καὶ πᾶσα ἡ Ἰουδαία καὶ πᾶσα ἡ περίχωρος τοῦ Ἰορδάνου. (6) καὶ ἐβαπτίζοντο ἐν τῷ Ἰορδάνῃ ποταμῷ.

> Important witnesses (ℵ B C it vg . . .) read δέ after ἐν in v. 1. It is much more likely that this word was inserted later than that it dropped out of the original text. Obviously someone wanted to ameliorate the asyndeton.

This chronological remark, placed at the beginning of the narrative, actually has nothing to do with chronology, because chapter 3 does not connect temporally with chapter 2. We are dealing here with a connection that is utterly lacking in specificity, along the lines of "in those days," i.e., in the time known to Christians, as it was referred to in the oral stories. We are going to encounter more such "chronological" notices in Matthew, and it is important for us to have before us, right from the beginning, an especially clear case of a chronological date that amounts only to a caesura, nothing more than the introduction to a pericope. Matthew's repeated use of this formula for connecting stories shows that he himself originated it, although we can still trace the origin of this style even further back. Folk-narration works comfortably with indefinite links of this sort, and thus one cannot ask about literary dependence, but in the case of Matthew such questions are not out of place. For Matthew knew the Old Testament and the Hebrew folk narrative that was its prototype. Countless places in Genesis and Exodus (cf. also the LXX) show that the narrators of those texts likewise gave no thought to precise indicators of time. Just so, in the Gospel of Mark, John the Baptizer (instead of ὁ βαπτιστὴς he is called ὁ βαπτίζων) appears in the desert, which Matthew describes more precisely as ἐν τῇ ἐρήμῳ τῆς Ἰουδαίας. It is illustrative that Matthew also expands on Mark, by saying that not only the people of Jerusalem and Judea, but indeed the population of the entire region of the Jordan came out to see him. Still more frequent is τότε—which basically says nothing at all—and this too is to be credited to Matthew's account. All of these are small glosses on Mark. There still remains the discrepancy in the geographical scenery, where Matthew draws a larger scene than Mark. If worst came to worst, one could attempt to resolve the problem by suggesting that Matthew mistakenly located the Jordan in the Trans-Jordan plateau, but the "Judean desert" referred to by Matthew certainly did not extend all the way to the Jordan. As we have seen, Mark does not go so far as to stipulate the location of the desert. It is Matthew who pursues a geographical interest, with unimpressive results.

Luke 3:1–6 is quite different. While Matthew tries to bridge the yawning chasm between Jesus' early history and the beginning of his public ministry with an utterly vague indicator of time, Luke inserts something entirely new into the narrative: a precise stipulation of the time that synchronizes Jesus with secular history. Regarding the distinctiveness of this verse I will have no more to say here, but one point does need to be mentioned, a point that puts the authorial work of Luke in its clearest light from the very beginning: this synchronizing of Jesus with secular history has an educated look about it, as if it is genuine. "The fifteenth year of Tiberius" suggests a strongly formed tradition, and the other indicators of time are similarly confident and specific. We need not—indeed we cannot—accept the impression of careful scientific research conveyed by the word ἀκριβῶς in Luke 1:1. Closer examination of the individual details shows that the evangelist plainly did not have a clear picture of the matters with which he was dealing. That is especially true of his enumeration of the lands of northern Palestine. We have here before us a literary product of Luke, of the same sort that we will later see in the introduction of the Baptist as the son of Zacharias. The setting for Jesus' ministry is described by Luke as follows: ²ἐγένετο ῥῆμα θεοῦ ἐπὶ Ἰωάννην τὸν Ζαχαρίου υἱὸν ἐν τῇ ἐρήμῳ ³καὶ ἦλθεν εἰς πᾶσαν τὴν περίχωρον τοῦ Ἰορδάνου κηρύσσων. Clearly two actions that took place in different locales are being distinguished here: the call in the desert, and the preaching and baptizing ministry in the Jordan. Otherwise the prophetic word that accompanies this description would have no real point, for Luke never says anything at all about anyone βοῶν ἐν τῇ ἐρήμῳ. There can be no doubt, then, that the third evangelist wanted to do away with the vague localization offered by Mark. He betrays this literary effort when he deletes the exaggerated details in Mark 1:5 (= Matt 3:5). Verse 3 mentions only the region around the Jordan, and as a result Luke's description is relatively bland. It may be that the citation of Judea and Jerusalem did not seem reliable to Luke, but it cannot have been the case that Matthew and Mark wanted to remove something from Luke. The first two evangelists offer, as it were, the more difficult (and therefore the original) reading. If the desert location is historical, then Luke's description may be as well, but that does not alter the fact that the earliest report is found in Mark.

Matthew and Luke's description of John's preaching of repentance goes beyond Mark, coming as it does from Q (Matt 3:7-10 = Luke 3:7-9). The narrative is polished, as many Pharisees and Sadducees come to be baptized but are turned away with sharp words from John. The form of the narrative—ἰδὼν δὲ πολλοὺς τῶν Φαρισαίων καὶ Σαδδουκαίων ἐρχομένους . . . εἶπεν αὐτοῖς—goes back to Matthew, for he loves to introduce a scene (which is of minor importance) with a brief participial construction, and then put the saying (which is of major importance) in the foreground.

As in Mark 1:7-8, the messianic proclamation of John is reported: Matt 3:11-12 (= Luke 3:15-18) uses the word for "winnowing fork," vividly evoking the native rural background without linking the rural setting to any specific place. There is definite local color in v. 9, which speaks of λίθοι from which God is able to raise up children of Abraham. Perhaps in that case we can think of an actual desert.

John's preaching of repentance and the Messiah is directed toward the Pharisees and Sadducees, an audience that fits well with the wording of vv. 7-10, but not as well with vv. 11-13. This difficulty would be resolved if Matthew had received Mark 1:1-8 as a separate pericope: Matt 3:11-2, like Mark 1:7-8, is spoken to the Jews in general. When the preaching of repentance was inserted, this connection became confused. We might ask, however, whether the reference to the Pharisees and Sadducees originated with Matthew or was handed down to him in the tradition. I cannot answer that question with certainty, but we can consider the possibilities. The saying about "a brood of vipers" may have been handed down without a specific addressee. Matthew would then have directed it specifically toward the Pharisees and Sadducees, because he regarded the Baptist as the forerunner of Jesus, and Jesus certainly often argued with those Jewish groups. On the other hand, if the addressee was included in the saying as it came to Matthew, then two further possibilities suggest themselves: either the addressees were named in the pericope from the beginning, or they were introduced into the tradition at some point along the way. In my judgment Matthew found them in the tradition, because the descriptions of the audience in the texts are so vague and general. If Matthew himself introduced our first reference to "Pharisees and Sadducees"—and he would have done so only in the saying about the brood of vipers—it would have been easy for vv. 11ff to be directed once more to the people in general. But if the Pharisees were already named in the tradition, then it is easily conceivable that the indeterminacy emerged later. But Matthew gave no thought to such questions; he simply wrote down what the tradition brought to him. My explanation—so full of "ifs" and "buts"—may seem complicated, but it cannot be otherwise, since the facts of the case are so complicated.

The setting of the material in Luke neither supports nor contradicts Matthew's presentation, because the third evangelist has stylized and glossed over the connections. If Pharisees and Sadducees were mentioned in Q, then it is not hard to believe that this author has set them aside. For him it is a very simple scene: here is the Baptist, and there are the Jews. They are the ὄχλοι (vv. 7, 10) or the λαός (v. 15), and the saying about the brood of vipers applies to all of them. Differentiation does not appear until v. 10-11, when people of various circles come in with their requests. The whole report flows so smoothly that it is hardly noticeable that a new narrative from a different source begins in v. 7: ἔλεγεν οὖν (D improves it to δὲ) τοῖς ἐκπορευομένοις ὄχλοις. For clarity, ἐκπορευομένοις was added, as it connects directly with these people's question in v.10: καὶ ἐπηρώτων αὐτὸν οἱ ὄχλοι. Next come the tax collectors and the soldiers with their own particular questions: ἦλθον δὲ καὶ τελῶναι (v. 12), ἐπηρώτων δὲ αὐτὸν καὶ στρατευόμενοι (v. 14). In typical Lukan authorial style, neither noun has the article. Usually this excerpt (vv. 10-14) is traced back to a special Lukan source, but I think it very likely that the words of the Baptist recorded here were handed down to the third evangelist in the tradition, and that he formed the present narrative out of that material. He wanted to create a lively scene with a protagonist and an antagonist. The messianic proclamation is strongly bound, both internally and externally, with what has preceded: προσδοκῶντος δὲ τοῦ λαοῦ καὶ διαλογιζομένων πάντων ἐν ταῖς καρδίαις αὐτῶν περὶ Ἰωάννου, μήποτε αὐτὸς ὁ Χριστός . . . This introduction has been extracted from what follows. John's proclamation of "one who is stronger" was associated with his (i.e., John's) image in popular messianic expectations. Unlike Matthew and Mark, Luke does not naively place the stories right next to each other, but provides a historical foundation in the form of an historical construct that had to be in agreement with what people had actually said in the days of the Baptist. Verse 15 is thus not special tradition, but a creation of the author. Verse 18 is to be judged the same way: πολλὰ μὲν οὖν καὶ ἕτερα παρακαλῶν εὐηγγελίζετο τὸν λαόν. The use of οὖν is noticeable, as is εὐηγγελίζεσθαι, a concept that is not at home in the Synoptic tradition. In a similar way, vv. 19ff (the arrest of the Baptist) are a highly condensed version of the tradition about the end of the Baptist (cf. Mark 6:17–18 = Matt 14:3–4). At this point Luke wants to bring the story of John to its conclusion, and not return to it again. Thus the story of Jesus in direct contact with the ministry of the Baptist actually begins in 3:21. Verses 19ff (actually vv. 18–20 as well) are, from Luke's point of view, a parenthesis. It is peculiar that the death of the Baptist is not narrated. Luke 9:9 will treat it as a known fact, and 3:19ff takes it for granted that the reader knows about the affair with Herodias. This could mean that in the circle of the third evangelist's readers, i.e., where Theophilus lived, these matters were already well known. But that is not the most important point, for sometimes Luke does narrate well-known facts. That he leaves out this information about the Baptist is not a matter of authorial license: it only means that Luke had no interest in the Baptist per se, and for that reason he narrated only what was essential to the story of Jesus. He overlooked (or included only in a brief parenthesis) the story of the death of John.

The Baptism of Jesus
(Mark 1:9–11; Matt 3:13–17; Luke 3:21–22)

After Mark 1:8 there is a clear break in the text. Verse 9: καὶ ἐγένετο ἐν ἐκείναις ταῖς ἡμέραις ἦλθεν Ἰησοῦς ἀπὸ Ναζαρὲτ τῆς Γαλιλαίας καὶ ἐβαπτίσθη εἰς τὴν Ἰορδάνην ὑπὸ Ἰωάννου.

> The καί is lacking in B. Bernhard Weiss (17) wants to delete the word as a mere connective. Cf. however the remarks above on p. 15. If B, D, vg, etc. bring ἐκείναις to ἡμέραις, that is by assimilation to Matt. Instead of Ναζαρέτ important witnesses read Ναζαρέθ (cf. also Ναζαράτ, Ναζαρά). The most plausible form of the name in Mark is Ναζαρέτ. The isolated readings εἰς Ναζαρέτ and εἰς τὴν Γαλιλαίαν are very strange.

Like John the Baptist, Jesus is introduced here as a character already known to the reader. It would have been easy for the evangelists to introduce Jesus, telling us about his home, family, and vocation. That they had information about such matters is established by texts like Mark 3:21ff (Jesus' relatives) and 6:1ff (exact enumeration of his family members; his and Joseph's vocation as carpenters). But all of that is mentioned only in passing, and only when it is essential to the story at hand, depending upon the situation. As we have already seen, the tradition—which highlighted the individual stories—was not interested in biographical details as such, and Mark did nothing to change it. As in the previous cases, however, Luke tried to make literary improvements: in 3:23 he is the only evangelist to report on the age of Jesus, and (like Matthew) he also records a genealogy of Jesus. With these literary corrections he outdoes the author of the Gospel of the Ebionites, who reports: ἐγένετο τις ἀνὴρ ὀνόματι Ἰησοῦς, καὶ αὐτὸς ὡς ἐτῶν τριάκοντα. The usual exegesis, which takes ἀπὸ Ναζαρὲτ τῆς Γαλιλαίας as an adverbial designation, seems doubtful to me, since the words can also be taken as an attribute of Ἰησοῦς. The absence of the article does not speak against this interpretation (in spite of Mark 15:43; cf. for example 1 Thess 1:1, where ἐν θεῷ is an attribute of τῇ ἐκκλησίᾳ). A stronger objection would be that Mark prefers to call Jesus ὁ Ναζαρηνός, but this argument is not convincing, because the narratives that Mark put to use were not linguistically consistent, and Mark did not need to make them so. The generally accepted interpretation holds—consciously or unconsciously—that according to the Gospel of Mark Jesus hurried directly out from his hometown to the places where John was active. But it appears highly doubtful that Mark was paying any attention to topographical connections. Our story is tied to the preceding pericope with a chronological note: ἐν ἐκείναις ταῖς ἡμέραις. Upon closer examination these words prove to be not the least bit chronological; indeed, they could be removed from the text without affecting its meaning. Thus they are the same as a simple καί, a caesura remark. It can be asked, however, where this caesura comes from. It was already in the oral tradition, along with καὶ ἐγένετο. That Mark did not coin the phrase is shown by the fact that he expressed himself differently than the first evangelist, who leaned very heavily on Old Testament patterns of usage. The phrase εἰς τὸν Ἰορδάνην appears unnecessary, because according to the preceding narrative only the Jordan River can possibly be the setting. An extraneous detail of this sort leads us to recognize that this text originally was a self-contained narrative, independent of 1:1–8. The account in 1:4–11 is not a *fluxus orationis*; rather, Mark has artlessly combined here two originally separate pericopes. A story of Jesus is directly attached (καὶ εὐθύς, v. 10) to the baptism, and καὶ εὐθύς is, of course, a favorite expression of Mark. In this case there may be reason to regard it as meaningful, because in the parallel passage Matthew also has εὐθύς (3:16), even though he usually shies away from that expression.

Matthew (3:13–17) introduces the baptismal narrative with his typical τότε. Ναζαρέτ he lets drop, keeping only ἀπὸ τῆς Γαλιλαίας. Perhaps that can be explained by the fact that Matthew has earlier mentioned Nazareth as the hometown of Jesus (2:22–23), an indication that here in the main body of his gospel Matthew is taking into consideration his pre-history of Jesus. Luke (3:21–22) shapes this pericope in his own distinctive way. He never actually narrates the baptism itself, referring to it only indirectly, in order to report the one event that is important to him—the descent of the Holy Spirit. The introduction is stylistically rough and awkward, not like Luke at all. The explanation for this problem is that in this text the author's pen has been driven by religious and/or dogmatic interests, because the baptism of Jesus by John was understandably a difficult matter (cf. the apologetic efforts of Matt 3:15, as well as the Gospel of the Ebionites and the Gospel of the Hebrews). While Mark and Matthew begin a new section with the baptism narrative (thus the topographical and chronological caesurae), Luke leaves out the caesura in order to conceal the pericope, as it were. The third evangelist, who knew so well how to narrate logical developments and how to display biographical events, found this story something of an embarrassment.

The Age of Jesus
(Luke 3:23)

Luke's authorial aspirations also make themselves evident at the close of the baptism pericope, where a list of Jesus' ancestors is given, including a statement about his age (3:23): καὶ αὐτὸς ἦν Ἰησοῦς ἀρχόμενος ὡσεὶ ἐτῶν τριάκοντα. Of course the tradition behind these words is not uniform; the word ἀρχόμενος is especially uncertain, but that is the way that the matter is stated by Luke. We cannot say where he obtained this information about Jesus' age, but this number has played a leading role in the debate about the age of Jesus and the duration of his public activity. Any attempt to determine the exact year of Jesus' birth, however, founders on the word ὡσεὶ ("about, approximately"). In addition, the round number thirty has a rather indefinite quality about it: it certainly does not appear to be precise.[1] Th. Zahn's comment on this point is not completely convincing, but is still worthy of mention: Luke certainly expressed himself very strangely, unless he was aware that a series of years had passed between the baptism and the death of Jesus. For no intelligent person would say, "When he set out, he was about thirty years old," of a man who died in the same year that he began his

1. Cf. a papyrus owned by the New Testament Seminar at Berlin University, cited by Paul M. Meyer, *Greichische Texte au Aegypten* (1916), 27–28. A. Deissmann remarks that "Among the instructive elements in the papyri is the formula ὡς ἐτῶν, followed by a numerical determination, which is informative for the well-known text in Lk 3:23 ... Although the age of an Egyptian could be determined, the exact date of birth does not appear in the recording of the scribe. Over and over we see round numbers ... 'about 40,' 'about 50 years old.'" If we take the assertion of Luke 3:23 in this sense, then it is not as significant for the chronology of early Christianity as it is often thought to be.

ministry. This text thus offers some support to the view that Jesus was active not for merely one year, but for several.

The Temptation of Jesus
(Mark 1:12–13; Matt 4:1–11; Luke 4:1–13)

Closely connected to Mark 1:9–11 is a little report about the temptation of Jesus: καὶ εὐθύς τὸ πνεῦμα αὐτὸν ἐκβάλλει εἰς τὴν ἔρημον . . . (v. 12). The connection with what precedes (except for εὐθύς) is so strong that perhaps it might be proper to regard the baptism and temptation stories as originally one pericope. I have already discussed the designation of place in the expression εἰς τὴν ἔρημον; here it has its ordinary meaning, namely, that Jesus made his way up from the Jordan into the desert. The temporal designation τεσσεράκοντα ἡμέρας is strikingly detailed, and it has been asked whether Jesus really was tempted for a full forty (40) days. The question is prompted by Matthew's version of the story, in which the temptation only begins after the forty days, but perhaps the issue cannot be fully resolved, or even seriously debated. No value at all can be placed on the exact number, since forty (40) is a very typical number (cf. especially the story of the forty-year wandering of the children of Israel), and thereby it loses all its chronological significance here.

Matthew (4:1–11) marks off his temptation narrative with the now familiar τότε. There follows a temptation story in three acts: in the desert (vv. 3–4), in the Holy City (introduced by another τότε; vv. 5–7), and atop a high mountain (introduced by πάλιν; vv. 8–10), followed by the conclusion (where?) introduced again by τότε; v. 11. The expression ἁγία πόλις is obviously a pattern of speech used by those of Jewish background. The location of the "high mountain" is of no interest to the narrator, but others soon took up the task of locating and identifying it, as in the Gospel of the Hebrews: ἀνήνεγκέ με εἰς τὸ ὄρος τὸ μέγα τὸ Θαβώρ.

Luke (4:1–13) contains exactly the same material as Matthew. Both τότε (Matt 4:1) and καὶ εὐθύς (Mark 1:12) are missing, but these bits of verbal patchwork really mark more of a separation than a connection, at least that is what Luke seems to have thought. He forged a connection stronger than the one given by the tradition when he introduced the words ἀπὸ τοῦ Ἰορδάνου. He reports the three acts of the temptation in a different order, probably geographically, and he intends to make a substantial improvement over Matthew. τὸ ὄρος is lacking, and the Jewish-Christian (Jewish) expression εἰς τὴν ἁγίαν πόλιν is replaced with εἰς τὴν Ἰερουσαλήμ. The chronological conclusion (v. 13) is typical: ὁ διάβολος ἀπέστη ἀπ᾽ αὐτοῦ ἄχρι καιροῦ.

With this sequencing remark Luke sets the developments that will follow in a parenthesis: although the devil will have no part to play in Luke's narration of the public ministry of Jesus, he will come back on the stage at the beginning of the Passion Narrative (cf. Luke 22:3).

2

Jesus' Activity in Galilee

(Mark 1:14–45par.)

Jesus' Entry into Galilee
(Mark 1:14–16; Matt 4:12–17; Luke 4:14–15)

CLEARLY A NEW SECTION begins here: μετὰ δὲ τὸ παραδοθῆναι τὸν Ἰωάννην ἦλθεν ὁ Ἰησοῦς εἰς τὴν Γαλιλαίαν.

> δέ is so well-attested (א A L ... lat pesh arm eth) that it deserves preference over καί (B D syr). Mark always prefers to begin a pericope with καί, so here it has been supplemented. In this text, it cannot be the residue of a καί from an old pericope-caesura, because 1:14–15 is, as has been demonstrated, the work of the evangelist. If καί were original, then δέ would have to be an atticizing gloss, but it is not clear why such a gloss would appear here, and only here.

The introduction includes a designation of time, but that designation is too vague to be of any significance. We hear nothing about when the arrest of John took place, nor about how much time had elapsed between Jesus' temptation and this παραδοθῆναι. Not only is there an absence of any external chronological connection, there is also a complete lack of any internal link with what has preceded. Jesus' entry into Galilee seems to have been unmotivated; the most we can say is that he was returning to his homeland. The exact circumstances under which the Baptist departed the stage are also not described. Apparently all of this could be regarded as well-known. The same goes for the topography: every kind of geographical detail is wanting. Should we conclude that Jesus came straight from the desert, which was either in or right next to Galilee? Even the designation "Galilee" is not very specific. Thus the contents of vv. 14–15 are general and imprecise; they make up a summary statement that we should credit to the account of the evangelist. He constructed this statement in order to secure an introduction for the individual scenes that will follow. The style is quite different from the two preceding pericopes, as well as from the following one, a fact that is especially evident in the much-discussed account in Mark 3:7–12. There too we find not the smooth narrative style of epic, which does not describe actual facts, but idiosyncratic summaries and remarks.

It is significant for our purposes that a seam lies between 1:13 and 1:14. J. Weiss is correct to speak of a salvation-historical chronology here, according to which the entry of Jesus follows upon that of the Baptist. It is well-known that the fourth evangelist has Jesus and the Baptist working side by side. As has been demonstrated, however, the historical course of events cannot be reconstructed with certainty on the basis of Mark. Jesus did not necessarily move directly into Galilee after the baptism and temptation. The account as it appears in the Gospel of John, with Jesus and the Baptist working alongside each other, can be put in its proper place without too much difficulty. I do not say this in order to rescue the Gospel of John as a historical source, as if we could incorporate its narratives into the synoptic outlines at specific points in a harmonizing kind of way. Methodologically, it is instead a matter of the tendencies in the report of the fourth evangelist: as part of a polemic against disciples of John the Baptist, he wants to describe Jesus and the Baptist as working alongside each other (John the Baptist was not the only one to baptize: Jesus also baptized, and at the same time!). Whether anything historical can be extracted from this tendency is a different question. It seems to me that what is historical here is not the baptismal activity of Jesus, upon which the fourth gospel places so much weight, but rather that Jesus had begun his own public ministry while the Baptist was still active. This can be inferred from a proper evaluation of the non-chronological character of the Gospel of Mark: schematization is the driving force here, a salvation-historical schema that is based on the idea that the old must give way so that the new can unfold. John the Baptist must exit, so that Jesus can enter. On the whole, this schema is historical, and the first Christians kept their eye on this important line of development. But in its details the development did not proceed so clearly and schematically. The possibility thus persists that Jesus did work alongside the Baptist, and it remains questionable whether 1:14–15 reports the real beginning of his public ministry.

Matthew and Luke glossed over the seam between Mark 1:13 and 1:14, but for very different reasons. Matthew offers a distinctive form of the summary statement (4:12–17): ἀκούσας δὲ ὅτι Ἰωάννης παρεδόθη, ἀνεχώρησεν εἰς τὴν Γαλιλαίαν.

Some mss. insert ὁ Ἰησοῦς after δὲ (C* E L Γ Δ, it . . .). Supplements of this sort usually indicate the beginning of a pericope. The individual narrative has been lifted out of its context, and the subject of the saying must be named.

This introduction, like that of Mark (1:14), can be understood as a purely chronological statement. It is possible that Matthew may have given this indicator of time as an explanation of Jesus' motivation: ἀκούσας means "because he had heard." ἀνεχώρησεν also poses difficulties, since Mark obviously does not say that Jesus withdrew from the region in which John had been imprisoned. Galilee lay within the territory ruled by Herod Antipas. Do we perhaps have to insert "as it were" before "he withdrew," in order to weaken it? It looks as if Matthew has gotten the historical details all wrong, yet in fact he is often not very particular about such things: a similar oversight occurs when he has Joseph flee from Archelaus, the son of Herod the Great, into Galilee, without thinking that this region was also ruled by one of the sons of Herod. Thus it is better not to ask the question, "Whence did Jesus withdraw?" The context indicates that Jesus withdrew from the desert, which was the stage for the action up to 4:11. Here, however, the desert is a simply an out-of-the-way place. A gap thus lies between 4:11 and 4:12. The ongoing itinerary, which is found only in Matthew (vv. 13–16), is odd, in that there is no transition from v. 12 to v. 13: καὶ καταλιπὼν τὴν Ναζαρὰ κατῴκησεν εἰς Καφαρναοὺμ τὴν παραθαλασσίαν ἐν ὁρίοις Ζαβουλὼν καὶ Νεφταλείμ. It appears to presuppose the idea that when Jesus returned to Galilee, he naturally went first to his hometown of Nazareth. After Jesus left Nazareth—what he had done there is not recounted—he moved to Capernaum, the city by the lake in the territory of Zebulon and Naphtali. A citation from Isaiah follows, to substantiate the activity of Jesus, and then (ἀπὸ τότε) Jesus begins to proclaim the Kingdom of God. Here we can clearly see the work of the evangelist. One fact is at his disposal: Jesus began his preaching of the Kingdom in Galilee (cf. Mark 1:14), and he wants to establish this important event with a proof-text: a prophecy of Isaiah that speaks of Zebulon and Naphtali in Γαλιλαία τῶν ἐθνῶν will suit just fine. For the town of Capernaum, which plays such a large role in the Jesus tradition, was in Galilee, and so he has Jesus move to Capernaum. But since it could appear unseemly to have Jesus (who came from Nazareth) not go back there after his baptism, Nazareth is briefly mentioned in a participial construction. For Matthew, all of this is prelude: the Old Testament, the book of the fathers, says that a light shines in the northern part of the land. The activity of Jesus is to be dated from that point on (n.b. the forceful ἀπὸ τότε, rather than merely τότε).

When the text of Matthew is analyzed in this way, one no longer ventures to ask how much of it goes back to a good historical tradition. The historian can no longer ascertain where Jesus went after his baptism—whether to Nazareth, to Capernaum, or to some other place. Only this much is certain, and absolutely so: Jesus appeared in Galilee. The depiction in the Gospel of Matthew makes this fact unmistakably clear. For the first evangelist, who looks toward Jerusalem, Galilee is a Gentile land (Γαλιλαία τῶν ἐθνῶν), and he is surprised that Jesus began his ministry there, so he is pleased to be able to ground this curious circumstance in a quotation from the fathers.

Luke alters the summary statement of Mark 1:14-15 is his own characteristic way (Luke 4:14-15): καὶ ὑπέστρεψεν ὁ Ἰησοῦς ἐν τῇ δυνάμει τοῦ πνεύματος εἰς τὴν Γαλιλαίαν, φήμη ἐξῆλθεν καθ' ὅλης τῆς περιχώρου περὶ αὐτοῦ· καὶ αὐτὸς ἐδίδασκεν ἐν ταῖς συναγωγαῖς αὐτῶν δοξαζόμενος ὑπὸ πάντων.

> Instead of περιχώρου, ℵ and the Latin versions read χώρας, which reduces the hyperbole. D deletes the apparently extraneous αὐτῶν after συναγωγαῖς; but αὐτῶν is a *constructio ad sensum* in reference to the inhabitants of Galilee.

The alteration is so great that we might almost begin to doubt whether Luke actually had the text of Mark in front of him at this point. But there are indications that Luke's version has been developed from specific features in Mark. No reference is made to the Baptist's imprisonment (contrast Mark and Matthew), because Luke's outline has already brought the story of John the Baptist to its conclusion in 3:19-20. In this context ὑπέστρεψεν does not mean, "he went back," but rather, "he drew back" (cf. 4:1). The phrase ἐν τῇ δυνάμει τοῦ πνεύματος, which is unique to Luke, is the means by which he explains the sudden change of location indicated by the tradition. 4:3ff is similar, and in the Acts of the Apostles (written by this same Luke) it is often the Spirit that suddenly moves the disciples of Jesus from one place to another. Recall, for example, the story of Philip in Acts 8 (v. 26: ἄγγελος κυρίου ἐλάλησεν; v. 39: πνεῦμα κυρίου ἥρπασεν τὸν Φίλιππον), or the missionary journey of Barnabas and Paul in Acts 13 (v. 4: αὐτοὶ . . . ἐκπεμφθέντες ὑπὸ τοῦ ἁγίου πνεύματος κατῆλθον εἰς . . .). It is the Spirit who also prevents Paul and his companion Silas from undertaking a journey they had planned in Acts 16 (cf. v. 6: κωλυθέντες ὑπὸ τοῦ ἁγίου πνεύματος λαλῆσαι τὸν λόγον ἐν τῇ Ἀσίᾳ). This evidence is sufficient to establish with a very high probability that both the phrase ἐν τῇ δυνάμει τοῦ πνεύματος, which is lacking from Mark and Matthew, as well as the phrase ἐν τῷ πνεύματι in 4:1, go back to the evangelist.

By the way, even before the particulars of Jesus' ministry are described, it is steadfastly affirmed that he aroused attention in the entire region of the Galilee. Once again this is a matter of Lukan formulation, as in Acts 9:31, 42. In that case both the former (καθ' ὅλης τῆς Ἰουδαίας) and the latter (καθ' ὅλης τῆς Ἰόππης) are details introduced by Luke.

In what follows, Luke uses the phrase ἐν ταῖς συναγωγαῖς αὐτῶν, and in v. 16 he begins his opening synagogue scene. In a similar way δοξαζόμενος ὑπὸ πάντων also finds its explanation in the story (cf. v. 22). While both Matthew and Mark describe the content of Jesus' proclamation as the preaching of the kingdom, Luke says nothing about that. Apparently it was to him too narrow a depiction of the content of Jesus' preaching; Jesus certainly also spoke of other things. Luke's version has much more the character of a heading to what follows than the reports of Matthew and Luke. As a result, every effort to calculate the length of the activity of Jesus described in this verses falls to the floor. A remark made in a literary heading cannot serve to fill out a span of time in the real world.

Jesus' Inaugural Sermon in Nazareth
(Luke 4:16–30)

We continue to follow the outline of the Gospel of Luke, which next relates Jesus' so-called "inaugural sermon" in Nazareth. The burning question here is how and why Luke altered the outline of Mark, which must have appeared insufficient to him, since his alterations of it at this point are so thorough and far-reaching. The narrative begins: καὶ ἦλθεν εἰς Ναζαρά οὗ ἦν ἀνατεθραμμένος καὶ εἰσῆλθεν κατὰ τὸ εἰωθὸς αὐτῷ ἐν τῇ ἡμέρᾳ τῶν σαββάτων εἰς τὴν συναγωγὴν καὶ ἀνέστη ἀναγνῶναι.

> If D reads ἐλθὼν δὲ instead of καὶ ἦλθεν, this reading is still not true to Luke's style, which strives for a continuous narrative. To give the location so incidentally in a participial construction is typical of Matthew. With good reason von Soden cites the reading of Matt 13:54 here. —A few mss insert ὁ Ἰησοῦς. I have already (cf. above, p. 27) discussed the introductions to pericopes. Tischendorff (Editio VIII) confirms that "F G M (*initio lectionis*) al aliq add ὁ Ἰησοῦς. —ἀνατεθραμμένος καὶ εἰσῆλθεν is missing from D.

To begin, this introduction must be regarded from top to bottom as the work of the evangelist. The phrase οὗ ἦν ἀνατεθραμμένος is an introductory comment on the part of the author. And what does it introduce?

Simply this: that Jesus made his inaugural appearance right in Nazareth, the city in which he grew up. κατὰ τὸ εἰωθὸς αὐτῷ is similar, serving as Luke's explanation for the fact that Jesus went to the synagogue. Acts 17:2 confirms that this is a distinctly Lukan expression. Exactly what Luke meant by this phrase, "according to his custom," is more difficult to ascertain. Some exegetes think of the Jewish custom of visiting the synagogue on the Sabbath, but it is more likely that Jesus was in the habit of going to the synagogue as a teacher. It is somewhat disturbing, though, that Luke should refer back to previous synagogue visits while narrating Jesus' first visit to a synagogue. Thus it becomes clear that Luke inserted this story about Jesus preaching in Nazareth in its present location. He put this special tradition here in order to achieve an intensification in the unfolding movements of Jesus. Jesus begins his ministry in his home town, and Luke obviously takes that as a given. He is the only one of the evangelists who asks about the original starting point for the activity of Jesus. At the same time he offers an answer to the question of why Jesus did not make his home town the center of his work. Only after Nazareth can Capernaum come into view, and after that the entire region of the Galilee. Thus the ministry of Jesus moves outward in ever-widening circles, in a development from the lesser to the greater. Luke wants to put the story of Jesus into a sequence and thereby to describe it as much as possible as a biography. It is all the more surprising that in v. 23 the people of Nazareth ask for miracles like those he has done in Capernaum (ὅσα ἠκούσαμεν γενόμενα . . .), since to this point Luke has said nothing about any such activity in Capernaum. From this evidence it is clear that this story originally belonged to a later section in the ministry of Jesus, in a chronological setting that we cannot recover. Luke obviously did not notice the contradiction. I simply do not believe that he noticed it but was too conservative to set it aside.

It appears questionable whether v. 24 was spoken on the same occasion as that which precedes. Luke has brought the saying (Mark 6:4; Matt 13:57) into this setting, and it does not fit well here; v. 25ff matches up very well with v. 23. The phrase ἐν τῷ πατρίδι in v. 23 will have been the reason that Luke put the well-known, oft-cited saying of Jesus about a prophet in his own country in this context. The overall theme of Luke is thus somewhat different from that of Mark and Matthew: while in those gospels the Nazarenes reject Jesus, here Jesus rejects the Nazarenes. This theme illumines everything that will follow: what Jesus does here, he will do everywhere—like Elijah and Elisha, he will turn away from the hard-hearted and bring salvation to the Gentiles. It seems unlikely that this was the actual course of historical events. Certainly the primitive Christian community, under the influence of its break with Judaism, came to look at it that way. Thus Luke did not come upon any strong chronological indicator for this question about the success of Jesus among his nearest neighbors; instead, he designed it, and his design did not get the chronology right.

Perhaps we should go still further in this direction: can we be certain that this scene, which means so much to us, really played out in Nazareth? The question has to be asked, since v. 23 (the phrase ἐν τῷ πατρίδι σου stands elsewhere in Mark) and v. 22b (the detail certainly originates with Mark) have to be removed. Only the opening phrase εἰς Ναζαρά points toward Nazareth. But is the narrative really set in Nazareth? Many stories were handed down without any indication of their location. From among the many possibilities I select only one, a synagogue scene that now stands recorded in Mark 3:1ff. Even if the oral tradition had not already localized the story, then Luke could have done it, on the basis of the motives discussed above. In other cases localizations attached themselves to pericopes, and that also could have happened here. Critical questions of this sort can be posed quite forcefully here. Gospel criticism is all too used to irrationalities, including miracles with which our modern scientific outlook is totally unfamiliar. Most of the time it is a matter of criticism of content and outlook, usually to the neglect of genuine literary criticism. Questions such as the one I have just raised here are regarded as unimportant. I can hear the objection: why in the world would this scene not have happened in Nazareth? And the answer is: because an analysis of the oldest Jesus tradition, a peek into the workshop of the author Luke, forces this question upon us. It has already been demonstrated that localizations often attached themselves to stories. In fact it would not be remarkable if over the course of the centuries everything had been localized! Every detail in the Holy Scripture found its fixed abode, to which pilgrims could journey—and still do. Medieval travel narratives piled tradition upon tradition. Modern scholarship (including Catholicism) looked into this material critically and disregarded most of it. Thus it has not been made sufficiently clear that this process of localizing events in the story of Jesus was not post-biblical, or even post- or extra-canonical. On the contrary, it is as old as the earliest traditions themselves. Luke lived in that era, and therefore he could set the inaugural sermon of Jesus in Nazareth. We take none of the shine off the story if we disconnect it from its location. Certainly it cannot be said that the story of Jesus preaching from the prophet Isaiah has anything in particular to do with Nazareth. Such stories are essentially timeless and place-less, and we are attuned to its content if we hear the pericope as part of the worship service in the form of the Sunday reading. That is where this story belonged from the very beginning. The introductory designations of place and time are only ornamentation, only the framework, and they must not distract our attention from the splendid picture itself.

Marcion's placement of the Nazareth story shows just how loose the chronological sequence in the Gospels is, even in Luke, who took some care with arrangement. In Marcion the pericope is located between 4:39 and 4:40. Marcion probably wanted to make sense of the remark in 4:23, which mentions Jesus' activity in Capernaum, but his efforts do not give us the original arrangement. At one stroke a whole series of closely-related narratives (Mark 1:21-38 = Luke 4:31-43) is shattered, and Luke 4:40ff takes place not in Capernaum but in Nazareth. Worse yet, the remark in 4:23 is still not adequately explained. For the ministry in Capernaum that it introduces is so insignificant that the Nazarenes could hardly have brought it up. Yet Marcion's rearrangement is very instructive for a correct understanding of the outline of the Gospels. The narratives could be repositioned, and the framework would not be damaged. The introductory remarks about chronology and topography remained intact. What Marcion did to Luke, Luke and Matthew had already done to Mark—and before that, Mark had done it to the oral tradition. It all comes down to the individual narratives, not to their chronological connections. Hunting for firm chronology in this kind of material is like chasing after a ghost.

It seems to me that these literary observations are of primary importance, and they can be further reinforced by precise information about the topography of Nazareth. At this point I must rely upon authorities who have actually seen the place. Pölzl, for example, states: "To the west of Nazareth there are several steep slopes where a fall can be life-threatening. The tradition that locates the attempt on Jesus' life at the current site of the Maronite church is categorically better than any that locates it at "the mount of the precipice" (about an hour down from the town—too far away)." M. Brückner, on the other hand, writes: "Nazareth does not sit atop a mountain, but rather is an inhabited slope; the town is situated on the southern side of the hill, and there is no precipice that fits the description in Luke 4:29. Of course they will show you one today." In a similar vein, Merx remarks: "I note that there are no cliffs atop the height of Gebel-Siqh, which I visited on 21 Mar 1891, and that the only rock faces in the town are above the Greek church and the Maronite church, although legend has not seen fit to locate the story there. Legend places it (implausibly) two English miles southeast of the town upon a cliff that overlooks the Jezreel Valley . . . but only because the hill above the town does not fit the description ἕως ὀφρύος τοῦ ὄρους." In sum, there is no getting around the topographical difficulties.

The Call of the First Disciples
(Mark 1:16–20; Matt 4:18–22; Luke 5:1–11)

καὶ παράγων παρὰ τὴν θάλασσαν τῆς Γαλιλαίας εἶδεν Σίμωνα καὶ Ἀνδρέαν τὸν ἀδελφὸν Σίμωνος ἀμφιβάλλοντας ἐν τῇ θαλάσσῃ.

With these words begins the first individual report of the Galilean ministry.

The reading περιπατοῦν δὲ (Α Γ Δ ... syr) comes from Matt 4:18.

Here we begin by taking notice of an absence, i.e., what the narrative does not have. First of all, it lacks any chronological and topographical transition. We hear nothing about how long Jesus has been preaching, or where, or how he has come to be at the Sea of Galilee. The text of 1:14 does not specify in what precise locality we should place him. The author writes as if he is relating something that is already known. As in 1:4–8 and 1:9–13, we are dealing with a story that was told by and for those who already knew all about it. Mark simply took over a pericope that already existed, and he did not change or expand it. At most τῆς Γαλιλαίας might be an explanatory comment by the evangelist. The strength of the pericope is especially evident in the names of the two brothers Simon and Andrew. As was previously the case with John the Baptist and Jesus, the two do not receive any kind of introduction. It seems as if the brothers were already acquainted with Jesus, or that they had heard some of the preaching described in 1:14–15, but we are actually reading such things into the text through a kind of psychological reflection. The individual gospel narratives are a long way from drawing this type of connection between the individual stories and the larger overall framework. Nor did Mark do anything to change that. Of course it could have been handled differently; the gaps could have been glossed over, as is shown by the other two evangelists, who place this narrative in a different form and context. But Mark preserves the original local color of the scene, so that in this narrative we find ourselves taken back into the earliest circle of Jesus' disciples. J. Weiss has perceptively observed that the word παράγων is spoken more from the perspective of fishermen on the water, who see Jesus passing by on the shore, than from the perspective of Jesus. This way of introducing a pericope had staying power: cf. Mark 2:14 and John 9:1. But Matthew changed the opening. The absolute ἀμφιβάλλοντας is a *terminus technicus* that is especially appropriate on the lips of the fishermen who are telling this story. Matthew explained it with the phrase βάλλοντας ἀμφίβληστρον. In my judgment the term θάλασσα is a native expression: fishermen who lived by and on this lake would have called it a "sea," but not an author who was at home in the wider Mediterranean world. It is significant that Luke, who thinks like a Greek, and the author of the Gospel of the Ebionites both use λίμνη rather than θάλασσα (Luke 5:1; Epiphanius, *Haer.* 30.13). καὶ εὐθύς is already known to us. Here too it can be asked whether the term might be fraught with meaning. That is possible, since Matthew preserved the sense of "immediately" (εὐθέως).

Καὶ προβὰς ὀλίγον εἶδεν Ἰάκωβον τὸν τοῦ Ζεβεδαίου καὶ Ἰωάννην τὸν ἀδελφὸν αὐτοῦ (v. 18).

> B, along with ℵ* (although without ὀλίγον) A, C, Γ, Δ, and Vg, reads ἐκεῖθεν after προβάς. This insertion originates from Matt 4:21.

Once again our curiosity about chronology and topography is left unsatisfied. Certainly ὀλίγον was firmly settled in the tradition that Mark has taken up, for the second evangelist hardly ever introduces this kind of connection. On this basis one could argue that 1:16-18 and 1:19-20 originally belonged together, since the two scenes are otherwise completely parallel to each other. In that case, all the comments that I have made above about 1:16ff would apply here as well. The use of the definite article in the phrase ἐν τῷ πλοίῳ is striking, and it may indeed be possible that it corresponds to our expression "on board." On the other hand the article may also indicate that this vessel was already known to the earliest narrators and listeners. In view of what we have already seen, the style in which this report is delivered is not surprising, and we are going to continue to encounter this use of the definite article in expressions like ὁ οἶκος and τὸ ὄρος.

Matthew (4:18-22) agrees with Mark in content and structure, but is slightly more polished: περιπατῶν δὲ παρὰ τὴν θάλασσαν τῆς Γαλιλαίας εἶδεν δύο ἀδελφούς, Σίμωνα τὸν λεγόμενον Πέτρον καὶ Ἀνδρέαν τὸν ἀδελφὸν αὐτοῦ, βάλλοντας ἀμφίβληστρον εἰς τὴν θάλασσαν.

> D, following Mark, reads παράγων here. Some manuscripts read ὁ Ἰησοῦς after δέ.

Matthew's transition into this pericope is smoother than Mark's. Since Jesus has already been preaching beside the sea (4:12), the phrase παρὰ τὴν θάλασσαν has a familiar ring. Yet the episode does not fit particularly well into Matthew's outline, for the first evangelist goes to some lengths to give a comprehensive picture of Jesus' ministry. In this story, however, he could not quite get himself entirely free of Mark's order. Thus he substituted δέ (vv. 18, 20) for Mark's καί, and εὐθέως (vv. 20, 22) for Mark's εὐθύς, and in v. 19 he dropped ὁ Ἰησοῦς as unnecessary. In v. 21 Matthew's transition to the next scene is smoother than Mark's, which is marked by ἐκεῖθεν. It is the same with the character treatment: Matthew provides them with something like an introduction, whereas in Mark they appear on stage with no announcement at all. Two different times Matthew says, "two brothers," but in each case he then follows the name of the second brother with the phrase τὸν ἀδελφὸν αὐτοῦ. These words are utterly superfluous, but they are important for our purposes because they show that Matthew is dependent upon Mark's text. Zebedee is also mentioned, yet another gloss on Mark.

Luke (5:1–11) narrates a version of the call story that is essentially different. Here we do not meet two pairs of disciples; instead only the call of Simon is reported, and the story is placed in an entirely different position than in Mark. A miracle story is the narrative's most important feature: ἐγένετο δὲ ἐν τῷ τὸν ὄχλον ἐπικεῖσθαι αὐτῷ καὶ ἀκούειν τὸν λόγον τοῦ θεοῦ, καὶ αὐτὸς ἦν ἑστὼς παρὰ τὴν λίμνην Γεννησαρὲτ καὶ εἶδεν δύο πλοιάρια ἑστῶτα παρὰ τὴν λίμνην.

> ς reads (along with C D vg) τοῦ ἀκούειν. The articular infinitive is a later gloss, as is the reading ἑστῶτος αὐτου in D. The spelling of the name Gennesaret varies: Γεννησαρέτ, Γεννησαρέθ, Γεννησαρέδ. In some mss ὁ Ἰησοῦς appears after ἑστώς. The Gospel lectionaries read that way. These books, structured as they were by pericopes, needed to use Jesus' name near the beginning of each pericope.

Verse 10 only hints at the calling of James and John, the two sons of Zebedee, rather than actually narrating it. Simon is in the foreground throughout the scene. In fact his calling is the only one that is narrated. The difficulty of this special tradition is further reflected in the variations that arose in the textual tradition. Thus in D it is not Simon alone who is called, but rather the two brothers as well (ὁ εἶπεν αὐτοῖς, δεῦτε . . .), a reading that corrects the apparent contradiction between v. 10 and v. 11 in the text of Mark.

Excursus: Luke's Configuration of
the Outline of the Story of Jesus

Our evaluation of the transition from chapter 4 to chapter 5 in the gospel of Luke will depend upon whether the reading in 4:44 is τῆς Ἰουδαίας or τῆς Γαλιλαίας. If it is τῆς Ἰουδαίας, then the transition is quite remarkable. For even though Luke is trying to report an itinerary, with Jesus traveling from place to place, here he sets us down in a completely new scene without any preparation at all. The dissonance would be reduced if the correct reading in

4:44 is τῆς Γαλιλαίας, for then the narrative would move forward smoothly: "as Jesus was by the Sea of Galilee, this and that happened." In that case we could be certain that we are on Galilean soil. The reasons for Luke opening his narrative in this way can carefully be made clear. Earlier we referred to the fact that Luke is following a topographical arrangement in his first chapter: Nazareth—Capernaum—Galilee (i.e., the region around Capernaum). Thus it was matter of necessity for Luke to begin his narration of the ministry of Jesus by the Sea at this point.[1]

This re-ordering of the outline of the story Jesus—or, one might say, Luke's critique of the earlier arrangement of the stories in the gospel of Mark—is important. It is clear from the report in Mark that Jesus called his first disciples *before* the beginning of his public activity, but Luke does not recount the course of events that way. Thus Mark's description was subject to criticism from very early on, and it absorbed some heavy blows. In fact historical probability is actually on Luke's side.[2] At the beginning of his ministry Jesus would surely have worked for a time without disciples, and the notion that he hurried from southern Palestine to the Sea of Galilee and immediately called two pairs of disciples cannot possibly be historical. Here Luke helps us recognize the problem, but he does not give us the oldest version of the story.

Merx has neatly summarized the outline of the gospel of Luke:

> Inspired by the Baptist movement, Jesus leaves Nazareth where he was brought up, goes to the Jordan to be baptized and then withdraws into the desert (4:1). Then he travels around in Galilee, teaching and becoming well-known (4:14). At this time he comes back to his hometown of Nazareth and (as was his custom) delivers a sermon on the Sabbath there (where he was well received). A dispute arises between him and the residents,

---

1. Commentators appraise this narrative in various ways, because they do not adequately understand Luke's plan. Some (B. Weiss, *Markus und Lukas*, 349, e.g.) maintain that Luke is thinking here of a different event than the one related in Mark 1:16–20. Meyer (350) says Luke is harking back to Simon's connection with Jesus that was narrated in 4:38. All these explanations correctly recognize the difficulty, but solve it very awkwardly.

2. Loisy disagrees (*Les Évangiles synoptiques*, 1:439): "Jesus could not have stayed in Simon's house at Capernaum until after Simon had become a disciple." But Loisy's historical judgment relies heavily upon Mark. Why should Jesus not stay with Peter, even if Peter had not yet become a Christian?

forcing him to flee and resettle in Capernaum, where he teaches every Sabbath and performs miracles (4:31). The family and business partners of Simon, who later came to be called Cephas, live there, and Jesus becomes friendly with them (4:38). Jesus' first disciples were Simon and his business partners, James and John, the sons of Zebedee. All of this is reasonable, coherent, and believable. The call of the first disciples is natural and normal.[3]

Elsewhere Merx speaks of "a biographical arrangement in Luke," a phrase that correctly describes the distinctive character of the third gospel. This characteristic is too often misconstrued, however, especially by advocates of the Markan hypothesis. For even though Luke's arrangement looks to us like a well-grounded account of Jesus ministry—and even if it does actually give us a better version of the historical reality—that does not change the fact that Luke's account is a product of his own construction. We cannot overlook the fact that Luke's arrangement contains discrepancies—literary discrepancies, rather than errors of content. Merx is so favorably predisposed toward Luke that he misses this point altogether, but Spitta (whose overall assessment of Luke is generally the same as Merx) has a sharper eye. He concludes that the pericope in Luke 5:1–11 "interrupts the original context," and he speaks of the "comprehensive weight of the inconsistency, which does not reflect well on Luke's authorial abilities."[4] Spitta wants to find a continuous narrative that could have served as the basis for the Synoptic gospels, and he naturally thinks that Luke, the most biographical of the evangelists, is the gospel in which this document is to be found. Yet even Spitta cannot get around the fact that there are certain inconsistencies in Luke's text, and he has to resort to theories of interpolation in order to smooth them out. It seems to me, however, that we must always remember that Luke found himself in a very difficult situation: he did not want to alter the traditional outline of the story of Jesus very much; indeed, perhaps he *couldn't*.

---

3. Merx, *Markus und Lukas II/2*, 28–29.
4. Spitta, *Die synoptische Grundschrift*, 53.

In the Synagogue at Capernaum
(Mark 1:21-28; Luke 4:31-37)

καὶ εἰσπορεύονται εἰς Καφαρναούμ. καὶ εὐθὺς τοῖς σάββασιν ἐδίδασκεν εἰς τὴν συναγωγήν.

The text is uncertain here. A few mss read εἰσπορεύεται, making the story a Jesus pericope.others (A B D Γ lat arm eth) insert εἰσελθών after τοῖς σάββασιν. The expression διδάσκειν εἰς is not unusual in the Koine, which often used εἰς and ἐν interchangeably. A later Atticist would have regarded this text as disconnected, and would have wanted to correct it. The readings of syrs will be discussed below.

In this case there are strong topographical and chronological connections, but as soon as we try to trace out those connections in detail, difficulties begin to surface. Commentators end up proposing various dates for this event, dates that often stand in direct contradiction with each other. As a matter of fact this passage cannot be explained clearly. Jesus and his newly-won disciples move from the shore to Capernaum and immediately go into the synagogue on the Sabbath. Are we to suppose that they arrived in Capernaum on a Sabbath? If so, then the call stories must also have taken place on the Sabbath. This seems unlikely, since it would mean that the disciples would have been hard at work, fishing, on the Sabbath. To avoid this impossible conclusion, an indefinite interval of time is usually inserted either right *before* or right *after* καὶ εἰσπορεύονται εἰς Καφαρναούμ. B. Weiss[5] starts from the observation that εὐθύς has to create a connection with that which follows εἰσπορεύονται, and on that basis he argues that there is nothing here about a direct movement from the sea to the village. Other exegetes[6] place a gap in the narrative between the arrival and the entry into the synagogue. On this view, Jesus came into Capernaum with his disciples and taught on the next Sabbath after their arrival. Wohlenberg[7] finds the following chronological connection:

> The onset of the Sabbath took place soon after the Lord had arrived in Capernaum with his four disciples. Thus their arrival in Capernaum was sometime on Friday afternoon, and the story that we read took place during the services held on that Sabbath ... Otherwise we will have to assume that this description refers

---

5. B. Weiss, *Markus und Lukas*, 21.
6. J. Weiss, *Das älteste Evangelium*, 141; Windisch, "Die Dauer," 143.
7. Wohlenberg, *Markus*, 56-57.

not to the evening or opening service, but has to do with the Saturday evening gathering or gatherings.

All of these explanations (of which Wohlenberg's seems to be one of the more reasonable and plausible) argue that we are dealing here with a close sequence of chronological events, which nevertheless must be softened at those points where difficulties arise. But in view of what we have already discovered about the framework of the story of Jesus, it appears that Mark's chronology is nothing more than a postulate, from which we will have to make a clean break. In our studies to this point there is nothing to indicate that εὐθύς is meant literally (in the corresponding text, 4:31, Luke has neither εὐθύς nor εὐθέως). Most of all—and this is the decisive point—there is a seam between 1:20 and 1:21, a seam that cannot and must not be filled in.[8] Nothing at all is told to us about what happened to Jesus and his new disciples right after their call. A new pericope begins in 1:21, a new pericope that forms a piece entirely separate from 1:16-20. Recall as well that 1:16-20 is not in its proper place in the outline of the story of Jesus.[9]

When we consider the report of Jesus' synagogue preaching as a whole, it appears so similar to summary statements like 1:14-15 that it seems best to regard it too as a piece of the evangelist's construction. It may be pointed out in this regard that the phrase ἐν τοῖς σάββασιν does not necessarily designate one particular Sabbath. The linguistic function of the phrase is not so simple: sometimes τὸ σάββατον and τὰ σάββατα were used interchangeably (cf. within these narratives 2:23-24 vs. 2:27-28), and the plural meaning is not necessarily excluded here either. The generalizing plural would be better suited for a summary statement that intends to introduce what follows. And this verse is rather more concrete than 1:14-15. There, for example, a specific place is mentioned, Capernaum, and a specific location, the synagogue. It can be asked whether these local details should not be credited to the evangelist's account. It may be that 1:21b (from καὶ εὐθύς on) and 1:22 were inserted by Mark, who expanded a pure summary statement (as it appears in Matt 7:28b-29) into the subsequent narrative of 1:23-24. Or it is equally possible that vv. 23-28, which form a well-rounded narrative, may have originally been an independent pericope that Mark found in some other

---

8. That Jesus came to Capernaum from Nazareth is an insupportable hypothesis. It arises from the effort to square Mark with Luke, where Jesus does indeed first appear in Nazareth (Luke 4:16ff).

9. J. Weiss (*Schriften*, 76) appends καὶ εἰσπορεύονται εἰς Καφαρναούμ (v. 21a) to 1:16-20 to conclude the call story, and Wendling agrees (cf. *Urmarkus*, 43). Nothing specific can be said against this partitioning of the pericopes (it is a matter of taste and style), but differences in interpretation do not change the point I have been making: two pericopes meet each other here!

setting and placed here in this location. Verse 29 certainly links up smoothly with v. 22. These kinds of solutions are fairly easy because of Mark's strongly paratactic style, but this is a situation that calls for considerable care and restraint. It has to be borne in mind that 1:27a might point back to 1:22. Ultimately the Gospel of Mark requires a restrained kind of criticism: this evangelist arranges the individual stories that have come down to him in the tradition, putting them into a series, one after another. It was not his style to make artistic interpolations.

The second act begins in v. 23.[10] The new beginning is clearly marked: καὶ εὐθὺς ἦν ἐν τῇ συναγωγῇ αὐτῶν ἄνθρωπος ἐν πνεύματι ἀκαθάρτῳ. A definite unit, the healing of a demoniac, is recounted here. There is no reason to take the word εὐθύς literally (it is missing, by the way, from ς A C D Γ Δ it vg arm aeth go). Its use here clearly exemplifies its insignificance:the meaning of the sentence is not changed by its presence or absence.[11] Verse 27 depicts the immediate consequences of the miracle, and also of Jesus' preaching, and v. 28 relates those consequences more widely: καὶ ἦλθεν ἡ ἀκοὴ αὐτοῦ εὐθὺς πανταχοῦ εἰς ὅλην τὴν περίχωρον τῆς Γαλιλαίας. As in 1:5, the place designation here is hyperbolic in form and content (παντ-, ὁλ-; the "region of Galilee" extends beyond the borders of Galilee). On the one hand, expressions of this sort should not be weakened,[12] but on the other hand they are not necessarily trimmings put on the narrative by the evangelist.[13] Certainly this statement reaches beyond the framework of the narrative, and perhaps even beyond all the material we have treated to this point, but it might express an attitude characteristic of the earliest tradition. Our pericope describes the first appearance of Jesus in the gospel of Mark, a single act of preaching and

---

10. It is noteworthy that the early gospel lectionaries began a new pericope here, and that they therefore replaced the αὐτῶν after ἐν τῇ συναγωγῇ with τῶν Ἰουδαίων. Cf. Tischendorf, *Editio VIII*, sub loc.

11. With good reason, then, J. Weiss translates the εὐθύς of this text with the word "now": "Now there was a man in the synagogue . . ." (J. Weiss, *Schriften*, 78).

12. That is to say, the expression refers to the region of Galilee all around Capernaum.

13. In several publications (*Das älteste Evangelium*, 141; *Schriften*, 83; and "Synoptische Evangelien," 187), J. Weiss has asserted that this depiction of spreading rumors goes so far beyond the temporal and topographical framework of the narratives about the first Sabbath that it cannot possibly come from the narrator of this series of stories. It must be an interpolation by the evangelist, in preparation for the travels and actions of Jesus in 1:39 and 3:7ff. Weiss further points out that it usually takes some time for rumors to spread, but here the subsequent narratives play out only a few hours later. The first point is well taken, but Weiss does not see that this is a trait of the earliest tradition, rather than of the evangelist. His objection is based on an overly mechanical view of the gospel. 1:28 can be understood as a parenthesis, so that Wohlenberg's stylistic observation still stands: "The connection with what follows would almost be smoother without v. 28."

healing that cannot possibly have had such a substantial impact. This historical judgment is certainly right, but it does not mean that the inclination of the tradition was not original. The narratives of Jesus' synagogue miracle and the subsequent events were created out of a fund of stories about Jesus' actions, a fund that is no longer available to us. The actual chronology, therefore, remains (for us) an insoluble riddle.

We have already touched upon the question of whether it was the evangelist who situated this pericope in Capernaum. In the case of Luke's Nazareth narrative, I argued that the location was a later addition. Here, however, the situation is different. Despite what follows—especially the mention of the house of Peter—the Sabbath narrative (vv. 21–28, or vv. 21–22 and vv. 23–28) is not necessarily connected to Capernaum. Yet it is not necessarily tendentious for the story to be located there, in the town that was Peter's home, with specific traditions related to what Jesus did there. The reading of syr^s, as Merx[14] has pointed out with great emphasis, does not change this fact. In syr^s the reading καὶ εἰσπορεύονται εἰς Καφαρναούμ is lacking, and Merx asserts: "This reading can be explained only on the supposition that the original narrative taken up by Mark, which had no details about location, has been arranged according to Matt 4:13 and Luke 4:14, 16, and 31." But how did the ancient tradition answer the question about Jesus' hometown? To that question Mark gave no answer, but simply handed on the tradition, whether it was localized or not. This non-literary method is in fact a literary characteristic of Mark. Therefore, the mention of Capernaum in 1:21 is original, in spite of its absence from syr^{sin}. That manuscript let the designation of place drop out, because it seemed unusual that Jesus would have called fisherman who lived by the sea at Capernaum without ever having visited the town himself. As we have seen, Matthew and Luke smooth out these difficulties, and syr^{sin} has simply done so in an especially radical way. It attempts a similar improvement in 1:21, where it leaves out εὐθύς.[15] Thus the two scenes, 1:16–20 and 1:21–28, which appear to have a strong connection, should be separated from each other. From this point of view the reading of syr^{sin}, which deviates so sharply, is in fact quite important. It opens up the very exegetical problem in which we are most interested.

There is nothing particularly astonishing about the fact that the location of a particular scene might disappear. Some narratives, which are no longer linked to any specific place in the gospels, were originally situated in or around a definite location. Often, however, the topographical setting

---

14. Merx, *Markus und Lukas*, 15–16, 28–29. At this point Merx is heavily influenced by his favoritism toward Luke.

15. Merx, *Markus und Lukas*, 16ff.

was not essential to the point of the story, which depended instead upon the content of the narrative. Yet we have also seen that descriptions of place could attach themselves to stories and be taken up into them, not because any value was laid upon such details, but in fact because they were regarded as a matter of indifference. This is the situation with the gospel of Mark. We cannot construct a canon by which to evaluate the topographical details in this gospel, but we can lay down the following general rule: the fact that Mark sometimes localizes a scene (more or less) and sometimes does not, shows that these designations of place were already there in the tradition that Mark had at his disposal. It is the same with his designations of time. As we have seen, we cannot speak of chronological connections in Mark. Too often we try to solve problems that are not really problems at all. If Mark told the call stories first and then related a series of events in Capernaum, and Luke later reversed that order, there is no need to imagine some sort of special tradition that led Luke to do so. A proper understanding of the outline of Mark shows that there is no relationship between 1:16–20 and 1:21–28, and it will not do to assert that even though there is a break between 1:20 and 1:21, the event described in 1:16–20 still was chronologically prior to the scene in Capernaum. On the contrary, we must go even further: both events could just as well have been reversed in the sequence. The earliest writers of the gospels were not bound by these kinds of concerns and therefore had no scruples about them. Luke simply transposed the two narratives. If that is the case, then we cannot answer the question of what the actual course of events in Capernaum might have been. Mark describes for us only one sojourn in Capernaum in 1:21ff. Matthew fits two stories (1:29ff and 1:32ff) into a report of a second visit to Capernaum. Even here it is not a matter of some "improper" alteration of the Markan narrative, because Mark himself gives us no information about the order and series of events during the visit to Capernaum.[16] Advocates of the Markan Hypothesis cannot smash the framework of the story of Jesus in Matthew and Luke, nor can those who favor Luke (Merx and Spitta, e.g.) do the same to Matthew and Mark. The framework has to be smashed all the way around, in all three gospels. The Markan Hypothesis suffers no damage thereby to its essential kernel, i.e., that Mark is the oldest gospel. Those who prefer Luke, however, and who believe they can find therein support for the framework of the story of Jesus, will find that this support has been irretrievably snatched away.

We have already discussed Matthew's reworking of this outline. It is striking that he completely omits the narrative in Mark 1:21–28, beginning

---

16. Comments like Klostermann's are unproductive: "It appears that Jesus comes to Capernaum with his companions for the first time" (Klostermann, *Markus*, 12).

instead with the next story. Mark 1:22 is relocated to the conclusion of the Sermon on the Mount (Matt 7:28–29), and we can only guess at his reasons for omitting the healing of the demoniac. In the position where he might have told that story from Mark (i.e., chapters 8 and 9, *after* the Sermon on the Mount), Matthew put another narrative from his special tradition, which exemplifies Jesus' exorcisms (9:32–33).[17]

Luke, by contrast, presents the exorcism in the same context as Mark. Luke 4:31 reads: καὶ κατῆλθεν εἰς Καφαρναοὺμ πόλιν τῆς Γαλιλαίας καὶ ἦν διδάσκων αὐτοὺς ἐν τοῖς σάββασιν.

> After κατῆλθεν we find in some manuscripts, in good style, ὁ ις. Tischendorf points out: "In Mmg the initial reading is notated with τῷ καιρῷ ἠλθεν ὁ ις." This τῷ καιρῷ offers strong support to the thesis offered above, namely, that chronological specifications of this sort are at bottom nothing more than introductions to pericopes." After τῆς Γαλιλαίας D reads as a supplement to Matt 4:13: τὴν παραθαλάσσιον ἐν ὁρίοις Ζαβουλὼν καὶ Νεφθαλείμ.

The choice of the verb κατῆλθεν rises from Luke's method for the presentation of the setting: Jesus has left Nazareth, which lies on higher ground, and moved to Capernaum, which lies on the Sea of Galilee. From Luke's point of view this topographical movement also has a spiritual aspect: in Nazareth, Jesus' hometown, no one wanted to learn from the master; so he turned toward Capernaum, which also was in Galilee. πόλιν τῆς Γαλιλαίας is an explanatory addition by the evangelist, whose readers appear to have been generally uninformed about the geography of Palestine.[18] Capernaum has already been mentioned in 4:23, showing once again that the reference to Capernaum in chapter 4 did not fit neatly into the framework Luke wanted to construct. ἐν τοῖς σάββασιν does not designate any particular Sabbath, and should be identified with a preaching ministry of Jesus that lasted for some length of time. The construction ἐν διδάσκων points in this same direction (cf. ἐδίδασκεν in Mark 1:21). When Luke wants to designate a specific Sabbath day, he usually says ἐν τῇ ἡμέρᾳ τῶν σαββάτων (4:16). The healing of the demoniac concludes in v. 23 in almost exactly the same way as it does in Mark—only εὐθύς is missing. Luke tones down Mark's exaggerated description of the success of Jesus' ministry, saying only καὶ ἐξεπορεύετο ἦχος περὶ αὐτοῦ εἰς πάντα τόπον τῆς περιχώρου. According to Mark 1:28, Jesus' activity affected the entire region of Galilee, but here it is restricted to the

---

17. Cf. Loisy, *Les Évangiles synoptiques*, 1:447.

18. Spitta (*Die synoptische Grundschrift*, 57) also suggests that the description of the location was introduced into the narrative by Luke, in order to orient his readers, who were unfamiliar with Galilee.

area around Capernaum. While we might often be inclined to regard exaggerations about the success of Jesus' ministry as secondary, in this case it appears that Luke has altered Mark's depiction for his own particular reasons. Whether Luke has also thereby come closer to the actual facts of history is an entirely different question.

Marcion's text of Luke began with 4:31, which he combined with 3:1. Everything prior to the Nazareth pericope (4:16–30) is missing. To what, then, does the κατά in κατῆλθεν refer? To heaven, apparently, from which Jesus came down to earth at Capernaum. Clearly the introductory pieces of the framework, which Luke uses to create a strong topographical context (from Nazareth down to Capernaum) have been picked up rather unreflectively. In this way Marcion introduced the problem of how to interpret the place designations within the framework of the story of Jesus.

The Healing of Peter's Mother-in-Law
(Mark 1:29–31; Matt 8:14–15; Luke 4:38–39)

Καὶ εὐθὺς ἐκ τῆς συναγωγῆς ἐξελθόντες ἦλθον εἰς τὴν οἰκίαν Σίμωνος καὶ Ἀνδρέου μετὰ Ἰακώβου καὶ Ἰωάννου.

> The well-attested reading ἐξελθὼν ἦλθεν (B, cf. D) looks to me like a later stylistic improvement upon the original text. B. Weiss, by contrast, regards ἐξελθόντες ἦλθον as conforming to 1:21 (B. Weiss, *Markus und Lukas*, 24).

The degree to which this scene is bound to the one that precedes it is quite striking. The designation of place, for example, is clearly similar. We are led out of the synagogue and taken straight to a person who was well-known in the circle of the disciples, the mother-in-law of Peter. Unlike the other stories, this narrative does not hover in the air either chronologically or topographically. Of particular note is the enumeration of the four brothers, only two of whom accompany Jesus; the other two are mentioned only as co-owners of the house. We would expect either "Jesus and his disciples" or "Jesus with his disciples," but despite Matthew's and Luke's varying conceptions of it, Mark's text cannot be improved upon. On the contrary, as Th. Zahn has pointed out in a fine study,[19] Mark produced this text by trans-

---

19. Zahn, *Einleitung*, 2:251ff. Wohlenberg (*Markus*, 63) points out that Klostermann had made this argument before Zahn. In my view the unbalanced construction originated during the translation from Aramaic to Greek, a view that is reinforced by Merx, when he writes: "It is not certain whether syrs should be understood 'They came to the house of Simon Peter; Andrew, James, and John were with him'" (Merx, *Markus und Lukas*, 32).

forming Peter's original report from the first person plural into the third person plural. Mark altered the original report so slightly (and awkwardly), that it is possible for us to reconstruct Peter's report.

As has already been mentioned, Matthew brings this narrative into the complex of healing stories in chapters 8 and 9: καὶ ἦλθον ὁ Ἰησοῦς εἰς τὴν οἰκίαν Πέτρου εἶδεν τὴν πενθερὰν (Matt 8:14–15). In Matthew, then, the narrative has the following context: the preceding story takes place at the gate of the city, while this one takes place inside the city. Matthew attaches no significance to this difference. The place designation is given only because—and only in so far as—it is necessary for understanding the story. For that reason it is presented in a participial clause, as a matter of lesser importance.

Luke (4:38–39) follows Mark's thread, except that he simplifies the circumstantial clause in Mark 1:29: ἀναστὰς δὲ ἀπὸ τῆς συναγωγῆς εἰσῆλθεν τὴν οἰκίαν Σίμωνος.

> While ς A Γ Δ . . . it vg remove only Mark's ἐκ, D conforms more thoroughly: ἦλθεν ε. τ. οἰκίαν Σίμωνος καὶ Ἀνδρέου, as this codex typically glosses it. A and other codices read ὁ ις before εἰσῆλθεν.

The dependence of Luke on Mark shows up in v. 38b, where τοῦ Σίμωνος from Mark 1:30 is repeated in a rather clumsy way. In that verse the repetition had a point, because other names had previously been mentioned. But Luke could not name the four disciples, since in his gospel the disciples had not yet been called.[20]

Healings in the Evening at Peter's House
(Mark 1:32–34; Matt 8:16–17; Luke 4:40–41)

Ὀψίας δὲ γενομένης ὅτε ἔδυσεν ὁ ἥλιος . . . Once again there is a precise specification of time, and the chronology is spelled out in detail. Yet the impression of specificity is based entirely upon the presumption that ὀψίας refers to the late afternoon and should be taken to mean that the Sabbath was ending, so that the sick could now be brought to Jesus. δέ is conspicuous, and Mark took it up just as it was. In this context, then, the designation of time is highly relevant. The topographical connection with what precedes is also preserved, in

---

20. Spitta (*Die synoptische Grundschrift*, 60–61) rightly argues against the view that the plurals ἠρώτησαν αὐτὸν περὶ αὐτῆς and ἀναστᾶσα διηκόνει αὐτοῖς are a thoughtless appropriation of Mark's text (so B. Weiss, *Markus und Lukas*, 347). In Mark, Jesus enters the house with four apostles, while in Luke he appears all by himself: "Even if Jesus came in alone, there were nevertheless people in the house who could ask on behalf of the sick, especially Simon and his wife." I would translate ἠρώτησαν as "he was asked." αὐτοῖς refers to Jesus and Peter and the other guests.

two ways: ὅλη ἡ πόλις (v. 33) refers to Capernaum (1:21), and πρὸς τὴν θύραν refers to the house of Simon (1:29). We can therefore think only of Simon's house here, and not of a house that belonged to Jesus, to which he might have retired for the evening. Mark does not know whether Jesus lived in Capernaum. These localizations, parenthetical as they are, are thus all the more significant, because they are neither studied nor artistic: they have grown up unintentionally, as it were, from the depiction itself.

In the context of a pericope about Peter's mother-in-law, Matthew follows Mark and reports that the healing in the evening (8:16-17). He condenses several reports into one and concludes with a biblical quotation. The designation of time says only ὀψίας δὲ γενομένης. For Matthew, who is not bound to the idea that the event took place on a Sabbath, it is enough to say that it happened late in the day. He has brought the events in Mark 1:29-34 together, not as two complete pericopes but as only one. Matthew's condensation of the narrative stems from the fact that he is more interested in the miracle than in its attendant circumstances.

Luke, too, follows Mark's thread (Luke 4:40-41). The time is denoted by the circumstantial expression δύοντος δὲ τοῦ ἡλίου. The manner in which the sick are brought to Jesus in each of the three Synoptics is noteworthy. In Mark they are *all* brought, and *many* are healed; in Matthew *many* are brought, and *all* are healed; in Luke *all* are brought, and *all* are healed. When Mark distinguishes between the number of sick and the number of those who were healed, it indicates that he is working with an older version of the report, while Matthew and Luke ratchet the story up into something more miraculous. In contrast to Mark, Luke adds details (4:41, e.g.) that make the scene rather more dramatic: he speaks first of all the sick who were brought to Jesus, and then of the demon-possessed. Here too we get the impression that Luke has polished up Mark's account.[21]

Jesus Escapes into Solitude
(Mark 1:35-38; Luke 4:42-43)

καὶ πρωῒ ἔννυχα λίαν ἀναστὰς ἐξῆλθεν καὶ ἀπῆλθεν εἰς ἔρημον τόπον.

While the adverbial use of the accusative plural is remarkable, ἔννυχα is preferable to ἔννυχον (Α Γ Δ). Ἀναστάς and καὶ ἀπῆλθεν

---

21. Spitta, *Die synoptische Grundschrift*, 62), by contrast, rightly elaborates on the distinctiveness of Luke's version: "Thus the text of Luke is thoroughly complete and comprehensible . . . It arranges in tidy sequence the healing of the sick and then the exorcism of demons."

are to be retained, even if important mss. may have omitted such artistic features.

Once again we have here a surprisingly precise description of the time: very early, while it is still night, Jesus gets up and goes out. This narrative depiction has something especially vivid about it, as if "the scent of an oriental morning lies upon it."[22] An isolated place is the goal, and though the exact location is not stated, the description of the place is vivid enough to be more than sufficient. The disciples hurry after him and find him, and the words that Jesus then speaks are also specific with regard to location: ἄγωμεν ἀλλαχοῦ εἰς τὰς ἐχομένας κωμοπόλεις,[23] "Let us go somewhere else in the area around here, not back to Capernaum." In my judgment ἦλθον is a christological term and does not refer to leaving a house.[24]

Matthew omitted this story about Jesus' withdrawal. It was simply not possible for him to put it in here, where he had already located the two preceding narratives. On this basis it may legitimately be asked whether Matthew put much store in this entire episode. In his presentation, topographical and chronological details are suppressed in favor of sayings material and miracle stories. This was not the place for a story about Jesus escaping into solitude.

In Luke 4:42–43, by contrast, Mark's narrative is recounted with only slight stylistic alterations. Nothing is said about Jesus praying: we hear only that γενομένης ἡμέρας Jesus went to an isolated location, and the crowds (οἱ ὄχλοι) followed him there. In Mark it is the disciples who find him, and in Mark their effort to locate him is understandable, since according to this account there were many sick people who had not yet been healed. Jesus should heal all the sick. In Luke this connection is not as clear. In addition, in Luke the disciples have not yet been called, and thus cannot come into view here. In place of Mark's peculiar description of the locations to which Jesus will go, Luke has the more understandable expression, ταῖς ἑτέραις πόλεσιν.[25]

---

22. Wohlenberg, *Markus*, 66.

23. Regarding the deletion of ἀλλαχοῦ from some Mss., cf. the text critical remarks above. Κωμόπολις, which appears only here in the New Testament, is a city that is constitutionally in the position of only a κώμη (Schürer, *History of the Jewish People*, 2:179). κώμας καὶ εἰς τὰς πόλεις would be an easier expression for this relatively rare word.

24. Cf. B. Weiss, *Markus und Lukas*, 27; Wohlenberg, *Markus*, 68–69.

25. In this text it is obviously difficult for Spitta to maintain that Luke gives us the oldest version of the text. It shows us something interesting about Spitta's method when he says: "It has already been shown (in the report of Jesus' activity in Capernaum) that Mark's account is based upon Luke's, so the same goes also for the report of Jesus' departure" (Spitta, *Die synoptische Grundschrift*, 64).

Jesus' Preaching Tour in Galilee
(Mark 1:39; Matt 4:23-25; Luke 4:44)

καὶ ἦν κηρύσσων εἰς τῆς συναγωγῆς αὐτῶν εἰς ὅλην τὴν Γαλιλαίαν καὶ τὰ δαιμόνια ἐκβάλλων.

> The well-attested reading καὶ ἦλθεν is certainly an attempt to make the sentence read more easily. The recurrence of εἰς may seem harsh, but it coheres well with ἦλθεν and the second designation of place, εἰς ὅλην τὴν Γαλιλαίαν. The words ἐν ταῖς συναγωγαῖς (E F . . .) are another effort to improve the reading.

This description of Jesus' ministry joins smoothly with what precedes, and we cannot exclude the possibility that it belonged to the original content of the pericope. In general, however, individual narratives of this type tend not to include such details, so we would do well to take v. 39 as a summary statement that should be credited to the evangelist. The incongruity of the words καὶ τὰ δαιμόνια ἐκβάλλων is striking, since to this point Jesus' mission has been described as preaching, not healing. Yet Mark mentions this here in a momentary *fluxus orationis*: he wants to give a general picture of Jesus' activity, rather than fine-tuning it for particular details.[26] It is of interest that Luke does not preserve the phrase καὶ τὰ δαιμόνια ἐκβάλλων, and it is also noteworthy that the text refers only to exorcisms of demons. Mark certainly includes healings that from our perspective have nothing to do with possession (cf. Acts 10:38 concerning the healing work of Jesus). Matthew changes that (4:23). This text is a summary statement that was later appended to the pericope, a fact that is confirmed by its style. The construction is not entirely clear, and difficulties are created, for example, by the repetition of εἰς. We have already made similar stylistic observations about Mark 1:14ff, where the pericope also lacked simple and clear style. In its place we noted a form of description that sought to connect the events but in so doing produced clutter and incongruity.

We find an echo of Mark 1:39 in the summary statement of Matt 4:23-25, which arose from the overall plan of the evangelist, as we have already demonstrated.

---

26. On the basis of these perceptions J. Weiss (*Das älteste Evangelium*, p. 151) and Wendling (*Das Enstehung des Markusevangelium*, p. 4) delete καὶ τὰ δαιμόνια ἐκβάλλων as a later addition. Rauch argues that the addition begins with εἰς ὅλην τὴν Γαλιλαίαν; cf. Rauch, "Bemerkungen zum Markustexte," 301. It appears to me to be more important (and more correct) to bear in mind the generalizing character of 1:39 and not to be so distracted by bumps in the details of the content that nothing in the verse can be taken as incidental.

The situation is different with Luke 4:44. This evangelist, following the framework of Mark very closely, was not inclined to interrupt the progression of the narrative. He notes only: καὶ ἦν κηρύσσων εἰς τὰς συναγωγὰς τῆς Γαλιλαίας (the reading ἐν ταῖς συναγωγαῖς in A C and L is a later improvement). Mark's hyperbolic εἰς ὅλην τὴν Γαλιλαίαν is suppressed, and as we have already pointed out, Luke deletes the troubling words καὶ τὰ δαιμόνια ἐκβάλλων. So far, so good, but now there arises a very substantial text-critical problem, one with significant implications for the issues we are exploring. The manuscript tradition swings back and forth between τῆς Γαλιλαίας and τῆς Ἰουδαίας. The former is read by such manuscripts as A D Γ and Δ, and is followed by the editions of Lachmann, Tischendorf, and Weymouth. The latter is read by B C and L, and is followed by the editions of Westcott-Hort, B. Weiss, Nestle, and von Soden. This external evidence supplies no basis for hope that a solution can be found. But what about internal considerations? Here the tools of higher criticism can be decisive. The conventional rule "i.e., the more difficult reading (τῆς Ἰουδαίας) is to be preferred[27]" is insufficient in this case. That Luke could have regarded the region of Judea as the stage for Jesus' ministry is ruled out by the context.[28] We know that Luke is attentive to the need for a pragmatic progression in the plot, so it is conceivable that by "Judea," Luke is not thinking of the province of Judea, but rather all the Jewish territory apart from Galilee. This possibility cannot be ruled out, because Luke did not have precise geographic information and might therefore have expressed himself in ways that were incorrect. The expressions and descriptions in Luke and Acts often indicate a degree of uncertainty. On numerous occasions the meaning of the term "Judea" is not entirely clear: Luke 1:65; 2:4; 3:1; 5:17; 21:21; Acts 1:8; 8:1; 9:31; 11:1; 11:29; 12:19; 15:1; 21:10; 26:20; 28:21. These statistics should not be pressed too far, however, because they do not fully acquaint us with Luke's use of the term. For the text as we have it rises from the pieces that Luke took up from the tradition without making any alteration in their geographical significance. The expression "Jewish land" stands for Palestine in the following verses: Luke 1:5; 6:17; 7:17; 23:5. In Luke 1:5 the text reads: ἐγένετο ... βασιλέως τῆς Ἰουδαίας, referring to Herod the Great, who ruled over all of the Jewish territory, over

---

27. Several scholars opt for the principle, "incomprehensible, therefore correct!" Cf. Zahn, *Lucas*, 247–48; B. Weiss, *Markus und Lukas*, 349; Wellhausen, *Luke*, 13; Merx, *Markus und Lukas*, 217; Spitta, *Die synoptische Grundschrift*, 66ff.

28. Spitta maintains that according to Luke 4:15 Jesus had to this point been preaching in the synagogues of Galilee and must have now intended to go into the areas of the Jewish land outside of Galilee. But that is a *petitio principii*, and Spitta admits as much when he writes, "the translation 'Jewish land' is meaningless" (Spitta, *Jesus und die Heidenmission*, 68).

all of Palestine. Thus the term "Judea" could be used here in a broader sense to describe the entire holy land, as it was used in the Hebrew Bible during the pre-Davidic era. Luke 6:17 has this wider sense.[29] In this context it makes no sense to think only of the Jewish countryside. This point is even clearer in Luke 7:17, where it simply cannot be the case that the miracle stories involving the centurion of Capernaum and the widow of Nain should be thought of as having taken place in the province of Judea.[30] In Luke 23:5 Jesus is charged before Pilate with having carried out his ministry καθ' ὅλης τῆς Ἰουδαίας καὶ ἀρξάμενος ἀπὸ τῆς Γαλιλαίας ἕως ὧδε. The word ὅλης makes clear that the total compass of ἀπὸ τῆς Γαλιλαίας ἕως ὧδε, and not the individual province, is in view here. Likewise Acts 2:9, where the list of the nations includes Judea, cannot mean only the province of that name.[31] Acts 10:37 is reminiscent of Luke 23:5.[32] All of these texts show that when Luke 4:44 uses the term Ἰουδαία, it does not necessarily refer to the province of Judea. It is hardly surprising that this unusual form of expression disappeared from some later manuscripts. Certainly this reading in no way suggests that the source of Luke's narrative should be relocated to Judea.[33] Luke 4:31 and 5:1 strongly connect the story of Jesus with Galilee.

29. The textual tradition is uncertain here. In place of the words καὶ Ἰερουσαλήμ ... οἳ ἦλθον, D reads καὶ ἄλλων πόλεων ἐληλυθότων. Perhaps καὶ Ἰερουσαλήμ should be deleted, since it does not cohere with the use of the term "Judea" in a wider sense.

30. Spitta (*Die synoptische Grundschrift*, 142ff) so thoroughly alters the material that he asserts that both Galilean pericopes "the centurion of Capernaum and the widow of Nain" were not in the document from which the Synoptics have arisen.

31. Here Spitta overindulges his penchant for speculation by proposing Ἰνδίαν or Ἰδουμαίαν in place of Ἰουδαίαν. His predecessors in this effort include some of the church fathers: Jerome read "Syria," while Tertullian and Augustine read "Armenia." Von Harnack feels that the difficulty is so serious that that Ἰουδαίαν should be deleted as meaningless; cf. von Harnack, *Die Apostelgeschichte*, 65. These efforts with regard to Ἰουδαίαν are all misguided. In vv. 9-11 the narrator is giving us a catalogue of nations, in which the Jews are included, and that is all he is thinking about. With a certain *fluxus orationis* he counts off the various peoples in what he regards as a sequence.

32. Even Spitta has to admit that 10:37 might be the one place where Ἰουδαία could carry a wider sense of meaning (Spitta, *Die synoptische Grundschrift*, 70).

33. "But the reading τῆς Ἰουδαίας compels a conception of Jesus' activity different from the customary one, in which Galilee will no longer be preferred, which owes its origin to the customary view" (Merx, *Markus und Lukas*, 217). Spitta, who deletes the story that follows in 5:1-11 (cf. above), has a similar, and likewise very complicated, perspective. He thinks that the document from which the Synoptics arose did not mention Judea, but the author of Luke obviously understood Ἰουδαία in the sense of the Jewish land, as Mark plainly did, since he can use it in place of Γαλιλαία. As will become clear from my subsequent investigations, I regard it as very significant that Merx and Spitta oppose the "customary conception" of Jesus' activity. Their thesis finds no support in Luke 4:44.

The Healing of a Leper
(Mark 1:40-45; Matt 8:1-4; Luke 5:12-16)

The first question is: does the new section begin with v. 40? Or is the break perhaps at v. 38, so that vv. 39-45 should be viewed as a unity? It is possible that vv. 39-45 is a unified section, and it is conceivable that this complex was once read as a separate pericope. Boundaries between pericopes could sometimes be moved, and the introductions and conclusions to the pericopes were not clearly marked. Yet the narrative, at least as it existed independently before being incorporated into the Gospel of Mark, certainly began with v. 39. There are two reasons for this: 1) if v. 39 refers backward, then this verse would have belonged to the original arrangement of the narrative about Jesus' withdrawal and ongoing work in a different place. Verse 39, in other words, would have been a self-contained little summary statement from the hand of the evangelist. Yet the second reason is more important: 2) vv. 40-45 have not the slightest internal connection with v. 39. The designation of place in v. 39, which is generally held to be correct, is not anchored in the event described in vv. 40-45. But might not the word ἐξέβαλεν in v. 43 (Jesus sent the healed man away), along with the word ἐξελθών (the man went out), indicate a specific place, a particular building? Can we not think of the same synagogue that was mentioned in v. 39?[34] If Mark had intended this connection, he would have marked it much more clearly. A reader who is reading the stories in sequence, or even one who is merely skimming, will not think of the synagogue mentioned in v. 39. These simple narratives do not pose riddles of that sort.[35] It makes no difference to our understanding of the pericope whether the building, which we infer from the preposition ἐξ, was a synagogue or some kind of house. Neither option affects our understanding of the pericope, and this negative result is of prime importance. At the end of the day it is doubtful whether the ἐξ

---

34. B. Weiss (*Markus und Lukas*, 38) says: "According to v. 39 Jesus is preaching in a synagogue when the leper comes in... In fact these unfortunates, even though entry into the synagogue was generally forbidden to them, did have access to the synagogues under certain restrictions (cf. Lev. 13:46; Num 5:2)." But this explanation will not suffice, because it is built upon historical and psychological deliberations. If Mark thought that these legal stipulations were correct, he would have been led to include them here in this narrative. Wohlenberg (*Markus*, 70) offers additional historical-psychological notions, but takes them in a completely different direction: "He (the leper) came to Jesus, risking therefore the breaking of the legal rules that required lepers to avoid contact with healthy people."

35. "In Mark the event appears to take place in a house" (J. Weiss, *Schriften*, 88). "He is in a house, although that is not explicitly stated" (Wellhausen, *Mark*, 15). "We are not informed that the event takes place in a house, but that would be reasonable according to v. 43 and v. 45" (Lagrange, *Évangile selon Saint Marc*, 26).

in ἐξελθών really carries the meaning of "out" (from an inner room out into the open).³⁶ We know of no Aramaic correlate. The word ἐξελθών can be understood as "he went out" or "he went away," and it is related to the word ἐξῆλθον in v. 38. Yet another sense may lie hidden behind the word ἐξέβαλεν: perhaps the exorcism of the demon, with which Jesus clearly was angry, is in view. The original phrasing, which conceived of something along these lines, strikes me as utterly nonsensical.

Nor did Matthew and Luke, the earliest interpreters of this story, think of a synagogue as the setting. For them the narrative began with v. 40, and so they inserted a break between v. 39 and v. 40. In both stories the setting is certainly somewhere out in the open: according to Matt 8:1ff the healing takes place as Jesus comes down from preaching the Sermon on the Mount, and in Luke 5:12 it occurs in "one of the cities" (ἐν μιᾷ τῶν πόλεων).³⁷ With these localizations both evangelists have put something into the story that they thought that it lacked.

What is missing is any chronological or topographical specificity in this narrative. The scene floats free in the air: it has no location, and there is no indication of the time. As a result we cannot recover even an approximate chronology for this story. The setting unfortunately provides no information about the year of Jesus' ministry in which it took place. Mark found the pericope without any specification about time or place, and he regarded it as a fitting illustration of Jesus' movements in 1:39, even though it had nothing to do with either preaching in a synagogue or casting out a demon. He used it to fill the gap between 1:39 and 2:1.³⁸

Yet perhaps the following consideration of its content can help us to identify at least an approximate location for this narrative. Jesus instructs the healed man to show himself to the priest and to bring the purity offering commanded by Moses. Certainly there were priests who had no cultic

---

36. Wohlenberg rightly observes: "ἐξέβαλεν—out of the surroundings in which he found himself (cf. v. 12; 5:40; 11:15; John 6:37; 9:34–35; 10:4)—does not indicate that Mark imagines these events to have taken place in a house" (Wohlenberg, *Markus*, 71). On the same page he asserts that ἐξελθών corresponds to ἐξέβαλεν. But Wohlenberg's further comments are overdone and emphasize elements that play no role in the narrative. Thus he says that the passage can also be explained by the possibility that the man who was healed may have gone back to the house in which he was confined during his illness, "that this house would not have been far away is obvious," and then he came out of this house again, in order to proclaim what had happened to him.

37. "Luke senses the gap in Mark and fills it with a vague hypothesis" (Loisy, *Les Évangiles synoptiques*, 1:463). According to Spitta (*Die synoptische Grundschrift*, 70–71), Mark 5:12 connects directly with 4:44, and ἐν μιᾷ τῶν πόλεων refers to a Jewish city.

38. "This story does not belong to the framework of the first day, but serves rather as an example of 1:39" (Wellhausen, *Mark*, 15).

position and thus lived in various places across Palestine. Zacharias (Luke 1) comes to mind in this regard. One of these priests could pronounce the declaration of purity. The offering, however, could only be brought to Jerusalem (Lev 14:3ff). Does the story thereby suggest a location somewhere near the city of Jerusalem? It surprises me that more exegetes have not touched upon this point.[39] If the story took place in Galilee—and this can be presumed from its present placement in the Gospel of Mark—is it not remarkable that Jesus sends the healed man to Jerusalem? We often speak of Jesus' journeys to Jerusalem. Is not just such a journey required of the healed man in this story, and right away? The distance of such a journey is typically overestimated. The trip from Galilee to Jerusalem could be completed in a day. Obviously a lively commerce went on between the two regions, and there would have been nothing particularly remarkable about the fact that a man who had just experienced the most important moment in his life, the healing of an incurable disease, would travel to Jerusalem from Galilee. Although geographical observations can be important, in this case they are unproductive. We are left with a situation in which we know neither the time nor the place of this remarkable story (in which region? inside a house? outside?).

In spite of Jesus' command, the healed man reported what had happened to him, and as a result μηκέτι δύνασθαι φανερῶς εἰς πόλιν εἰσελθεῖν, ἀλλ᾽ ἔξω ἐπ᾽ ἐρήμοις τόποις ἦν. καὶ ἤρχοντο πρὸς αὐτὸν πάντοθεν (v. 45).

> The placement of φανερῶς after πόλιν in some mss is not significant. The reading ἐν in ς is a gloss upon ἐπί and does not originate with Luke for πάντοθεν, ς reads πανταχόθεν.

The accent lies upon φανερῶς, which is emphatic. We expect the continuation: "he could only enter a city secretly (λάθρᾳ)," but instead it says, "He did not go into a city, but rather withdrew to an isolated area."[40] I am inclined toward the view that φανερῶς has been inserted by the evangelist, so as to ensure the ongoing movement of the narrative. Then in 2:1 Jesus goes into a city. That he entered Capernaum secretly can be seen in the expression ἠκούσθη ὅτι ἐν οἴκῳ ἐστίν. Even this does not remove the difficulty, however, for in 2:1ff nothing at all is said about a secret journey back to Capernaum or a residence there. The idea that Jesus could not enter a city but had to remain in the desert, supplies a better conclusion to the narrative than the impression produced by φανερῶς. That impression—that

---

39. Wohlenberg (*Markus*, 72) raises the question but does not try to answer it.

40. This inner contradiction in v. 45 is itself the important point. Most exegetes who notice the contradiction here, think too much of the contradiction that follows between 1:45 and 2:1ff.

Jesus had to withdraw but was continually sought by the crowds—is widely regarded as a "dogmatic conception"[41] on the evangelist's part. But I would like to propose two ideas: 1) with all due respect to this theory, which may indeed be present in the Gospel of Mark as a whole, 1:45 actually seems to connect quite naturally with the story. It should not be tangled up with such theories. And 2) it is possible to separate the whole of v. 45 from the original content of the pericope. Verse 44 is certainly not the proper conclusion of the narrative; v. 45 is much better. If this is correct, then it will suffice to remove all the words from ὥστε to ἦν, so that we are left with a conclusion to the narrative that is nicely rounded off: the healed man proclaimed Jesus' great deed, and everyone streamed toward Jesus, the helper.

Matthew, who put the story about the centurion of Capernaum right after this narrative (8:5–13), made no use of Mark 1:45. For him, living and moving in a Jewish world, the high point of the narrative was the phrase that had originally served as its conclusion: ὃ προσέταξεν Μωϋσῆς εἰς μαρτύριον αὐτοῖς. Luke certainly used Mark 1:45; indeed he handled the text more conservatively than Matthew did, turning it back upon itself: the people stream to Jesus (not in the desert, but openly and in public), and Jesus withdraws, but only to a quiet area (Luke 5:15–16).

Excursus: The Complex of Mark 1:14–45

This complex should be regarded as a coherent whole.[42] It begins with the response of the Baptist in 1:14 and ends with the new set of narratives that starts in 2:1. Most interpreters are in agreement about these boundaries. Disagreements arise only when the topic turns to the chronology of these stories. Thus far our discussions have concluded that v. 15, 20, and 39 are breaks in the narrative,

---

41. So J. Weiss, *Das älteste Evangelium*, 152. The issue has been framed in especially strong terms by Wrede, *The Messianic Secret* [BM: German ed.]), 126. Wendling (5) follows him, arguing that the disconnection between 1:45 and 2:1 concludes the course of events in 1:35ff. J. Weiss (*Das älteste Evangelium*, 152) asserts: "The conclusion of 1:45 was not part of the original narrative, for it cuts across the agenda of 1:39." In my view, however, the narrative must be understood primarily as an individual narrative. If we keep this fact in mind, we will not try to bring all these narratives together under one roof. Wendling has noted that 1:45 "is put together like a mosaic out of individual phrases in the original report," but it seems to me that in this case his keen observations are not conclusive. His methodological principle, by contrast—that the evangelist put together his report from individual narratives—is quite right.

42. Cf. B. Weiss, *Markus und Lukas*, 30; Wellhausen, *Mark*, 9. On the other hand Wohlenberg, *Markus*, 69, divides the complex rather artfully into seven sections and contrasts it with another sevenfold complex of narratives in 1:40—3:6.

recognizable as sutures. In this regard vv. 21-39 occupy a particularly significant position. Our examination has shown that this section has a strong chronology, within which the individual narratives were bound to each other from the beginning with specific markers of time, indicating that these events took place on a Sabbath and the following morning.[43] This chronological data cannot have originated with the evangelist. If he had found the individual narratives without temporal connections and then supplied what was lacking, it would have been a simple thing for him to rearrange 1:40-45 into a better order. The evangelist's technique is clear: he positions the narratives just as they were handed down to him, one after the other, foregoing any effort to provide chronological or topographical brackets. Matthew, and especially Luke, are in this regard not merely redactors, but rather authors, to a degree.

Each of the individual reports (1:16-20; 1:21-39; 1:40-45) arrives at a conclusion, and this is noteworthy: in 1:20 they follow after him; in 1:39 Jesus is active in Galilee; and in 1:45 the people stream to him. The conclusions lead into the flow of the action, and the flow of the action conveys a general impression of time. Each individual event encompasses a particular length of time, but the subsequent climactic conclusion of the pericope entails a greater, indefinite span of time that cannot be computed chronologically. We despoil the circumstantial character of the picture when we try to put these narratives together through a mishmash of calculations.[44]

---

43. J. Weiss rightly refers to the famous remarks of Papias, who states that traditions from Peter underlie 1:16 and 1:20ff. Spitta, once again in opposition to our view, asserts that Mark put all the events from the call of the disciples to the healing of the sick into the framework of a *single* day: "This depiction is a reorganization of the oldest tradition" (Spitta, *Die synoptische Grundschrift*, 69). In response I pose this question: how could Mark come up with the idea of *one* day, if he found the stories loosely arrayed in the tradition?

44. Cf. by contrast Wohlenberg: "The length of time that elapsed was, as we read in 1:35, not limited to one day (cf. 1:39, εἰς ὅλην τὴν Γαλιλαίαν, 1:45). Weeks or months could have gone by. It would be inappropriate to conclude that Jesus had been away from Capernaum for any length of time. Any intelligent reader can make the connection here" (Wohlenberg, *Markus*, 73). In my judgment, an intelligent reader would not be likely to make this connection, and the hyperbole in εἰς ὅλην τὴν Γαλιλαίαν should not be pressed. Even the considerations that Windisch advances, albeit hypothetically, lead to vague results (cf. Windisch, "Die Dauer," 143-44). He asserts that it is difficult to determine the length of time taken up by the preaching tour in 1:39. If we wanted to suppose that Jesus only taught on Sabbath days, it would involve several weeks, maybe

Excursus: The Complex of Mark 1:14-45 in Matthew:
Jesus' First Acts in Galilee
(Matt 4:12-9:34; Matt 4:12-8:17 = Mark 1:14-45)

We have already discussed the ways in which Matthew and Luke each treat the complex Mark 1:14-45, along with the motives that led them to rearrange the narratives in a new formation and framework. But we have not yet outlined the overall plan that underlies this authorial effort.

Matthew 4:12—9:34 is a self-enclosed unit that describes Jesus' opening activities in Galilee. The description of Jesus' public appearance and call of the first disciples (4:12-22) is only the prelude to the first great act in the ministry of Jesus. The perspective from which this is described is indicated by Matthew himself in a summary statement in 4:23-25: Jesus moves all around Galilee, sometimes as a teacher (teaching in synagogues and preaching the kingdom of God), and sometimes as a miracle worker. His call extends all the way to Syria. From all directions the sick are brought to him, and many people from Galilee, the Decapolis, Jerusalem, Judea, and Perea come to be near him. Matthew develops this general description by using different parts of the Gospel of Mark (cf. 1:28, 32, 29, 45; 3:7, 8), and that thus serves as a headline for the entire section, even as it is repeated as a caption to the conclusion (9:35). Not surprisingly, more thorough depictions of this general perspective follow: 1) the teachings of Jesus (chaps. 5-7), and 2) the healings of Jesus (chaps. 8 and 9). Jesus' first day in Capernaum (Mark 1:21-39) is smashed to pieces, and the story of the leper (Mark 1:40-45) is reshuffled.

---

months, but it is more likely that the evangelist means that Jesus roamed from place to place without regard for the Sabbath. "We have to think of a restless movement rather like that described in Matt 10:23. If Jesus only went to the towns and villages closest around Capernaum (1:38), then it could have been taken care of in two weeks ... As little as three weeks would have elapsed between his first and second visits to Capernaum." In my judgment, the literary properties of Mark's report will not bear such theories, even when they are advanced hypothetically. Certainly Windisch is right to remark upon the scant distances between these locations along the sea. It is indeed a fact that a journey through these places could have been completed in two weeks. But a stay in any particular town could have been shorter or longer. This kind of historical-psychological speculation has led another scholar to a completely different result: "Even four months would still not be enough time for this very intense preaching activity" (Homanner, *Die Dauer*, 94).

Jesus' Teaching: The Sermon on the Mount
(Matthew 5–7)

Matthew's first section, the so-called "Sermon on the Mount," is introduced with the words ἰδὼν δὲ τοὺς ὄχλους ἀνέβη εἰς τὸ ὄρος. The identity of the audience is not quite clear. According to 5:1 it seems that Jesus has withdrawn from the crowds and is speaking only to his disciples, but 7:28 indicates that other people are also present. This variation can be accounted for by the fact that Matthew took the presence of the crowds from the report in Mark, but derived the sermon itself from the Sayings Source Q, in which only the disciples were witnesses to Jesus' words. Even there not merely the Twelve were meant, but rather a larger band of followers (cf. Luke 6:20). No specific "mount" is named.[45] There are many traditions, but no specific geographic location is traceable. Does the designation "mount" originate with Matthew, or are we dealing here with an older tradition? In Mark, Jesus often withdraws to a mountain in order to be alone and to pray, and that happens in Matt 14:23 as well. The first evangelist could easily have taken up this motif, but Luke 6:17 ("to a level place on the mountain," "a mountain hillside") indicates that there may be an older tradition here, from the Sayings Source, which Matthew somewhat reduced and at the same time amplified. There is not much more to say in this regard about the Sermon on the Mount, which is already widely regarded as a composition by Matthew. Some places clearly betray a local coloring: the saying about birds, for example, which "neither sow nor reap" (6:23); or about the lilies of the field, which grow without cares (6:28); or about the son, who asked his father for a fish (7:10); about the prophets who are wolves in sheep's clothing (7:15); about the grapes and the thorns, the figs and the thistles (7:16); about the house upon the rock, upon which the wind and the rain had no impact (7:24). The word "sand" (ἄμμος) was typically used for the beach (cf. Rom 9:27; Heb 11:12; Rev. 12:18, 20:8). Thus it has to do with a house on a shore. Did this saying therefore have to originate in a region near the seashore, or is it conceivable that Jesus was using a familiar image that may have been at home on the coast but was also known in the Galilee? Ποταμός can be understood as a sea current. The nautical character of the saying

---

45. Cf. Wellhausen, *Matthew*,13: "The mount is an open stage."

is clear in Luke 6:48, where the word πλημμύρη appears, a word that means "high tide" as opposed to "low tide." And in Luke 6:17 other people are named as bystanders ἀπὸ τῆς παραλίου Τύρου καὶ Σιδῶνος.[46] The altar mentioned in 5:23 (θυσιαστήριον) is to be found in Jerusalem, so the hearer of that saying lived in Jerusalem. If the saying did not take on its form in circles of the community in Jerusalem, then Jesus must have first spoken it in Jerusalem. The mention of the fish in 7:10, by contrast, points to the region around the Sea of Galilee as the setting for that saying; indeed, the blooming of the lilies may be a reference to a specific season of the year. If the phrase "lilies of the fields" means (as some have suggested[47]) the flowers that we know as irises, then these flowers would have bloomed in April. In that case the Sermon on the Mount, whatever its setting might have been, would have been preached not three or four months before Jesus' death, but rather eleven or twelve months.[48] This one calendrical datum would by itself rule out the theory that Jesus' ministry was very short, perhaps lasting only a few months. It is too bad that we do not have more material with which to determine the seasons of the year in the stories of Jesus, for it is precisely these involuntary indigenous indicators of time that are the most valuable. But even apart from all that, it is abundantly clear that the so-called "Sermon on the Mount" is a mosaic of sayings. We are dealing here with sayings of Jesus that may come not only from locations in the Galilee but also just about anywhere else (the north, Perea, Samaria, Judea), and whose time period cannot be determined within several months or even within a year, but only within several years in the story of Jesus. In Matthew the Sermon on the Mount concludes with the words καὶ ἐγένετο ὅτε ἐτέλεσεν ὁ Ἰησοῦς τοὺς λόγους, ἐξεπλήσσοντο ... In Mark this same wording is used to describe the impact of Jesus' preaching in the synagogue (1:22). Other "sermons" of Jesus in the Gospel of Matthew also conclude with the words καὶ ἐγένετο ὅτε ἐτέλεσεν, indicating that these "sermons" were constructed by the evangelist. We have

---

46. But here we must beware of being too clever, as Spitta is, by far: "It (the picture in its Lucan form) confirms that according to the document that became the basis for the Synoptic tradition, the Sermon was not delivered on a mount in Galilee, but in a valley in Judah, near the seashore" (Spitta, *Die synoptische Grundschrift*, 46). In my judgment, the sermon cannot be regarded as a self-enclosed complex.

47. Cf. Christ, "Nochmals die Lilie der Bibel."

48. "Die Dauer der oeffentliche Wirksamkeit Jesu" *ZNW* 12 (1911), 158.

to reckon with the possibility that similar expressions may have already existed in the Sayings Source. The likelihood of this possibility is increased the fact that in Luke 7:1, the Sermon on the Plain comes to an end with the words ἐπειδὴ ἐπλήρωσεν πάντα τὰ ῥήματα.

Jesus' Deeds: The Centurion from Capernaum
(Matt 8:5–13; Luke 7:1–10)

Next in importance after the teachings of Jesus is his miracle-working activity, of which Matthew reports a selection of stories in chapters 8 and 9. The collected stories are put together in a continuous series that takes up and expands upon bits and pieces of the framework from Mark. In most cases a participial construction contains information about place and time of the event. The number of miracles reported may be schematized: nine stories could have been published (3 x 3), or perhaps ten. The stories may come from an older tradition that Matthew has taken up here.[49] In the *Pirqe Aboth*, for example, we read: "Ten miracles happened to our fathers in Egypt, and ten at the sea . . . ten miracles happened to our fathers in the sanctuary" (*m. Aboth* 5.4). We may well be dealing with that kind of symbolism here. In Matthew, however, the schema is disrupted by the insertion of other non-miraculous stories, since Matthew is following Mark's thread. We have already seen that two or three miracle stories from the complex of Mark 1:14–45 have been brought over into chapters 8 and 9 of Matthew. The pericope about the cleansing of the leper (Mark 1:40–45) is the best example, in Matt 8:1–4. Since it carries no indication of its location, it can fit easily between the end of the Sermon on the Mount and the entry into Capernaum.

Next comes the pericope about the centurion of Capernaum (Matt 8:5–13), also taken from the Sayings Source and introduced, in typical Matthean style, with a participial construction: εἰσελθόντος δὲ αὐτοῦ εἰς Καφαρναούμ προσῆλθεν αὐτῷ ἑκατοντάρχης.

> εἰσελθόντι δὲ αὐτοῦ (E Δ . . .) is an improvement, as is the reading in ς: εἰσελθόντι δὲ τῷ ιυ. The introduction of Jesus' name can be attributed to an *initium lectionis*, as can

---

49. Cf. Klostermann, *Matthäus*, 211.

the reading of syr^sin, which is based upon a text that read
μετὰ δὲ ταῦτα προσῆλθεν . . . Instead of ἑκατοντάρχης, it
reads χιλίαρχος, as do several Itala. mss. There is something more precise to observe about these remarkable variations. In some Latin mss., both of the readings are tied together: *post haec autem cum introisset*, etc.

Once again we pose the same question we asked earlier about Luke 4:16 and its location in Nazareth: is this tradition firmly situated in Capernaum? There seems to be no particular reason why Matthew should have located this story there, yet some details in the narrative do point to Capernaum as its setting. The presence of a centurion, for example, suggests some kind of garrison, which would fit well in Capernaum, since it was a city on the border with Iturea. We should not think of Roman soldiers, of course, but rather of troops in the service of Herod Antipas, most of whose soldiers were non-Jews. The ἑκατοντάρχης, a commander of one hundred men, was identical to the *centurio*, a low-ranking officer, and we meet such centurions several different times in the New Testament (cf. Matt 27:54 = Luke 23:47; in the Markan parallel the loanword κεντουρίων is used; later in Acts 10:1 there is the centurion Cornelius; cf. also Acts 21:32; 22:25, et.al.). Another version of our pericope, Luke 7:1–10, speaks of a centurion who is enthusiastically recommended to Jesus by the Jews, because he built their synagogue (v. 5). A gift of that sort would have been out of the ordinary for an individual centurion. Syr^sin, however, has χιλίαρχος instead of ἑκατοντάρχης. That term refers to a ranking officer, the Latin word for which is *tribunus*. Wellhausen remarks: "The term is, according to everything that I have ever been taught, not a military title but a civic responsibility. Matthew 8:9 and Luke 7:8 indicate the same thing."[50] The pericope is thus strongly reminiscent of the narrative about the raising of Jairus' daughter (Mark 5:21ff and par.), since in both cases an official comes to Jesus in order to ask help for a seriously ill family member, who cannot be brought to Jesus. These are the only officials for whom Jesus performs miracles, which raises the possibility that we might be dealing with a doublet here. The fact that, according to Luke, the centurion/chiliarch had founded a synagogue, would cohere well with the term ἀρχισυνάγωγος (Mark 5:22). In addition, the narrative in John 4:46ff also speaks

50. Wellhausen, *Matthew*, 35.

of a βασιλικός, who is much more like a chiliarch or head of the synagogue than a centurion. These considerations do not prove that Matthew has re-formed the tradition, but they do show that at an early stage of the tradition there were several narratives about an official who sought healing for a member of his household. These narratives were very similar in their personal details, their structure, and their content. The differences between ἑκατοντάρχης (Matt 8:5), ἀρχισυνάγωγος (Mark 5:22), ἄρχων (Matt 9:18), ἄρχων τῆς συναγωγῆς (Luke 8:41), βασιλικός (John 4:46) do not amount to much, nor do the distinctions between παῖς (Matt 8:6), θυγάτριον/θυγατήρ (Mark 5:23 par), and υἱός (John 4:46). These slight variations, which arise from oral repetition in the ongoing flow of the tradition, suggest that the various versions supported each other. In one version (Mark 5:22 = Luke 8:41) the official has a specific name; in Matthew and John he does not. Matthew 8:5ff and John 4:46ff are located in Capernaum, while Capernaum is not mentioned in Mark 5:22ff and par. Otherwise the story of Jairus, taken in and of itself, could easily have taken place in Capernaum. This localization makes it likely, especially in light of our other observations, that only one narrative from the story of Jesus underlies these different versions. We cannot tell precisely what this original pericope looked like, nor is it possible to make any chronological determinations about it. The closing remark in v. 10 reinforces this conclusion. The words οὐδὲ ἐν τῷ Ἰσραὴλ τοσαύτην πίστιν εὗρον are significant. Since according to Matthew's depictions to this point, Jesus has not had any opportunity to test the faith of the Israelites in the way that is suggested here, this story cannot have been one of the earliest miracles.[51] A similar chronological difficulty presents itself in v. 11, where the rejection of the Jews and the winning of the Gentiles is treated as the high point of Jesus' ministry, even though Jesus first came to this realization near the end of his activity. The connection between vv. 11 and 12 thus dissolves. Luke brought them together much later (13:28ff), which may not have been correct historically, but that was still correct. Obviously the story of Jesus was being treated with a certain pragmatism. It is

---

51. Cf. Loisy, *Les Évangiles synoptiques*, 1:646: "The story of the centurion cannot be placed in the early period of the Galilean ministry." Cf. also Wellhausen, *Matthew*, 36: "The closing sentence includes the inappropriate suggestion that at this point Jesus can look back on a long period of activity." I am not so sure that we can call the suggestion "inappropriate."

conceivable that the kinds of words that Jesus speaks in the conclusion of this pericope retained their liveliness in the tradition and became normative for the Christian community. The fact that Jesus had thought differently at the beginning, that he had indeed fought for the soul of his people, could not have permanently fixed itself in the consciousness of the earliest community. In their eyes Jesus had been perfect from the very beginning, and his words and deeds were all at the same level. This awareness is decisive for correctly evaluating the chronology of the story of Jesus. Nothing but the statement about the location is strongly fixed in the tradition. It makes no difference that the Syriac makes no mention of Capernaum here. We may not be able to tell exactly why this or that localization for the narrative subsequently came up, but we can positively affirm that the account itself points to Capernaum as its location.

Luke 7:1–10, a version of the story into which we have already looked briefly, connects the story (as Mark does) with a great sermon of Jesus and with his arrival in Capernaum. But Luke puts the pericope about the demon in a different place. His description of the situation is also slightly different in content, for the official sends his servant rather than coming himself. Whether this was the original version or a later elaboration I will not venture to guess.[52] As in Matthew, the narrative is located in Capernaum.[53]

The two brief stories that Matthew places after this narrative (8:14–15 and 8:16–17, which we have already discussed) also point to Capernaum.

In addition we may also briefly consider here the overall narrative from Matt 4:12–8:17. This complex, which runs parallel to Mark 1:14–45, clearly shows that Matthew has rearranged and expanded upon the material at his disposal. We have therefore no

---

52. Zahn (cited by Klostermann, *Matthäus*, 212) speaks here of a "believable lifelikeness." Loisy, on the other hand, declares: "Luke is secondary to Matthew, and his modifications ... seem artificial" (Loisy, *Les Évangiles synoptiques*, 1:648ff).

53. The mention of Capernaum here creates a painful problem for Spitta, because according to his theory of a Synoptic *Grundschrift*, Jesus has been in Judea since Luke 4:44 (Spitta, *Die synoptische Grundschrift*, 143). "All at once the scene changes, and we find ourselves in the same region in which Jesus gave the Sermon on the Mount. We cannot avoid the conclusion that the place-name was inserted by Luke after Matthew; perhaps the original reading was εἰς Καισαρίαν, since there are many connections and contacts between this story and Luke's account in Acts 10. John 4:46 brought in the reference to Capernaum independently of the Matthean rescension." Spitta excludes Luke 7:1b from the Synoptic *Grundschrift*.

choice but to abandon the idea that a chronology—even a general and approximate one—can be extracted from this complex.[54] Matthew himself gave no thought to the amounts of time that may have been involved.

Excursus: The Complex Mark 1:14–45 in Luke

With respect to the outline of Mark, Luke (4:14–5:16) is more conservative than Matthew, but when does make changes, he usually goes deeper than the first evangelist. For Matthew valued the individual pictures from the story of Jesus, putting them together in a specific sequence, with a method that was plainly based on connections by content. Luke, by contrast, places his emphasis on sequencing and psychologizing the course of events. He does this so energetically and skillfully that it almost appears as if his particular arrangement of the framework of the story of Jesus might represent a special tradition that is superior to the Markan outline.[55] We have demonstrated in these pages, of course, that Luke's framework is the result of his intentional effort to improve the Markan outline.

Excursus: Literary and Historical Evaluation of Mark 1:14–45par

The alterations that Matthew and Luke made to Mark's threads have the effect of shining the beam of a searchlight on those gospels. Is it possible that alterations of this sort could have taken shape right away, in the same generation? In that case we would have to regard Matthew and Luke as interpreters of Mark. Advocates of the Markan hypothesis and the Two-Source theory are inclined to find in Mark, the oldest evangelist, an account that reproduces the development of Jesus generally correctly, as it unfolds in the sequence of events. The course of the history of Jesus is frequently described on the basis of the Gospel of Mark, even

---

54. Cf. Windisch, "Die Dauer der öffentliche Wirksamkeit Jesu," 154: "this opening period, which Mark indicates was certainly more than two weeks, may have lasted an entire month or more." Zahn thinks in terms of months: "we understand why he has nothing more to report about this period of work that lasted for weeks: it was less significant than the one sermon." Zahn, *Matthäus*, 173.

55. So Merx and Spitta.

though the events in Mark are only loosely strung together.[56] Our analysis of this Gospel, supported by an analysis of parallel excerpts in Matthew and Luke, has shown that beneath the veneer of a chronological arrangement in Mark 1:15, 1:20, and 1:39, we have been able to find only gaps, and nothing else. The sequence of events in these stories is in fact highly uncertain. Many of the historical circumstances are doubtful, including the "fact" that Jesus called his disciples before his ministry in Capernaum. All we can say is that these narratives, anchored in Capernaum and its environs, belong together and may have taken place around the same time. The story of the possessed man cannot be located either chronologically or geographically. It could have taken place either before or after the events in Capernaum. Yet Mark himself put no stock in chronological, topographical, or psychological connections between individual stories. His references to time and place arise only from coincidences in the tradition, and no hard and fast rules can be laid down about them, since they appear and disappear through the course of the tradition. We have seen that there was certainly an effort to localize stories that were merely floating in the air, but it is equally clear that such details quickly fell off the table. They seem to be the result of a certain educated interest in the tradition, but they disappear under the influence of the primitive Christian worship, in which the story, apart from its framework, was all that mattered. Textual variants can be highly instructive, for they provide us with evidence of these tendencies, and from them we can draw conclusions about the treatment of the Jesus tradition during its earliest origins. This negative result is therefore a positive achievement. If Matthew and Luke did alter the Markan outline, it is not as though they destroyed some perfect historical chronology and thereby eclipsed historical facts. From now on synoptic criticism will have to be more complex and simple. The Markan/Two-Source hypothesis asserts that Mark wrote the oldest Gospel, which both of the other evangelists then used and supplemented with additional special sources. It seems to me that this is now an assured result of the literary criticism of early Christianity. But this certainty provides no information at all about the actual historical sequence in the story of Jesus. It is understandable that efforts have been made to find the original outline in the Gospel

---

56. Cf. especially J. Weiss, Wellhausen, Loisy.

of Luke, and Spitta's work is particularly illustrative in this regard. So are Catholic attempts to harmonize John with the Synoptics, even if they are in rather bad taste. The Markan framework of the story of Jesus does have gaps, and on that basis, these kinds of efforts seem to acquire an aura of legitimacy, but in fact they are chasing after phantoms that never existed in reality. Occasionally we may harmonize this or that issue and thereby come up with genuine historical content, but it generally does no good at all to lay the various frameworks of the four Gospels up against each other. It is begging the question (*petitio principii*) to assume that a smooth chronological thread can be extracted from the Gospels. Efforts at harmonization depend upon the hypothesis of an Ur-Mark, which may have been longer or shorter than our Mark. By failing to see the actual sequence of the narratives in Mark, we assume that the sequence must have originated in Ur-Mark.

3

Jesus' Conflicts with the Leaders of the People

Mark 2:1—3:6 and par.

The Healing of a Paralytic
(Mark 2:1-2; Matt 9:1-8; Luke 5:17-26)

ΚΑΙ ΕΙΣΕΛΘΩΝ ΠΑΛΙΝ ΕΙΣ Καφαρναοὺμ δι' ἡμερῶν ἠκούσθη ὅτι εἰς οἶκόν ἐστιν. This opening sentence is thoroughly transitional.

> The reading εἰσελθών πάλιν is represented in B D L 33 cop arm and eth. Most of the uncials resolve the construction into εἰσῆλθεν ... καί. A C E Δ, and F have ὁ ις after εἰσῆλθεν. Most of the minuscules, the Vulgate and ς have πάλιν εἰσῆλθεν. The lectionaries tend to drop this πάλιν, which usually refers backward to what has preceded. Despite good witnesses (B D L 33 latt cop), the reading ἐν οἴκῳ should be regarded as an atticizing improvement. A C Γ Δ offer εἰς οἶκον (cf. εἰς τὴν συναγωγήν, 1:21).

The grammatical resolution of this sentence, however, is disputed, as it depends upon whether δι' ἡμερῶν is to be connected with εἰσελθών or with ἀκούσθη. The former is more likely.[1] Δι' ἡμερῶν, rendered by the Vulgate as *post dies*, means "in the course of (some) days," or "after (some) days."[2] Since the event that follows took place during Jesus' second visit to Capernaum, the difference in time has to be indicated. But this chronological reference is not specific, and thus is best regarded as evidence of a caesura that has been inserted here by the evangelist. The word πάλιν is another

---

1. Contra Wohlenberg, who alternates on the question of whether ἠκούσθη is used personally or impersonally (Wohlenberg, *Markus*, 73), and B. Weiss, who confidently chooses the latter option and regards εἰσελθών as an anacoluthon (B. Weiss, *Markus und Lukas*, 31).

2. One codex gets the sense just right when it inserts the word ὀλίγων.

such insertion, one of Mark's favorite expressions (he uses it about thirty times). We cannot tell whether the verse contains any further compositional work on the part of the evangelist, but we can observe that from the very beginning it did contain one designation of place: εἰς οἶκόν. The details that follow (no room in front of the door, removing the roof, and the word καθήμενοι)³ all indicate that Jesus has entered a house. Exactly what, however, does εἰς οἶκόν mean? Although the definite article is missing, perhaps we should not think of a generic house, but of one particular house. At that time εἰς οἶκόν and εἰς τὸν οἶκόν were used interchangeably, and in this context, a reference to a "house" in Capernaum is probably a reference to the house of Peter, which has already been mentioned in chapter one.⁴ That is why the evangelist introduced Καφαρναούμ, along with πάλιν and δι' ἡμερῶν. The word ἠκούσθη, which is missing from Matthew and Luke, can be ascribed to Mark's redactional activity. Some sort of transition had to be created from 1:45 to 2:1: Jesus goes into the city, but not openly; he comes to Capernaum secretly, and the people hear that he is εἰς οἶκον. The original narrative would have begun simply with the words καὶ ἦν εἰς οἶκον (or ἐν οἴκῳ). Nothing more is necessary in order to understand the narrative that follows. The details of time and place are not firmly anchored in the narrative itself, and the narrative loses none of its character when literary and compositional analysis shows that we have to remove those details. They are nothing more than stopgaps that fill in the obvious break between chapter one and chapter two.

The other two Synoptics show how easily such "fill-ins" could be revised or changed. Matthew puts the story in a completely different position, after the healing of the demoniac in Gadara. To that end he has to insert a journey on the sea: καὶ ἐμβὰς εἰς πλοῖον διεπέρασεν καὶ ἦλθεν εἰς τὴν ἰδίαν πόλιν (Matt 9:1).

> The tradition swings back and forth between πλοῖον and τὸ πλοῖον. No final answer is possible here, since the use of the article in the κοινή is highly irregular. C F et.al. insert ὁ ἰς after ἐμβάς.

---

3. Translations and interpretations vary. The Vulgate has *in domo*; Luther, "im Hause." Weizsäcker, "zu Hause"; Klostermann: "zu Hause"; Loisy: "à la maison"; Lagrange (*Évangile selon Saint Marc*, 30), "dans une maison." Lagrange rightly notes that the expression is "probably synonymous with οἴκοι, or in Latin, *domi*." Cf. 1 Cor 11:34, where ἐν οἴκῳ means "at home," as it also does in 1 Cor 14:35. Wellhausen is correct when he writes: "In such expressions the article can easily drop in or out, sometimes in different manuscripts of the same text. Like the desert or the mountain, the house is at his disposal" (Wellhausen, *Mark*, 16). Cf. also Loisy, *Mark*, 83.

4. J. Weiss confidently observes: "We can hear the narrative style of Peter in this short and vague expression. Even though it was his house, he does not describe it any more precisely" (J. Weiss, *Das älteste Evangelium*, 155).

The idiosyncratic reading in F, which has Ἰουδαίαν πόλιν instead of ἰδίαν πόλιν, must have been caused by a misunderstanding.

Matthew offers no designation of time, because his arrangement of the stories makes the phrase δι' ἡμερῶν superfluous. ἰδία πόλις is to be understood as "his city," i.e., Capernaum (not Nazareth, as Jerome mistakenly thought), since it has already been mentioned as Jesus' base of operations in 4:13, but there is no reference to a house. We encounter this kind of disregard for locations frequently in Matthew (cf. Matt 12:23; 15:15, 21; 17:19; 19:9 vs. Mark 3:20; 7:17, 24; 9:28; 10:10). The pressure of the crowd is also missing. Matthew drops these painterly details, because he is interested only in the words and deeds of Jesus, yet his shorter version of the story is just as understandable as the earlier one.[5]

Luke 5:17 is quite different. It makes a chronological detail out of δι' ἡμερῶν by turning it into ἐν μιᾷ τῶν ἡμερῶν.[6] Luke also does not name Capernaum as the location for this event, for as we have already seen, Luke presents the Galilean ministry of Jesus according to a clear plan: first Nazareth, then Capernaum, then the area around Capernaum. After Jesus leaves Capernaum at the end of chapter 4, it would have been inappropriate for him to go back again to that city. In Luke he does not come back to Capernaum until 7:1, after a long ministry in the open country and only after his great sermon on the plain.[7] In his introduction Luke says nothing about an οἶκος, even though (as it does in Mark) the whole story plays out in a house.

Thus there is no firm itinerary in this tradition, nor any firm or clear chronology. While the result of our analysis of Mark 2:1 may be negative, these results are important.

In the course of the narrative (Mark 2:6), γραμματεῖς step onto the stage, and their arrival is somewhat unexpected. Of course we have already seen that the oldest narratives had no interest in pragmatic treatments of characters. In this regard Luke is different from the other evangelists, as he sets the scene by connecting these γραμματεῖς (or νομοδιδάσκαλοι) with the Φαρισαῖοι, and he tells us whence they have come: οἳ ἦσαν ἐληλυθότες ἐκ πάσης κώμης τῆς Γαλιλαίας καὶ Ἰουδαίας καὶ Ἰερουσαλήμ (Luke 5:17). This is due not to some special Lukan tradition, but rather to the fact that Luke

---

5. Wellhausen is of the opinion that this "abbreviation of Mark 2:1-4 makes Matt 9:2 (ἰδὼν τὴν πίστιν) seem unnatural or even supernatural" (Wellhausen, *Matthew*, 40).

6. Loisy is especially observant here: "Luke bleaches out and transforms the real and living character of the narrative" (Loisy, *Les Évangiles synoptiques*, 1:471). Compare ἐν μιᾷ τῶν ἡμερῶν here with ἐν μιᾷ τῶν πόλεων in 5:12.

7. Wellhausen is incorrect when he comments on this passage by suggesting that Luke was indifferent about Jesus' itinerary.

the author is putting things together here, and he may have managed to put them together correctly.⁸

In Mark's version of the story we cannot tell whether the scribes came from Jerusalem, but there is another way to produce a perspective that is oriented to Jerusalem. Those who stick to the outline of Jesus' ministry as presented in the Gospel of John do so by inserting a trip to Jerusalem right here, before Mark 2:1. Jesus then comes back to Capernaum from that trip.⁹ It goes without saying that these kinds of efforts at harmonization are desperate attempts to fill in the gaps in Mark's account with whatever insertions might be necessary. Of greater significance is the fact that even the harmonizers can see the gap in the text at this point. Awareness of that gap points us toward both a correct understanding of the literary style of this Gospel and a proper evaluation of the techniques by which it was composed. Perhaps there are times when a harmonizer may actually be seeing the text more clearly than a scholar who thinks the phrase δι' ἡμερῶν is a strong chronological indicator and means "after a few days."

The Call of Levi and Dinner with the Tax Collectors
(Mark 2:13-17; Matt 9:9-13; Luke 5:27-32)

¹³ Καὶ ἐξῆλθεν πάλιν παρὰ τὴν θάλασσαν· καὶ πᾶς ὁ ὄχλος ἤρχετο πρὸς αὐτὸν καὶ ἐδίδασκεν αὐτούς. ¹⁴ καὶ παράγων εἶδεν Λευεὶν τὸν τοῦ Ἀλφαίου καθήμενον ἐπὶ τὸ τελώνιον.

> Some manuscripts (D, e.g.) have dropped πάλιν and inserted ὁ ις after ἐξῆλθεν, and there may also be other changes here that

---

8. Spitta says: "Here we are plainly being guided into the region of Judea... In Mark and Matthew this contrast in the pericopes is hinted at only once, anticipating what comes later" (Spitta, *Die synoptische Grundschrift*, 74). Wellhausen recognizes that Luke describes the opponents of Jesus as having come from a distance. He says that the people—not the Pharisees and scribes—have gathered from all of Galilee—not Judea and Jerusalem (Wellhausen, *Luke*, 17). In my judgment Codex D, upon which Wellhausen depends here, conforms to the text of Mark and Matthew. That is also to disagree with Merx, who argues on the basis of this variation in the tradition that Luke 5:17 is overdone and fragile (Merx *Markus und Lukas*, 219). On the other hand Spitta places great value on the fact that τῆς Γαλιλαίας is an insertion. Luke 5:17, he says, is clear evidence for the fact that according to the Synoptic *Grundschrift*, of whose characteristics traits the canonical Mark and Matthew were ignorant, the healing of the paralytic took place in a city in Judea (Spitta, *Die synoptische Grundschrift*, 76).

9. So esp. the Catholic exegetes. Cf. J. Belser, "Zur Evangelienfrage," 363: "In this turn of phrase (δι' ἡμερῶν) we can glimpse an indication of the fact that during these intervening days Jesus has undertaken a journey to Jerusalem, for the feast in John 5, after which he returned to his beloved place, Capernaum."

have been brought on by the lectionaries. In a lectionary, for example, the backward reference in the word πάλιν would have a disruptive effect (cf. Mark 2:1). The insertion of ὁ ἰς is very strong evidence that the pericope originally began with v. 13. On the other hand the presence of ὁ ἰς in v. 14 of some manuscripts, after παράγων (F G Γ, and some lectionaries), indicates that some versions of the pericope began with v. 14.

As we have already seen in another story (cf. 1:39), here too we can ask whether v. 13 is the conclusion of the preceding pericope or the introduction to this one. In this case the second possibility is more natural, for v. 12 provides a good conclusion to the story of the paralytic, and the πάλιν (which functions here like the πάλιν in 2:1)[10] points toward a new beginning, connecting this story with 1:16, just as in 2:1 it connected that story with 1:21. Yet here too (as in v. 1), we can see the redactional work of the evangelist. Indeed the entire verse can be identified as a summary statement, producing the same construction we have already found in 1:14 and 1:16-20. Once again the decisive consideration is that the scene that follows has no internal connection at all with the details of v. 13, but is fully comprehensible in and of itself.[11]

Both Matthew and Luke understood this, and for both of them Mark 2:13 simply drops out of the picture. Matthew adds only the bare necessities as to the location, contenting himself with a vague ἐκεῖθεν (9:9).

> The predominant reading is ὁ ἰς ἐκεῖθεν. D cop it rearrange the order to read ἐκεῖθεν ὁ ἰς. ℵ* L ("item evv initio pericopae") drop ἐκεῖθεν.

This pericope basically does not fit very well into the outline of Matthew (chapter 8 includes only miracle stories), but it is located here primarily because Matthew is not at liberty to cut himself completely free from

---

10. "πάλιν ... need only be described as a transition word" (Wellhausen, *Mark*, 18). "The transition formula is artificial" (Loisy, *Mark*, 90).

11. Blass seems to have been sensitive to this when he asserts that Jesus was not teaching while he walked along the sea in v. 14 (Blass, "Textkritische Bemerkungen zu Markus"). Wohlenberg thinks the tax collectors and sinners who are named later must have been among the listeners in v. 13 (Wohlenberg, *Markus*, 81). In my judgment that is reading into the text. B. Weiss is of the opinion that the narrative is completely given overto describing events by the seashore and is expressly distinguished from any temporal connection with the preceding narrative (B. Weiss, *Markus und Lukas*, 35). None of these exegetical notes is based on a correct insight into the compositional techniques of the evangelist, who used summary statements as transitional pieces (both conclusions and introductions). J. Weiss understands this; he ascribes 1:13 to the editor (J. Weiss, *Das älteste Evangelium*, 159).

Mark's thread. Here he shows that he knows how to fit in a story that is not especially well suited to the context.

Luke (5:27) approaches this problem differently. As we have seen, he does not pay much attention to specific details of place and time. For him a simple μετὰ ταῦτα will suffice, so as not to disrupt the flow of the narrative.

> In some manuscripts ὁ ις is inserted after ἐξῆλθεν or ἐθεάσατο. The sharply divergent reading of D has been conformed to the text of Mark.

From Luke's point of view the influx of the crowds is an interruption, and the mention of the sea, which plays no part in what follows, is superfluous or (even worse) incorrect.

The pericope originally began with καὶ παράγων (Mark 2:14), as did 1:16 as well.[12] Levi does not receive much of an introduction, since the first hearers of this story already knew him and his work at the τελώνιον.

In both of the other Synoptics, Matthew is introduced personally. The Gospel of Matthew links this scene with what precedes by means of the word ἐκεῖθεν (we have already seen that he dropped Mark 2:13), describing him as ἄνθρωπον ... Ματθαίον λεγόμενον.[13] And Luke, who reconfigures the story more thoroughly, says (in better style than Mark) τελώνην ὀνόματι Λευείν.

Mark 2:15-17 describes for us a meal with tax collectors and sinners, at which Pharisaic scribes are also in attendance.

> The text of what follows has come down to us in a variety of forms. The occurrence of ἐγένετο in place of γίνεται appears to be in conformity with ἠκολούθησεν. The construction γίνεται ἐν τῷ κατακεῖσθαι is well-attested; it appears very frequently in Acts. Tischendorf argues that the reading κατακειμένων αὐτῶν (D it) is an accommodation to the text of Matthew, which also has a genitive absolute. The aorist ἠκολούθησαν (A C D . . .), instead of the imperfect ἠκολούθουν (B) can also be explained as an accommodation to v. 14. With Tischendorf and Westcott-Hort we must put a punctuation mark after πολλοί and take ἠκολούθουν with what follows (cf. also Wendling, *Die Enstehung des Marcusevangelium*, 8). The word ἀκολουθεῖν is better suited to an expression about the followers of Jesus. Instead of the unusual

---

12. "καὶ παράγων transports us into this situation without any indication of time . . ." (B. Weiss, *Markus und Lukas*, 35). Wohlenberg also sees the gap when he says: "As Jesus went along beside the sea, naturally he had finished his teaching" (Wohlenberg, *Markus*, 81).

13. At this point I will not go into the "Matthew-Levi" question.

(and frankly incomprehensible) οἱ γραμματεῖς τῶν Φαρισαίων (X B L Δ 33), A C D have the more typical οἱ γραμματεῖς καὶ οἱ Φαρισαῖοι. The definite article οἱ (B) should be kept.

The time of day at which this meal took place is left indefinite, so there is no way to connect this episode with what precedes. As in 1:18 and 1:20, the call story reaches its climax and resolution with the words καὶ ἀναστὰς ἠκολούθησεν αὐτῷ. A new entity, with no connection at all to 2:13–14, begins in 2:15. A few remarks about the character of the narrative itself will confirm this observation: it is a story about disciples of Jesus, about most of whom we have heard nothing before. Since the previous report mentioned only the calling of two pairs of brothers, where did all these other disciples come from?[14] 2:14 appears to describe the process by which Jesus called his closest circle of disciples, and v. 15 depicts a gathering of all of them. The brief remark, ἦσαν γὰρ πολλοὶ καὶ ἠκολούθησαν αὐτῷ, does not change the situation. These words are a transitional comment of the evangelist, who uses them to establish the existence of a broader circle of disciples.[15]

Without any announcement οἱ γραμματεῖς τῶν Φαρισαίων appear on stage in v. 16 and address their question to the disciples.[16] The presentation of this scene is vague, and we cannot tell when or where the scribes came to the disciples. Are they asking their question during the meal, to which the disciples were not invited? Or was it after the meal? Or were the scribes included in the group gathered around the table? The article οἱ before γραμματεῖς is also significant: these "scribes" are already known to hearers of this story as opponents of Jesus. In general we can make two observations about this story:

1) Jesus sits with his disciples in a group of tax collectors and sinners. His opponents pose a trick question and receive a surprising answer. Temporal and geographical details are completely lacking.

2) The story can be understood on its own, with no connection with what precedes. True, the details relate to what has been narrated to this

14. J. Belser believes that a trip to Jerusalem has been removed from the story at this point. John 5:1ff tells us about the great number of Jesus' disciples. Cf. J. Belser, "Zur Evangelienfrage," 362.

15. "There were many others besides the first four" (B. Weiss, *Markus und Lukas*, 36). Other exegetes take πολλοί to refer to the tax collectors and sinners, but in my judgment that makes little sense. Mark does not need to establish the fact that there were many tax collectors and sinners in the house.

16. "In the original report the amazed expression, 'Is he eating with tax collectors and sinners?', was placed on the lips of unspecified members of the public" (Wendling, *Die Enstehung des Evangeliums*, 8). But Wendling removes from the original story not only the end of v. 15 (from ἦσαν to αὐτῷ) but also οἱ γραμματεῖς τῶν Φαρισαίων. In my opinion this misunderstands the way Mark has worked over this story.

point, but it is impossible to make any precise specification as to the chronology. Clearly the story does not come from the early stages of Jesus' ministry. On close examination the place designation ἐν τῇ οἰκίᾳ αὐτοῦ proves to be unclear, although in this context it most naturally refers to the house of Levi. In the original narrative the phrase may have been only ἐν τῇ οἰκίᾳ (so Matt 9:10). That would be a house that was at Jesus' disposal, about which we cannot be more precise. Thus the story floats free in the air, and since it mentions tax collectors, Mark could easily link it with a story about the call of a tax collector.[17]

The construction of the parallel pericope in Matthew (9:10-13) is generally the same as in Mark. The construction καὶ ἐγένετο αὐτοῦ ἀνακειμένου ἐν τῇ οἰκίᾳ καὶ ἰδού ... recalls the style of the LXX for the Hebrew expressions והיה והנה. The early chapters of Genesis offer many comparable examples. Matthew drops Mark's transitional remark, ἦσαν γὰρ πολλοὶ καὶ ἠκολούθησαν αὐτῷ. Perhaps the word ἐλθόντες in v. 10 is a vestigial remnant of this sentence, which Matthew regarded as superfluous. οἱ Φαρισαῖοι stands in for the phrase οἱ γραμματεῖς τῶν Φαρισαίων and can be regarded as an improvement upon Mark's text. αὐτοῦ drops out after τῇ οἰκίᾳ, perhaps intentionally, because Matthew is not thinking of the house of Matthew the tax collector, but rather of Jesus' own house, i.e., the house in which he performed the healing of the paralytic (9:1-8). Certainly Jesus' house *can* be meant by the phrase ἐν τῇ οἰκίᾳ.

While the call scene and the meal hang together only loosely in both Matthew and Mark, Luke creates a close relationship between them in 5:29: καὶ ἐποίησεν δοχὴν μεγάλην Λευεὶς αὐτῷ ἐν τῇ οἰκίᾳ αὐτοῦ. We need not waste time discussing whether this text (instead of Mark's) was touched by exegesis and combination. Even the *dramatis personae* have been improved upon by the third evangelist: he speaks of an ὄχλος πολὺς τελωνῶν καὶ ἄλλων. This term ἄλλων includes the Φαρισαῖοι καὶ οἱ γραμματεῖς αὐτῶν mentioned in v. 30, yet even in Luke the identities of the characters in the scene are not

---

17. The groping of exegetes at this point is striking. Older exegetes (cf. B. Weiss, *Markus und Lukas*, 35) connect the αὐτοῦ with Jesus. Others think it refers to the house of Simon. Most of the time αὐτόν is connected with Jesus and αὐτοῦ with Levi. Wohlenberg, by contrast, disagrees and connects both pronouns with Levi (Wohlenberg, *Markus*, 82). Wellhausen rightly observes: "If Levi got up and followed Jesus after 2:14, it would not fit very well for Jesus to turn around and go to Levi's house. There really is no connection" (Wellhausen, *Mark*, 18). Loisy has also laid out the incongruity of the text (Loisy, *Mk*, 91). Only a proper comprehension of the techniques by which this unit was composed can overcome all these chronological and topographical problems. Wellhausen's opinion, i.e., that vv 15 and 16 introduce the situation "as an occasion for the saying in v. 17" (Wellhausen, *Mark*, 18), cannot be confirmed. Why could vv. 15-17 not have been an independent narrative from the beginning?

entirely clear. The phrase πρὸς τοὺς μαθητάς in v. 30 suggests that μετ' αὐτῶν in v. 29 must refer to Jesus and his disciples. Thus while Luke's report is more cohesive than either Mark's or Matthew's, it is still not seamless.

The Question about Fasting
(Mark 2:18-22; Matt 9:14-17; Luke 5:33-39)

Καὶ ἦσαν οἱ μαθηταὶ Ἰωάννου καὶ οἱ Φαρισαῖοι νηστεύοντες. καὶ ἔρχονται καὶ λέγουσιν αὐτῷ· διὰ τί οἱ μαθηταὶ Ἰωάννου καὶ οἱ μαθηταί τῶν Φαρισαίων νηστεύουσιν, οἱ δὲ σοὶ μαθηταὶ οὐ νηστεύουσιν; καὶ εἶπεν ὁ Ἰησοῦς . . .

א A B C D vg cop arm go read οἱ Φαρισαῖοι, but ς E F L Γ Δ 33 aeth have οἱ τῶν Φαρισαίων, a reading that is a later accommodation to v. 18b, as οἱ Φαρισαῖοι in some manuscripts is an accommodation to 18a. The readings οἱ τῶν Φαρισαίων 18b D Γ Δ vg), οἱ δὲ μαθηταί σου (E it vg cop) especially the omission of μαθηταί (B; cf. Luke 5:33), are attributable to efforts to smooth out the style. In D, ὁ Ἰησοῦς is lacking from v. 19a.

There is no connection here, either temporal or topographical, with what has preceded.[18] It is not clear who the questioners are, as the subject of the verb λέγουσιν is "the people," i.e., an indeterminate "somebody." We can see quite plainly that our story owes its current position to its content, because it deals with the ongoing conflict between Jesus and his opponents. As in the preceding story, Jesus is guilty of committing an offense against pious custom. And not only him: he and his free-thinking outlook are situated at the center of a wider circle of disciples. In this regard the story breaks the boundaries of the preceding framework, which had thus far described only a small band of disciples. The original story must have conceived of a broader circle, since the non-fasting of Jesus' disciples is contrasted with the practice of the followers of the Pharisees and John the Baptist. The unusual expression οἱ μαθηταὶ τῶν Φαρισαίων speaks for the fact that this narrative is very early. In this context it refers not the Pharisees themselves, who are usually depicted only schematically, but to their followers, the *Haberim* as opposed to the *am-haAretz*. The most important point, however, is to recognize that

---

18. B. Weiss rightly observes: "Καὶ ἦσαν—νηστεύοντες once again cuts off every temporal connection. Only that which is essential to the beginning of a new episode is reported. Clearly this narrative was arranged in this order purely on the basis of its content" (B. Weiss, *Markus und Lukas*, 37). Wohlenberg also sees that our story need not be connected temporally with the preceding. Wohlenberg adds: "But the possibility of such temporal connections cannot be ruled out, and the point of the story would only be sharpened by such details" (Wohlenberg, *Markus*, 84). That is not quite convincing.

the pericope breaks free from the preceding framework because it stems from an old, primitive, independent story. We can even entertain the question of whether the first half of v. 18 might be an insertion on the part of the evangelist. It all comes down to the way in which this first sentence is understood. Either it means that the disciples of John and the Pharisees were fasting at that particular time for some specific reason,[19] or it means that they customarily fasted, thereby making a general statement about them.[20] Perhaps the periphrastic construction νηστεύοντες ἦσαν speaks in favor of the former. καὶ ἔρχονται in v. 18b would make a good beginning for the pericope, rendering v. 18a disposable, but v. 18a could also have been the start of the pericope in the tradition. In this case we will have to content ourselves with the conclusion, *non liquet*. Verse 18a may even have been the beginning of the pericope in the tradition that Mark received. After all, why could not an individual narrative begin with a general remark that directs the reader's attention right to the main point? It does not matter that the flow of the description (from v. 17 to v. 18) would be disrupted: in composing this Gospel, Mark gave no thought to smooth narration.[21]

It is uncertain whether v. 21-22 might originally have been placed at this point; i.e., it is unclear whether the verse was spoken by Jesus on this occasion or some other. Perhaps it was a stray saying, which Mark attached here because it fit the general context.

Matthew (9:14-17) follows Mark's line and forms the introduction as follows: ¹⁴τότε προσέρχονται αὐτῷ οἱ μαθηταὶ Ἰωάννου λέγοντες· διὰ τί ἡμεῖς καὶ οἱ Φαρισαῖοι νηστεύομεν, οἱ δὲ μαθηταί σου οὐ νηστεύουσιν; ¹⁵καὶ εἶπεν . . .

> A C D E L Δ vg and cop insert the word πολλά. That is a later addition, but good exegesis. Syr^sin adds σπουδαίως. Merx (*Markus und Lukas*, 1:151-52) argues energetically (actually a bit too

---

19. Various efforts to fix this more precisely have come to nothing. B. Weiss reports on some of the proposals: that particular day may have been a feast day (W. Beyschlag, *Die Christologie des Neuen Testaments*, 37f.) or the disciples of John might have been fasting in mourning for the death of their master (Holtzmann, *Die synoptischen Evangelien*). B. Weiss himself thinks it was just one of the traditional holidays (cf. B. Weiss, *Markus und Lukas*, 37).

20. Thus many older and more recent exegetes (cf. B. Weiss, *Markus und Lukas*, 38).

21. J. Weiss (*Das älteste Evangelium*, 160) and Wellhausen (*Mark*, 20) take v. 18a as an editorial addition. Wendling (*Markus*, 8) disagrees with this view, but he does regard the mention of the Pharisees as a later insertion. Yet both of these scholars are too concerned with the connection between our story and what precedes. Even Windisch ("Die Dauer," 144) stands under the spell of this misdirected idea when he says: "The inquiry about fasting would have taken place at the same time and in connection with the previous complaint."

much so) against the view that πολλά was an addition in order to improve the construction. Some Mss lack Ἰησοῦς in v. 15b.

In Matthew it is the people who ask the question, not the disciples of Jesus, and they ask it on behalf of both themselves and the Pharisees. In this way Matthew tried to clarify the issue at stake in the conversation. With the word τότε Matthew has, as is characteristic of him, connected the scene with what precedes.

Luke (5:33-39) extensively reconfigured the story: οἱ δὲ εἶπαν πρὸς αὐτόν· οἱ μαθηταὶ Ἰωάννου νηστεύουσιν πυκνὰ καὶ δεήσεις ποιοῦνται, ὁμοίως καὶ οἱ τῶν Φαρισαίων· οἱ δὲ σοὶ ἐσθίουσιν καὶ πίνουσιν. ³⁴ὁ δὲ Ἰησοῦς εἶπεν πρὸς αὐτούς . . .

> A C D Γ Δ Λ it vg go arm aeth have διὰ τί in front of νηστεύουσιν. After Ἰωάννου, D has the words καὶ οἱ τῶν Φαρισαίων, but drops the phrase ὁμοίως καὶ οἱ τῶν Φαρισαίων. A Γ Δ Λ it vg go drop ὁ δὲ Ἰησοῦς.

Luke wants to create a chronological connection here, and his method of doing so is rather simple: he allows the conversation that took place in vv. 27-32 to continue, so that οἱ δέ could be the Pharisees, even if "the people" might be a better interpretation.[22] In v. 36 Luke inserts a parenthetical remark into Mark's narrative: ἔλεγεν δὲ καὶ παραβολὴν πρὸς αὐτούς. This is a clear signal that vv. 36-39 (= Mark 2:21-22) do not arise from the context.

Plucking Grain on the Sabbath
(Mark 2:23-28; Matt 12:1-8; Luke 6:1-5)

Καὶ ἐγένετο αὐτὸν ἐν τοῖς σάββασιν παραπορεύεσθαι διὰ τῶν σπορίμων.

> D and Vg add πάλιν after ἐγένετο. Elsewhere we have identified this πάλιν as an addition by the evangelist. Here its insertion strengthens the chronology. The import of the expression παραπορεύεσθαι was variously misunderstood, so that changes like διαπαραπορεύεσθαι were introduced by B C D, following Luke 6:1, or παραπορεύεσθαι in a few manuscripts, following Matt 12:1. The Vulgate translates it with *ambulare*. Even Luther translated it too generally: "He traveled there."

The story is a classic example of an independent narrative that has no close links with its context in time or location, the sort of narrative we have already

---

22. Of course Spitta (*Die synoptische Grundschrift*, 85-86) places special emphasis on the close connection here and finds in it the earliest tradition.

gotten to know in several other examples (cf. 1:40-45; 2:18-20). It begins with a clear purpose: it is an anecdote about a disagreement between Jesus and his opponents. ἐγένετο with the infinitive is a characteristic introductory formula in Luke, but occurs only here in Mark. Perhaps at this point the transmission of the text of Mark was influenced by the text of Luke.[23] The time designation, "on the Sabbath," and the place designation, "through the fields," are anchored in the narrative itself. We might ask: which Sabbath? which fields? where? But such questions cannot be answered and should not be posed to anecdotes of this kind. There is no connection between this pericope and what precedes, and nothing further can be determined about the time or the place in which it occurred. There is, however, something in the content of this story that does allow us at least to identify the season of the year during which it took place. It was during the season of the harvest, i.e., in the weeks after Easter between the beginning of April and the middle of June. Here we have come upon the only specific calendrical information in the entire synoptic tradition—outside of the Passion Narrative.[24] Because it offers such a rare clue to the chronology of Jesus' life, this detail has played a prominent role in efforts to determine the length of Jesus' public ministry. It suggests that all of the experiences that have been narrated up to this point had to have taken place during the harvest season, i.e., in the period of time immediately after Easter. It cannot have been otherwise, since the Synoptics only mention one Passover (the one when Jesus dies). All of the other events in the Gospels had to take place before that Passover, and in the Synoptics Jesus' ministry cannot have lasted longer than one year. In fact the narratives in these Gospels come nowhere close to filling up even that much time. If for the moment we were to leave Mark 2:23 out of consideration, the rest of the narratives in the Gospel of Mark would take up only about three, four, or perhaps five months—and the same would be true of Matthew and Luke as well.[25] For Mark was not paying any attention to the chronological details in this story, and he had not the first idea about the actual length of Jesus' ministry. We, by contrast, on the basis of coincidental details in this story, can correct his mistake. In this way various attempts are made at reckoning the

---

23. Cf. Moulton, *Einleitung in die Sprache des Neuen Testaments*, 18-24, for a discussion of the Hebraic background of this formula. ED: see the English original: *Introduction to the Language of the New Testament*.

24. Cf. Wellhausen, *Mark*, 22: "The time is after Easter; we have here the only determination of the season in the Gospel."

25. In this regard see esp. Windisch, "Die Dauer," 141-42, where he tries to answer the question of how the Gospel narrative relates to the framework of the Gospels, and how it fills it out.

chronology of Jesus' life more or less precisely,[26] although this way of reading the story is hopelessly misguided, because it insists on clinging tightly to the framework, especially as it is depicted in Mark, correcting that framework only slightly. This study, however, has already demonstrated that there is no strong framework or outline at all in Mark. The individual narratives are loosely arranged, one after the other, sometimes *with* and sometimes *without* specifications of time and/or place. It would be pure speculation to assert that the various narratives leading up to the Passover of Jesus' death took up at most one year of time. Exactly when did they take place? To that question the evangelists (except perhaps for Luke) offer no reply, and therefore historians have to remain silent. It may occasionally be possible to situate one or another of the stories near the beginning or the end of Jesus' ministry, but most of the time such efforts are doomed to fail. That is the very essence of a collection of anecdotes: it has no interest in chronology or topography. One narrative may have some details in its introductory framework, and another (like the one we are considering here) may coincidentally include something that places us in a specific season of the year, but the framing pieces and specific details are so few and far between that they cannot support any chronological calculations about the length of Jesus' ministry. We can be grateful for the mention of the harvest season in this story, since it establishes that the Synoptic story of Jesus lasted at least one year. If that detail had not been handed down to us, it might have been possible to argue, on the basis of the Gospel of Mark, that as a matter of historical fact, the ministry of Jesus lasted only a few months. Yet we cannot build anything even upon this minimum. Too bad there is not another pericope that contains a detail that might blow up the one-year framework, for then the fragility of the chronology would be jolted into clarity.

Some scholars still try to take the Johannine chronology as authentic and to reconcile it with the Synoptics, as though the outline of Mark has not been destroyed. But these efforts, which we find especially among advocates of harmonization, miss the point. Before the three-year Johannine chronology, which has much more to commend it psychologically than the beloved one-year theory, can be appraised historically, it first has to be evaluated as a literary phenomenon. The criteria for this evaluation cannot be derived from the Synoptics. Certainly the Synoptics are not without

26. Cf. Zahn, *Matthäus*, 444, where he argues (on the basis of this story) against the idea that Jesus' ministry lasted only a few months by situating this story eleven or twelve months before the Passover when Jesus died. Similarly Loisy writes: "This anecdote cannot be set in the later period of Jesus-ministry in Galilee; on the contrary, it fits into the middle of the year that preceded the death of Jesus, twelve months before the passion" (Loisy, *Mark*, 100).

value for understanding John, but the two cannot be brought together, as they usually are, by playing one against the other. Too often scholars try to hold onto the so-called "chronology of the Gospels" in a more or less rationalistic fashion, instead of giving free rein to literary study of the composition techniques of the evangelists.

Let us return then to the story of the Sabbath controversy. Unfortunately we have no evidence upon which to fix the point in Jesus' ministry at which this event occurred, other than to note that it took place during harvest season. Was it during the early period, one of his first encounters with his opponents, somewhere in Galilee? These opponents step onto the stage in v. 24 without any introduction: καὶ οἱ Φαρισαῖοι ἔλεγον αὐτῷ. Luke eases their abrupt entry slightly with τινὲς τῶν Φαρισαίων, but the appearance of the Pharisees at this point in the story remains unexplained and without motive. That, of course, is typical of the style of these narratives—characters can be mentioned without any introduction, and it is simply presumed that they are known to the readers (or hearers).[27] Over and over again the opponents of Jesus are not clearly differentiated from each other, because in the Christian communities within which these stories were formulated, it was simply a matter of Jesus on one side and his enemies on the other. His enemies included the Pharisees and the scribes in an undifferentiated mass. We do not have to imagine that these circles were confined to Jerusalem and Judea; they were present in Galilee as well. The distances involved are not so great that a Pharisee could not have moved from the south to the north. We know, for example, that Pharisees often traveled for the purposes of making proselytes, and in this story we also have to reckon with μαθηταὶ τῶν Φαρισαίων, i.e., with their wider following in the land. It is not surprising that such fine distinctions have disappeared from the narration of the stories here and there (but cf. 2:18).

We have already mentioned that in Palestine the harvest season begins at Easter. In this story it is not clear whether the harvest has already gotten underway, so the Sabbath referred to here may have been prior to the Passover. It might be possible on that basis to situate this narrative in Jerusalem, shortly before the Passover when Jesus died. If, by contrast, the Sabbath in question took place shortly after the spring festival, then our story would still be located in Jerusalem or its surroundings. For according to Deut 15:5-6, the Passover sacrifice had to be celebrated in Jerusalem, and Pharisees, who believed so strongly in the Law, would naturally be in

---

27. Of course, it makes no sense at all to ask how, or on what road, Jesus met the Pharisees. Some exegetes think that a group of Pharisees just ran into Jesus and his disciples, and Jesus made way for them (cf. παραπορεύεσθαι, v. 24). Others think that Jesus cut a path through a field, and his disciples followed (cf. Wohlenberg, *Markus*, 91).

Jerusalem at this time. If, however, the Sabbath in question fell later in the harvest season, there would be no way to know where the story took place.

Matthew (12:1-8) introduces it with the following words: ἐν ἐκείνῳ τῷ καιρῷ ἐπορεύθη ὁ Ἰησοῦς τοῖς σάββασιν διὰ τῶν σπορίμων.

> D drops τοῖς, which is surely a gloss, since it is not a matter of some specific sabbath.

Matthew locates this and the subsequent story in a different context. He treated the first conflict story (Mark 2:1-2) as a miracle story, placing it in the context of a series of miracle stories (9:1-8), and he stayed with Mark's pattern by putting the second and third conflict stories there as well (Mark 2:13-17; 18-22 = Matt 9:9-13;14-17). But he relocates the fourth and fifth of Mark's conflict narratives. Why this rearrangement? We cannot know for sure. Perhaps these two narratives would have made for too long a series of miracle stories; or perhaps, having already devoted a long section to Jesus' activity in Galilee (4:12-9:34) and the mission of the disciples (9:36-10:42), Matthew now wanted to devote the next section (chaps. 11-13) to the unbelief and opposition of the Jews. Having shown that Jesus understood himself as having been sent not to the whole people but rather to the powerless and the minorities, Matthew now presents Jesus in conflict with the leaders—the wise and the learned—of the people. Thus can we reasonably approximate the layout of Matthew, even if the arrangement of the various stories is not always completely clear. Our lack of clarity stems from the fact that Matthew, it would be fair to say, generally follows the narrative framework of Mark, except for that fact that here and there, in order to add his own contribution to the material, he thoroughly rearranges it, rather than following Mark conservatively.

By this time we know quite well how to evaluate the chronological reference, ἐν ἐκείνῳ τῷ καιρῷ (12:1). As in other places, it has been inserted by the evangelist, perhaps under the influence of the Old Testament, to mark the beginning of something new. It is, however, of no real chronological significance; it has the same force as the word τότε, which we have already encountered several times. In this context Matthew uses it to re-connect with his source, Mark, after having followed the Q source for awhile. The alterations that Matthew typically makes to the text of Mark tend to be of a stylistic nature. As usual (cf. 3:13), he avoids the construction καὶ ἐγένετο with an infinitive and substitutes the finite verb ἐπορεύθη.

Luke (6:1-5), follows Mark's lead and offers a highly unusual chronological introduction: ἐγένετο δὲ ἐν σαββάτῳ δευτεροπρώτῳ διαπορεύεσθαι αὐτὸν διασπρίμων. The word δευτεροπρώτῳ is a text-critical crux that cannot be solved by text-criticism alone. It appears in A C D E Γ Δ Λ . . . vg go arm, etc., but it is missing from ℵ^B L 33 cop pesh aeth. The shorter reading δευτέρῳ is scarcely attested, and codex Palatinus (cf. Metzger, p. 73) has *sabbato mane*. Editors of the Greek New Testament run the gamut: Tischendorf, Westcott-Hort, and Nestle include the word, while Lachmann and von Soden enclose it in brackets, and B. Weiss deletes it. Patristic writers offer a variety of explanations (cf. Tischendorf, 8th ed, 475–77). Ancient and modern exegetes argue over whether δευτεροπρώτῳ was even a word, an issue that has become a sticking point in Catholic discussion.[28] The old text-critical motto, *difficilior lectio potior*, provides little assistance here, since the word appears to be nonsense and is an absolute *hapax legomenon*. In all the rest of ancient literature it occurs only once, and that reference, which speaks of a δευτεροπρώτη κυριακή (Eustratius, *Vita et conversio Eutychii* 95; cf. Migne PG LXXXVI, 2381), probably goes back to this text in Luke. Lexicographers and grammarians are at a loss to explain the word. It has been suggested that it is a combination of two originally separate words, like the compound δευτερέσχατος ("penultimate").[29] Yet that example does not account for our word in this context. Perhaps it is an unknown *terminus technicus*; the fact that it is anarthrous does not rule out this possibility. Or it may be that, since the story takes place during the harvest season, δευτερόπρωτος designates a particular Sabbath that fell between Easter and Pentecost. None of these suggestions is well-founded, of course, and all we have to rely on are guesses and speculations.[30] It is highly unlikely that

28. Cf. Belser, *Tübingen ThQ* (1903), 59ff; Zellinger, *Die Dauer*, 69; Fendt, *Die Dauer*, 103; Chwolson, "Der Prolog des Johannesevangelium," *Das letzte Passahmahl Christi*, 59ff (he thinks the Sabbath in question is the Sabbath of Easter week); Dausch, "Neue Studien," 160 (he combines the Easter festival of Luke 6:1 with the one in John 6:4!).

29. Blass, *Grammatik*, 115.2.

30. For the opinions of ancient exegetes, cf. B. Weiss, *Markus und Lukas*, 361. The most widely held view is that of Scaliger: the word refers to the first Sabbath after the second day of Passover, since seven Sabbaths were counted from the second day of Passover (when the mature first-fruits were offered) until Pentecost. Alternatively, it may refer to the second Sabbath after the first Sabbath of the Jewish festival year, i.e., between 8 and 14 Nisan, or shortly before the Passover; cf. Zahn, *Einleitung*, 448. Wellhausen (*Luke*, 20) thinks it refers to the Sunday after Easter. Schlatter prefers 1 Nisan, i.e., the second day of the New Year festival; cf. Schlatter, *Markus und Lukas*, 206. Wohlenberg (*Markus*, 90) and Spitta (*Die synoptische Grundschrift*, 94) align themselves with Scaliger. All of these explanations regard the term as a designation for some specific particular day during the Easter season. Strack, by contrast, treats it as the first Sabbath in the second year of a Sabbath cycle, a Sabbath that had an especially clear significance because of the higher tax that began in that year (cf. Josephus, *Antiquities XIV*, 199–207); cf. Strack, "Briefliche Mitteilung an J. Belser," 59. According to another possible hypothesis, a Sabbath period ended in the fall of 781, i.e., in the fifteenth year of the emperor Tiberius, so that the second year of a new

JESUS' CONFLICTS WITH THE LEADERS OF THE PEOPLE 85

Luke had a more exact chronological specification than Mark.³¹ We simply do not know where Luke found the word or how he would have expected his readers to understand this kind of *terminus technicus*. Lukan special tradition is usually not very helpful when it comes to a chronological problem like this. Even on those occasions when Luke provides a more exact chronological fix than the other Synoptics, he typically does not work it out with much care. We have already seen this in the case of Luke 3:1. Is it perhaps possible that Luke himself coined the expression in this context, not in order to designate one specific Sabbath day, but rather to distinguish one Sabbath from another? Etymologically, the term does create a distinction between two Sabbath days, designating one as the first and the other as the second. Luke 6:6 mentions a Sabbath, but 6:1 has already mentioned one, so on that basis the Sabbath referred to in 6:6 would be the "second first" one. Yet it is hard to believe that Luke would have reckoned it that way, and this suggestion cannot be taken very seriously.

Was the word perhaps introduced into the story at a later stage in its development? Since this kind of insertion can happen unintentionally, the rule *difficilior lectio potior* does not always apply. In this regard it is surprising that the truly exceptional reading of codex e, "*sabbato mane*," has not received more attention.³² In Greek the manuscript reads σαββάτῳ πρωΐ. Should we take this as the original reading? Perhaps a glossator looked back to 4:31, where one Sabbath is mentioned, and inserted here the word δευτέρῳ. Later, the word πρωΐ was misunderstood, and it was combined with δευτέρῳ. Or perhaps πρωΐ was mistakenly thought to mean the same thing as πρώτῳ and thus came to be combined with δευτέρῳ. It is possible (and this possibility is often overlooked) for a technical expression to be expanded upon with a gloss. In the *Kerygma Petri*, for example, amid a discussion of Jewish festivals, there is mention of a "first Sabbath" (τὸ σάββατον τὸ λεγόμενον πρῶτον).³³ This expression must have been customary in the

---

Sabbath period began on 1 Tishri 782. Thus the season in question would not have been Easter, but the fall.

31. The exception to this is Spitta (*Die synoptische Grundschrift*, 94), who thinks he can see here a *terminus technicus* from the Synoptic *Grundschrift*.

32. Cf. J. H. Moulton, *Introduction to the Language of the New Testament* (1911), 144n1: "Interpreters of this passage (as well as John 1:41) now have to reckon with the reading that Lewis recently discovered in syr^sin, which suggests πρωΐ instead of πρῶτον, as likewise b and e in the Latin (*mane*). Cf. my remarks in "Contributions and Comments," 230 and 428, where I discuss another example of this same variant (Luke 6:1 in manuscript e, *sabbato mane*)."

33. Cf. E. Preuschen, *Antilegomena*, 90. For an explanation of the difficulty, cf. E. von Dobschütz, *Das Kerygma Petri*, 42ff. It has been argued that just as the expression δευτερόπρωτη κυριακή (in Eustratius) is related to the phrase πρώτη κυριακή, so

early Christian period. A later scribe did not understand it, however, and thinking it was a mistake, inserted the prefix δευτέρῳ (based on 4:31), which then became attached to the word πρώτῳ. I would find this explanation plausible, were it not for an objection that has already been raised: how likely is it that Luke would be the only Gospel writer who preserved this term? Isn't it more likely that Mark would have known this word too, and decided to leave it out? There are many good reasons to think that a later scribe would have felt compelled to insert πρώτῳ, on account of 6:6, where a Sabbath is mentioned. πρώτῳ was then replaced (on account of 4:31) with δευτέρῳ, and eventually δευτέρῳ was combined with πρώτῳ to produce δευτεροπρώτῳ.[34] Yet we cannot solve the problem with a simple reference back to 4:31. If for some reason a glossator did try to count the Sabbaths in Jesus' ministry, why did he begin here, and not with 4:16, or 13:10, or 14:1? If we would rather not trust a glossator with the carving knife, then this unusual enumeration of Sabbaths must have arisen from 6:6. A new expression was coined because one of these two narratives had to be designated as the first. That is not the work of a glossator, who for some reason displayed his skills only on this one narrative. It is the result of the practice of early Christian worship, in which the reading of a lectionary was customary. We have already observed that *initia lectionis* played a role in shaping the form in which texts were handed down. In this case these two narratives in the Gospel of Luke—6:1–5 and 6:6–11—were often read one after the other, and in that context the two narratives would have come to be known as the first and the second, respectively.

This rather extensive explanation has been necessary in order to get a clear picture of the facts in this case. But the complications involved in δευτεροπρώτῳ—a word of explanation, and a monster of a word at that—do not affect the outcome. With only a slight stylistic alteration we can see that the original text, like that in Mark, ran: ἐγένετο δὲ ἐν σαββάτῳ διαπορεύεσθαι αὐτὸν διὰ σπορίμων.

Mark 2:27 starts a new section: καὶ ἔλεγεν. Two sayings follow, as the controversy about the Sabbath comes to an end with the reference to David. Of the two sayings, the first—about people and the Sabbath—is a logical extension of the preceding story, although not an essential part of that story. The second saying, about the Son of Man, has a totally different

---

also δευτεροπρώτον σάββατον is related to πρῶτον σάββατον; cf. Westberg, *Die biblische Chronologie*, 120ff.

34. Cf. B. Weiss, *Markus und Lukas*, 361. In personal conversation A. Deissmann has told me that δευτεροπρώτῳ may be a later contamination driven by embarrassment, like δωένδεκα in 1 Cor 15:5. On that text, Tischendorf observes "E D* and D^c have created this monstrosity: μετὰ ταυεῖτα τοῖς δωένδεκα."

orientation. We must consider the possibility that, in order to answer questions about the Sabbath, the evangelist has brought together here two sayings that were spoken by Jesus on different occasions. Thus, as in 2:21–22, we have here a saying that roamed the tradition without a specific setting. The introduction καὶ ἔλεγεν is similar to those in 4:9, 11, 13; 7:9, 20; 8:21; and 9:1. Codex D has preserved the introduction as λέγω δὲ ὑμῖν, thereby linking v. 26 with v. 28.

This reading conforms to the parallel passages in Matthew and Luke. Matthew (12:5–8) arranges vv. 5 and 6 in such a way that they come to a climax in the statement, "Something greater than the Temple is here." There follows a quotation from the Hebrew Bible that Matthew has already used in 9:13. By dropping the premise of Mark 2:27, Matthew is able to create a stronger connection with 12:8 (Mark 2:28). The train of thought is completely different, but it is exquisitely consistent. Both of the sayings given by Matthew may come from a special source (not Q, since this material is missing from Luke), but it is more likely that Matthew himself constructed these sayings. As an expert writer, it seemed suitable to him to unite two biblical quotations with the story about the priests and a prophetic saying, in order both to justify the conduct of the disciples and to offer a proof from the Law and the prophets.[35]

Luke (6:5) leaves out Mark 2:27 and offers only Mark 2:28. Luke can de-emphasize Mark's premise here because later on, in his so-called "Travel Narrative" (13:10ff; 14:1ff), he will introduce a set of stories that illustrate the point of Mark 2:27.[36] Luke's dependence on Mark is evident in the fact that the καί in front of σαββάτου is incomprehensible except with reference back to Mark 2:27. As we would expect, Sinaiticus B pesch cop aeth and Matthew all drop this καί. There is no reason for its appearance here, at least not within the verse itself. Recalling an earlier story in which the topic was similar (Luke 5:24) we can see that, even though the pericopes originally existed independently of each other, it is not always necessary to interpret each one independently. As in Mark, the saying in Luke 6:5 is isolated.

Codex D provides an instructive example of the fact that the Gospels were composed through techniques that allowed individual sayings to come to rest in various settings. In this codex Luke 6:5 is isolated even more than in the standard text. It is separated from 6:3–4 and located after

---

35. Cf. Loisy, *Les Évangiles synoptiques*, 1:509: "This accumulation of proofs has the scent of a school and is the result of redactional combination."

36. At this point we need not enter into a discussion of the complicated problem with the phrase υἱὸς τοῦ ἀνθρώπου (does it designate the "son of man" as messianic, or merely human?), although strata in the tradition and redaction can be identified on this basis.

6:10, thus placing it at the end of the next Sabbath story. The possibility of this kind of transposition shows just how loose the structure actually was. Matthew welded a loose framework together. In Codex D, 6:3 is followed by yet another little Sabbath story that appears only here in the tradition: τῇ αὐτῇ ἡμέρᾳ θεασάμενός τινα ἐργαζόμενον τῷ σαββάτῳ . . . The time designation τῇ αὐτῇ ἡμέρᾳ does not sound original. In Luke it does not appear that these stories happened at the same time.[37] He could just as well have used here the expression that appears after 6:6, "on another Sabbath." This verse is thus a supplement to the original text, a fact that has no implications at all for the historicity of the saying itself. It may be just as historical as any other *agraphon*.

The Healing of the Withered Hand
(Mark 3:1-6; Matt 12:9-14; Luke 6:6-11)

There follows in Mark 3:1-6 another sabbath story, which supplies a fifth episode of conflict between Jesus and his opponents: καὶ εἰσῆλθεν πάλιν εἰς συναγωγήν. καὶ ἦν ἐκεῖ ἄνθρωπος . . . καὶ παρετήρουν αὐτόν, εἰ τοῖς σάββασιν θεραπεύει αὐτόν. After the healing and Jesus' threatening words to his opponents, the story concludes with: καὶ ἐξελθόντες οἱ Φαρισαῖοι εὐθὺς μετὰ τῶν Ἡρῳδιανῶν συμβούλιον ἐποίησαν κατὰ αὐτοῦ, ὅπως αὐτὸν ἀπολέσωσιν.

> Sinaiticus and B read εἰς συναγωγήν. The reading εἰς τὴν συναγωγήν, which is offered by ς, supported by A C D and L, is plainly an accommodation to Matthew and Luke. Various Latin versions tried to enliven ἦν ἐκεῖ with translations like *accessit* or *venit*. ℵ C and D read ἐν τοῖς σάββασιν, while A B L Γ Δ drop the ἐν. In v. 6 the tradition varied in innumerable small ways.

No details of time or place connect this narrative with what precedes.[38] In fact no time or place is mentioned at all. The word πάλιν naturally points

---

37. Cf., of course, two places in the so-called "Travel Narrative": Luke 10:21 and 13:31.

38. In my judgment Windisch misunderstands Mark's plan when he writes: "The synagogue visit and the healing that took place there are of course situated by Mark on one and the same Sabbath" (Windisch, 144). This chronological connection has rightly been disputed by B. Weiss (*Markus und Lukas*, 44), Klostermann (*Mark*, 26), and Wohlenberg (*Markus*, 96). Wohlenberg adds: "It is scarcely likely that this happened on the same Sabbath, the one on which the previous story took place, because in 2:23 the disciples went out for a long walk, which presumably began after the worship service in the synagogue" (Wohlenberg, *Markus*, 96). But that comment leads nowhere. These stories cannot be pumped for that kind of information. By the way, J. Belser maintains that a journey to Jerusalem was omitted right after 3:1.

back to 1:21 and Jesus' visit to the synagogue in Capernaum, but it also evokes 1:39, where it was reported that synagogue visits were customary for Jesus. We have already found this little word πάλιν in 2:1 and 2:13, and here in this context it has once again been inserted by the evangelist. Which town the synagogue might have been located in, we are not permitted to ask. The absence of the article discourages the notion that it is some specific or particular synagogue. While we cannot rule out the possibility that this was the synagogue in Capernaum, it is quite pointless to imagine that it is, solely on the basis of the word πάλιν. When the opponents of Jesus come on stage in v. 2, they are not named, yet it is unmistakably clear that we are dealing here with his enemies.

The pericope could end with v. 5, with v. 6 limping along behind, as the Pharisees and the Herodians leave together, rather abruptly. But this unusual detail actually speaks for its own authenticity: it is outside the typical template, according to which Jesus' opponents are the Pharisees and the scribes. Here we have reached not only the conclusion of this pericope, but also the climax of an entire series of conflict stories: the Pharisees have strongly disagreed with Jesus several times, and now they seek to destroy him, and in that effort they find allies. Opposition to Jesus has reached its high point. The "Herodians" were functionaries or agents of Herod Antipas, ruler of Galilee. Perhaps therefore this story could have taken place in Galilee, but a setting in Jerusalem cannot be ruled out. We should think of the Herodians as a powerful leading party in Antipas' court; Josephus describes them as τὰ Ἡρῴδου φρονοῦντες (*Ant.* 14.450). Mark mentions them in 12:13, a reference that reappears in Matt 22:16. There too we see them in concert with the Pharisees. Jesus' saying about the yeast of the Pharisees and of Herod (Mark 8:15) is relevant here as well, since Matthew refers the saying to the Sadducees (Matt 16:6) and Luke does not mention Herod (Luke 12:1). Herod himself came into some contact with Jesus: as Mark 6:14par indicates, he had heard of and thought about Jesus. The only strong rejection of Herod by Jesus, when Jesus calls him a "fox," is reported in Luke (13:32). Here the Pharisees are also portrayed as working in concert with Herod. It is also only Luke who reports the scene of Jesus appearing before Herod during the Passion Narrative (23:6ff). We will have more to say about the details of that scene later on, but at this point the most important consideration is that Jesus consistently had a conflicted relationship with both Herod and the Herodians.[39] The tradition consistently

---

39. Cf. Zahn, *Matthäus*, 533n44: "It could equally well have been Sadducees or Herodians." Catena on Mark 12:13: the Herodians were at that time οἱ τὸν Ἡρῴδην Χριστὸν εἶναι λέγοντες, ὡς ἱστορεῖται, ἄλλοι δὲ Ἡρῳδιανούς φασι τοὺς Ἡρῴδου στρατιώτας. For similar patristic comments, cf. Klostermann, *Markus*, 27.

emphasizes this fact. A comparison of the Gospels with each other shows that some of the details may not be significant, and others may have been lost, but the early picture of Jesus and his opponents was certainly livelier than the broad strokes in which it later came to be rendered. The opposition between Jesus and the Pharisees remained alive in a form different from that of the later conflicts between Jews, Jewish-Christians, and Gentile Christians. By that point the Herodians had vanished. How fortunate that at least a little of it has survived.

The specific reference to the Herodians makes it possible for us to determine the time of this story somewhat more precisely, for in this scene we no longer find ourselves in the early stages of Jesus' Galilean ministry. Herod and his people have certainly heard about Jesus, but they have taken little notice of him. The situation with the Pharisees is totally different: Jesus' liberalism was always a thorn in their side. In this story the Pharisees have formed an alliance with the Herodians, a detail that indicates that it took place in a later period of Jesus' ministry. Perhaps the Pharisees told the Herodians that Jesus was seeking to bring about an earthly kingdom, and thus that he was dangerous to Herod Antipas. Whether this alliance would have taken place at or shortly before the end of Jesus' Galilean ministry, or in what year it was begun, we do not know.

As we have already noted, Matthew (12:9-14), like Mark, connects the narrative of the healing of the withered hand with the story about picking grain on the Sabbath: καὶ μεταβὰς ἐκεῖθεν ἦλθεν εἰς τὴν συναγωγὴν αὐτῶν, καὶ ἰδοὺ ἄνθρωπος . . .

> C and E, along with some other Mss., insert the familiar phrase
> ὁ ις after ἐκεῖθεν.

The alteration in the introduction is typical of Matthew. The word μεταβαίνειν, which Mark never uses, occurs five times in Matthew: 8:34, 11:1, 12:9, 15:29, and 17:20. A similar transition is also found in 15:29. The word ἐκεῖθεν is another of Matthew's favorite expressions, occurring twelve times (versus only five in Mark, three in Luke, and two in John). We first saw it in 4:21. This introduction seems to set up a precise chronological and topographical relationship: both this and the preceding scene (1-8 and 9-14) fall on a Sabbath. Upon closer examination, however, these details turn out to be very loosely fastened. The preceding story was not situated in any specific location, and thus it is not possible to identify from what direction Jesus has come. From unspecified fields he enters into a synagogue, which is identified as belonging to those people who have already been named (n.b., αὐτῶν), i.e., the Pharisees. Since Matthew, like Mark, puts the definite article before συναγωγήν, perhaps he is thinking of the synagogue in Capernaum. The story itself, however, is quite different from the one in Mark. Mark 3:2 is recast here into a direct question, which Jesus answers with the well-known saying about rescuing a sheep that has fallen into a well on the Sabbath. This Q saying, which Luke placed in a later context (14:5), is in its original setting here in Matthew. We have seen a similar case in the earlier pericope, Matt 12:5-7. Along the way, Mark 3:3-6 is very briefly summarized by Matthew: specific details drop out, and the Herodians are not named. The reasons for this are not entirely clear, since in a later context (Matt 22:16) the Herodians do appear in Jerusalem. Perhaps Matthew believed that it should not be presupposed that these people would have been in Galilee.

In Luke's treatment of the framework of this narrative (6:6-11), Mark's text is carefully reformed: ἐγένετο δὲ ἐν ἑτέρῳ σαββάτῳ εἰσελθεῖν αὐτὸν εἰς τὴν συναγωγὴν καὶ διδάσκειν καὶ ἦν ἄνθρωπος ἐκεῖ . . .

> D has a widely variant reading: καὶ εἰσελθόντος αὐτοῦ πάλιν εἰς τὸν συναγωγὸν σαββάτῳ ἐν ᾗ ἦν ἄνθρωπος ξήραν ἔχων τὴν χεῖρα . . . This restructuring can partially be explained as a look back toward Mark 3:1 (cf. εἰσελθεῖν, πάλιν); its use of the participle is also reminiscent of the style in which Matthew often fashions the introductions to his pericopes. Within the Gospel of Luke, however, which is known for its smooth descriptions and which puts such a premium on the flow of the narrative, this reading cannot possibly be genuine. ς along with A and Δ has simply δέ instead of the more frequent δὲ καὶ.

The work of the evangelist Luke clearly betrays itself here. He loves the construction ἐγένετο, and he puts the phrase, ἐν ἑτέρῳ σαββάτῳ, which comes later in Mark, right at the beginning. Unlike Matthew, Luke makes it explicitly clear that this event took place on a Sabbath different from the one in the preceding story. We can and should attribute the word ἑτέρῳ to Luke, who wants to distinguish clearly between two stories that both begin with the phrase ἐν σαββάτῳ. Thus he inserted the word ἑτέρῳ here.[40] As in Matthew, the synagogue is a specific one (without the modifier αὐτῶν), yet we cannot tell whether the synagogue in Capernaum is meant, since the

---

40. J. Belser offers here a masterpiece of far-reaching harmonization ("Zur Hypothese von der einjährigen Wirksamkeit Jesu," 60). According to Matt 12:9, both the picking of grain and the healing of the withered hand took place on the same Sabbath. In the morning, Jesus went to the synagogue with his disciples. At noon the worshipers were on empty stomachs, and the disciples were hungry. In the afternoon they returned to the synagogue (cf. πάλιν, Mark 3:1) and spent the rest of the afternoon there, in accordance with Jewish custom. In view of these considerations Belser regards it as likely that ἑτέρῳ is an addition by a later glossator. If we compare this line of reasoning with those of other interpreters, we find ourselves wondering which might be correct. In my opinion it is a pointless question.

phrase εἰς τὴν συναγωγήν can be used like our phrase, "in church." Luke enlivens the scene with the addition of καὶ διδάσκειν, which explains why Jesus has gone into the synagogue. The extent to which the third evangelist was interested in artful formulation of the setting is evident in the unfolding of the narrative: παρετηροῦντο δὲ οἱ γραμματεῖς . . . In Mark the opponents are not immediately named, and only in retrospect do we learn who they are. Luke, by contrast, introduces us to Jesus' opponents right away. We have already seen this kind of authorial effort in 5:17-18, as well as in 5:29-33. But why are the Herodians not listed among the opponents of Jesus, along with the scribes and the Pharisees? An important clue appears in the closing sentence: αὐτοὶ δὲ ἐπλήσθησαν ἀνοίας, καὶ διελάλουν πρὸς ἀλλήλους τί ἂν ποιήσαιεν τῷ Ἰησοῦ. In Mark the narrative looked forward to Jesus' death, but Luke erases all of that, for reasons that are clear: in his view it is not yet time to mention the plot against Jesus. Only much later (13:31) will he speak of such a plot, and instead of the Pharisees it will be Herod himself who moves against Jesus. Pragmatic and chronological considerations cause Luke to alter the scene that he has before him.[41]

Conclusion: Mark 2:1—3:6par

In closing there is something more to be said about Mark 2:1—3:6. It has become clear that the stories in this section are arranged purely on the basis of their content. Five separate narratives—the reports of five conflicts between Jesus and the Pharisees—stand loosely connected with each other. We might even say that it is the opponents who hold the series together, for they are always there, ready to fight, and to that end they sometimes receive a special introduction. Individual sayings are inserted into these stories. The framing pieces, so far as they are evident, are varied: one story is localized with visible details, while another is framed without any specifics. This kind of variation is typical of stories that have a strongly anecdotal character. It is more or less an accident that we have any evidence at all of the trellis on which these anecdotes grew. The people who told these stories and passed them down paid little or no attention to their framing, and this helps to account for the variety in the framing details. Was the arrangement of the stories the work of the evangelist, or did it belong to the preceding tradition?

---

41. This pericope appears to me to be a masterpiece of Luke's literary artistry. The changes that he makes are obvious. Spitta is quite wrong to assert that the pre-Lukan text is preserved here in its truest form (Spitta, *Die synoptische Grundschrift*, 100ff). He finds Luke's conclusion to the story quite sensible: "They do not issue a death threat—although they would have gladly done so—because of their utter helplessness" (102).

The latter is more likely. There is little to suggest that Mark arranged the ministry of Jesus in a consistent way under specific topics. It is more likely that he found the arrangement of the stories in 2:1—3:6 in the tradition. The Christian community needed these kinds of stories for its proclamation and for its disagreement with Judaism, and so it arranged them on practical grounds. As an author, Matthew is on a higher level than Mark. His plan, in which these five stories played a role, has been made clear in our discussion of Matt 12:1-8 above, but on the whole he rearranged the framework of the individual narratives only slightly. Often he provided extra chronological and topographical details, but only in those cases where such details served to separate the stories from each other. He supplied introductions to pericopes, as well as pieces that would bridge gaps. For his part, Luke followed Mark's order in this section of the narrative, using skillful introductions to build a kind of chain, made up of stories that originally stood side by side. Yet even with this kind of sequencing, he still re-formed the stories only slightly. The fact that the tradition was based on individual narratives is clearly evident in Luke, even without looking at Mark.[42]

---

42. We can dismiss, therefore, all attempts to arrange these various stories in any kind of temporal or topographical order. Such efforts refuse to die out, even though we now know that the arrangement of the material is topical. Commentators are forever trying, if possible, to work out a chronological sequence.

4

Jesus and the People

(*Mark 3:7—6:13par.*)

Crowds and Healings
(Mark 3:7–12; Matt 12:15–21; Luke 6:17–19)

⁷ καὶ ὁ Ἰησοῦς μετὰ τῶν μαθητῶν αὐτοῦ ἀνεχώρησεν πρὸς τὴν θάλασσαν· καὶ πολὺ πλῆθος ἀπὸ τῆς Γαλιλαίας ἠκολούθησαν, ⁸ καὶ ἀπὸ τῆς Ἰουδαίας καὶ ἀπὸ Ἱεροσολύμων καὶ ἀπὸ τῆς Ἰδουμαίας καὶ πέραν τοῦ Ἰορδάνου καὶ περὶ Τύρον καὶ Σιδῶνα πλῆθος πολύ, ἀκούοντες ὅσα ἐποίει, ἦλθον πρὸς αὐτόν· ⁹ καὶ εἶπεν τοῖς μαθηταῖς αὐτοῦ, ἵνα πλοιάριον προσκαρτερῇ αὐτῷ διὰ τὸν ὄχλον ...

The tradition of this piece varies widely, and both the extent and punctuation of the text are uncertain. D, for example, has readings that are well off the beaten path, but understandable as attempts to smooth out the style: ὁ δὲ ις, for example, instead of καὶ ὁ ις; εἰς instead of πρός, (or εἰς could also have been softened to πρός, since it is an uncharacteristic expression for Mark and thus a more difficult reading; cf. 2:13; 7:21); πολὺς ὄχλος instead of πολὺ πλῆθος (so D, it, vg: *multa turba*); ἠκολούθησαν, a word that destroys the construction, is dropped out (so also syr^sin); καὶ οἱ πέραν instead of καὶ πέραν; καὶ οἱ περί rather than καὶ περί (as in A Γ vg); ἀκούσαντες instead of ἀκούοντες (cf. A C L Γ). In a *constructio ad sensum*, the word ἠκολούθησαν is replaced with the singular in A B L Γ vg. The placement of this word also varies: Sinaiticus, C Δ vg read it after Ἰουδαίας. Sinaiticus, syr^sin arm drop out the phrase καὶ ἀπὸ τῆς Ἰδουμαίας. In v. 9, B reads πλοιάρια in place of πλοιάριον.

Along with his disciples, Jesus returns to the sea, followed by a large crowd from all the land, indeed, from all the adjoining lands. He heals many people, and it is the demons, those emissaries from the spiritual realm, who recognize him. This is a very general sort of description, a kind of summary statement, the only details of which lie in the rising number of people who follow Jesus and in the demons who recognize him as the Son of God and are commanded to be silent. Our investigation can begin from an observation of the difference between the general description in these verses and the more detailed reports that have preceded it. We note, for example, that individual anecdotes are likely to be older than summary statements. Individual stories have a long and vibrant life in the tradition, but summary statements do not. Even though we cannot always determine the exact origin of a particular anecdotal narrative (they often grow naturally, as if on their own), we can be sure that a summary statement is the product of a particular author. It is a kind of artistic production, fixed in a written text. In this case that author was the evangelist, who arranged these individual stories, buttoned them up with a summary statement, and incorporated them into a larger framework. The evidence that an author has been at work here is not hard to see: the summary statement includes not one specific tradition. The events recounted here are in fact strewn through several different stories and narratives. The fact that Jesus carried out a significant healing ministry is evident in various individual narratives (cf. 1:23ff; 1:40ff; 2:1ff; 5:1ff; 9:14ff). Mark 3:10 is reminiscent of 5:27 and 6:56. Its connection with 3:11, in which unclean spirits see Jesus and fall down before him, recalls 5:6 or 9:20. Even the choice of words sounds familiar: the verb κράζειν, for example, also appears in 1:23, 5:7, and 9:26, and the cry of the demons recalls 5:7 (υἱὲ τοῦ θεοῦ τοῦ ὑψίστου). A new element, however, is the fact that Jesus wants his identity as Messiah to remain secret.[1] When Jesus says φιμώθητι (1:25), the demon is fully restrained. It is noteworthy that although Jesus calls for a boat be prepared, he makes no use of that boat. Later, in 4:1, Jesus boards a boat, but only to be able to preach to the crowds, not to get away from them. Of course, the evangelist might well be referring in advance to that boat, but we have already become well acquainted with the fact that in these individual narratives, which were originally independent, a scenic detail that is introduced in one setting may not begin to make sense until much later.

Yet there remains the fact that these geographical names are not typical. Do the names perhaps point back to a specific tradition? In the immediate context the evangelist is trying to paint a picture of the extent—the downright amazing extent—of Jesus' success. For Jesus has made a powerful impression everywhere in Palestine, and Jews from all over the land are being drawn to him. That is why, in addition to Galilee, all the other inhabited regions of Palestine are also named: first Judea and its capital city of Jerusalem (naturally),

---

1. Wrede's thesis about the messianic secret finds support here; cf. also Wendling, 16.

then Idumea, which lay further south but at that time belonged to the province of Judea and was judaized,[2] Perea to the east (πέραν τοῦ Ἰορδάνου, as the LXX had already put it), and finally, to the far north, the region of Tyre and Sidon. According to the Gospel accounts, Jesus had already been active in all these areas. Samaria is missing, which actually fits these circumstances quite well. The evangelist would not have needed any special tradition in order to construct this picture. On the contrary, a certain schematization is clearly evident, as no less than seven different geographical names appear, and the descriptions of people pressing around Jesus—and perhaps other details in the story as well—are certainly based on the general outline of the Gospel to this point. This report in Mark 3:7-12 is a long way from being anchored in any strong connection to what precedes it.

There is therefore no chronological sequence here. It is not stated whether the story we are reading is directly related to the Sabbath healing in 3:1-6, and we cannot make out the locale from which Jesus has come, since the previous scene was not set in any specific location. In all likelihood the connection is based on content; or, to put it more precisely, there is a contrast between this story and what has preceded. The Pharisees do not want to know anything about Jesus, but the people recognize him. This portrait serves as a foil for what will come next: Jesus selects disciples from the people, and from these disciples he selects those who will follow him full-time. That much is clear, but now in 3:20ff Jesus raises the level of tension between himself and his opponents. Why did the evangelist insert 3:7-12 right here, and why did he connect it with 3:13-19? The reason for the summary statement in 1:14ff was plain: at that point (i.e., after 1:13) there needed to be a headline over the ministry of Jesus, beginning with the baptism. But an internal justification of that sort is not evident in this case. Perhaps the motivation might be external. I would like to suggest that there is a suture in the narrative in v. 7, so that: 1) a large number of people followed Jesus from Galilee, and 2) a large number of people also came from Judea, etc. The evangelist's account, in other words, is not smooth. The variants in the tradition (sometimes the opening verbs are omitted, other times they are transposed[3]) confirm this fact. Therefore v. 7a (up to and including ἠκολούθησαν) can be taken as the conclusion to the story in 3:1-6. It could have belonged to the original version of this pericope: the Pharisees, along with the Herodians, want to kill Jesus; Jesus, along with his disciples, withdraws to the sea; many people from Galilee follow him. That much is certain, but we also find here the opening lines of an independent pericope

---

2. Cf. Josephus, *Ant.* 13.9.1; also E. Schürer, *History of the Jewish People*, 1.181-82.
3. Cf. above, p. 92.

(cf. 1:28; 1:45), so the contrast that I mentioned above must lie in the tradition. Mark painted the contrast, using it as a foil for what would follow, and at the same time also fastened a clamp (πλοιάριον) between this story and the upcoming one. It would not make sense to argue that this story employed a highly unusual form of description that was incomprehensible to the evangelist.[4] That is not how the Gospels were handed down. As we said earlier, the contents of the pericope (3:7–12) are portable. It could just as well have been located arbitrarily in some other place.[5]

Matthew (12:15-21) picks up Mark's arrangement of the pieces and reports the summary statement as follows: ὁ δὲ Ἰησοῦς γνοὺς ἀνεχώρησεν ἐκεῖθεν. καὶ ἠκολούθησαν αὐτῷ πολλοί, καὶ ἐθεράπευσεν αὐτοῖς πάντας καὶ ἐπετίμησεν αὐτοῖς, ἵνα μὴ φανερὸν αὐτὸν ποιήσωσιν, ἵνα . . . A citation from Isaiah follows.

> Along with C D E L Γ and Δ, ς reads ὄχλοι πολλοί (cf. 4:25; 8:1; 13:2, and many others). The reading in D for v. 16, πάντας δὲ οὓς ἐθεράπευσεν, is a later gloss.

This is an abridged version of Mark 3:7a. The word γνούς makes clear that Jesus' withdrawal was motivated by the decision of the Pharisees in Matt 12:14. Matthew had already revised a summary statement in Mark 1:14-15 in a similar way, adding the word ἀκούσας to create a stronger connection with what follows. This time he also added ἐκεῖθεν, a word that we have come to recognize as one of his favorites (cf. 12:9). Matthew thus makes use here of a different tactic than he previously employed in 4:24-25: here he summarizes Mark 3:7b-10 very briefly and attaches to it a biblical citation. The reason, however, that Jesus' withdrawal is mentioned in the same breath as a description of his followers is even less clear here than in Mark. At that point the narrative simply stops and does not go further.

Luke (6:17-19) generally follows Mark's order. He makes use of an adapted version of Mark's text, which accounts for the place designation at the beginning and the personal details in the story. As in Matthew, here too there is no mention of the sea-voyage.

---

4. Recent critics are content to verify that this is an insertion; cf. Wellhausen, *Mark*, 24, 26; Klostermann, *Markus*, 27; Wendling, 14ff; Loisy, *Mark*, 108. Loisy described the situation clearly and correctly: "It looks like pieces of filling that the evangelist has written on his own because there were no precise memories, in order to elevate the biography of his hero and to fill the gaps in the tradition."

5. It does not follow that a summary statement is not historical simply because it is the work of the evangelist. If, on the basis of individual Gospel narratives, historians gain the impression that Jesus' activity was as comprehensive as the summary statement suggests, then Mark's description of that ministry is correct.

The Call of the Twelve Apostles
(Mark 3:13–19; Matt 10:1–42; Luke 6:12–16)

καὶ ἀναβαίνει εἰς τὸ ὄρος καὶ προσκαλεῖται οὓς ἤθελεν αὐτός, καὶ ἀπῆλθον πρὸς αὐτόν.

> Many manuscripts substitute the aorist tense for the present, due to the influence of parallels in Matthew and Luke on the one hand and stylistic glosses on the other. The insertion of ὁ ις after τὸ ὄρος suggests the beginning of a pericope.

With the mention of a "mountain," there arise again the same insoluble questions that came up in the Sermon on the Mount (Matt 5:1). Once again we cannot even approximate the location. One thinks in general of a mountaintop not far from Capernaum, since mountains of various heights rise from the northwestern shore of the Sea of Galilee.[6] Efforts to identify the mountain more precisely get nowhere.[7] It may be that no specific mountain is intended. The translations vary: Luther renders it "on a mountain," and Weizsäcker has "on the mountain," and it could also be interpreted as "in the mountains," similar to expressions such as "on a ship," "on the sea," or "in the forest." Yet we must be careful not to water down the picture that should come into our minds here: Jesus stands alone on a mountain height, with only his disciples present. There is a strong contrast with the preceding scene, for Jesus has now left the pressing crowds of people and gathered only a small circle of followers around him. When we look more closely at what has happened, however, the scene becomes increasingly difficult to comprehend. When Jesus left the crowds, was he alone, or with his disciples, or with the common people? How are we supposed to understand his summons and their response? If Jesus called the disciples, where had they been until then: at the foot of the mountain, or did they follow him up? Such gaps are similar to the presentation in Mark 9:2, where Jesus leads some disciples up onto a high mountain. In this case, however, the description, with its catalog of the

---

6. A tradition from the sixteenth century identifies the Horns of Hattin, about four hours from Capernaum, as the site of both the call of the apostles and the Sermon on the Mount. An early Christian tradition identifies a hill about three kilometers north of Tabgha, which is about an hour from Capernaum, as the Mount of the Beatitudes.

7. H. A. W. Meyer calls it "the mountain there," while Keil prefers "the mountain of the Sermon on the Mount," and Volkmar has "the New Testament Sinai" (all quoted in B. Weiss, *Markus und Lukas*, 49). Or "the mountain that was known to the evangelist, in his mind's eye" (Wohlenberg, *Markus*, 104). H. B. Swete, *The Gospel according to St. Mark*, 55, recalls the expressions in Gen 19:17 and Judg 1:19. But in both of those texts the reference can only be to a mountainous land. Spitta asserts, without justification, "Matt 5:1 and Mark 3:13 are parallels" (Spitta, *Die synoptische Grundschrift*, 106).

12 disciples, is highly schematic. There is no shortage of contradictions with the preceding stories. On the one hand the disciples are already there (or should we imagine yet another circle of disciples?), but on the other hand the story mentions the commissioning of the disciples to preach, preparing the way for a later scene in which they will begin their mission (6:7-13). Here we arrive at some familiar internal chronological inconsistencies. If we adopt Mark's outline for a moment, this story stands at or near the beginning of Jesus' ministry. It seems unlikely that he would have already had a close circle of twelve disciples. A calling of this sort would be more conceivable at a later point in Jesus' shared experience with his disciples. At what point in the ministry should this story be situated, then? Somewhere in the final part of Jesus' activity? That answer has problems of its own, since neither Mark nor any of the other evangelists describes a process of development in the relationship between Jesus and his disciples. At whatever point in the narrative we might locate this story, it always comes across as unexpected, and that is its essential quality: it is not just timeless in relation to its context, it is completely timeless. This historical narrative is trans-historical.[8]

But then who created this narrative? It is a schematized picture built upon details that only appear to come from real life, so it does not necessarily rest upon a specific memory of an actual event. There was a general tradition about the twelve apostles after the death of Jesus, for example, and there was a circle of twelve disciples, which is sufficient to explain the origin of our story.[9] It was created by a desire to give the institution of the apostolate a slightly more precise date and locale. This may have been done by Mark, but it could also have been done by someone earlier than Mark. There is good reason to think that Mark took up an existing tradition, since this tradition is of a different species from the other stories that Mark handed down.[10]

In this regard our judgment about the absence of historicity in this narrative can be sharpened a little further. Nothing significant has been

---

8. The story is "the working out of a dogmatic idea" (J. Weiss, 165), and "not an historical event but rather a statistic in historical depiction: a formal drawing of a scene on a mountain" (Wellhausen, *Mark*, 25). It is "a model of the evangelist's style, which was especially recognized by Wrede" (Wendling, 19).

9. It would take us too far afield to go into the question of the apostolate at this point.

10. Advocates for the "Ur-Mark" hypothesis are inclined to view this story as the work of the evangelist. J. Weiss demurs (J. Weiss, 166), as does Loisy (*Mark*, 110f). Wellhausen glimpses an earlier story in 3:13-19, a story that is nonetheless, like 3:7-12, a work of redaction. A clearer view, but one that still misses an important point, is that of Wendling, who regards 3:13-19 as a story that the redactor assembled, for two reasons: 1) Jesus withdraws with selected confidants into splendid isolation; and 2) Jesus calls his disciples (Wendling, 19).

damaged by our conclusion. The narrative has been separated not only from its immediate context, but from the Gospel of Mark altogether, yet nothing important has been lost. For the twelve men named here are simply that and nothing more: twelve names. They are not clearly defined personalities about whom we know anything. At bottom, all we have here is a list with no life in it.

Matthew, by contrast, does not tell a special story about the call. We noted above that Mark's account of the call foreshadows the later mission of the twelve, a problem that Matthew corrects. In chapter 10 he puts the two events together, constructing a scene that is a kind of call. Here too, however, the mention of the twelve comes without any preparation: the construction of the first verse in chapter 10 is not coherent. The list of names is presented as a parenthesis, showing that the evangelist is combining two different traditions. This fact is especially clear in v. 5a, which picks up the thread of v. 1 again after the parenthesis in vv. 2-4.

Luke (6:12-16), as usual, follows Mark's order more closely than Matthew, but he changes this account even more thoroughly: ἐγένετο δὲ ἐν ταῖς ἡμέραις ταύταις ἐξελθεῖν αὐτὸν εἰς τὸ ὄρος προσεύξασθαι, καὶ ἦν διανυκτερεύων ἐν τῇ προσευχῇ τοῦ θεοῦ καὶ ὅτε ἐγένετο ἡμέρα, προσεφώνησεν τοὺς μαθητὰς αὐτοῦ καὶ ἐκλεξάμενος ἀπ' αὐτῶν δώδεκα, οὓς καὶ ἀποστόλους ὠνόμασεν . . .

> D and other mss read ἐκείναις, as does the Vg: *illis*. Instead of ἐξελθεῖν αὐτόν, ς Ε Γ Δ Λ all read ἐξῆλθεν (cf. Matt 20:30; Mark 1:35, et al). In addition, D has ἐφώνησεν in place of προσεφώνησεν, and ἐκάλεσεν instead of ὠνόμασεν. As in the text of Mark, here too several mss have ὁ ις after εἰς τὸ ὄρος.

Unlike the other two evangelists, Luke narrates a genuine call story. In contrast to Mark, the narrative is directly connected with the story of the healing of the withered hand (6:6-11). Phrases like "in those days," "he spent the night in prayer," and "when day came" are chronological insertions on the part of the evangelist, which help to create a temporal link with the preceding story, as well as to situate this narrative at a specific point in time. The depiction is deeply psychological, as Jesus spends all night long in prayer before the important step of calling his apostles. It is also characteristic of Luke that the Twelve are described as a group selected from a larger circle of disciples. In Mark 3:13 that point is not really clear, and as a result Luke is more vivid. Luke also keeps the reference to an unidentifiable mountain.

There is thus a sequential connection with the next pericope (6:17-19): Jesus comes down from the mountain with his disciples and arrives at a level place: καὶ καταβὰς μετ' αὐτῶν ἔστη ἐπὶ τόπου πεδινοῦ, καὶ ὄχλος πολὺς μαθητῶν αὐτοῦ, καὶ πλῆθος πολὺ τοῦ λαοῦ ἀπὸ πάσης τῆς Ἰουδαίας καὶ Ἰερουσαλὴμ καὶ τῆς παραλίου Τύρου καὶ Σιδῶνος ...

ς along with A D Γ Δ Λ it and vg leaves out the word πολύς after ὄχλος. This omission may be attributable to the fact that scribes did not understand the use of the word πολύς in connection with the word μαθηταί. Instead of καὶ Ἰερουσαλήμ κτλ, D reads καὶ ἄλλων πόλεων ἐληλυθότων. I cannot find a good explanation for the origin of this simplifying reading.

What the "level place" might have been is not entirely clear. We can think of a plain as opposed to a mountain, or of a level spot on a mountainside. Luke obviously thought (and previously the saying was in Q) that there would not have been enough room for many people at the top of a mountain, so he situated the scene on a hillside in a kind of meadow.[11] Luke's enumeration of the people who are following Jesus is somewhat different from Mark's. Galilee, Idumea, and Perea are missing. Obviously when Luke says "Judea" he means all of Palestine, and thus he only gives a proper name to the region along the sea near Tyre and Sidon.[12]

By transposing the two scenes in the text of Mark (Mark 3:7-12; 13-19), Luke produces a three-fold audience: 1) the twelve apostles; 2) the wider circle of disciples; and 3) the crowds of people. Previously we saw that the activity of Jesus in his hometown of Nazareth spread through Capernaum into all of Galilee, and now once again we see a development *a minori ad maius*. The circle of the disciples forms a middle term between the apostles and the people. Luke, who wrote with psychology in mind, does not owe this construction to any special source.[13] It may even be historical, but rearranging Mark's loosely structured narrative posed no particular problem for Luke.

---

11. For the controversy about this phrase, which is frankly not very important, cf. B. Weiss, *Markus und Lukas*, 366-67. According to Spitta, this text shows that Luke is older than the other Synoptics, because its geographic description is more precise than theirs. The τόπος πεδινός may be the Plain of Sharon, which lies along the sea. The region of the παραλία goes all the way to Caesarea Maritima (Spitta, *Die synoptische Grundschrift*, 114). Spitta's observations here are very perceptive, but there is no evidence to support his thesis that this scene occurred during the period of Jesus' activity in Judea.

12. A fully convincing explanation founders on the difficulty of the manuscript tradition.

13. Such sources have often been suggested; cf. Loisy, who refers to "another source" (Loisy, *Les Évangiles synoptiques*, 1:525).

Excursus: A Lukan Insertion
(Luke 6:20—8:3)

The Sermon on the Plain
(Luke 6:20–49)

For Luke, the section 6:17-19 serves as an introduction to a long discourse by Jesus, the so-called "Sermon on the Plain" (6:20-49). According to Luke, this sermon was delivered to a large public audience (cf. 6:17; 7:1), which means that the introduction in v. 20 does not fit especially well: καὶ αὐτὸς ἐπάρας τοὺς ὀφθαλμοὺς αὐτοῦ εἰς τοὺς μαθητὰς αὐτοῦ ἔλεγεν (the text of D is slightly different). The difficulty cannot be interpreted away, and we can see it even more clearly in Matthew's version. It appears that Luke is following his source Q, in which the Sermon on the Mount was delivered to the disciples, even though he himself pictures a much larger audience. The same problem appears again in 12:1 and 20:45. This difficulty, while significant, is not insurmountable, since the term μαθηταί certainly refers to the next concentric circle out from the Twelve. We will go no further into the question of the relationship between Luke's "Sermon on the Plain" and Matthew's "Sermon on the Mount," except to observe that the text of Luke is closer to the original in both form and content. For our purposes here it will suffice to lay out the framework of this compilation of sayings.

The entirety of Luke's insertion, from 6:20 until 8:3, abandons both the Markan outline and most of the parallels in Mark. In addition to the "Sermon on the Plain" (6:20-49), the following pericopes are also absent from Mark: the centurion from Capernaum (7:1-10), the young man from Nain (7:11-17), John the Baptist's question to Jesus (7:18-23), Jesus' testimony to the Baptist (7:24-35), the sinful woman (7:36-50), and Jesus' journey with the apostles and the women who served him (8:1-3). Let us take a closer look at the framework of these individual narratives. We have already dealt with 7:1-10.

The Young Man from Nain
(Luke 7:11–17)

Luke 7:11-17 is introduced as follows: καὶ ἐγένετο ἐν τῇ (τῷ) ἑξῆς ἐπορεύθη εἰς πόλιν καλουμένην Ναΐν, καὶ συνεπορεύοντο αὐτῷ οἱ μαθηταὶ αὐτοῦ ἱκανοὶ καὶ ὄχλος πολύς· ὡς δὲ ἤγγισεν τῇ πύλῃ τῆς πόλεως, καὶ ἰδοὺ ἐξεκομίζετο τεθνηκὼς ...

> At the beginning syr^sin has the plural: "they (i.e., Jesus and his followers) went." Syr^sin, eth, and D have dropped ἐγένετο, an attempt at a gloss. D drops ἐν as well. τῇ is read by ℵ C D go cop arm and eth; while τῷ is read by ℵ^c, A B E F vg and cf. also syr^sin. ℵ and B have ἐπορεύθη; while ς A C D Δ and Λ have ἐπορεύετο, as does vg, which reads *ibat*. This reading is conformed to συνεπορεύετο in the following verse. Several mss insert ὁ ις. The tradition of the place name is not entirely certain. In addition to the predominant Ναΐν we also find Ναείν (E Γ Λ), and some have Ναείμ. The reading *capharnaum* in e and l* is quite peculiar. ἱκανοί is missing from ℵ B D F vg cop and arm. Instead of ὡς δὲ ἤγγισεν D has ἐγένετο δὲ ὡς ἤγγιζεν. καὶ ἰδού is missing from from D gr and eth, and at this point syr^sin has a text that diverges sharply from the Greek, and Merx (*Markus und Lukas*, 230) puts the excess words in brackets: καὶ συνεπορεύοντο αὐτῷ οἱ μαθηταί αὐτοῦ (ἱκανοί) καὶ ὄχλος πολύς (ὡς δὲ) ἤγγισεν τῇ πύλῃ τῆς πόλεως. The text of syr^sin becomes completely uncertain after this point. Merx (*Markus und Lukas*, 230) suggests: "Nearing the gate of the city, he saw that they were bringing one who had died ..." and so on. Obviously the introduction to this pericope has been changed and corrected in so many ways that we can no longer see it with certainty.

The pericope stems from a special tradition of Luke and is noteworthy for its location, since Nain is never mentioned elsewhere in the primitive Christian tradition. "Nain" means "meadow," and today the village is a tiny wide spot in the road, as it may have been in the days of Jesus. It lies about two and a half hours south of Nazareth at the foot of Mt. Tabor, at the northern end of the Mt. Hermon range. Nain is firmly fixed in the tradition.[14] As was previously the case with Nazareth, we

---

14. The etymology of Nain suggested by Nestle (i.e., Nain comes from the Hebrew

cannot identify any reason why Luke would have made up his mind to set the story in this location. Why did he pick Nain? It is a striking fact that this location is mentioned absolutely nowhere else. We cannot help thinking that perhaps in the earliest Jesus tradition the story was set in some other tiny hamlet in Palestine, which somehow dropped out of the narrative along the way. It is noteworthy that in some mss, Capernaum has replaced Nain as the setting of the story. It appears that Capernaum, which stood out in the foreground of the Jesus tradition, attracted to itself one or another of the stories. We cannot say with certainty how far the evangelist adapted or altered the introduction to this pericope. The phrase πόλιν καλουμένην should probably be credited to his account, because it clarifies the story (cf. 2:4; ἥτις καλεῖται Βηθλεέμ). Luke loves this kind of elucidation (e.g., 4:16; 4:31). The construction καὶ ἐγένετο ... ἐπορεύθη has a parallel in Luke 1:59, although it could be original to the tradition. ἐν τῇ (or τῷ) ἑξῆς looks a lot like a comment by the evangelist, who wants to add chronological detail at this point, and ἑξῆς (along with καθεξῆς) appears in the NT only in the writings of Luke. I will not venture a guess as to whether the correct reading is ἐν τῇ ἑξῆς or perhaps τῇ ἑξῆς, or ἐν τῷ ἑξῆς. The first would mean "on the following day" (understand ἡμέρᾳ), and the second would mean "in the subsequent period of time" (understand χρόνῳ or καιρῷ). The first sense of the phrase is found three times in Acts (21:1; 25:17; 27:18). We can compare the phrase τῇ ἑξῆς ἡμέρᾳ (Luke 9:37), which in the light of the parallel passages in Mark and Matthew is clearly a Lukan insertion. On the other hand the second sense of the phrase is found in Luke 8:1, ἐν τῷ καθεξῆς. In spite of the "Lukan" characteristics of this phrase, it is not impossible that they belonged to the tradition that was taken up by the evangelist. In both cases, however, we are dealing with the introduction to a pericope, which has no chronological value. Even if the situation did seem to confirm a real chronology, that would still not prove anything. The distance between Capernaum, where the preceding story was set, and Nain, where this story is set, is about eight or nine hours, i.e., a day's journey. Jewish funerals took place in the evening, so Jesus could have been coming into Nain in the evening, to spend the night. If the reading is ἐν τῷ ἑξῆς, then there

---

nahim and means "one who has been awakened") is highly unlikely. Cf. Nestle, "Chorazin, Bethsaida," 185.

is one extra day with which to reckon. Make of it what you will, it is still not possible to determine to what period in Jesus' ministry this pericope belongs. It is utterly timeless. Perhaps it was an excerpt from a longer story about a journey to Jerusalem, since Nain lay on the route that ran from the north through Samaria to Jerusalem.[15] The narrative mentions that others were traveling with Jesus, but they play no role in the story, a fact that suggests that it originally belonged in another context. It has been placed in its current context by a specific authorial interest on the part of Luke. After the healing of someone at death's door, a dying slave in Capernaum, there now follows an even greater demonstration of Jesus' power: the resuscitation of someone already dead, a deceased son. This is because Luke wants to provide support for the saying of Jesus in 7:22 (νεκροὶ ἐγείρονται).[16] The story then concludes in v. 17 with the spreading fame of Jesus on the basis of the miracle: καὶ ἐξῆλθεν ὁ λόγος οὗτος ἐν ὅλῃ τῇ Ἰουδαίᾳ περὶ αὐτοῦ καὶ πάσῃ τῇ περιχώρῳ. Obviously "Judea" is a designation for all of Palestine, and the "surrounding region" refers to the Gentile lands that border on Palestine. This closing is the kind of codicil that we have often seen at the end of individual pericopes (cf. Mark 1:28; Luke 4:37). It belongs to the original version of the narrative.[17]

John the Baptist's Question and Jesus' Testimony
(Luke 7:18–35; Matt 11:2–19)

The next pericope is the story of John the Baptist's question to Jesus, and Jesus' testimony to John the Baptist (7:18–35): καὶ ἀπήγγειλαν Ἰωάννει οἱ μαθηταὶ αὐτοῦ περὶ πάντων τούτων. καὶ προσκαλεσάμενος δύο τινὰς τῶν μαθητῶν αὐτοῦ ὁ Ἰωάννης . . .

---

15. Some Catholic exegetes think here of a journey to Jerusalem for the festival (Pentecost?) in John 5:1. Cf. Homanner, 99–100. Pölzl recalls John 5:21 as well (*Lukas*, 164)

16. In Matthew, the story of Jairus' daughter (9:18–26) provides this kind of support for the saying in Matt 11:5.

17. Merx recognizes that we have here "an un-stylish, illogical mess" (*Markus und Lukas*, 232). There is no place for the Nain pericope in Spitta's pre-Synoptic document, as it does not fit into the framework (Jesus in Judea). Spitta skips from Luke 7:1a to 7:16, which he regards as the conclusion to the Sermon on the Plain (Spitta, *Die synoptische Grundschrift*, 144–45).

In D the text of v. 18 is as follows, connecting it closely with the preceding narrative: ἐν οἷς καὶ μέχρι Ἰωάννου τοῦ Βαπτιστοῦ...

The link between this scene and the preceding one is obviously very close: John the Baptist's disciples have told him about Jesus, and the Baptist sends two of them to him, but this transition loses all its significance when we notice that the original temporal setting of these stories cannot be confirmed. The present shape of v. 18 certainly comes from Luke himself, while the narrative as a whole comes from Q. Thus it is highly instructive to study the treatment of this story in Matthew, who sets us down right in the middle of the scene: ὁ δὲ Ἰωάννης ἀκούσας ἐν τῷ δεσμωτηρίῳ τὰ ἔργα τοῦ Χριστοῦ πέμψας διὰ τῶν μαθητῶν αὐτοῦ (Matt 11:2). If there was any connection between these stories prior to Luke, it was different from the one in Luke. Matthew puts the narrative **after** the speech in which Jesus commissions his disciples (Matt 10), but in Luke it comes **before**, and we have no way of knowing which of the chronologies is correct.[18] By τὰ ἔργα τοῦ Χριστοῦ, Matthew means the events in chapter 8 and 9. In those chapters Matthew gave examples of all the types of miracles referred to in 11:5 (cf. 8:1-4; 9:1-8; 9:18-34). According to Matthew, John the Baptist was at this time confined in prison. Based on what we know of ancient jails and prisons, however, there would have been nothing particularly unusual about him sending a message out or receiving one in return.[19] Luke does not mention the prison, but it is clear from the descriptions in Luke 3:1-17 and 18-21 (which are supposed to be taken as chronological) that he too thinks the Baptist is in prison. We have to reckon, however, with the possibility that Q knew nothing about an imprisonment of John the Baptist—ἐν τῷ δεσμωτηρίῳ could have been inserted by Matthew—and thus the Baptist might still have been moving about freely. Certainly the fourth gospel describes contemporaneous ministries of Jesus and John. Luke 7:20-21 heightens the drama of the scene, and thus may be judged to be an insertion on the part of the third evangelist.

---

18. As Wellhausen does when he declares: "Lk rightly sets this piece ahead of the sending out of the disciples" (Wellhausen, *Luke*, 29).

19. Cf. also Matt 25:36, ἐν φυλακῇ ἤμην καὶ ἤλθατε πρός με. See also the exposition in Deissmann, *Paulus*, 20n5. Spitta disputes this conclusion, arguing (incorrectly) that Luke refers to events that transpired while John was free, not in prison.

In both Gospels there follows a speech by Jesus about John the Baptist to the people: τούτων δὲ πορευομένων (Matt 11:7) = ἀπελθόντων δὲ τῶν ἀγγέλλων (Luke 7:24). This connection was certainly present in the Sayings Source, but of course it does not necessarily follow that Jesus actually spoke these words, for the speech itself is not a unit. In Luke 7:29–30, for example, Jesus continues with a remark that, at bottom, is a narrative. ἀκούσας is especially difficult to understand; it has to be translated with something like "obeyed." But since v. 29 is connected with what precedes it, it also has to be taken as part of the speech by Jesus and not a comment inserted by the evangelist. The expression βάπτισμα Ἰωάννου is peculiar; it sounds as if back then it might have also referred to a Christian baptism. Matthew makes a similar point at the end of the parable of the two sons (Matt 21:32). It is not certain whether Luke 7:29 and Matt 21:32 go back to one and the same tradition, although that is widely believed, but it is highly unlikely that Matt 21:32 was originally in its current position. Matthew 11:12–15, on the other hand, has the so-called "stormy saying," which Luke does not introduce until 16:16, in shorter form and with two other sayings about the Law. Matthew 11:16–19 is thus exactly parallel to Luke 7:31–35. The first saying (Matt 11:7 = Luke 7:24) refers to the desert (εἰς τὸν ἔρημον), giving it enough local color to suggest that the original setting of these words was in the vicinity of the ministry of John the Baptist. That would be, of course, the lower Jordan Valley, near Machaerus, the fortress where (according to Josephus) John was imprisoned. With its mention of the οἶκοι τῶν βασιλέων (Luke 7:25 = τὰ βασίλεια), Matt 11:8 prompts the question of where Jesus could have acquired the knowledge of such things. Could he have learned about "the palaces of kings" in Jerusalem?

The Sinful Woman in Simon's House
(Luke 7:36–50)

Without any transition there follows immediately the narrative about the sinful woman in Simon's house (7:36–50): ἠρώτα δέ τις αὐτὸν τῶν Φαρισαίων, ἵνα φάγῃ μετ᾽ αὐτοῦ· καὶ εἰσελθὼν εἰς τὸν οἶκον τοῦ Φαρισαίου κατεκλίθη· καὶ ἰδοὺ γυνή, ἥτις ἦν ἐν τῇ πόλει ἁμαρτωλός...

Luke has obviously reported this story just as he found it in the tradition. The city is not named, and it would be pure speculation to think that it might have been Nain or Capernaum: any other city might just as well be in mind here. Of course Luke was not thinking of Jerusalem, since he puts this story in the Galilean portion of Jesus' ministry. Equally speculative are questions about whether the sinful woman might have been Mary Magdalene (a widespread inference, although 8:2 speaks more against it than in favor), or whether the Pharisee invited Jesus to dinner out of friendly or unfriendly motives. The view that this pericope is a doublet of the story of Jesus' anointing in Bethany (Mark 14:3ff; Matt 26:6ff) is widely held, but this view overlooks the fact that despite their similarities, the two narratives have sharp differences: one is a story about an act of repentance, while the other is a story about an act of loving respect. John 12:1–8 is the true parallel to the second narrative. Perhaps Luke himself, through a process of elision, came to identify the two stories and worked them together into one narrative. In both stories, for instance, the host is named Simon, and it is noteworthy that his name is introduced only in passing in v. 40. Apparently Luke was reminded of Mark 14:3 and introduced the name at this point. If the original story did not give the Pharisee's name in v. 36, he could hardly have suddenly and all at once been called Simon at this point in the middle of the story. Some Pharisee invited Jesus one can imagine it was customary to entertain traveling teachers of the law after they had spoken in the synagogue. Some woman showed up: she was obviously an onlooker at the festivities surrounding the guest, as is still customary in the East. Her name is unknown and cannot be deduced,[20] and it all happened in some unidentified city at some indefinite time. We cannot know why the story was placed in the narrative at this point. It might have been to support the assertion in 7:34 that Jesus is a φίλος ἁμαρτωλῶν, or it might also prepare for the following pericope, in which the subject is the various women around Jesus. This justification is not very compelling, for it establishes a link of

---

20. The Roman Catholic Church identifies the three people about whom an anointing story was told as follows: 1) in Luke 7:37, the sinful woman is Mary Magdalene (cf. Luke 8:3); 2) in Mark 14:3, she is a woman in the house of Simon; and 3) in John 12:1ff, the woman is Mary, the sister of Lazarus. The Roman breviary prescribes our pericope for the feast of Mary Magdalene. There is no agreement on the number of anointings, either one, two, or three.

rather trivial significance, but in the relaxed structure of the Jesus tradition such motives could be enough to insert stories into the narrative and to rearrange stories within the narrative.

The words of Jesus in v. 40ff are not necessarily a unit, and the parable in vv. 41-43 and the new paragraph in vv. 44-46 do not hang together well. The parable may have originally been independent.

Controversy Stories
(Mark 3:20-25; Matt 12:22-50; Luke 11:14-31, 8:19-21)

At this point we pick up Mark's thread again, which Luke returns to after 8:1, or at least after 8:4. After the pericope about the selection of the apostles (Mark 3:13-19), Mark appends a collection of "controversy stories" (3:20-35):

²⁰ καὶ ἔρχεται εἰς οἶκον καὶ συνέρχεται πάλιν (ὁ) ὄχλος, ὥστε μὴ δύνασθαι αὐτοὺς μήτε ἄρτον φαγεῖν. ²¹ καὶ ἀκούσαντες οἱ παρ' αὐτοῦ ἐξῆλθον κρατῆσαι αὐτόν. ἔλεγον γὰρ, ὅτι ἐξέστη. ²² καὶ οἱ γραμματεῖς οἱ ἀπὸ Ἱεροσολύμων καταβάντες ἔλεγον, ὅτι Βεελζεβοὺλ ἔχει... ²³ καὶ προσκαλεσάμενος αὐτοὺς ἐν παραβολαῖς ἔλεγεν αὐτοῖς... ³¹ καὶ ἔρχονται ἡ μήτηρ αὐτοῦ καὶ οἱ ἀδελφοὶ αὐτοῦ καὶ ἔξω στήκοντες ἀπέστειλαν πρὸς αὐτὸν καλοῦντες αὐτόν. ³² καὶ ἐκάθητο περὶ αὐτὸν ὄχλος καὶ λέγουσιν αὐτῷ· ἰδοὺ ἡ μήτηρ... ἔξω ζητοῦσίν σε. ³³ καὶ ἀποκριθεὶς αὐτοῖς λέγει... ³⁴ καὶ περιβλεψάμενος τοὺς περὶ αὐτὸν... λέγει...

> V. 20: ἔρχεται: ℵ* B Γ... (also 10:1); ς reads ἔρχονται, based upon ℵᶜ C L Δ and the Vg (*veniunt*). But that is a later improvement, because the subject of the preceding story was Jesus *and* his disciples. Dᵍʳ reads εἰσέρχονται. There is an isolated reading of εἰσέρχεται. ὄχλος appears in ℵ* C E F Γ, ὁ ὄχλος in A B D Δ, and is picked up in the earlier editions of Lachmann and Tischendorf; von Soden and Nestle conclude, *non liquet*. V. 21: D it go read: καὶ ὅτε ἤκουσαν περὶ αὐτοῦ οἱ γραμματεῖς καὶ οἱ λιποί. This variant is an obvious attempt to clarify οἱ παρ' αοὐτοῦ, which is not exactly clear, and at the same time to establish a closer connection with what follows. In v. 31 the tradition vacillates between ἔρχεται and ἔρχονται. A and Γ read οὖν in place of καί.

As in many other cases, there are no chronological or topographical connections with what has preceded.²¹ And as in many other cases, questions can be raised about the house. Perhaps we should translate ἔρχεται εἰς οἶκον as "he went home," and think of Peter's house, which was referred to in 2:1. πάλιν was added by the evangelist and points back to 3:7. In this episode, which appears only in Mark, the meaning of the phrase οἱ παρὰ αὐτοῦ is difficult, and several different linguistic explanations are possible. Literally, οἱ παρὰ αὐτοῦ means "those who are from him," which in classical Greek would mean "his messengers." But that cannot possibly be what is meant here. Instead, the phrase goes back to an expression in Hellenistic literature that means "his own" (cf. οἱ παρὰ αὐτῆς, Prov 29:29, Susanna 33). Especially instructive is 1 Macc 9:44, where ℵ and V read τοῖς παρ' αὐτοῦ, and A has τοῖς ἀδελφοῖς αὐτοῦ (cf. also 1 Macc 13:52).²² In all these cases the meaning is "relatives." There are other expressions that mean "countrymen," "slaves," "fellow members," and "employees" (cf. Josephus, *Antiquities* 1.10.5; also 1 Macc 9:58; 15:15; 16:16). It is conceivable that the expression might refer to the apostles, but in this context it is more natural to understand it as a reference to Jesus' relatives.²³ They arrive on the scene in an effort to get to Jesus, saying "He is out of his mind."²⁴ We simply cannot

---

21. Cf. the remark of Wohlenberg, *Markus*, 108-9: "As a function of the independence and importance of the report about the selection of the apostles (v. 13ff), there is a long interval of time between this and the next episode, i.e., between vv. 19 and 20. For it is not likely that Jesus would have taken the twelve with him into the house without further instruction and training." Windisch (144) seeks to counter Wohlenberg's interpretation on the basis of Mark's style of description, which arranges events closely together. Who is right? I regard the whole dispute as pure speculation.

22. Swete, *The Old Testament in Greek*, 3:629.

23. Catena 297 identifies οἱ παρ' αὐτοῦ with οἱ περὶ αὐτόν (Mark 4:10), taking the phrase to mean "the scribes" (as does Codex D).

24. Naturally this text is especially problematic for Catholic exegetes, who are suspicious of the reference to the relatives of Jesus. The scholarly literature records an almost incomprehensible discussion (and disagreement) over this reference. Pölzl, for example, interprets it this way: those who were with Jesus came out of the house in order to restrain and calm down the crowd; and they said, "the crowd is out of its mind" (Pölzl, *Marcus*, 98, 100; cf. also his article in *BZ* 7 (1909) 427; and Hartmann, "Mark 3, 20f.," 249ff). Zorell, by contrast, is more stylish: "When his family members realized that they could not begin their meal without him, they came to notify him and invite him to the table; then they said, 'He is completely exhausted'" (Zorell, "Zu Mark 3, 20, 21," 695-96). Spitta also thinks that some of the disciples left the house in order to hold back the mob of people (Spitta, *Die synoptische Grundschrift*, 107-8). He further asserts that a gap, not intentional but a scribal accident, lies behind the words ἔλεγον γὰρ, ὅτι

say anything about where they might have come from—whether Capernaum or Nazareth or Cana—not least because relatives in those locations could scarcely have heard so quickly about the situation described in v. 20.[25] More importantly, those kinds of questions never entered the mind of the narrator of this story. He wanted to draw a picture for us: Jesus in a house, so overrun by crowds that he cannot even eat with his disciples, with his relatives thinking that such behavior is crazy.

A second picture also fits in here. It may seem awkward to bring in the Pharisees into the scene in the house along with the crowds, without any introduction at all, but it is actually quite well-coordinated. Jesus' relatives think he is crazy, and his opponents think he is possessed by the devil. This is an important development in the plot, whether it was in the tradition or was created by the evangelist. It is noteworthy that the word γραμματεῖς has the definite article οἱ: these are the scribes about whom the reader has already heard, who are always there and who need no further introduction. They have come from Jerusalem, toward which Jesus' call is beckoning him. The connections between Jesus' ministry in Galilee and the capital city of Jerusalem may have been greater than we usually think, based on the sources. The remark by the scribes elicits a response from Jesus. The introduction to v. 23, with the word προσκαλεσάμενος, appears to be formulaic (cf. 7:14; 8:1, 34; 12:43; also 6:7).

A new scene begins in v. 31, and this scene is completely independent, having nothing to do with the episode about the scribes. Jesus' mother and brothers stand outside (the story presupposes that he is in a house) and call for him, but he is surrounded by so great a crowd of people that the message from his relatives has to be relayed to him. With two aphorisms Jesus rejects his kinfolk and declares who his real relatives are. It is a consensus of recent criticism that vv. 22–30 are an insertion into a scene that began in v. 21 and resumes in v. 31.[26] This insertion came either from the tradition or from the work of the evangelist.

---

in 3:21.

25. Wendling has thought of this, and concludes that the object of the verb ἀκούσαντες in 3:21 is the chain of events in 2:1–3:6 (Wendling, 20).

26. "The pause between the relatives' departure from home (v. 21) and their arrival on the scene (v. 31) was deftly filled" (B. Weiss, *Markus und Lukas*, 54). Cf. Wellhausen, *Mark*, 27. "Vv. 20–21 and vv. 31–35 are one in tenor and location" (Wendling, 21). Cf. also Loisy, *Mark*, 113; Klostermann, *Markus*, 30; J. Weiss, *Schriften*, 102.

Thus vv. 22-30 can be cut loose from their connection to this narrative, but that does not mean that vv. 20-21 and vv. 31-35 constitute a unity. On the contrary, v. 31 is an entirely new beginning. Certainly Jesus' mother and brothers are identified by the expression οἱ παρ' αὐτοῦ, but there is a difference in formulation that is noteworthy and decisive. When vv. 20-21 and vv. 31-35 are read together, they do not give the impression of being a unified story. It is not clear, for example, why the expression οἱ παρ' αὐτοῦ suddenly changes into μήτηρ, etc. We are dealing with two different traditions here. The structure of this chapter as we now have it is not a-b-a, but a-b-c. These three stories have been brought together solely on the basis of their content: Jesus is homeless among his own people, and his own relatives disturb his peace. The scribes are even worse, so he rejects them, but he also withdraws from his relatives.

The parallel complex to Mark 3:20-35 is Matt 12:22-50. As in Mark, it comes after reports about throngs and healings. Luke puts most of it in a later context, but closely follows Mark's order, and here he seems to have been working with a collection of material in Q. We can best compare the accounts by setting the frameworks of the two evangelists alongside each other:

Matthew	Luke
12:22 τότε προσηνέχθη αὐτῷ δαιμονιζόμενος τυφλὸς καὶ κωφός· καὶ ἐθεράπευσεν αὐτόν...	11:14 καὶ ἦν ἐκβάλλων δαιμόνιον, καὶ αὐτὸ ἦν κωφόν.
	(Healing)
12:23 καὶ ἐξίσταντο πάντες οἱ ὄχλοι καὶ ἔλεγον· μήτι οὗτός ἐστιν ὁ υἱὸς Δαυείδ;	καὶ ἐθαύμασεν οἱ ὄχλοι
	Vacat!
12:24 οἱ δὲ Φαρισαῖοι ἀκούσαντες εἶπον· (saying about Beelzebul)	11:15 τινὲς δὲ ἐξ αὐτῶν εἶπον (saying about Beelzebul)
Vacat! (but cf. v. 38)	11:16 ἕτεροι δὲ πειράζοντες σημεῖον ἐξ οὐρανοῦ ἐζήτουν παρ' αὐτοῦ.
12:25 εἰδὼς δὲ τὰς ἐνθυμήσεις αὐτῶν εἶπεν αὐτοῖς. (speech for the defense, incl. v. 30)	11:17 αὐτὸς δὲ εἰδὼς αὐτῶν τὰ διανοήματα εἶπεν αὐτοῖς. (speech for the defense, incl. v. 23)

Matthew	Luke
12:31 διὰ τοῦτο λέγω ὑμῖν (saying about the sin against the Holy Spirit; v. 32)	12:10 (in a different context, the same saying in abbreviated form)
12:33–35 (without introduction, the saying about a tree and its fruit)	6:43–45 (the saying within the Sermon on the Mount)
12:34 γεννήματα ἐχιδνῶν	Vacat!
12:36–37 λέγω δὲ ὑμῖν ὅτι . . . (saying about human speech and judgment)	Vacat!
12:38 τότε ἀπεκρίθησαν αὐτῷ τινες τῶν γραμματέων καὶ Φαρισαίων λέγοντες· διδάσκαλε, θέλομεν ἀπὸ σοῦ σημεῖον ἰδεῖν.	11:29 τῶν δὲ ὄχλων ἐπαθροιζομένων. Vacat! (but cf. v. 16)
12:39 ὁ δὲ ἀποκριθεὶς εἶπεν αὐτοῖς (saying about the request for a sign)	ἤρξατο λέγειν (the same saying)
12:43–45 (without introduction, the saying about relapse)	11:24–26 (the same saying at a different point in the same chapter)
12:46 ἔτι αὐτοῦ λαλοῦντος τοῖς ὄχλοις, ἰδοὺ ἡ μήτηρ καὶ οἱ ἀδελφοὶ αὐτοῦ εἱστήκεισαν ἔξω (to v. 50)	8:19 παρεγένετο δὲ πρὸς αὐτὸν ἡ μήτηρ αὐτοῦ καὶ οἱ ἀδελφοὶ αὐτοῦ, καὶ οὐκ ἠδύναντο συντυχεῖν αὐτῷ διὰ τὸν ὄχλον καὶ . . . (to v. 21)
Variants	
12:22 προσηνέχθη . . . κωφός: ℵ C D Γ Δ προσήνεγκαν . . . κωφόν: B syr cop eth	11:14 ὁ ις after ἦν: F. D provides a transition: ταῦτα δὲ εἰπόντος αὐτοῦ προσφέρετε (Tischendorf) αὐτῷ δαιμοιζόμενος κωφός. Some Latin mss are similar.
12:25 ὁ ις: ς C E Γ Δ. Cf. it vg: *Jesus autem sciens*.	
12:38 B omits καὶ Φαρισαίων	

Matthew	Luke
12:46 After ἔτι, ς (along with C E F ΓΔ) reads δέ.	11:15 καί τινες: D
	Instead of ἐξ αὐτῶν some Lat mss have *ex Pharisaeis*.
	8:19 παρεγένοντο: ℵ A L Γ Δ Λ. In a similar way, in Mark 3:20 the tradition alternates between ἔρχεται and ἔρχονται. The entire verse 8:19 is lacking in Marcion and can be dispensed with. Cf. Th. Zahn, *Geschichte des neutestamentlichen Kanons*, II.2, 464.

At the beginning of this pericope we encounter Matthew's typical introduction: τότε. On the whole, his narrative is a combination of Mark 3:20–35 and Q, in which there was a version of the Beelzebul saying. Luke 11:29ff shows that the piece that begins with τότε in v. 38 must have been followed in Q by the Beelzebul saying. For that reason Matthew took it up in this context. That Matthew drew upon both Mark and Q is evident in the fact that when he repeats Mark 8:11ff (in Matt 16:1–4), he includes the admonition about seeking a sign. Matthew got the pericope about the relatives of Jesus (12:46–50) from Mark, although the introduction with a participle is his own work. The mention of ὄχλοι comes from Mark 3:22 (καὶ ἐκάθητο περὶ αὐτὸν ὄχλος), but it does not fit very well in this context, since to this point Jesus has not been speaking to a crowd. The setting is in a house (as in Mark), although that is not made explicit. Luke 8:19–21 does not mention the setting, either. In Luke, Jesus does not live in a house in Capernaum, nor does he go into a house at the end of a day of traveling. In Luke, the story plays out in the open. Without comment he simply puts it in a different location. In Matthew and Mark this pericope leads into a series of parables, but in Luke it follows them. To the third evangelist this arrangement seemed more effective, and as a matter of fact it actually is. It connects Jesus' saying about his family with a series of agricultural parables, showing that Jesus' true relatives are not his physical kin, but rather those who hear and obey the word of God, i.e., those who are like the good soil.[27]

27. Spitta develops this point well, but he is wrong to try to use it in support of

Matthew's version of this pericope was not a unit, as is shown by the fact that in Luke some pieces are either missing or placed elsewhere in the narrative. In Matt 12:31, for example, the saying that begins with διὰ τοῦτο λέγω is in a different context in Luke (Luke 12:10). In Matt 12:33–35, the saying about a tree and its fruit has no introduction, but in Luke 6:43–45 it appears in the midst of the Sermon on the Plain and is parallel to Matt 7:16–20. In Matt 12:36–37, the saying about human words and divine judgment, which also begins with the introductory formula λέγω δὲ ὑμῖν, does not appear in Luke at all. Finally, the sayings about the demand for a sign in Matt 12:38–42 and the return of an unclean spirit in Matt 12:43–45 appear in reverse order in Luke, separated by the blessing of Jesus' mother in Luke 11:27–28. That blessing is introduced by the typically Lukan formula ἐγένετο δὲ ἐν τῷ λέγειν αὐτόν.

Over and above all these differences, however, we can clearly see significant agreement between Matthew and Luke. This agreement indicates that the charges of the Pharisees, Jesus' defense, his response to their request for a sign, and the saying about the return of the unclean spirit were all connected with each other in Q. But was this outline original? The fact that it was not is made evident in the fact that Matthew's version is internally unbalanced. He basically sets Jesus against the Pharisees, and it is important to pay attention to how they are described. In v. 23, οἱ ὄχλοι enter, at which point they immediately cease to be important to the conversation. In v.24, the Pharisees appear (to whom the expression "that brood of vipers" applies), with the scribes and some more Pharisees coming along in v. 38. This is not exactly a smoothly flowing narrative. In Luke, by contrast, all of this is so well arranged that, if not for Matthew's version, we would scarcely be able to detect the tradition which lies so close to the surface here. In Luke the opponents of Jesus are only the ὄχλοι, and they are mentioned only once in 11:14. Since he leaves out the saying about David (Matt 12:23), Luke divides the ὄχλοι into two groups: τινές δὲ ἐξ αὐτῶν (v. 15) and ἕτεροι δέ (v. 16). What the τινές say is contradicted in v. 17ff, and what the ἕτεροι say is refuted in v. 29ff. Thus two themes are artfully developed and resolved, one after the other. On the basis of Q, both evangelists take as their starting-point the healing of a demon-possessed

---

Luke's outline; cf. Spitta, *Die synoptische Grundschrift*, 108.

blind and lame man (so Matthew), or of a demon-possessed lame man (so Luke). But in Mark that healing is not connected in any way with the Pharisees and their attacks on Jesus. The oral tradition that preceded Q may have preserved (as Q and Mark nearly did) the connection between their attacks and his response, and that connection may well have been historical. The important event—a miracle of Jesus—is thus set into a narrative context, but the actual course of events is unfortunately lost to us.

Parables of Jesus
(Mark 4:1–34; Matt 13:1–52; Luke 8:4–18)

¹καὶ πάλιν ἤρξατο διδάσκειν παρὰ τὴν θάλασσαν. καὶ συνάγεται πρὸς αὐτὸν ὄχλος πλεῖστος, ὥστε αὐτὸν εἰς πλοῖον ἐμβάντα καθῆσαι ἐν τῇ θαλάσσῃ, καὶ πᾶς ὁ ὄχλος πρὸς τὸν θάλασσαν ἐπὶ τῆς γῆς ἦσαν. ²καὶ ἐδίδασκεν αὐτοὺς ἐν παραβολαῖς πολλά, καὶ ἔλεγεν αὐτοῖς ἐν τῇ διδαχῇ αὐτοῦ . . .

> D reads πρός instead of παρά. ℵ B C L Δ have συνάγεται, while some other mss. read συνέρχεται. ς D have συνήχθη, and it vg read *congregata est*. A syr: συνήχθησαν (cf. Matt 13:2). In place of ὄχλος D has ὁ λαός. ℵ B C L Δ read πλεῖστος; ς A D have πολύς; it vg read *turba multa vel magna*. ℵ B* C syr^sin πλοῖον, ς A B² D Δ τὸ πλοῖον (cf. also 1:19–20, 3:9). Due to the difficulty of the question of the article in hellenistic Greek, these specific cases cannot be resolved. For ἐν τῇ θαλάσσῃ D has πέραν τῆς θαλάσσης; cf. in that regard traditions such as *circa mare, super mare, circa litus maris, ad litus, proxime litus*. "Does πέραν, or its Aramaic correlate mean just *beside*, or does it mean *on the shore of*?" (Wellhausen, *Mark*, 31). That is made more likely by the reading in D^gr, which has simply πέραν τῆς θαλάσσης in place of πρὸς τὴν θάλασσαν ἐπὶ τῆς γῆς. ς A Dgr read ἦν instead of ἦσαν, relieving the difficulty.

All at once Jesus is back by the sea. Mark's use of the word πάλιν here connects back to 2:13 and 3:7. How Jesus got to the sea is not stated, nor is anything said about a change in his situation. There is no bridge from 3:35 to 4:1. The general picture is all that matters: Jesus, surrounded by the masses, teaching in a boat. It is a scene that artists have often painted.[28] We do not know where the disciples are "in the boat" or "on the shore," but the narrative

---

28. Early Christian exegesis had the right feel for this; cf. Catene: ἵνα μετ' ἀκριβείας συνθῇ τὸ θέατρον, καὶ μηδένα ἀφῇ κατὰ νώτου, ἀλλὰ πάντας ἀντιπροσώπους ἔχει. Cf. Wohlenberg, *Markus*, 120n8.

is not interested in that question. We ourselves produce that kind of question on the basis of of our well-developed conceptions of the outline of Jesus' ministry, even though we cannot prove that at the time of this event Jesus even had any disciples, since it is not certain that this story took place after Jesus had chosen the Twelve. Anyone who wants to try to answer questions like these—anyone, that is, who wants to be an artist and paint a picture of the disciples—will find plenty of leeway here. An earlier story mentioned a boat (3:9), but as far as this story is concerned, that does not matter. The summary statement in 3:9 connects itself with this story, but this story does not connect itself back. The localization of this scene stands on the ground of an early tradition, which Mark has taken up. The evangelist surrounds this scene with local details, but they are not his creation. The pericope certainly could have begun with 4:2, but in 4:1 there hangs a tale. The individual stories from the life of Jesus had no interest in identifying the locations of the events. Sometimes local details were given, sometimes not. In this regard the anecdotal tradition was consistently uneven, yet in certain stories—especially narratives about Capernaum (cf. esp. 1:16ff) or stories about the sea—the scenic details can be strikingly precise, and those pericopes played a special role in the oldest Jesus tradition. The tradition that connects Mark with Capernaum, and to Simon Peter who lived there, is especially fascinating. While other stories about Jesus were handed down without any designation of place, the connections of Mark to Capernaum force us to slow down as we assess the stories about Capernaum and the sea. It appears that the evangelist did know something of an itinerary for Jesus, at least as far as the Sea of Galilee was concerned. The broken pieces of that itinerary are in the tradition, but we cannot fully reconstruct them, because other narratives (which did not belong to that itinerary) have been interposed. In this case, 4:1 is strongly anchored in the tradition: Jesus preaches to the people at the Sea of Galilee. Whether the entire sermon belongs here, or whether it continued over more than one day, is a further question.

Let us first consider the parallel passages. Matthew 13:1ff follows Mark, except that Matthew puts a local (ἐκ τῆς οἰκίας) and a temporal (ἐν τῇ ἡμέρᾳ ἐκείνῃ) clamp on the event: ¹ἐν τῇ ἡμέρᾳ ἐκείνῃ ἐξελθὼν ὁ Ἰησοῦς ἐκ τῆς οἰκίας ἐκάθητο παρὰ τὴν θάλασσαν. ²καὶ συνήχθησαν πρὸς αὐτὸν ὄχλοι πολλοί, ὥστε αὐτὸν εἰς πλοῖον ἐμβάντα καθῆσαι, καὶ πᾶς ὁ ὄχλος ἐπὶ τὸν αἰγιαλὸν εἱστήκει. ³καὶ ἐλάλησεν αὐτοῖς ἐν παραβολαῖς λέγων . . .

ς C D E F insert δέ at the beginning. D changes Matthew's characteristic participle into ἐξῆλθεν . . . καί. Instead of ἐκ (read by ℵ), ς C E F L Γ Δ have ἀπό (cf. vg.: *de domo*). B drops the word ἐκ, and D drops the whole phrase ἐκ τῆς οἰκίας.

In 13:1-52 Matthew follows Mark's arrangement, for this collection of parables fits his plan nicely at this point, as it makes the unbelief of the people more visible. We have here the first sustained discourse from Jesus since the Sermon on the Mount, but we dare not make a chronological assertion here, as if the parables belonged to a later period in the Galilean ministry of Jesus.

With this pericope Luke takes up again Mark's thread, which he had dropped back in 6:19. In 8:1-3 Luke gave a report about the **women who served Jesus**. This brief note was a fitting counterpoint to the story of the sinful woman that had immediately preceded it, yet these three verses also introduced something new: Jesus had left Capernaum and begun to travel. The present form of the introductory verse (8:1, καὶ ἐγένετο ἐν τῷ καθεξῆς καὶ αὐτὸς διώδευεν) certainly comes from Luke, as does the phrase κατὰ πόλιν καὶ κώμην.[29] 8:1 bears the marks of a summary statement, but what follows has a thoroughly distinctive coloring. Among the many women who served and followed Jesus, three (3) are named: 1) Mary Magdalene, i.e., Mary from Magdala. That may be the same as the Magadan/Magdala named in Matt 15:39. 2) Johanna, the wife of Herod Antipas' adminstrator, Churza; and 3) Suzanna. We know just the names of the last two, while it is said of Mary Magdalene that Jesus had exorcised seven demons from her. She is mentioned again in Mark 15:40 (= Matt 27:56), along with Mary the mother of the younger James and Joses (or Joseph), and Salome, the mother of the sons of Zebedee. These are the women who follow Jesus from Galilee and witness his crucifixion. In those other texts Luke does not mention names, which makes it seem as if he may have transposed Mark 15:40 to Luke 8:1-3. In arranging the ministry of Jesus into periods, he put one of Mark's parenthetical remarks at the beginning of Jesus' travels. Certainly these details were not created by Mark, although we cannot tell whether Luke was following an oral tradition or a written one. But if we are going to arrive at an appropriate evaluation of the outline of the story of Jesus, it is important for details such as these to produce an insight: the circumference of Jesus' ministry was obviously greater than what we would think, based upon the individual Gospel stories.

In Luke 8:4-18 the parables are introduced by: Συνιόντος δὲ ὄχλου πολλοῦ καὶ τῶν κατὰ πόλιν ἐπιπορευομένων πρὸς αὐτὸν εἶπεν διὰ παραβολῆς . . .

---

29. In Spitta's opinion 8:1 marks Jesus' departure from Judea, where he had previously worked, toward the north. In my judgment the text gives us nothing to stand on. Spitta assesses the whole episode correctly, although he concludes (without any support) that it is original in its current position (Spitta, *Die synoptische Grundschrift*, 157).

Instead of the singular Συνιόντος D has Συνελθόντος, and κατὰ τὴν πόλιν instead of κατὰ πόλιν (perhaps having Capernaum in mind).³⁰

κατὰ πόλιν means "city by city," and that is the point of the verse: many people gathered together as inhabitants of city after city (from every city) came to him.³¹ Naturally there is no difference between two groups here. The καὶ is explicative, as the verse explains why the crowds keep growing. Mark's setting beside the sea is completely gone: Jesus is speaking to a completely arbitrary group of people. Mark's setting is not reduced thereby; Luke simply situates it in a wider framework. While in Mark Jesus returns again and again to the sea, Luke lets him roam more freely, which certainly corresponds to historical reality, even if in individual cases Mark's tradition is older and more historical.

Mark 4:10 introduces something new: καὶ ὅτε ἐγένετο κατὰ μόνας, ἠρώτουν αὐτὸν οἱ περὶ αὐτὸν σὺν τοῖς δώδεκα τὰς παραβολας· καὶ ἔλεγεν αὐτοῖς . . .

ς and A read ὅτε δέ for καὶ ὅτε. With the regard to the words οἱ περὶ αὐτὸν σὺν τοῖς δώδεκα, the tradition varies. Obviously there was a concern to distinguish the Twelve from other followers of Jesus. The whole phrase is missing from vg, while D has οἱ μαθηταὶ αὐτοῦ, as do the lectionaries, which tend to follow the form of the text in Luke. D improves upon τὰς παραβολάς with τίς ἡ παραβολὴ αὕτη, like ς and A, which have τὴν παραβολήν. Neither reading fits well with v. 11. These variants aptly illustrate the peculiar difficulties of transitional pieces.

A new picture rises before our eyes, which cannot be understood with reference either to what has preceded or to what follows: Jesus is alone, κατὰ μόνας, surrounded by his circle of followers, including the disciples (οἱ περὶ αὐτὸν σὺν τοῖς δώδεκα), and talking about the meaning of the parables. He has withdrawn from the masses and is joined only by those he trusts. Any further questions about the location—the kinds of questions one tends to ask (indeed, *must* ask) of a continuous narrative—come to nothing. Where is this scene set: in a house? (cf. the various places where Jesus withdraws into a house:

---

30. Cf. the reading "Capernaum" in Luke 7:11, and the comment thereon above.

31. According to Spitta, the text "does not give the impression of being an original composition. It is instead a careful welding of pieces that originally did not belong together." Thus it can be improved to read: "καὶ περὶ τῶν κατὰ πόλιν ἐπιπορευομένων πρὸς αὐτὸν εἶπεν διὰ παραβολῆς . . . = but since they came to him from city after city, he spoke in parables" (Spitta, *Die synoptische Grundschrift*, 166). Other opinions are enumerated in B. Weiss, *Markus und Lukas*, 398.

7:17; 9:29; 10:10). On the shore of the sea? On the way home? Or in a boat? It cannot be in a boat, since there would be no room for this many listeners. For that matter, how did all these people come to be together with the Twelve in this location? They is no mention of them in the preceding narrative (4:1). It all adds up to this: here we have an especially vivid case of the fact that the tradition really did not bother at all with details of time and place. There is even an internal inconsistency in the story: it speaks of "parables" in the plural, but as a matter of fact only one parable is recounted.

As we have already seen, there is no connection with what precedes. But is there perhaps some kind of connection with what follows? How long should we imagine that Jesus remained basically alone? That would be a reasonable question for a critic who wants to understand an ongoing narrative. In Mark 4:33 the crowd of hearers is introduced, so at least part of the chapter between v. 10 and v. 33 must be directed toward the people, say v. 30ff, or also possibly vv. 13, 21, 24 or 26. On the other hand, vv. 13, 21, etc. could be connected with the setting in v. 10. Various critical operations could relieve the difficulty, the simplest and most radical of which is to take either vv. 10–12,[32] or vv. 10–20,[33] or vv. 10–25[34] as a later addition. But it is equally plausible to excise vv. 10–12 (or vv. 10–10 or even vv. 10–25) and relocate them after v. 32.[35] All of these suggestions arise from an effort to salvage some kind of order in the material, but in fact there is no order here. The three parables that remain after the excision of vv. 10–25 stand in no particular sequence. The second follows very loosely after the first (καὶ ἔλεγεν, v. 26), as so on to the third (καὶ ἔλεγεν, v. 30). The real question is whether the evangelist put the pieces in this order, or whether a later editor expanded upon an existing series by inserting some new material. Perhaps the evangelist re-worked some earlier document (Ur-Mark?), but the "Ur-Mark" that some have distilled out of this material turns out not to have any compelling logic to it, either. Thus is is most likely that it was the evangelist who put the pieces in this order.[36] 4:1–9, 10–12, 13–20, 21–23, 24–25, 29–29, and 30–32 are all individual pieces that have been arranged

---

32. Wellhausen regards vv. 11 and 12 as interpolations and v. 10 as a revision (Wellhausen, *Mark*, 32). Merx thinks vv. 1–12 are not original (*Markus und Lukas*, 46).

33. Cf. Klostermann, *Markus*, 34.

34. J. Weiss, *Schriften*, 109; Wendling, 28.

35. So Wendt, *Die Lehre Jesu*, 30ff.

36. Wendling regards 4:1–9, 26–29, and 33 as the original report, leaving out only two parables. That makes v. 33 (παραβολαῖς πολλαῖς) remarkable, and Wendling later expresses himself more cautiously: "We will not go wrong if we take the parable in vv. 26–29 as part of the oldest version of the narrative of the preaching beside the sea" (Wendling, *Die Entstehung*, 38).

at random, and that is why the discourse always seems to be starting all over again, as the formula καὶ ἔλεγεν repeats itself. It appears that the evangelist (who inserted the concluding remark in v. 33) thought of vv. 10–25 as a sermon of Jesus to his disciples: Jesus withdraws with them from the uncomprehending masses, gives them the explanation to the parable of the sower, and closes with some words about the use of parables. The excerpts in v. 13ff, v. 21ff, and v. 24ff are thoroughly independent, and it is clear that they had a different audience in both the tradition and in historical reality than the one they have now.[37]

Did the individual pieces collected in chapter 4 come from the same layer of the tradition? The answer to that question has to be No. The allegorical interpretation of the parable of the sower appears not to be as old as the parable itself; the testimony about the hardness of heart among the Jews looks like a theory that would not cohere well with the character of Jesus; the parable of the mustard seed (vv. 30–32) is secondary to Luke 13:18f (Q). Thus some of the traditional material in chapter 4 will have to be labeled as unhistorical.

Be that as it may, the outline of Mark 4:1–34 is not secondary. The material may come from different layers of the tradition, but different hands have not necessarily worked on this chapter. Even in its original outline it would have combined material that was both earlier and later, historical and unhistorical. When working with a tradition that is richer than we might suspect, we must guard against arriving too quickly at a verdict of "impossible," "psychologically incomprehensible," or "unhistorical." A backlash against Jülicher's theory of the parables—which seeks to separate the historical Jesus from anything allegorical—is already well underway, based on Jewish parallels from the period,[38] and Wrede's picture of Jesus is certainly one-sided. He and his followers have underestimated the tensions that were present in Jesus himself. Doubts about the historicity of the tradition, and in many cases there are no right answers, are having an undue influence on literary analysis of the Gospels.[39] It is as if scholars are trying to produce the original relationships by following a recipe.

37. This is the judgment at which we arrive if we are attentive to the compositional techniques of this Gospel. If we are inattentive to these techniques, the results are tortured and torturous. For example: "We definitely regard the words reported in vv. 21–32 as originally intended for the disciples. That does not exclude—in fact it includes—the possibility that they found their way to other people as well . . ." (Wohlenberg, *Markus*, 134).

38. Cf. Eissfeldt, *Der Maschal im Alten Testament*, 30–31.

39. Wendling is exempt from this criticism, for he expressly says that he is pursuing "formal criteria," yet even he does not get off scot free. He is aware that the tradition comes in pieces, but still he works with historical postulates: "With regard to content, there is an unbridgeable gulf between the narrative about the true relatives and the

Mark's loose configuration in 4:10ff is restructured by Matthew and Luke. Matthew 13:10 does not pick up the change of scene in Mark 4:10; instead it says: καὶ προσελθόντες οἱ μαθηταὶ εἶπαν αὐτῷ· διὸ τί ἐν παραβολαῖς λαλεῖς αὐτοῖς; The phrase κατὰ μόνας, which causes so many headaches, drops out, but the plural ἐν παραβολαῖς stays in, a vestigial remnant of Mark's version and thereby also of the original independent pericope. Verse 12 is a saying that Mark puts in a later context (4:25), and in v. 14 there follows a citation from the Old Testament (Matthew's own method of citation) and a saying to the disciples about the blessedness of eyewitnesses. Luke links this saying, which came from Q, with the cry of jubilation in 10:23-24, giving it a short introduction: καὶ στραφεὶς πρὸς τοὺς μαθητὰς κατ' ἰδίαν εἶπεν. In Matthew the meaning of the parable of the sower is presented to the disciples more clearly than in Mark: ὑμεῖς οὖν ἀκούσατε... (Matt 13:18). The saying about the use of parables drops out, except for Mark 4:25, which Matthew has already used in 13:12, along with the saying about the growing seed (Mark 4:26-29). In its place Matthew brings in from his special source a parable about weeds among the wheat (Matt 13:24-30) with the introduction, ἄλλην παραβολὴν παρέθηκεν αὐτοῖς λέγων. Next, and introduced the same way, in Matt 13:31-32 comes the parable of the mustard seed, a parable that is in Mark but that Matthew presents here in the original form in which it came to him from Q.[40] The introduction to the parable of the leaven (Matt 13:33) is similar: ἄλλην παραβολὴν ἐλάλησεν αὐτοῖς. This parable also came from Q (cf. Luke 13:20-21).[41] As in Mark 4:33-34, Matthew closes with a note about speaking in parables, and the form of this note comes from Matthew himself: Mark's reference to κατ' ἰδίαν drops out, and the whole thing finishes off with a biblical citation.

It is striking that still more follows. Matthew 13:34-35 is a well-rounded conclusion, and yet Matt 13:36-52 goes on to add material that can be traced back to the evangelist himself. The parable of the weeds, which came from Matthew's special source, now receives its own explanation: τότε ἀφεὶς τοὺς ὄχλους ἦλθεν εἰς τὴν οἰκίαν· καὶ προσῆλθον οἱ μαθηταί αὐτοῦ λέγοντες... ὁ δέ...

ς C E F Δ insert ὁ ις.

---

scene in 4:10ff, between the saying in 3:34ff and the saying about hardness of heart in 4:11-12. It is not hard to see which one sketches the character of Jesus" (Wendling, 32n1). But in these texts the character of Jesus has been pressed out with a template. It appears to me that the "formal criteria" that Wendling cites are of value, except for the fact that they point toward an Ur-Mark and exaggerate some things too much.

40. D L* read ἐλάλησεν; cf. Matt 12:33. After αὐτοῖς L* has ὁ ις.
41. ℵ C L insert λέγων, and some also ὁ ις. D has only: ἄλλην παραβολήν.

By the word οἰκία, Matthew does not refer to any particular house; the term merely serves to separate Jesus from the crowds.

Three more parables, all from Matthew's special source, are spoken in a context that includes only the disciples, but it is not at all certain that these parables were situated this way in the tradition: first 13:44, about the treasure ὁμοία ἐστὶν ἡ βασιλεία τῶν οὐρανῶν; second 13:45 about the pearls, introduced the same way, plus πάλιν; and third 13:47–50 about the fishing nets, introduced just like 13:45. After them comes a concluding passage (13:51–52) that Matthew shaped on the basis of a traditional saying. διὰ τοῦτο, however, is not anchored in this tradition; Matthew brought it in from elsewhere and used 13:51 to tie it to the parables.

The total complex consists of seven (7) parables, not counting two interpretations of parables, and the saying about hardness of heart. This arrangement is of course not a coincidence, even if the plan is not consistent in all its details. We have to say that the framework is rather carelessly constructed, which explains a lot, as does the fact that Matthew depends upon Mark more than just a little.

Luke 8:9–18, by contrast, is much more independent, and vv. 9, 11, and 16 all take up Mark's sequence. Only κατὰ μόνας (Mark 4:10) drops out. παραβολάι changes to παραβολή, in order to smooth out the transition to the following scene, in which the disciples ask about the meaning of just one parable. καὶ λέγει αὐτοῖς in Mark 4:13 also drops out, and the discourse goes on uninterrupted after δέ. The same treatment repeats itself in v. 16. The parable of the growing seed is missing from Matthew, and Luke puts the parables of the mustard seed and the leaven in a later context (chap. 13) with the simplest of introductions, ἔλεγεν οὖν and καὶ πάλιν εἶπεν. We cannot tell why those two parables were put there.

But Luke's overall project is clear. Traditions that lacked chronological and topographical settings were grouped by Mark and (especially) Matthew on the basis of their content. But Luke, because he was an author, worked differently. To the extent that such complexes of individual traditions had been formed, Luke proceeded to dissolve them again, for he wanted to lay out the ministry of Jesus more consistently, through separate stories. To that end he generally followed Mark's thread, but often he needed to change it slightly, as in this case, where he worked more substantially with material that had already been rolled together. As a result, individual remarks like Mark 4:33–34, which only make sense in the broader context of a complex of material, simply had to be ignored.[42]

42. Spitta arrives at exactly the opposite conclusion, because he does not take sufficient notice of this characteristic in Luke's method of writing history. In his opinion the Lukan parallel arose from the situation described in 8:1–3 (cf., by contrast, my early

Three Stories on and around the Sea of Galilee
(Mark 4:35—5:43 par.)

The Storm at Sea
(Mark 4:35–41; Matt 8:23–27; Luke 8:22–25)

³⁵καὶ λέγει αὐτοῖς ἐν ἐκείνῃ τῇ ἡμέρᾳ ὀψίας γενομένης· διέλθωμεν εἰς τὸ πέραν. ³⁶καὶ ἀφέντες τὸν ὄχλον παραλαμβάνουσιν αὐτὸν ὡς ἦν ἐν τῷ πλοίῳ, ἄλλα δὲ πλοῖα ἦσαν μετ' αὐτοῦ. ³⁷καὶ γίνεται λαῖλαψ μεγάλη ἀνέμου . . .

> ς E F and L have πλοιάρια (cf. John 6:23). D has ἐγένετο instead of γίνεται (cf. Vg.).

This story is marked by unusually specific designations of time and place, and by vivid details. The temporal phrase, ἐν ἐκείνῃ τῇ ἡμέρᾳ, is especially striking. In Matthew and Luke a remark like this ("on that day") would have to be regarded as a link created by the evangelist, but not so in Mark, for whom this kind of composition is not typical. "On that day" is unusual, and so is "when evening had come." These are chronological details that come from the deepest layers of the tradition that Mark was using. The same goes for all of the following details in the setting: Jesus wants to cross to the other side of the sea with his disciples, the disciples leave behind the crowds, the boat sets sail, other boats follow. This narrative begins with a highly unusual level of detail.

One of those details presents a problem. How are we to understand the sentence, παραλαμβάνουσιν αὐτὸν ὡς ἦν ἐν τῷ πλοίῳ? Grammar and usage allow for two possibilities: first, ἐν τῷ πλοίῳ could go with ἦν, in which case the sentence would mean, "the disciples took him along, as he was already in the boat," recalling the fact that Jesus had gotten into the boat to preach. Our story would then connect nicely with the scene in 4:1–9 (but not 4:10ff). But ἐν τῷ πλοίῳ could also go with παραλαμβάνουσιν, and in that case the sentence would mean, "the disciples took him in the boat, as he was." In Hellenistic Greek εἰς and ἐν were interchangeable, and the scene could then be imagined as follows: Jesus was exhausted from his preaching and needed rest. Seeing his condition, the disciples took him into the boat.[43] For my part,

---

remarks on those verses). Luke muddied the sequence there. As Spitta rightly recognizes, there is a connection here in Luke, whereby the parable of the different kinds of soil "grew out of a concrete historical situation" (Spitta, *Die synoptische Grundschrift*, 167). But Spitta does not realize that Luke himself constructed that concrete situation.

43. Spitta takes παραλαμβάνουσιν as a textual lacuna (Spitta, *Die synoptische Grundschrift*, 181). But Luke 8:22 is crystal clear; many indictments have been issued against Mark 4:35ff.

I cannot decide between these two possibilities, as both are equally shaped by a desire to connect this scene with what has preceded it. Yet is there really any such connection here? The phrase "that day" appears to suggest that there is, especially in the light of ὀψίας γενομένης. It appears that Jesus must have preached to the crowds until evening, and then decided to cross the sea. But this connection is not solid, and given the loose structure of Mark's outline, here (as elsewhere) we have to consider other possibilities just as carefully. I see two: 1) 4:1ff (especially 4:1–9) may have been linked with 4:35ff in the pre-Markan tradition, possibly because of similarities in their settings. ἐν ἐκείνῃ τῇ ἡμέρᾳ would then be either a patch sewn on by this redaction, or it may have originally been part of 4:35ff. We cannot really tell, for such patches certainly arose at some point, but even after they appeared, the stories carried their introductions with them as they landed, unchanged, at new locations in the framework.[44] Or: 2) Mark himself might have inserted the travel story into the narrative here, attaching a sea voyage to a setting in which Jesus was preaching by the sea. The apparent connection with what precedes may not be real, and it may not have been in the pre-Markan tradition either. Interpreters have to respect those words, *may not*. Even when two narratives are chronologically connected, we may still have good reason to regard those connections as uncertain. It is essential to keep in mind that the stories are sealed up in individual pericopes, and from that point of view, even those chronological connections that turn out to be genuine are actually quite coincidental and secondary.[45] We always have to ask why the evangelist

---

44. Wohlenberg recognizes this when he says: "The specific chronological indicators in Mark can only have originated from the personal reports of an eyewitness. Probably the Lord taught the people late into the evening" (Wohlenberg, *Markus*, 144).

45. Even scholars who correctly understand that the Gospel of Mark has the general character of a compilation are still influenced by the impression of chronology in this Gospel. They recognize that they are dealing with framing pieces that, even though they are only a framework, seem to have been taken up from the tradition pretty much just as they were. And if that framework collapses, then there is no way to go any further. What then should we say to the following roster of comments?

On ἐκείνῃ τῇ ἡμέρᾳ: "The connection in 4:35 comes from the redaction" (Wellhausen, *Mark*, 38). "This story was linked with the parable scene in the earlier tradition" (J. Weiss, 181).

On ὀψίας γενομένης: "The evening is mentioned because visibility was declining and Jesus was going to sleep" (Wellhausen, *Luke*, 38). "Certainly this is a bit of ornamentation by the editor, of whose style it is characteristic. But the addition is minimal, since the following scenes supposedly played out on the same day; thus time was growing short" (J. Weiss, *Das älteste Evangelium*, 181).

On παραλαμβάνουσιν αὐτὸν ὡς ἦν ἐν τῷ πλοίῳ: "The sentence contains an internal contradiction" (Wellhausen, *Mark*, 38). "This link looks like it goes back to a very concrete memory" (J. Wesiss, *Das älteste Evangelium*, 181).

On ἄλλα δὲ πλοῖα ἦσαν μετ' αὐτοῦ: "The detail adds nothing to the context and thus

has arranged the individual stories as he did. Only when we cannot answer that question should we begin to entertain the possibility that there might have been an outline that held them together. We have already seen what this procedure can do, in our discussion of 1:21–39 and 2:1—3:6. The first of those complexes was a chronological sequence not constructed by the evangelist, but the second was certainly arranged by him, and thus its chronology was rendered doubtful, unlikely, even impossible. And what about this case? In the section that occupies us now (3:7—6:13), Jesus is depicted as busily working among the people, who generally reject him. The narrative about Jesus' sea voyage has nothing to do with this theme, unless we were to suppose that it emphasizes the fact that even the disciples had little faith, so that even Jesus' own followers ultimately were not necessarily committed to him. But that is a rather elaborate level of interpretation. The real point of the pericope is that Jesus works with miraculous power. When the evangelist locates this story here, is he perhaps simply following the tradition, which had already put 4:1ff and 4:35ff together?

Matthew 8:23–27 places the story of the storm at sea in the series of miracles in chapters 8 and 9: καὶ ἐμβάντι αὐτῷ εἰς τὸ πλοῖον ἠκολούθησαν αὐτῷ οἱ μαθηταὶ αὐτοῦ.

> In isolated cases we find τῷ ιυ for αὐτῷ. ℵ^b B C 33 drop τό from before πλοῖον (cf. Luke 8:22).

Just ahead of this passage, in Matt 8:18–22, there are *two sayings about discipleship*, which Luke puts in a different framework (Luke 9:57–60[46]) at the beginning of his long Travel Narrative. Luke's introduction sounds a lot like Mark 4:35: ἰδὼν δὲ ὁ Ἰησοῦς πολλοὺς ὄχλους περὶ αὐτὸν ἐκέλευσεν ἀπελθεῖν εἰς τὸ πέραν.

> B reads ὄχλον, ℵ* cop have ὄχλους.

The pause between the command and the carrying out of that command is filled up by a conversation. The Markan framework of the pericope is on the whole preserved (ὀψίας γενομένης drops out, because in Matthew

---

points back to genuine tradition" (Wellhausen, *Mark*, 39). "A second contribution of the editor is the presence of other boats" (J. Wesiss, *Das älteste Evangelium*, 181).

It seems to me that these scholars are indulging in impressionism, which certainly has its place. Wellhausen's description is particularly clear and fresh. But we should point out the difference between the tradition and the compositional work of the evangelist.

46. According to Luke 9:57, Jesus has left his "stronghold" in Capernaum. The question of which evangelist has arranged the sayings in their correct chronological order cannot even be discussed. Wellhausen finds the arrangement in Mark to be "suitable" (Wellhausen, *Matthew*, 39).

that phrase has already been used in 8:16), but the narrative itself is set in an entirely new context. Here we should recall that Matthew arranges his material on the basis of content, but that does not necessarily mean that Mark is chronological. Is not Mark's chronology also full of holes, if another evangelist can treat it with so little respect?

Luke 8:22-25 has the following introduction: ἐγένετο δὲ ἐν μιᾷ τῶν ἡμερῶν καὶ αὐτὸς ἐνέβη εἰς πλοῖον καὶ οἱ μαθηταὶ αὐτοῦ, καὶ εἶπεν πρὸς αὐτοῖς· διέλθωμεν εἰς τὸ πέραν τῆς λίμνης.[47] καὶ ἀνήχθησαν.

Various mss. have ὁ ις after ἀνέβη. F reads καὶ αὐτὸς ὁ ις ἀνέβη.

Clearly we have here the precursor to Mark, which Luke has altered in two ways. First he says ἐν μιᾷ τῶν ἡμερῶν: the story takes place on some arbitrary day, not on the same day as the parable story, as Mark seems to think. Earlier we suggested that Luke made an effort to spread the stories of Jesus over a wider geographical area, and here we can see that even more clearly. One after another the following events played out in sequence: Jesus takes his seat in a boat (Luke drops the τό from Mark), the destination is stated, and off they go, as daylight is fading. In Luke there are no previous stories about the sea, so the connection with what precedes is even weaker than in Mark.

The Gerasene Demoniac
(Mark 5:1-20; Matt 8:28-34; Luke 8:26-39)

[1] καὶ ἦλθον εἰς τὸ πέραν τῆς θαλάσσης εἰς τὴν χώραν τῶν Γερασηνῶν· [2] καὶ ἐξελθόντος αὐτοῦ ἐκ τοῦ πλοίου εὐθὺς ὑπήντησεν αὐτῷ ἐκ τῶν μνημείων ἄνθρωπος ἐν πνεύματι ἀκαθάρτῳ, [3] ὃς τὴν κατοίκησιν εἶχεν ἐν τοῖς μνήμασιν . . . [5] καὶ διαπαντὶς νυκτὸς καὶ ἡμέρας ἐν τοῖς μνήμασιν καὶ ἐν τοῖς ὄρεσιν ἦν . . . [6] καὶ ἰδὼν τὸν Ἰησοῦν ἀπὸ μακρόθεν ἔδραμεν . . . [11] ἦν δὲ ἐκεῖ πρὸς τῷ ὄρει ἀγέλη χοίρων μεγάλη βοσκομένη . . . [13] τὰ πνεύματα . . . εἰσῆλθον εἰς τοὺς χοίρους, καὶ ὥρμησεν ἡ ἀγέλη κατὰ τοῦ κρημνοῦ εἰς τὴν θάλασσαν . . . [14] καὶ οἱ βόσκοντες αὐτοὺς ἔφυγον καὶ ἀπήγγειλαν εἰς τὴν πόλιν καὶ εἰς τοὺς ἀγρούς. Of the residents who were gathering it says: [17] καὶ ἤρξαντο παρακαλεῖν αὐτὸν ἀπελθεῖν ἀπὸ τῶν ὁρίων αὐτῶν. [18] καὶ ἐμβαίνοντος αὐτοῦ εἰς τὸ πλοῖον παρεκάλει αὐτὸν ὁ δαιμονισθείς, ἵνα μετ' αὐτοῦ ᾖ. [19] καὶ οὐκ ἀφῆκεν αὐτόν, ἀλλὰ λέγει αὐτῷ· ὕπαγε εἰς τὸν οἶκόν σου πρὸς τοὺς σοὺς . . . [20] καὶ ἀπῆλθεν καὶ ἤρξατο κηρύσσειν ἐν τῇ Δεκαπόλει . . .

---

47. Merx regards λίμνη as the original text and says that Luke "as we know had very old sources" (*Markus und Lukas*, 250). He did? In my judgment λίμνη is an effort to improve on θάλασσα.

ἦλθεν for ἦλθον is well attested (C L Δ). The Gospel lectionaries read it that way, and they insert ὁ ις to make the narrative an independent pericope. The reading ἦλθεν itself may be an indication that a new pericope is indicated here. In this case I will not venture a guess which is original and which is later, and I have to regard Merx's astute observation as nonetheless still uncertain: "If ἦλθον was old, ἦλθεν would not have developed from it. Here the τάξις of the narrative is evident, which Papias reports was not in his manuscript of Mark" (*Markus und Lukas*, 46). The designation of the territory varies: Γερασηνῶν (א* B D it vg), Γαδαρηνῶν (A C pesh go), Γεργεσηνῶν (א^c L Δ^gr 33 cop syr^sin arm aeth). For the opinions of the church fathers on this tradition, cf. the critical apparatus in Tischendorf. In place of ἐξελθόντος αὐτοῦ in v. 2, ς A et al. have ἐξελθόντι αὐτῷ, D has ἐξελθόντων αὐτῶν; both readings are efforts to improve the text. For εὐθύς ς A and D read εὐθέως; B drops the word, as do syr^sin pesh arm aeth. ἐκ τῶν μνημείων is lacking in syr^sin; it may seem to be superfluous. In place of μνήμασιν (v. 3), ς and D read μνημείοις. Similar alterations appear in v. 5. In v. 11, ς and a few witnesses read πρὸς τὸ ὄρη. In v. 18, ς E and F have the pedantic ἐμβάντος.

Let us temporarily postpone the discussion of the connections between this story and what precedes it, and begin instead by analyzing the story itself. Jesus and those who are with him land on the far side of the sea in the territory of the Gerasenes. The story that follows is full of highly vivid local details: tombs are nearby, the area is hilly, and a steep cliff leads straight down into the sea, with people coming to him from the surrounding area. At their request, Jesus leaves and gets back into the boat, telling the healed man to go back home and to proclaim his exploits in the Decapolis. Specific reference to the city of Gerasa is deeply rooted in the narrative; in fact it must have been named before v. 14 (n.b. τὴν πόλιν). Thus we find ourselves on the eastern shore of the sea, i.e., close to the region named in v. 20, the Decapolis. It should be added at this point that the herd of swine suggests a Gentile, or at least a strongly mixed, population, a detail that also fits the region of the Decapolis.[48]

Yet the name and location of the city of Gerasa is highly uncertain, so much so that the textual tradition staggers all over the place. Gerasa, today's Jerash, was the eastern boundary of Perea, but it lay too far from

---

48. According to *m. Baba Kamma* 7.7, Jews may not rear swine anywhere (cf. Merx, *Matthäus*, 145). Some recent interpreters take offense at the destruction of the herd and place the blame on the Jewish owners of the swine, who were violating this Mishnaic ordinance (cf. Wohlenberg, *Markus*, 156).

the sea (about 35 miles as the crow flies) to be referred to here. Gadara, which Origen famously confused with Gezer in Judea, is also too far away, to the south. The place that is known today as Umm Qais is located 1.25 miles from the seashore.[49] Thus we will either have to suppose that there was a second Gerasa, this one farther north along the sea, or else we will have to stay with the name "Gergesa." It is widely thought that this name originated from a conjecture by Origen, but that is in fact not certain. A site discovered by Thompson on the steep shore of the sea in 1860, which went by the name(s) of Kursi, Kersa, or Gersa, may have been called Gergesa in antiquity.[50] These problems with the place name, however, do not change the fact that the name—like the other local details—belongs to the tradition. Explaining details of this sort is not Mark's style.

How then did this narrative come to reside in its present position? Recall the theme of Mark 3:7—6:13: Jesus turns toward the people, to no avail. Now Jesus is rejected in this story too. While that is a rather minor similarity within the broader plot line, it may have been what mattered most to the evangelist. He may have done more than was necessary for his purpose.[51]

Now we can discuss the relation of our story to what precedes it. There can be no doubt that 4:35ff and 5:1ff belonged together in the tradition, for they link up topographically without any problems, although chronologically there is a certain difficulty. Since it is ὀψία in 4:35, the narrative that immediately follows must also take place on the same day, and that entails

49. Origen, *Commentary on John* 6.24. Cf. Klostermann, *Markus*, 40.

50. A precise treatment of the problem of Gerasa has been offered by Zahn, "Das Land der Gadarener, Gerasener, Gergasener." Cf. also Wohlenberg, *Markus*, 148; Pölzl, *Marcus*, 131; Buhl, *Geographie des alten Palästina*, 243, 257. J. Weiss (*Das älteste Evangelium*, 186) suggests that the evangelist replaced an unknown name, something like Gergesa, with one even more unknown. I cannot verify whether M. Brückner is exaggerating the topographical difficulties when he writes: "Today's Jerash lies ... much too far away to be connected with the narrative about the healing of the demoniac. Only the southeastern end of the sea fits the setting for a headlong rush by 2,000 pigs. Thus the setting of the narrative as it stands in Mark 5:1ff cannot be identified"; cf. Brückner, *Das fünfte Evangelium*, 34. Nestle thinks that the confusion may have started with a place name such as *ras el chinzir* ("head of the swine") = χωραζείν; cf. Nestle, "Chorazin, Bethsaida," 185. Furrer supports Kursi and argues that Origen would have known the place on the eastern shore of the sea from his many travels in the area; cf. Furrer, "Nochmals Gerasa am See Genezareth." Merx disagrees, pointing out that Origen was wrong on his conjecture about Bethabara in John 1:28 (*Markus und Lukas*, 1:146-47).

51. According to Wohlenberg, the evangelist obviously wanted to put our story in the context of the training of the disciples (Wohlenberg, *Markus*, 158; cf. also J. Warneck, *Die Lebenskräfte des Evangeliums*). O. Schmiedel draws upon the Tübingen School and suggests that the demoniac was Paul, and that Gadara was the place name because it lay on the road to Damascus!!; cf. Schmiedel, *Hauptprobleme der Leben-Jesu-Forshung*, 114ff. This idea is not worth discussing.

a degree of difficulty, even if ὀψία means "late afternoon" rather than "evening." Should we insert a night after 4:35ff, and place 5:1ff on the following morning, when they land? Before we can proceed any further along these lines, we will have to examine the following narrative, Mark 5:21–43.

Like Mark, Matt 8:28–34 links our narrative with the storm at sea and offers the following framework:

²⁸καὶ ἐλθόντος αὐτοῦ εἰς τὸ πέραν εἰς τὴν χώραν τῶν Γαδαρηνῶν ὑπήντησαν αὐτῷ δύο δαιμονιζόμενοι ἐκ τῶν μνημείων ἐξερχόμενοι, χαλεποὶ λίαν, ὥστε μὴ ἰσχύειν τινὰ παρελθεῖν διὰ τῆς ὁδοῦ ἐκείνης . . . ³⁰ἦν δὲ μακρὰν ἀπ' αὐτῶν ἀγέλη χοίρων πολλῶν βοσκομένη . . . ³²καὶ ἰδοὺ ὥρμησεν πᾶσα ἡ ἀγέλη κατὰ τοῦ κρημνοῦ εἰς τὴν θάλασσαν . . . ³³οἱ δὲ βόσκοντες ἔφυγον καὶ ἀπελθόντες εἰς τὴν πόλιν . . . ³⁴καὶ ἰδοὺ πᾶσα ἡ πόλις ἐξῆλθεν εἰς ὑπάντησιν τοῦ Ἰησοῦ καὶ ἰδόντες αὐτὸν παρεκάλεσαν, ὅπως μεταβῇ ἀπὸ τῶν ὁρίων αὐτῶν.

ς E L and Δ, reads ἐλθόντι αὐτῷ (an improvement!). Γαδαρηνῶν appears in ℵ* B C* Δ syr^sin pesh. Γερασηνῶν in it and vg; Γεργεσηνῶν in ℵ^c L cop go arm aeth.

The skeleton of Mark is still here, although some things have dropped out and others have been rearranged. The introduction gives only the barest details about the location, and even those are in the form of participles, which is Matthew's characteristic way of downplaying the setting of a story. For Matthew, v. 28 is the introduction to a pericope, rather than a statement about Jesus' itinerary. The end of v. 28 looks like a clarification, and v. 30, with μακράν instead of Mark's ἐκεῖ (5:11), heightens the effect of the miracle. The city (Gadara) is named only in v. 33. Mark's conclusion (5:18ff) drops out, including his mention of the Decapolis. This omission can be explained by the fact that Matthew sets this narrative within a series of miracle stories, and thus his version cannot be encumbered with such details. Matthew's other abbreviations of Mark's text can be understood the same way.[52] There is a more serious difficulty in the fact that two demoniacs are mentioned, and it will not suffice to explain this by saying that Matthew amplifies Mark. What if Matthew is more accurate, and Mark has left out part of the truth by concentrating on the more important of the two diseased men? Would this difference be irrelevant, just something of an oversight on Matthew's part, because he did not read Mark carefully? Or does the number two perhaps come from the story in Mark 1:23–26, a story that Matthew left out?[53]

---

52. "Matthew does not omit this unseemly story, but he does shorten it" (Wellhausen, *Matthew*, 39). J. Weiss thinks Matthew's report is curiously short, and he suggests that there might have been a later revision of Mark's text (J. Weiss, 187).

53. Cf. Klostermann, *Matthäus*, 217. Spitta offers a very complicated explanation (Spitta, *Die synoptische Grundschrift*, 187ff).

Luke 8:26-39, by contrast, expands upon the itinerary in Mark:

²⁶ καὶ κατέπλευσαν εἰς τὴν χώραν τῶν Γεργεσηνῶν, ἥτις ἐστὶν ἀντίπερα τῆς Γαλιλαίας. ²⁷ἐξελθόντι δὲ αὐτῷ ἐπὶ τὴν γῆν ὑπήντησεν ἀνήρ τις ἐκ τῆς πόλεως . . . καὶ ἐν οἰκίᾳ οὐκ ἔμενεν, ἀλλ' ἐν τοῖς μνήμασιν. ²⁸ ἰδὼν δὲ τὸν Ἰησοῦν . . . ³² ἦν δὲ ἐκεῖ ἀγέλη χοίρων ἱκανῶν βοσκομένων ἐν τῷ ὄρει . . . ³³ καὶ ὥρμησεν ἡ ἀγέλη κατὰ τοῦ κρημνοῦ εἰς τὴν λίμνην . . . ³⁴ἰδόντες δὲ οἱ βόσκοντες τὸ γεγονὸς ἔφυγον καὶ ἀπήγγειλαν εἰς τὴν πόλιν καὶ εἰς τοὺς ἀγρούς . . . ³⁷καὶ ἠρώτησαν αὐτὸν ἅπαν τὸ πλῆθος τῆς περιχώρου τῶν Γεργεσηνῶν ἀπελθεῖν ἀπ' αὐτῶν . . . αὐτὸς δὲ ἐμβὰς εἰς πλοῖον ὑπέστρεψεν . . . ³⁸ἐδέετο δὲ αὐτοῦ ὁ ἀνήρ . . . εἶναι σὺν αὐτῷ· ἀπέλυσεν δὲ αὐτὸν λέγων· ³⁹ὑπόστρεφε εἰς τὸν οἶκόν . . . καὶ ἀπῆλθεν, καθ' ὅλην τὴν πόλιν κηρύσσων ὅσα ἐποίησεν αὐτῷ ὁ Ἰησοῦς.

Later lectionaries, as several mss show, read ὁ ις after κατέπλευσαν; cf. the comment above on Mark 5:1. Γεργεσηνῶν is ready by ℵ* L 33 cop arm aeth; Γαδαρηνῶν by A Δ syr go; Γερασηνῶν by B D it and vg. In v. 27 D has καὶ ἐξῆλθον ἐκ τῆς πόλεως. These words are missing from some mss. In v. 32, ἱκανῶν is missing from D. In v. 37 D reads πάντες καὶ ἡ χώρα. With regard to Γεργεσηνῶν the tradition varies in both v. 26 and v. 37. Instead of πλοῖον in v. 37 (typically Lukan: without the article!), A and Δ have τὸ πλοῖον. In v. 39 D improves the text with πορεύου in place of ὑπόστρεφε.

Luke does not abbreviate Mark as much as Matthew does, making only a few stylistic alterations. While Mark reports Jesus' arrival in the land of the Gerasenes, Luke starts with his voyage there, which is a deliberate extension of the story.⁵⁴ "Ἥτις ἐστὶν ἀντίπερα is the sort of explanatory addendum that Luke loves, and whether the geography is correct is an entirely different matter, since the third evangelist does not appear to have had any clear idea about the setting. The word τις after ἀνήρ is typical of Luke (cf. Acts 5:1), and the mention of the fact that the man came from the city (ἐκ τῆς πόλεως) is a Lukan addition. The number of the pigs is toned down (as in Matthew) and described as ἱκανοί. Verse 37 is a clarification. The Decapolis is not mentioned; instead it is said that the healed man spread the word about Jesus throughout the city. I cannot find a valid reason for this change, although it may have seemed to Luke as if a new setting would disrupt the topographical arrangement.

---

54. Spitta notices this, but incorrectly interprets it as a sign that Luke's text is original (Spitta, *Die synoptische Grundschrift*, 184). He goes on to argue that Luke's reading ("Gergesenes") is the oldest, and that Mark grossly misunderstood it, turning it into "Gerasenes." Yet Spitta produces no evidence.

Jairus' Daughter and the Hemorrhaging Woman
(Mark 5:21-43; Matt 9:18-26; Luke 8:40-56)

In Mark there follow two stories that have been joined together with the following framework:

²¹ καὶ διαπεράσοντας τοῦ Ἰησοῦ ἐν τῷ πλοίῳ εἰς τὸ πέραν πάλιν συνήχθη ὄχλος πολὺς ἐπ' αὐτόν, καὶ ἦν παρὰ τὴν θάλασσαν. ²² καὶ ἔρχεται εἰς τῶν ἀρχισυναγώγων, ὀνόματι Ἰάειρος . . . ²⁴ καὶ ἀπῆλθεν μετ' αὐτοῦ καὶ ἠκολούθη αὐτῷ ὄχλος πολὺς . . . ²⁵ καὶ γυνὴ οὖσα ἐν ῥύσει αἵματος δώδεκα ἔτη . . . ²⁷ ἀκούσασα τὰ περὶ τοῦ Ἰησοῦ, ἐλθοῦσα ἐν τῷ ὄχλῳ ὄπισθεν ἥψατο τοῦ ἱματίου αὐτοῦ . . . (the healing takes place) . . . ³⁵ ἔτι αὐτοῦ λαλοῦντος ἔρχονται ἀπὸ τοῦ ἀρχισυναγώγου . . . ³⁷ καὶ οὐκ ἀφῆκεν οὐδένα μετ' αὐτοῦ συνακολουθῆσαι, εἰ μὴ τὸν Πέτρον καὶ Ἰάκωβον καὶ Ἰωάννην . . . ³⁸ καὶ ἔρχονται εἰς τὸν οἶκον τοῦ ἀρχισυναγώγου.

D and it lack ἐν τῷ πλοίῳ. The placement of πάλιν is uncertain: א D it pesh read εἰς τὸ πέραν πάλιν, so that πάλιν goes with συνήχθη; but A B C L vg read πάλιν εἰς τὸ πέραν, so that it goes with διαπεράσοντας. Instead of ἐπ' αὐτόν D has the easier reading πρὸς αὐτόν; cf. it and vg: *ad illum, ad eum*. καὶ ἦν, which interrupts the flow somewhat, is missing from D and eth. In v. 22, ς A C arm go read ἰδού after καὶ (cf. Matt 9:18; Luke 8:41). D has τις instead of εις; cf. vg: *quidam*. The words ὀνόματι Ἰάειρος are lacking in D. The early church began a new pericope with v. 24b; cf. the note in Tischendorf: *initio lectionis eccles*. In v. 25, τις is inserted after γυνή in ς D arm go. Instead of οὐδένα in v. 37, D has the stronger οὐδὲ ἕνα; cf. it and vg: *non quemquam*.

In contrast to the preceding narrative, here the location is not precisely specified. If the evangelist was paying attention to geography, then τὸ πέραν must mean the western shore of the sea, to which Jesus now returns from the eastern shore. We should probably think of a setting in the area around Capernaum, since Jairus, to whose house Jesus will go, likely came from Capernaum. As far as I can see, then, there are no exegetical problems with the scenic details; on the contrary, the text produces a reasonably clear picture. But there is a problem with the simple phrase εἰς τὸ πέραν. Is it really quite that simple? Does this expression really mean (as so many people think) "to the western shore of the sea"? In general, when we can identify the location to which this phrase refers, the far side of the sea is always in view, as if τὸ πέραν was the equivalent of the Hebrew word עבר. In the Galilean traditions the designation τὸ πέραν means the eastern shore of the sea (cf. Mark

4:35 = Matt 8:18, Matt 8:28; also Mark 6:45 = Matt 14:22; and Mark 8:13 = Matt 16:5). It is the same with εἰς τὸ πέραν τῆς θαλάσσης (Mark 5:1), τὸ πέραν τῆς λίμνης (Luke 8:22), and with the prepositional phrase πέραν τῆς θαλάσσης (John 6:1, 17, 22, 25). The expression πέραν τοῦ Ἰορδάνου (Mark 3:8; Matt 4:15; Mark 10:1 = Matt 19:1; John 1:28; 3:26; 10:40) is also instructive. In all of these cases the expression designates the eastern side of the sea, in Jordan, as it always does when the text presupposes a Galilean perspective. From this point of view, Mark 5:21 is quite unique. Of course from the eastern shore of the sea, the western side can also be referred to as τὸ πέραν. The only parallel for this might be in John 6:17, where it says ἤρχοντο πέραν τῆς θαλάσσης εἰς Καφαρναούμ; but on the basis of Mark 3:8 (where πέραν τοῦ Ἰορδάνου means "from across the Jordan"), John 6:17 can be translated "they came from the other side of the sea to Capernaum." Even less relevant is Mark 6:45, where Bethsaida is said to be on the eastern shore of the lake.[55] Whoever (and now I am thinking especially of the first listeners and readers, who spread and read the story as an independent episode) reads the phrase εἰς τὸ πέραν in 5:21 thinks of the place named in 5:1 as the eastern shore of the sea. It is significant that Luther unintentionally translated the same Greek expression in 5:1 and 5:21 with two different German phrases: "the far side of the sea" (5:1) and "over here" (5:21). But is the meaning "eastern shore" impossible, since "western shore" poses so many problems? Not in the slightest, if we stop thinking that there is a direct chronological connection between 5:20 and 5:21. It can be read in such a way that a new story, set on the eastern shore, begins in 5:21. We can look for the house of Jairus just as easily in Bethsaida, on the northeastern shore, as in Capernaum.

It cannot be denied, moreover, that the connection between v. 21 and v. 22 is not very strong. The narrative stops for a rest with the words καὶ ἦν παρὰ τὴν θάλασσαν. Verse 21 almost seems like a summary statement: Jesus goes here and there (cf. 2:13), always surrounded by a great crowd of people. The many variants in D, already cited above, show that the narrative is not flowing along smoothly here. The tradition may well have begun a new unit with v. 22, and v. 21 might be a piece of rubble from an itinerary, but the connection between v. 21 and v. 22 probably was already there in the tradition.[56] It is not Mark's style to introduce highly detailed descriptions of place, if v. 21 can be seen as a general designation of place.

55. In John 6:17, D reads εἰς τὸ πέραν, probably under the influence of Mark 6:45. The debate about Mark 6:45 must consider the question of Bethsaida more thoroughly.

56. B. Weiss rightly says, "Once again the general presentation of the situation . . . cuts away every temporal connection with what precedes" (B. Weiss, *Markus und Lukas*, 81). Harmonizers use gaps like these to bring in other material. Among Catholic exegetes, for example, Wohlenberg writes: "If Matthew's home and customs house

It is significant that both of these difficulties were picked up by Luke (8:40-41). Leaning heavily upon Mark he refashioned his introduction into:

⁴⁰ ἐγένετο δὲ ἐν τῷ ὑποστρέφειν τὸν Ἰησοῦν ἀπεδέξατο αὐτὸν ὁ ὄχλος· ἦσαν γὰρ πάντες προσδοκῶντες αὐτόν. ⁴¹ καὶ ἰδοὺ ἦλθεν ἀνήρ, ᾧ ὄνομα Ἰάειρος, καὶ αὐτὸς ἄρχων τῆς συναγωγῆς ὑπῆρχεν.

The reading ἐγένετο δὲ ἐν τῷ is widely supported, but B L 33 cop syr^sin pesh eth all have ἐν δὲ τῷ. ς A C D L Γ Δ Λ read ὑποστρέψαι, which is certainly an improvement.

Gone is εἰς τὸ πέραν, which had been so difficult and unclear, and now the situation is described in clear-cut terms: Jesus comes back (i.e., from the western shore of the sea to the east), and the people who waited for him eagerly now receive him. And since the comment that "Jesus was by the sea" has also dropped away, the story naturally begins with καὶ ἰδού.[57]

Within the narrative itself, a synagogue leader by the name of Jairus plays the leading role. The use of his name poses a problem. In addition to the fact that his name is missing from Mark 5:22 in D, it is also noteworthy that later (Mark 5:35, 38) he is only referred to by his title. That is not especially good style, and it raises the possibility that the isolated mention of his name in v. 22 might be a later addition. We have a similar situation in 10:46 with Bartimaeus and in 15:21 with Simon of Cyrene. In those cases the names were already in the tradition, and in this case also Mark probably got the name Jairus from the tradition, but since his name is only occasionally mentioned, it may be that at some point the name grew into the tradition. The fact that such things could happen is illustrated by the history of the story about the hemorrhaging woman. In chapter 7 of the Gospel of Nicodemus, we can see that later legend gave her the name Veronica. These kinds of legendary accretions may also have been added during the earliest period, before the origin of our Gospels. Keep in mind that an allegorical or symbolic significance can be detected behind the name Jairus, which comes from the Aramaic root יאיר, meaning "illuminator" or "awakener." But at this point we are getting into highly speculative territory.[58]

---

were at the harbor, there is plenty of room and time for both of the stories we read in Matt 9:9-17 (the call of Matthew) and in 9:1-8 to have taken place. The appearance of Jairus makes sense, since he would have been a dinner guest at Matthew's home, where the sayings of Jesus about fasting and not fasting took place (cf. 9:18, ταῦτα αὐτοῦ λαλοῦντος)" (Wohlenberg, Markus, 160-61). Hypotheses like this obviously have no foundation.

57. Spitta makes no mention of this point.

58. Merx argues for the right to look for a symbolic meaning here. Commenting on the textual variant Joàrasch in syr^sin, he proposes such meanings as "the prayer" or "the

We come then to the outline of the narrative itself. Jairus, a leader of the synagogue, comes to Jesus with a request that his daughter be healed, and Jesus goes with him, as a large crowd of people follows. Among them is a woman who has suffered a hemorrhage for twelve years. The narrative closely follows her as she makes her way to Jesus through the crowd from behind and touches his garment. She is healed. Jesus notices that "power has gone forth from him" and turns to ask the crowd. The woman throws herself at his feet. While they are talking, news arrives that Jairus' daughter is dead. Jesus goes into the house with only Peter, James, and John and raises the girl, whose age (twelve years) we have learned along the way.

I have only briefly recounted the course of the narrative in order to show that one story develops out of the other, and that the two stories are closely woven together. There is no doubt that the connection of the two stories pre-dates the Gospel of Mark. This kind of composition, especially one so tidy and thorough, is not his style. Is it possible that the pre-Markan tradition interwove two stories that originally had nothing to do with each other? That too is highly unlikely; it is pure coincidence that the daughter was twelve years old and the woman was sick for twelve years. The significant problem here rises from the fact that the gospel tradition fell out in separate and self-enclosed narratives. What then must have happened to produce this remarkable combination? There can be only one answer: it was based on real memories of an event that had actually happened. The healing of the woman took place on the way to Jairus' house.[59]

Both of the synoptic parallels preserve the interweaving of the two stories. Luke 8:40–56 limits itself to a few small stylistic alterations, such as in v. 44, where παραχρῆμα replaces εὐθύς. The depiction of the mourners at the house is also slightly abbreviated, but this kind of rearrangement is especially characteristic of Luke's authorial style: while Mark mentions the young girl's age more or less in passing at the end of the story, Luke puts it in the introduction.[60] Besides, she is the only daughter mentioned. It is totally superfluous to ask whether Luke made use of special tradition or just had better information. Luke could have easily distilled this

---

Lord be praised" (Merx, *Markus und Lukas*, 48).

59. This case is an instructive example of how valuable it can be to undertake literary investigations of the ways in which historical events have been elucidated in the narratives. The sequence of stories in Mark 3:20ff, to which Klostermann has referred, is however a completely different matter (Klostermann, *Markus*, 42).

60. Spitta is deeply impressed by the fact that Mark takes his time introducing the age of the girl (Spitta, *Die synoptische Grundschrift*, 195). But as I see it, this fact is decisive for recognizing that Mark's version of the story is original. The earliest narrator, an eyewitness, related what he had seen. So he did not mention her age until he had described what had happened.

information out of the total story that was reported by the father, the mother, and their friends.⁶¹

Matthew relocated the narrative (Matt 9:18-26) and drastically shortened it. The two changes go together:

¹⁸ταῦτα αὐτοῦ λαλοῦντος αὐτοὺς ἰδοὺ ἄρχων εἰσελθών . . . ¹⁹καὶ ἐγερθεὶς ὁ Ἰησοῦς ἀκολούθει αὐτῷ καὶ οἱ μαθηταὶ αὐτοῦ· ²⁰καὶ ἰδοὺ γυνὴ αἱμορροοῦσα . . . ²² ὁ δὲ στραφεὶς καὶ ἰδὼν αὐτὴν εἶπεν . . . καὶ ἐσώθη ἡ γυνὴ ἀπὸ τῆς ὥρας ἐκείνης. ²³καὶ ἐλθὼν ὁ Ἰησοῦς εἰς τὴν οἰκίαν τοῦ ἄρχοντος . . . ²⁵ ὅτε δὲ ἐξεβλήθη ὁ ὄχλος, εἰσελθὼν ἐκράτησεν τῆς χειρὸς αὐτῆς, καὶ ἠγέρθη τὸ κοράσιον. ²⁶καὶ ἐξῆλθεν ἡ φήμη αὕτη εἰς ὅλην τὴν γῆν ἐκείνην.

Verses 18-19: εἰσελθών (ℵᶜ C D E), εἰς ἐλθών (Δ), εἰς προσελθών (ℵᵇ B vg), προσελθών (ℵ*), τὶς προσελθών (L); ἠκολούθει (ℵᶜ C D 33; cf. Vg: *sequebatur*, which is better than ἠκολούθησεν in ς B F L Γ Δ). In v. 22, ὁ ις is inserted after ὁ δέ by ςᵇ B C vg. In place of αὕτη in v. 26, ℵ C 33 cop read αὐτῆς, and D has αὐτοῦ.

How did this narrative get to its current position in the Gospel of Matthew? Clearly it now stands within the report of Jesus' healing activity in chapters 8 and 9, but why was it separated from the story of the Gerasene demoniac? It is closely related to two other stories—the healing of two blind men (Matt 9:27-31) and of a mute demoniac (Matt 9:32-34)—and along with those stories it serves (as has long been suspected) as an illustration of Jesus' point in Matt 11:5, where he sends word to John the Baptist that the blind and deaf are being healed and the dead are being raised. As we interpret Mark, it is important to keep in mind that Matthew, the earliest interpreter of Mark, regarded these stories of the storm at sea and the Gerasene demoniac as a unit, even though he cut and rearranged the narrative at Mark 5:20. In my view, that is further evidence of the looseness in Mark 5:20-21. Matthew does not set this scene beside the sea. In his characteristic way, he introduces the story with a participial construction. The number of people who surround Jesus is not specified, and everything that laid the groundwork for the hemorrhaging woman has therefore also dropped out. While Mark and Luke both describe the little girl as sick and dying, according to Matt 9:18 she is already dead (Matthew is looking ahead to 11:5 and wants to narrate a genuine resurrection). The story is therefore much more condensed in Matthew than in Mark (only 9 verses long, as opposed to 23 in Mark). The father's title is also different

---

61. Here too Spitta is cautious (*Die synoptische Grundschrift*, 195). He suspects that the redactor of the Gospel of Luke, who had just inserted the story of the young man at Nain (7:11-17), got the word μονογενής (8:42) from there.

in Matthew: he is called ἄρχων, which can mean something along the lines of "community leader." Nor is it mentioned that Jesus was accompanied by only three of his most trusted disciples. There is no single explanation that can account for all these differences, which raises questions about how Matthew actually went about using Mark. Perhaps in telling this story Matthew made more frequent use of his own memory.

Matthew 9:26 is a clause that recalls the form of Mark 1:28.

Excursus: The Special Connection of the Three Stories: The Itinerary and Arrangement of Mark 4:35—5:43par.

The preceding discussion has made it abundantly clear that three stories—the storm at sea (I), the Gerasene demoniac (II), and the daughter of Jairus (III)—stand in a special relationship with each other. The connection is easiest to see in I and II, but (at least in Mark) it is also plainly evident in II and III. Thus I, II, and III went together in the tradition. From this perspective we can begin to explain how the stories came to be in their present position. Jesus was mocked in the house of Jairus, so he sought to conceal the miracle, a motif of opposition that is absent from I, but it is very strong in II. We might suspect that Mark would not have taken up I and II if they had not already been directly connected with the story of the young girl's resuscitation,[62] but there is another entirely different explanation. Scholarship has already rightly and repeatedly confirmed that in the long section about Jesus and the people (3:7ff), Mark wants to make one specific point, based on a specific theme: Jesus preaches and works in the face of opposition from the people. It would be pure speculation on our part to imagine that this idea has been thoroughly and completely worked into the Gospel. Here and there collections of stories that already existed in the tradition have disrupted the evangelist's compositional plans, so that Mark was not willing or able to execute his idea fully and totally. Yet one thing is certain: he put no particular effort into constructing a continuous itinerary. When it was possible to reconstruct an itinerary, i.e., when pieces of the tradition contained the traces of an itinerary in their

---

62. That is the opinion of J. Weiss (cf. J. Weiss, 179ff). Weiss gets himself caught in a contradiction when he says that I and II may have been brought in because of III, and then elsewhere he says that 4:35ff was always closely bound to 4:1–34. Wendling disagrees with Weiss (cf. Wendling, 44n1), but Weiss does not seem to notice.

introductions, he arranged those pieces in roughly chronological order. This resulted partly from the stories themselves: stories of the sea were put alongside each other. But it is impossible for us to be able to tell whether they all happened at the same time, and it also remains unclear whether (for example) the Gerasene demoniac and Jairus' daughter belong together chronologically. After all, 5:21ff could have originally been situated in some other historical context.

In matters like this we must guard against overestimating the Markan outline. Advocates of the Markan Hypothesis tend in that direction when they say that Matthew damaged the connections by relocating Mark 5:21ff. Scholars examine the individual stories and pose questions to this supposed chronology in Mark: Jesus preaches among the people (4:1ff), in the evening (or late afternoon) of the same day he sails to the land of the Gerasenes (4:35), upon his arrival he heals a demoniac (5:1ff), then he sails back, is called by Jairus, heals a woman along the way and then raises Jairus' daughter at his house (5:21ff). And all of that is supposed to have happened on one day. A rather significant chunk of the public ministry of Jesus in Mark supposedly all took place on one and the same day.[63] With so many reasons to regard that

---

63. Wohlenberg is typical: "Probably there is no temporal gap between 5:21 and 5:22 . . . Chapters 4 and 5 look like a chronological unit" (Wohlenberg, *Markus*, 119). He proceeds to follow the chronology still further back. Mark 4:1 does not contain any information about time, but in the Matthean parallel (Matt 13:1ff) there is a clear indication: ἐν τῇ ἡμέρᾳ ἐκείνῃ. Wohlenberg takes this phrase over to Mark and concludes that the story in Mark 4:1 must have taken place on the same day as the Beelzebul saying in Mark 3:20ff.

Wendling usually has a very sharp scholarly eye, but even he does not recognize how loose the composition in 5:21ff really is. He only wants to show that 4:35—5:43 is an earlier form of the narrative taken from Ur-Mark. He settles unfairly into a perspective that is rather dogmatic: "In the grouping of 4:35—5:43, teaching is not the subject anymore; miracles suddenly are the main event." Reimarus Secundus is quoted with approval: "In Pseudo-Mark the mysterious person of Jesus steps into the foreground" (Wendling, 47). He summarizes his literary analysis in the following table (Wendling, 50):

1:16–21	Sea Scene	4:35–41
1:23–28	Exorcism	5:1–20
1:29–34	Miracles	5:21–42
1:29–31	Healing a Woman	5:25–34

It would take us too far afield to offer a detailed response here. Yet the content of that response should already be clear from the textual analyses I have offered so far. The table is a masterpiece of far-fetched sophistry. It doesn't even fit in with what Wendling himself has already said about the difference between this "earlier layer" and the report

conclusion as absurd, scholars are forced to begin slicing up the narrative. The phrase ὀψίας γενομένης looks suspicious to some,[64] while others insert a break between 5:20 and 21.[65] These are embarrassing particulars, and much as we might want to hang on to a chronological thread in Mark, that thread has been stretched beyond the breaking point, and scholars end up with a serious misunderstanding of the techniques of composition actually used by the second evangelist. Others prefer to read the stories from Matthew's point of view, who puts the parables in chap. 13, the pericopes about the storm at sea and the Gerasene demoniac in chap. 8, and the story of Jairus a little later in chap. 9.[66] Still others fall back on Luke, who pulls apart the events described by Mark, puts them into a different sequence, and thereby arouses an impression of historicity.[67]

But the chronology and topography that are contained in the Gospels have the status of a framework. Individual pieces of that framework could easily be altered, and they could just as easily drop out. This is one of the characteristic properties of folk-narratives, i.e., that they contain hardly any chronology or topography, and often none at all. In other words, sometimes their pictures are framed, and sometimes they are not. On the whole the collectors of these narratives did not substantially change them.

Jesus' Rejection in Nazareth
(Mark 6:1–6; Matt 13:53–58)

¹καὶ ἐξῆλθεν ἐκεῖθεν καὶ ἔρχεται εἰς τὴν πατρίδα αὐτοῦ, καὶ ἀκολουθοῦσιν αὐτῷ οἱ μαθηταὶ αὐτοῦ. ²καὶ γενομένου σαββάτου ἤρξατο διδάσκειν ἐν τῇ συναγωγῇ· καὶ οἱ πολλοὶ ἀκούοντες ἐξεπλήσσοντο λέγοντες ...

ℵ B C L Δ read ἔρχεται, while ς A go read ἦλθεν; it and vg read: et egressus inde abiit (cf. Luke 4:16). The past tense is a stylistic

about the day in Capernaum.

64. J. Weiss, Das älteste Evangelium, 181.

65. "Did Jesus spend only one night in Perea? The evangelist can hardly have meant that" (Windisch, Die Dauer, 145).

66. "Matthew introduces this story in a completely different context and that most unfortunately" (Loisy, Les Évangiles synoptiques, 1:813).

67. As I have already demonstrated several times, this is typical of Merx and especially Spitta.

gloss. D has καπῆλθεν, a corruption of either καὶ ἦλθεν or καὶ ἀπῆλθεν. Perhaps the scribe who wrote D just made a mistake. For the present tense ἀκολουθοῦσιν, it reads *secuti sunt* and vg has *sequebantur*. In place of γενομένου σαββάτου (vg: *facto sabbato*), D has ἡμέρᾳ σαββάτων (cf. Luke 4:16). Several mss. insert ὁ ις after ἤρξατο, an indication that the pericope began with 6:2. B and L read οἱ πολλοί; ς ℵ C D Δ drop οἱ. But the article is original, since it refers to the crowd, a crowd that may not have understood Jesus but was certainly known to readers and hearers of the story. In a similar way most witnesses drop τούς from before πολλούς in 9:26, and ℵ and D drop ὁ from before πολύς in 12:37.

At first glance this story seems to fit well with the one that precedes it, but upon closer examination, we can detect a seam between 5:43 and 6:1. The word ἐκεῖθεν is usually taken as having only a general meaning, but if in this case we take it more literally, it is a reference to the house of Jairus, from which Jesus has emerged, in order to go back to his hometown. Statistical analysis of ἐκεῖθεν, which appears fifteen times in the Gospel of Mark, suggests that the word was in the tradition prior to the writing of the Gospel. We had to draw the opposite conclusion about Matthew, who uses the word some twelve times. While Matthew certainly used this kind of clamp, we have already become familiar with Mark's style of redaction, whereby he arranged the narratives in the same order in which he took them from the tradition. As a result, we cannot reach any conclusions about the chronological relationship of this pericope with what precedes it. By "his hometown" Mark means Nazareth (cf. 1:9, 24). This village is located about thirty kilometers from the See of Galilee, and thus it can be reached by foot in about a day. Since the Sabbath (v. 2) begins on Friday evening, Jesus could been home by the evening.[68] Did the evangelist have these kinds of temporal connections in mind? Not at all. We understand him better if we notice that this story in Nazareth forms the climax of 3:7–6:13: Jesus carries out his ministry among the people with misunderstanding and opposition on all sides, and now even the people in his own home want nothing to do with him. So he leaves his hometown; indeed, he leaves Galilee altogether. Our pericope thus has no genuine chronological setting, and there is a seam between 5:43 and 6:1.[69]

---

68. Wohlenberg, *Markus*, 169.

69. Cf. B. Weiss, *Markus und Lukas*, 88; Wellhausen, *Mark*, 47; Loisy, *Mark*, 167; J. Weiss, 198. Even here Klostermann cannot break entirely free from the effort to protect the Markan outline: "Luke is totally wrong to put this effort by Jesus to minister in his hometown at the beginning of his activity" (Klostermann, *Markus*, 45). Cf., by contrast,

It is striking that the names of the disciples who accompany Jesus are specifically listed here, and all the more so because they are not the subject of what follows. This kind of detail speaks for a strong and true tradition, for Jesus was obviously not always and everywhere accompanied by his disciples (cf. 1:35-36; 2:1). Here it is different, and the tradition has held on to that. Or the disciples may be named here because the community imagined that Jesus was always surrounded by his disciples. But then why aren't they mentioned every time? In this regard it is important to observe that however much the Christians may have thought about the disciples, at the end of the day they heard, told, and passed on pericopes about Jesus. That is why the disciples are not mentioned in Matt 13:53, for example.

Thus v. 3 looks like genuine tradition and historical reality. The particulars about persons must come from the old Galilean tradition. Mary, the mother of Jesus, is named, as are his brothers James, Joses (or Joseph),[70] Simon, and Judas. And of Jesus' sisters it says, "Are they not here with us?" Perhaps this detail might be taken to mean that the brothers of Jesus lived elsewhere (in Capernaum?) and maybe his mother too. That conclusion is often drawn, but in my opinion it is mistaken. For v. 3 includes a kind of parallelism: 1) mother and brothers, 2) sisters. Thus in the second line of the parallelism, the form of expression is altered, but that does not mean there is any special accent on εἰσὶν ὧδε πρὸς ἡμᾶς. The verse does not rule out the idea that Jesus' mother and brothers lived in Nazareth.

Jesus himself is described as ὁ τέκτων. It would be most interesting if we could be certain about that: unfortunately here we cannot establish a confident connection between the original tradition and historical fact. Matthew has here ὁ τοῦ τέκτονος υἱός, as do several good manuscripts of Mark, so the uncertainty cannot be resolved text-critically. Nor do historical deliberations cut any ice. Based on the usage of this terminology in common speech and in the rabbinic literature, Jesus could have been pursuing the vocation of anything from a carpenter to a construction worker, or a builder, or a blacksmith. The meaning of the term τέκτων is not clarified by its Aramaic correlates either. The early Christian tradition is known to have told all kinds of stories about Jesus' vocation.[71] Some people may have taken offense at the idea of Jesus as a day-laborer, and therefore they have sought to weaken

---

my remarks above on Luke 4:16-30.

70. Matt 13:55 reads "Joseph." Clearly Joseph and Joses could be used interchangeably. The form Ἰωσῆς has a more elegant ending than Ἰωσήφ, which is a mere transliteration of the Hebrew.

71. On this point, cf. B. Weiss, *Markus und Lukas*, 89; Pölzl, *Marcus*, 146. There is a very interesting definition in the Gospel of Thomas 13; cf. Hennecke, *Neutestamentliche Apokryphen*, 73.

the offense by calling him the son of a day-laborer. Or perhaps the text has been influenced by the doctrine of the virgin birth: an effort was made to evade the impression that Jesus was the son of his father, so here he is not called the son of the τέκτων, but the τέκτων himself. We often have to reckon with these kinds of adjustments. Sometimes we cannot tell when they were inserted (before or after our Gospels?) and therefore sometimes the original text cannot be reconstructed. The popular notion that Jesus followed in his father's vocation may in fact correspond to historical reality.[72]

But this one difficulty does not change the fact that in 6:3 we find ourselves standing upon the lowest layer of the best tradition. It was certainly not in the interests of the early church to depict such negative conduct on the part of Jesus' relatives, especially not of James, who plays the key role. The same goes for the rather unreflective comment at the end of the narrative, that Jesus could not perform any miracles in his hometown. The whole story is slightly incoherent. On the one hand it reports Jesus preaching on the Sabbath, which provokes objections from his hearers, so that he comes up with the saying about a prophet in his own hometown (vv. 2a, 4). On the other hand, it says that the Nazarenes argued with each other about Jesus, who had come back to town. That is why Jesus cannot do any miracles there (vv. 2b, 3c, 5, 6a). It would be best to put v. 3a, b with v. 2. The first report is anchored in a specific situation. The second report can then be understood only if we keep in mind the various miracles that have already been narrated in chapter 5. It is not coincidental that 1 and 2 are woven together. These stories about Jesus were told by Christians, for whom Jesus was the great teacher and miracle worker. If a particular pericope did not contain anything about his miracles, those miracles could still be referred to, and his δυνάμεις τοιαῦται could still be mentioned. In such ways these narratives effectively burst the bonds of their own framework. The narrative in Mark 6 is thus understandable as a first draft written by the early Christian community. True, in a papyrus from Oxyrhynchus there are two disconnected sayings of Jesus, the first of which is found in Mark 6:4 and the second in Mark 6:5; but that does not mean that Mark created a context for the sayings here, or that he transposed the actual order. Mark 6:4 grew out of a specific situation. By now we are so familiar with this saying outside of its framework, that (as has already been mentioned) Mark 6:5 seems to have a certain lack of coherence about it. Jesus may have been in Nazareth

---

72. So the Acts of Peter 23: "Jesus, who was the son of a carpenter, was also himself a carpenter." On the problem of Jesus' relatives, cf. Th. Zahn, "Brüder und Vettern Jesu," 225-26. On the details, cf. also Klostermann, *Markus*, 46; Wohlenberg, *Markus*, 170; Merx, *Markus und Lukas*, 49-50. An excursus on the Catholic interpretation of Jesus' cousins can be found in Pölzl, *Marcus*, 148-49.

at various times, and the report as we now have it may be a conflation of two of th`ose occasions, but the tradition had long depicted a definitive conflict between Jesus and Nazareth. In this case the combination of the sayings gives the impression of being in the earliest tradition, which is narrating the story for the first time, rather than of a later addition. Whatever Mark's evaluation of these sayings might have been, he found them in the tradition and recorded them here in his Gospel.[73]

We have already explained that the "hometown" mentioned in 6:1 is Nazareth. In any case Mark is thinking of Nazareth, for he knows of its existence (1:9; Ἰησοῦς ἀπὸ Ναζαρὲτ τῆς Γαλιλαίας), and in 1:24 he calls Jesus Ναζαρηνός. So he thinks of him as a man from Nazareth, but it is not at all clear that Ναζαρηνός or Ναζωραῖος always have this meaning. Certainly the early Christians looked for a deeper meaning in these names. Matthew 2:23, for example, cites "the prophets" (probably Isa 11:1, נֵצֶר = son, branch) and calls Jesus "a Nazarene." Does this suggest the possibility that there was no place called Nazareth? Not any more than the words Γαλιλαία τῶν ἐθνῶν in Matt 4:15 suggest the possibility that there was no place called Galilee. I can see two possibilities: 1) the place name Nazareth already had a meaning that leaned in the direction of "branch"; and 2) in popular etymology (and because of the similarity in the sound) the place name took on this connotation. But why should this have been the case? This is not an instance of high-verbal wordplay on the part of Matthew, as we have already seen in Matt 4:15. It is a matter that occupied the attention of wider circles in primitive Christianity, for it was a problem for the early Christians that the Messiah had come from tiny Nazareth.[74] The name is mentioned in neither

---

73. Wellhausen starts with the contradiction between ἐξεπλήσσοντο and ἐσκανδαλίζοντο and asserts: "It appears that a false connection has been introduced into the narrative at 6:2" (Wellhausen, *Mark*, 44-45). In his translation he simply leaves out v. 4, with no comment. Spitta distinguishes between the two motives named above and projects the existence of a "pre-Lukan" document with a continuous narrative. But he misses the connection between chapters 5 and 6, and so he takes τοιαῦται δυνάμεις to refer back to what has preceded. He identifies v. 2a and v. 4 as secondary, and thus he is able to attribute 6:1-2b and 6:5 to his "pre-synoptic" document (Spitta, *Die synoptische Grundschrift*, 201ff). Wendling, by contrast, rightly holds onto the connection between chapters 5 and 6 (Wendling, 52). He thus regards the phrase τοιαῦται δυνάμεις as unseemly, but when he explains away the entirety of Mark 6:1-6 as a redactional insertion, his plan comes to grief. The idea that it derives from 1:21, 22 and 27 (cf. the table in Wendling, p. 52) is overdone. The saying from Oxyrhynchus does not weigh against Mark: it may have been distilled from Mark, or it may have existed in a parallel tradition. Literary studies of 6:1-6 can establish neither that this is the work of the evangelist, nor that it is some other kind of tradition.

74. Cf. the expression in John 1:47: "Can anything good come from Nazareth?" Some exegetes regard Mark 6:1-6 as the basis for this antipathy. Cf. Bauer, *Johannes*, 25.

the Hebrew Bible nor the Talmud, which refers to more than sixty (60) Galilean towns, villages, and cities. Nor is it mentioned by the Jewish historian Josephus or in the Apocrypha. Because the problem is serious, from the very beginning it was solved by resorting to allegories.⁷⁵ But the fact that Nazareth is not mentioned in our text should not be regarded as a *crux interpretum*, since Jesus' hometown is honored here with the designation ἡ πατρὶς αὐτοῦ, and the name Nazareth was naturally dropped. Furthermore, this is the only pericope set in Nazareth. As historians we must reckon with the distinctiveness of the tradition as it lies before us, and that distinctiveness is basic to the pericope in Mark 6:1ff.⁷⁶

The Markan outline had an effect on Matthew when he attached 13:53-58, the rejection of Jesus at Nazareth, to the great parable discourse. Since the story of the daughter of Jairus and the hemorrhaging woman had already been set in another context, Matthew fashioned an introduction that is typical of him (cf. 7:28; 11:1; 19:1; 26:1): καὶ ἐγένετο ὅτε ἐτέλεσεν ὁ Ἰησοῦς τὰς παραβολὰς ταύτας, μετῆρεν ἐκεῖθεν. The components of this introduction occur individually in other places, beginning with καὶ ἐγένετο ὅτε ἐτέλεσεν (7:28; 11:1; 19:1; 26:1). The verb μεταίρω occurs only in the NT, and only in Matthew (19:1). ἐκεῖθεν is one of Matthew's favorite transitional words. In this case it was already in the text of Mark 6:1-6. Similar details in 26:1 are understandable as the introduction to a pericope, and in 7:28; 11:1; and 19:1 the opening words are built into a summary statement about Jesus' ministry. All of these features can be explained as introductions to and transitions between pericopes. The same holds true in this case, since 13:54 is a good example of a narrative introduction: καὶ ἐλθὼν εἰς τὴν πατρίδα αὐτοῦ.⁷⁷ One can evaluate it in various ways, but 13:53 is simply a bridge between v. 52 and v. 54, and as such it has no chronological value whatsoever. The construction of the narrative is exactly the same as in Mark, except for the fact that the disciples of Jesus are not named as his companions. In my judgment this fact is evidence of a later development: Matthew wanted the

---

75. See A. Drews, *Die Christusmyth*, 25-26. According to Cheyne, the New Testament place name "Nazareth" is pure fiction. Drews may be correct that in ancient Christianity the name Ναζωραῖοι was not a reference to the town of Nazareth. The ancient world had a healthy appetite for all things symbolic and allegorical.

76. This takes care of Wendling's attempt to argue that since Nazareth is not mentioned here, the story must have been spun from the saying in 6:4 (Wendling, 56). Wendling cites W. B. Smith, *Der vorchristliche Jesus*, 44.

77. Syr^sin and other witnesses read "in their *synagogues*." On this point, Merx observes, curiously: "The Greek text has the singular, and thereby gives the wrong impression" (Merx, *Matthäus*, 224).

narrative to be about Jesus, and the disciples might draw focus, like extras in a stage production (which they certainly are in Mark).[78]

This pericope is missing from Luke, who put it into a report (which only he records) about Jesus' first visit to Nazareth (cf. above on Luke 4:16-30).

The conclusion of this pericope about Jesus in Nazareth has prompted an important discussion. Mark 6:6b reads: καὶ περιῆγεν τὰς κώμας κύκλῳ διδάσκων. For those who are able to follow Mark's compositional technique, a remark like this is very important. According to the verse divisions, it belongs to the pericope about Nazareth, and it makes good sense as a closing remark for that scene: because the Nazarenes do not want to have anything to do with him, Jesus goes out into the surrounding region and teaches there. We cannot rule out the possibility that this statement was part of the original form of the Nazareth pericope. Statistical analysis of the words used here is not very productive, but it can be pointed out that περιάγειν appears only here in the Gospel of Mark, and κύκλῳ is also a rare expression. Certainly we are not dealing here with the evangelist's pet vocabulary, which suggests that we may be standing on the ground floor of the tradition. In spite of this, most recent editors, translators, and commentators[79] take the sentence as the introduction to what follows, understanding it as a redactional comment. It is difficult to understand the confidence with which such assertions are made, for in other cases (cf. 1:39) the old verse divisions are left intact. The sentence can scarcely have belonged to the original version of the next pericope, 6:7-13. The individual units of tradition, as they were passed along orally, all went *in medias res* and did not begin with general and basically meaningless designations of place. Does that mean v. 6b should be regarded as an isolated transitional piece, a short summary statement inserted by the evangelist? There have been other cases like that: cf. 1:39; 2:13; 3:7ff. But could this short statement (and we take it that the Nazareth pericope ends with v. 6a) link two stories that originally had no chronological relationship? Some kind of connecting remark is needed in order to make plain the difference in the settings of the two stories. In the absence of any

---

78. Spitta looks for a deeper meaning for this difference, but his argument is not convincing (Spitta, *Die synoptische Grundschrift*, 202, 206).

79. See Tischendorf, von Soden, Nestle, Huck, Weizsäcker, B. Weiss (*Markus und Lukas*, 91), J. Weiss (*Das älteste Evangelium*, 199), Wohlenberg (*Markus*, 172), Pölzl (*Mark*, 150), Loisy (*Les Évangiles synoptiques*, 1:856), Klostermann (*Mark*, 47). Spitta (*Die synoptische Grundschrift*, xxviii) drops v. 6b without comment. Wendling does it first one way, then the other, but has nothing to say about the character of the sentence. In *Urmarkus* (73), he puts 6:1-6 together; then in his second book on page 55 he refers to 6:7-13 as a pericope, but on the very next page he speaks of 6:6-13 as a pericope. Alone among recent interpreters Wellhausen (*Mark*, 44) follows the old verse divisions.

designation of place, the entire scene has to have played out in Nazareth. Yet these details ought not to be pressed too far, or we might end up imagining things that the evangelist never had in mind. If we tackle this problem head-on, if we see in v. 6b something more than merely a connecting remark, we will attribute this sentence to the original version of the preceding pericope. The argument for that choice has already been explicated above.[80] Decide it whatever way you wish, but there is a suture here, lying hidden behind v. 6b, or in v. 6b itself, hiding in plain sight.

There are two reasons for the fact that confidence about this decision is not possible. First, there is the fact that the boundary around a pericope is not always clearly marked, so that sometimes the decision about the introduction and the conclusion may come down to a matter of taste. That shows up in the varying judgments of both ancient and modern interpreters. We have previously encountered this kind of uncertainty at 1:20-21; 1:39-40; 2:12-13; and 3:6-7. That leads us to a second reason: we cannot always tell to what extent the summary statements are the work of the evangelists. In comprehensive summaries like 1:14ff and 3:7ff we will likely answer this question in the affirmative, while shorter statements may possibly belong to the original closings of their pericopes. The question of why a summary statement has been inserted in any particular place can now be further illuminated, as we have seen in our earlier discussion of 3:6-7. These closing sentences, along with the summary statements that were either connected to them or developed from them, have absolutely no topographical or chronological value within the development of the story of Jesus.[81]

What has become of Mark 6:6b in Matthew and Luke? Do these two evangelists perhaps give us a clue to their compositional techniques here? Matthew explicitly tied the statement in 6:6b to the sending out of the disciples, and then he relocated this combination to a completely different position than Mark, creating a summary statement in Matt 9:35 that clearly shows traces of Mark 6:6b: καὶ περιῆγεν ὁ Ἰησοῦς τὰς πόλεις πάσας καὶ τὰς

---

80. J. Weiss sees the problem here, but he holds on to the connection between v. 6b and what follows (J. Weiss, 199). In his view Mark is bound by the tradition here: the sources from which he got the saying already contained it.

81. Unfortunately, efforts are still being made to reconstruct the chronology of Jesus' ministry. Pölzl wants to justify the Lukan outline here, particularly the transition from Luke 8 to Luke 9. The account does not rule out, he says, that "the Savior returned to Capernaum from his missionary journey, as he sent out the apostles for the first time" (Pölzl, *Marcus*, 150). And Wohlenberg thinks it significant that κῶμαι are mentioned here, whereas 1:38 spoke of κωμοπόλεις: "It is consistent with rational, healthy missionary work, to fill first and above all the cities with the ring of the gospel" (Wohlenberg, *Markus*, 173). Declarations of this sort about the course of Jesus' mission work with regard to towns and locations are, in my judgment, floating on thin air.

κώμας, διδάσκων ἐν ταῖς συναγωγαῖς αὐτῶν καὶ κηρύσσων τὸ εὐαγγέλιον τῆς βασιλείας καὶ θεραπεύων πᾶσαν νόσον καὶ πᾶσαν μαλακίαν.[82] This verse has many similarities to 4:23, which for its part developed from 1:39. The structure and content are identical: 1) place of activity: *all* of Galilee (4:23), in all the towns and villages (9:35), and especially in the synagogues (4:23; 9:35). 2) content of activity: a) proclaiming the gospel of the kingdom (4:23; 9:35), b) healing of all forms of disease and weakness (4:23; 9:35). Both summary statements are the work of an evangelist, but their uniformity suggests that traditional material probably lies behind them. We notice for example the term βασιλεία, while Matthew speaks of the βασιλεία τῶν οὐρανῶν. Mark 1:39 contains these same elements in a different order: preaching and healing in the synagogues of all Galilee. Compare that with Luke 4:15: καὶ αὐτὸς ἐδίδασκεν ἐν ταῖς συναγωγαῖς αὐτῶν, and Luke 4:44: καὶ ἦν κηρύσσων εἰς τὰς συναγωγὰς τῆς Ἰουδαίας, or Mark 6:6b and 6:56. The formulaic character is most evident in Acts 10:38: ὃς διῆλθεν εὐεργετῶν καὶ ἰώμενος πάντας τοὺς καταδυναστευομένους ὑπὸ τοῦ διαβόλου.

As in Mark 6:6b, we can again ask whether Matt 9:35 is connected with what precedes or what follows. Here too our editors, translators, and commentators do not agree.[83] Both options are possible: 9:35 could be a sign-off at the end of the Galilean activity of Jesus (4:23–9:34), or it could just as well be a heading for what is coming next. Yet the important thing to notice is that, either way, Matt 9:35 is a bridge between two larger complexes. Matthew 11:1 is exactly the same: a typical connecting verse, which both concludes a speech to the disciples and begins a narrative about Jesus and John the Baptist. Connections between pericopes always swing back and forth like that.[84] There is so much uncertainty in these transitional verses that no logical or chronological or geographical connections lie behind them. If we were to think it was an historical fact that after the healings of two blind men and a mute (Matt 9:27–34), Jesus was known as a teacher and healer in all the cities and villages, we would be spinning a chronological thread that is not there. It was Luke, the author, who took these independent pieces from Mark and used (only) some of them as subordinate conjunctions.

82. ℵ* and L continue with ἐν τῷ λαῷ (from 4:23) καὶ (πολλοὶ) ἠκολούθησαν αὐτῷ (from 4:25). "The addition of ἐν τῷ λαῷ, i.e., in Israel, is anything but harmless, nor is it disposed of with reference to 4:23. It means: he did not heal Gentiles" (Merx, *Markus und Lukas*, 1:155).

83. Von Soden, Nestle, Huck, and apparently Tischendorf connect 9:35 with what follows. But not J. Weiss (*Schriften*, 306): "This sentence, which reaches back to 4:23, forms as it were the signature of this section."

84. In spite of the chapter headings (chap. 10, chap. 11), which connect 11:1 with the pericope that follows, Huck attaches it to the following one. Nestle sets it apart from both the preceding and following verses, clearly showing that it is transitional.

Nor did the third evangelist make use of Mark 6:6 as an introduction to the sending out of the disciples. Since he has moved the Nazareth pericope forward in the story, the disciples are commissioned in a scene directly linked to the story of Jairus' daughter. Obviously Luke is thinking of the scene in Capernaum, which looked to him like the point of departure for Jesus' journeys. A remark about Jesus traveling through villages around the region would have destroyed that setting.

The Sending out of the Disciples
(Mark 6:7-13; Matt 10:1-42; Luke 9:1-6; 10:1-12)

Mark 6:7-13 is a pericope that floats in the air, both chronologically and topographically: καὶ προσκαλεῖται τοὺς δώδεκα καὶ ἤρξατο αὐτοὺς ἀποστέλλειν δύο δύο.

> For προσκαλεῖται . . . καί, D reads προσκαλεσάμενος and inserts μαθητάς after δώδεκα, as does syr^sin. We have here a labyrinth of variants like a spider-web (Merx, *Markus und Lukas*, 50).

The word ἤρξατο has been the occasion for a lot of unnecessary head-banging. Some have suggested that later on there must have been another commissioning of the disciples: this text describes only a first commissioning, which certainly would not have reached all of Galilee.[85] Yet a circumlocution like ἤρξατο ἀποστέλλειν is not so very different from ἀπέστειλεν.[86] In the pericope itself there is a conspicuous feature: the word κηρύσσειν does not appear in v. 7, even though preaching appears to be the main point of the actual words of commission (cf. v. 11, ἀκούσωσιν). This absence indicates that the report is not entirely unified, a fact that becomes clear in the rest of the pericope. After v. 9 the commands of Jesus begin to be reported in direct discourse, and v. 10 opens with an introductory formula, καὶ ἔλεγεν αὐτοῖς. As a result, this pericope does not appear to be a unified tradition, and there are schematic features that suggest that the evangelist may have created all of it. We have already identified προσκαλεῖσθαι (3:23) as an introductory formula that came either from the tradition or was crafted by the evangelist.

The summary healing report in 6:12-13 introduces no new factors, only issues with which we are already familiar from collections of healing reports in all the Gospels: 1:14ff (μετανοεῖν); 3:9-12 (δαιμόνια πολλά,

---

85. Wohlenberg, *Markus*, 173.

86. "Very often in Matt, Mark, and Luke, ἄρχεσθαι can barely be distinguished from κηρύσσειν. Mark 1:45 is a good example: ἤρξατο κηρύσσειν" (Blass, *Grammatik*, 231n1).

πνεύματα ἀκάθαρτα); and even 6:7. But *one* point of interest does come up: they healed many sick people with oil. We may be inclined to trace this back to a genuine tradition, as oil can easily strike us as more distinctive and rare than it really was. For olive oil ointment would have been very commonly used on the sick in Israel, as it is used today for that very purpose across the Orient.[87]

There remains, then, only the instruction to the disciples in vv. 8-11. Naturally this is traditional, but that does not mean it is a unit. A literary suture clearly lies between v. 9 and the words καὶ ἔλεγεν αὐτοῖς. Verses 8-9 and vv. 10-11 were necessarily together at the start, but there is nothing remarkable about the fact that the indirect discourse of v. 9 switches over to direct discourse in v. 10, and that change says nothing at all against the unity of vv. 8-9.[88]

In spite of this analysis, 6:7-13 can still be a pre-existing piece of tradition that was found by the evangelist.[89] It is likely that the current structure, along with its context, is his work. Thus the historicity of the pericope cannot be dismissed out of hand; on the contrary it even acquires stronger likelihood.[90] Recall our judgment about the call stories in 3:13ff. As in that case, the number twelve here remains coincidental. The general tradition that there were twelve apostles after Jesus' death, as well as the existence of an original group of twelve, both stand behind this story. The later story in 6:30-31 refers to ἀπόστολοι, not to the δώδεκα. This difference points to different forms of stratification in the two traditions, which indicate that the

---

87. See Wohlenberg, *Markus*, 177.

88. Commentators, obviously influenced by the unity of this complex in Q (Matt 10:9ff), generally do not notice this suture. On the other hand, the form of v. 9 stands out: "Obviously the presenter of these reports has abbreviated the even more thorough version of the sayings that he had before him" (Wohlenberg, *Markus*, 175). Similarly: "The comparison between Matt 10 and Luke 10 shows ... that his (i.e., Mark's) saying was only an excerpt from the report of the commission in the Sayings Source, which he used very freely and eclectically" (J. Weiss, 200). Cf. also Loisy, *Mark*, 145-46; Wendling, 57. It appears to me that at this point the assertion of independence from Q is not yet proven. How do we know that this is only an excerpt? Of the sayings that were circulating, Mark may have known only those given in 6:8-11.

89. It gets us nowhere to think that 6:7 is out of place, because Jesus has been accompanied by his disciples since 6:1.

90. Wellhausen (*Mark*, 46) goes too far when he does not find any real historical connection in the outline: "The Twelve ... try an experiment, but afterward they are just as unaware and passive as they were before, even though the experiment worked. Certainly Jesus was not conducting a training tour with a seminar." Here Wellhausen shows no understanding of the pre-historicity of the forms of description and looks for chronological accuracy from the evangelists. This kind of exegesis is a form of begging the question.

stories of Jesus sending out his disciples acquired a distinct form. We cannot make out the details of how much these sayings may have been influenced by the earliest Christian mission after Jesus. In its present location, Mark 6:7-13 is part of a general withdrawal of Jesus from the people: he leaves it to his disciples to carry out the actual ministry to Israel. Verse 11 in particular looks back to the Nazareth pericope.

As has already been stated, the sending out of the disciples in Luke 9:1-6 follows the story of the daughter of Jairus. Since Luke has made use of Mark, it is no surprise to see that all the details and difficulties of the Markan text reappear in Luke. Luke adds an explicit mention of preaching, which Mark does not have: καὶ ἀπέστειλεν αὐτὸς κηρύσσειν, etc. The report by the apostles is sharply curtailed, while in Mark the call pericope is reported as a commissioning (Mark 3:14). It is clearly evident, though, that Luke's commissioning story has made additions to the original. For after the statement in v. 1, the words καὶ ἰᾶσθαι are unnecessary, and v. 2 gives exactly the same formula about teaching and healing, so that it looks like a later insertion. The incoherence of the report is another sign that it was put together by Mark, although Luke covers up most of the evidence. Of particular significance is the fact that Luke drops the connecting phrase καὶ ἔλεγεν in Mark 6:10. As has been pointed out,[91] the infinitive ἔχειν at the end of Luke 9:3 does not fit with the imperative, but this difficulty disappears if the infinitive is not there, as in ℵ*. Verse 9:6 (= Mark 6:12-13) is stylized along Lukan lines. The mention of the anointing with oil has dropped out.[92]

The relationship between Mark and Q is determinative for chapter 10 of Matthew, where a long report is presented describing Jesus' activity after sending out the disciples. As has already been noted, the complex is introduced by a summary statement in 9:35. What follows is an impressionistic picture of Jesus' compassion for the masses, who are like sheep without a shepherd (9:36). With the typical Matthean particle τότε, a saying about the ripening of the vintage and the scarcity of the reapers has been appended to 9:37-38. The connection is, on the whole, a suitable one.[93] These circumstances indicate that, although this construction was put together by Matthew, both the setting and the saying were taken from Mark (6:34) and Q (cf. Luke 10:2).

This combination of the two sources is also evident in the ongoing report, where Matt 10:1, 9-11, 14 are exactly parallel to Mark 6:7-11 and

---

91. Wellhausen, *Luke*, 40.

92. Spitta's thesis (*Die synoptische Grundschrift*, 208ff), which erroneously asserts a comparison between Mark and Luke, is slightly more convincing here.

93. The word τότε points to the suture, which conceals a change of sources. But I cannot agree that we have here a "rough transition into a different picture" (Klostermann, *Matthäus*, 223).

Luke 9:1-5. After v. 1, the sign of an apostle is introduced at the end of Mark 3:16-19. The seam is still recognizable in v. 5, where the thread is picked up again. Verses 5-8 are distinctive to Matthew. In the center stands the directive of v. 5b: εἰς ὁδὸν ἐθνῶν μὴ ἀπέλθητε καὶ εἰς πόλιν Σαμαρειτῶν μὴ εἰσέλθητε. Ὁδὸς ἐθνῶν can refer either to a road that leads into a Gentile area or to a road within a Gentile area, but it cannot have referred to Gentiles in general, but rather only to the inhabitants of Hellenistic cities of Palestine, i.e., the Decapolis. The Gentile areas around Tyre and Sidon lay outside Jesus' circle of vision. The Samaritans are mentioned in the same breath as the Gentiles, because both groups were mixed half-gentile populations. The command, which closely fits Jesus' conduct in Matt 15:24 (although not the end of Matt 28), does not cohere well with the Gospel of Luke. For after this episode Jesus does not shun the mission to Jews and Samaritans, and he himself travels through Samaria (in agreement with John, but not with Mark and Matthew). If Matthew's wording is correct, then we cannot determine at what time or in what place Jesus uttered this saying. He could have said the words ὁδὸς ἐθνῶν and πόλις Σαμαρειτῶν on either Galilean or Jewish soil. Verse 9, where Matthew reconnects with Mark, is hardly a seam, since the saying is extended without any connecting remarks. Leaving Mark out of it, the report that follows has had some sort of contact with Luke 10:4-12. It has long been recognized that Matthew blended the variants of Mark and Q, while Luke keeps them separate (9:1-6 and 10:1-12). When Jesus speaks in v. 15 about Sodom and Gomorrah (in Luke 10:12 only Sodom is named), it may be that he is familiar with the region around the Dead Sea, but it is more likely that this saying is evidence of his piety and knowledge of the Bible.

In Luke the two reports about sending out the disciples differ from each other: one of them we have already discussed above; the other is in 10:1-12: μετὰ δὲ ταῦτα ἀνέδειξεν ὁ κύριος καὶ ἑτέρους ἑβδομήκοντα (δύο) καὶ ἀπέστειλεν αὐτοῖς ἀνὰ δύο πρὸ προσώπου αὐτοῦ εἰς πᾶσαν πόλιν καὶ τόπον οὗ ἤμελλεν αὐτὸς ἔρχεσθαι. ἔλεγεν δὲ πρὸς αὐτούς. Next come the saying about the harvest in v. 2, and the missionary instructions in vv. 3-12.

> The textual tradition of the introduction certainly fluctuates. Μετὰ ταῦτα is missing from D (ἐπέδειξεν δέ) and syr[sin]. In the Gospels the phrase ὁ κύριος is relatively rare as an expression for Jesus, and the individual manuscripts render it as ὁ ις, *dominus Jesus*, or without any marker at all. Καὶ ἑτέρους is found in ℵ A C D Γ Δ Λ it vg arm go; ἑτέρους without καί: B L 33 cop syr[sin] pesh eth. The second reading is certainly a gloss, but it does not change the meaning. Ἑβδομήκοντα: ℵ A C L Γ Δ Λ cop pesh go Iren Tert Eus. Ἑβδομήκοντα δύο: B D vg syr[sin] arm Ephiph. Αὐτούς is lacking in B; in B and some other manuscripts the δύο

after ἀνὰ δύο is the error of a copyist who thought of Mark 6:7 without noticing that the doubling is already expressed by ἀνά. Αὐτός before ἔρχεσθαι is missing from B it syr. Instead of δέ in v. 2 we find οὖν in ς A Δ, or there is no particle at all.

The pericope stands practically at the beginning of the so-called Lukan Travel Narrative, and it is introduced with the unspecific phrase μετὰ ταῦτα. As this remark has no chronological significance, but constitutes only a caesura, there is reason to ask exactly what the phrase "after this" refers to. We found the same situation in Luke 5:27. Here in 10:1 μετὰ ταῦτα can refer back to 9:57-62 or even to 9:56, but a connection with 9:51 or 9:1ff seems slightly artificial.

By contrast, what group is designated by the word ἑτέρους? In chapter 9 the topic of the saying was the sending out of the twelve apostles, so we naturally think that this must be a group parallel to the ἕτεροι. Both recent and older interpretations[94] have almost without exception identified this group as the twelve disciples, yet now another connection is also possible.[95] In 9:52 it was said that Jesus sent messengers ahead to prepare him a place to stay. Thus 10:1 appears to link up with that saying: Jesus now sends out some more people (καὶ ἑτέρους). Yet that does not fit well with the subsequent sayings about the mission, which suggest a longer and independent activity on the part of the disciples. A mediating interpretation, i.e., that the purpose of this activity by the disciples was to prepare the souls of humankind for Jesus, specifically by making room in their souls, does nothing to change the fact that there is an inconsistency here. The motif of the Lukan source L in 9:51-56, where Jesus sends out people to prepare the way, somehow has an after-effect on 10:1b. But the following saying about sending out has basically nothing to do with this motif. That saying belongs to Q, as we have already recognized it in Matthew 10. The manner of the insertion of material from L and Q is the solution to the riddle. Why Luke contrasts the two ἕτεροι cannot be determined on the basis of his authorial objectives. His special source (L) is thinking of the ἕτεροι in 9:52, and Luke picks this up, even though in so doing he has in mind a contrast with the twelve apostles.[96] A wider circle than just the Twelve is going to be necessary: for "the harvest is great, but the workers are few."

The number of those who are sent out is said to be either seventy or seventy-two. Two questions have kept researchers busy here, neither one of which admits of an easy answer, but the discussion will be fruitful and

---

94. For the opinions of early church leaders, cf. Tischendorf.
95. As convincingly demonstrated by B. Weiss, *Markus und Lukas*, 440.
96. B. Weiss recognizes this (*Markus und Lukas*, 440).

will bring us closer to a solution. The first question is about the tradition, namely, whether ἑβδομήκοντα or ἑβδομήκοντα δύο is correct. The familiar rule, *difficilior lectio potior*, is not helpful here, nor is the idea that a genuinely unremarkable number (72) was later changed into a holy number (70), because in Jewish tradition both numbers stand side by side and were interchangeable. Seventy-two can also be considered a holy and traditional number. Certainly the church fathers regarded both numbers as allusions to Jewish tradition. On the basis of the use of the number 72 in Jewish tradition, it may be the case that the number 72 here is a reference to the twelve apostles, times six. There have been many efforts to determine the original reading of this text on internal grounds, and in that regard I would like to offer the following proposal for debate: the mistake in the scribal tradition may arise from the fact that the word δύο appears in v. 1b, and during the copying process this δύο played a fateful role. A scribe may have been influenced by the words ἑβδομήκοντα δύο in v. 1b, or perhaps a scribe wrote the word δύο after ἑβδομήκοντα in v. 1b, and then, either mistakenly or intentionally, scratched it out. Similarly, it could be that the rounding of 72 down to 70 is analogous to a similar rounding down that previously took place within Jewish tradition (72 translators of the Old Testament, and 70 translators of the LXX). Yet on the other hand there is also the possibility that some literate scribe or theologian knew about the number 72 in Judaism and, putting his scholarship to work here, changed the number from 70 to 72.

There is a further question in this regard, namely, whether we are looking at history or construction, and if it is a case of construction, whether that construction was already in the tradition or was created by Luke. The Old Testament precedents do not argue against the historical existence of a wider circle of 70 disciples (I refer to 70, but of course the number 72 is also possible). In determining the size of the group, we can follow Jewish tradition, just as our modern picture of a group of twelve is based on repeated customary usage. In a similar way Jesus may have chosen exactly twelve apostles as a reference to the twelve tribes.[97] Decisively against the historicity of the number, however, stands the fact that in the entire gospel tradition the number 70 is spoken of only here. If Jesus really had selected 70 disciples, surely there would be some resonance of it somewhere else in the Gospels. In addition there is also the fact that the saying about the 70 cannot be a doublet of the saying about the twelve apostles in Mark 6 and Matt 10. This fact adds to our confidence that this saying is not historical. The later secondary traditions about the 70 disciples, especially the

---

97. *Epistle of Barnabas* 8:3 expresses this idea: οὖσιν δεκαδύο εἰς μαρτύριον τῶν φυλῶν ὅτι ιβ' αἱ φυλαὶ τοῦ Ἰσραήλ. Cf. A. Harnack, *Die Mission und Ausbreitung*, 1:267ff.

detailed lists of names, are based on Luke 10 and have no value in and of themselves. A circle of 70 disciples may have constituted itself during the days of the earliest community, and among that circle would have been people like Stephen, Philip, the Lord's brother James, and Barnabas. But there is no authentic report about this circle. The appointment of 70 such disciples has often been attributed to the time of Jesus, since Luke found an existing tradition and aligned it with the Q saying about commissioning the disciples, which he knew from Mark 6. It is therefore possible, but not likely, that Luke himself found out about the existence of the 70, or the tradition about them, in his own time. It is also possible that he found only a tradition about the 70 Jewish elders. Such traditions have a longer history and a deeper background than anyone can say, and one Christian (Luke) found them. Real history, and a fiction that was under the influence of long-practiced formulae, were working back and forth between each other in ways that we can no longer fully grasp.[98]

A large number of missionary sayings, which may or may not have actually gone back to Jesus, were gathered into two layers (Mark and Q). By their expressed rejection of a Gentile mission, all of these sayings show themselves to be related to the Jewish mission, and they seem to be addressed to the twelve apostles. On the whole Luke keeps these sayings, although he does allow some universalistic ideas to peek through (cf. Luke 10:8). The addressees are not merely the Twelve, but also a wider circle of people upon whom he pins the traditional number seventy. Certainly this was his interpretation, for by widening the idea of Jesus' mission, he created a picture that is in opposition to the Markan and Matthean tradition. This picture rightly does not limit Jesus' missionary instructions only to the Twelve, but rather lets them reach a wider circle. By limiting the commission only to the Twelve, Mark and Matthew present a form of description that is supra-historical, and this non-historical schematization deserves to be critiqued. Luke offers that critique, although even he himself does not overcome the absence of real historical materials in the schematization. Seventy (70) is a schematic number.

Yet none of this can fully explain the account of the instructions to the disciples in Matthew. The account follows 10:17-25, a series of loosely connected sayings about the fate of the disciples. They show strong similarity with words from the apocalyptic sayings of Jesus (Mark 13:9ff = Luke 21:12ff). In the parallel location at Matt 24:9ff, these words are for the most part missing. Clearly Matt 10 is a constellation of different sayings from very different

---

98. I cannot share the confidence of many commentators who are sure that the 70 disciples were created by Luke. "Luke assigns a specific number to τὸ πλῆθος τῶν μαθητῶν," as he puts it.

situations: 10:19-20 has its parallel in Luke 12:11, after the saying about supernatural knowledge, and Matt 10:25a appears in Luke 6:40, in the sermon on the plain within a complex of sayings about judging. At Matt 10:18 we can reasonably ask where Jesus got his conception of ἡγεμόνες and βασιλεῖς. Perhaps he is thinking here of Antipas and his retainers, but τοῖς ἔθνεσιν is suggestive of Gentile kings, and this very passage (v. 18) belongs not to the period of the first commissioning, but rather to a time of explicit persecution, such as those in which the Gentile government engaged.[99]

Additional sayings in Matt 10:26-33 make reference to fearless knowledge. Without any transition this complex joins itself to material that stands in a completely different context in Luke (12:2ff). Luke twice inserts the saying λέγω δὲ ὑμῖν (Luke 12:4, 8), clearly indicating that a collection of individual sayings lies behind the passage, an observation that is further confirmed by the fact that the sayings are arranged differently in Mark and Luke.

Be that as it may, Matt 10:34-36 is a parallel passage to Luke 12:51-53. The fact that this text this text is a compilation is particularly clear in the section about the stipulations for followers, i.e., Matt 10:37-39. These verses, which are unified in their content, appear as two separate sayings in Luke 14:26-27 and 17:33, and also have a parallel in Mark 8:34-35 and Luke 9:23-24. At that point, following the Markan sequence, Matt 16:24-25 again brings in this saying. The conclusion of the speech, Matt 10:40-42, ultimately includes ideas that also resonate with Mark 9:37 = Luke 9:48 = Matt 18:5, one of which (v. 42) recurs in Mark 9:41.

Excursus: Matthew 9:35—10:42:
A Transitional Piece in the Matthean Outline

As previously noted, the complex of Matt 9:35-10, 42 comes to an end at 11:1, having provided a transitional link from the Galilean activity of Jesus (Matt 4:12-9:34) to his ministry to unbelieving and hostile Jews (Matt 11:2-13:58). Why this link has been arranged precisely at this point is not fully evident. We do not know the sequence of the stories of Jesus in Q, but perhaps that sequence has had some secondary effects here.

99. Cf. Wellhausen, *Matthew* 49; Klostermann, *Matthäus*, 226.

Excursus: The Complex Mark 3:7—6:13 and
Its Rearrangement by Matthew and Luke

With the pericope in Mark 6:7-13, we close out the third section of the Gospel of Mark, which we have entitled "Jesus and the People: Mark 3:7—6:13." Jesus' movements among his fellow Jews, along with their negative attitude toward him, form the basic motif in this long series of individual stories. They were assembled here on the basis of their fundamental outlook: as the introductions to the pericopes were handed down, topographical details gave rise to a collection of sea-stories, even though a clear itinerary cannot be identified. From start to finish the dominant tone builds on the report about Jesus' rejection in his home town. Jesus is surrounded from the beginning by his disciples; in several situations he brings them with him, yet eventually he pulls back from them. Selecting the disciples, training them, sending them out—all of these make up a second motif closely interwoven with the first. This train of thought was circulating prior to Mark: he did not come up with it on his own, as is proven by the fact that the individual stories contain stray items that do not cohere with the evangelist's plan, but which he did not trim off.[100]

It is plain to see that both of the other evangelists, who did not have this Markan plan in mind, had to introduce a profusion of further material (Q and special material), in order to be able to free themselves from the Markan outline. This has been demonstrated in precise detail.

Matthew damns Mark's thread with faint praise: he includes only some of it. The chapter of parables is greatly expanded, but the miracle stories from this section of Mark had already been incorporated into the miracle stories in chapters 8 and 9. The call and sending out of the disciples together make up a bridge between two large excerpts: 4:12-9:34 and 11:2-13, 58, which run parallel to the three Markan excerpts 1:14-45; 2:1–3:6; 3:7-6:13.

Luke sticks close to Mark, but (following connections in the content) inserts the sermon on the plain, additional miracles

---

100. Along with syr[sin], which begins a new series with v. 6b with explicit Markan indicators, Wohlenberg links Mark 6:7-13 with the subsequent section (Wohlenberg, *Markus*, 172). But even without my remarks above, it can be argued that the collection was worked on by Mark. Although he does not mention it, Wohlenberg is clearly depending here upon his theory of sevens, for he finds fourteen stories (2 x 7) in 3:7—6:6, and another fourteen stories (7 + 7) in 6:6—8:26 (see Wohlenberg, *Markus*, VIII).

stories from Q and L, and the pericope about the repentant woman. Other Markan material, which Matthew inserted here, Luke placed in the so-called Travel Narrative.

5

Jesus Outside of Galilee in Gentile Territory

Mark 6:14—8:26par.

Herod's Judgment upon Jesus
(Mark 6:14-16; Matt 14:1-2; Luke 9:7-9)

¹⁴Καὶ ἤκουσεν ὁ βασιλεὺς Ἡρῴδης, φανερὸν γὰρ ἐγένετο τὸ ὄνομα αὐτοῦ, καὶ ἔλεγον . . . ¹⁵ ἄλλοι δὲ ἔλεγον . . . ¹⁶ ἀκούσας δὲ ὁ Ἡρῴδης ἔλεγεν . . .

> On the basis of this accepted text, the sayings in 14b and 15 are best understood as parentheses. To begin, ἔλεγον (= "they said") is the right reading (so B D). The reading ἔλεγεν (ℵ A C) is explicable as conforming to ἤκουσεν and to the text of Matthew. Merx notes a widely divergent text in syr^sin: "And when Herod the king heard (it), for his intellect (not 'the rumors about him' or 'his reputation' or even 'his wisdom') was widely known, and he said, '... but others say ...'"

The first question that comes up here has to do the object of the verb ἤκουσεν. The most likely possibility is that Herod has heard about the mission of the disciples, which was mentioned in 6:12. The reputation of Jesus, which was in fact the subject of that parenthesis, is thereby validated. A wide variety of opinions about him were circulating, and one of these opinions had apparently made its way to Herod. To the extent that the evangelist gave any thought at all to the continuity of his narrative, it was only to think about the connections with what preceded, and thus he laid out in the narrative only a vague progression of ideas. But this is not very helpful, since in this pericope Jesus does all the talking himself, and he cannot be referring to the activities of the disciples. There is therefore no clear connection between these verses and 6:6-13 (the commission of the disciples). Various efforts to determine the object of ἤκουσεν, particularly with reference to its grammatical and syntactical context, have all fallen short of their goal.

One explanation, i.e., to take φανερὸν γὰρ ἐγένετο as a parenthesis and to understand τὸ ὄνομα αὐτοῦ as the object of ἤκουσεν, is a bit too elaborate,[1] although it does have Matt 14:1 on its side. The only solution to the difficulty lies in recognizing that Mark 6:14-16 originally had no connection with the preceding story. The seam between v. 13 and v. 14 is unmistakable. To the extent that this narrative was ever situated within any chronological context, it was part of a report about the fact that Herod was surprised by the news of Jesus and his deeds (cf. v. 14: αἱ δυνάμεις ἐν αὐτῷ). Although we can no longer trace out this original setting, it is indeed an important chronological consideration. It is frankly astonishing that Herod, reigning over the land where Jesus lived, would have heard so quickly about his activity. Were there not other relationships, like the difficulties between him and his father-in-law Aretas, which would have absorbed his attention? Would he not have been largely indifferent toward Jesus' newly-aroused movement? It would be more likely and natural for Herod to have received reports quite soon after the sensational and exciting events in Capernaum. News may have radiated outward from there, especially in the direction of Tiberias. The real object of ἤκουσεν is thus, most likely, Jesus' debut in Capernaum.[2] Our stories rise from that context.

The story that unfolds from that point is quite clear: when Herod heard about Jesus and the various stories that were circulating, he was reminded of John the Baptist, whom he had put to death. There is nothing here to make us regard the people's testimony about Jesus as a doublet of 8:28.[3] Why could not the quite clear tradition of 6:14-16 have existed along with 8:28? And why could not this tradition actually correspond to historical reality? Certainly Jesus used that riddle about his people more than once, and more than once he reached back to his great predecessors Elijah and John the Baptist. If the present form of 6:14-16 is an independent story, or one that

---

1. Wohlenberg, *Markus*, 178. DeWette's opinion, i.e., that Mark forgot the object of ἤκουσεν because of the parenthesis, is not bad, but neither is it convincing (cf. B. Weiss, *Markus und Lukas*, 94).

2. Wellhausen points to Capernaum (*Mark*, 48), and says that the debut of Jesus in Capernaum was "the truth, even though it was delivered by way of redactional efforts on the part of an unknown person." Here he recognizes that the individual pericopes could appear in the larger narrative along with their framing pieces. That is true to the artfulness of such collections of individual traditions, and above all to the Markan tradition. But Wendling's effort to disconnect 6:14 from 6:1-13 and attach it to the Jairus narrative (Capernaum, again) does not work (Wendling, 59). Obviously Wendling would like to be able to tease out and disentangle a chronological pre-Markan report.

3. So J. Weiss, 200-201: "an early doublet of 8:28." So also Wendling, 61: 6:15 could be "an inserted doublet." He greatly overstates the difficulties of the construction in 6:14-16 (Wendling, 62).

stems from some other context, why then does it stand in its current location? This question will now find its answer.

Matthew 14:1–2 offers the following introduction: ¹ἐν ἐκείνῳ τῷ καιρῷ ἤκουσεν Ἡρῴδης ὁ τετραάρχης τὴν ἀκοὴν Ἰησοῦ, ²καὶ εἶπεν τοῖς παίσιν αὐτοῦ, etc. In Mark the preceding seam is filled up in two ways: first, what Herod hears is stated: he hears about the call of Jesus. Mark's simple καὶ ἤκουσεν is changed by Matthew into one of his customarily clear connections: ἐν ἐκείνῳ τῷ καιρῷ. The phrase looks like a chronological marker but is only a transitional phrase, as we have already identified in 3:1; 12:1; and 13:1. Matthew completely drops the difficult connection with what precedes, because he locates the commissioning discourse in a different place. What the first evangelist actually offers is simply an excerpt out of Mark. The lively scenery and the setting in the courtyard are of no interest to him.[4]

While in Matthew we can (in spite of the chronological bracketing) recognize the caesura as a connection between two scenes, in Luke 9:7–9 the text is closely attached to what precedes:

ἤκουσεν Ἡρῴδης ὁ τετραάρχης ὁ γινόμενα πάντα καὶ διηπόρει διὰ τὸ λέγεσθαι ὑπὸ τιννωὅτι Ἰωάννης ἠγέρθη ἐκ νεκρῶν.

ς rightly elucidates γινόμενα with ὑπ᾽ αὐτοῦ, adding various other stylistic alterations, as do A C³ Γ Δ Λ vg go aeth.

Just as in Mark, here also in Matthew our pericope is joined to the narrative about the commissioning of the disciples, although with πάντα and γινόμενα, Matthew sets it in a wider perspective than Mark: Herod has heard about the activity of Jesus. This arrangement substantially re-frames Herod's conduct, as Luke relies upon a report that he himself must have regarded as absurd, since it does not fit the character of Herod. In the process of transmission of the story of Jesus, upon which Luke places great value, on occasion the connections between scenes are stylistically satisfying. As we have already explained, there are chronological problems with placing this story at this point, but Luke lets them stand, revealing thereby that he is depending upon Mark.

---

4. If Wellhausen finds that "suitable" (*Matthew*, 74) and thinks that there is no popular gossip in Matthew, and that this is no great loss, this is obviously merely a matter of taste.

The Death of John the Baptist
(Mark 6:17-29; Matt 14:3-12)

There follows a report about the death of the Baptist, which takes the form of an insertion or an excursus. "Here begins the great parenthesis, which by every principle of logic, although perhaps not for the naive narrator, has exceptional value."[5] Since Mark 1:14 says that Jesus first stepped out into public view after the arrest of John the Baptist, 6:17ff has to come after 1:14. As we have previously seen, we must take seriously the possibility that Jesus and the Baptist had worked side by side. With the exception of John, the evangelists generally follow a schematic idea: the Baptist steps aside, and Jesus steps forward. But if that is not what actually happened, then we would not be able to determine at what point in the story of Jesus the arrest of John took place.[6] Verses 19-20 show that the execution of the Baptist did not immediately follow upon his imprisonment. How long he sat in jail, we do not know. The stories in Matt 11:2ff = Luke 7:18ff may well fit into that interval.

The narrative contains all sorts of data that could figure into an absolute chronology, if not for the fact that the historicity of the entire data-set is dubious in the extreme. Most seriously, it is difficult to reconcile this chronology with Josephus' account of the death of the Baptist in prison. According to Josephus (*Ant.* 18.5.2), the Baptist was executed at the desert fortress of Machaerus, located in southernmost Perea. But our scene clearly plays out in Antipas' palace in Galilee, probably in Tiberias. The phrase "the nobles of Galilee" (οἱ μεγιστᾶνες τῆς Γαλιλαίας) also points in that direction. There are two ways out of this difficulty: we can attribute to Josephus the entire episode about the party at Machaerus, which is not impossible. Or we can let the executioner (v. 27b and 28) travel from Tiberias to Machaerus and back. Since we cannot assume an interval of several days between the request of Salome and the return of the executioner, we have to accept the fact that the course of events has been poetically condensed.[7] On the other hand, this narrator may simply not have had an accurate sense of the geographical relationships

---

5. S. Klostermann, *Markus*, 49; Catena 325: οὐχ ὡς τότε γενομένων.

6. Pölzl (*Mark.*, 160) focuses on the Gospel of John and thereby places the imprisonment of John in the late summer of Jesus' first year of teaching, and his death at the end of the second year. That is not impossible, but neither is it demonstrable.

7. Cf. B. Weiss, *Markus und Lukas*, 99: "This conclusion (the journey of the executioner from Tiberias to Machaerus and back) may be necessary in order to round off the story, even if it did not actually take place. Loisy's comments are quite fine: 'This view reunites the location of the party and that of the murder with a place that was not unique or otherwise fixed: everything that happens is either a royal fantasy, a capital daydream, or the monstrous act of Herodias his adulteress, who becomes the murderer of a prophet.'"

involved. In any case, one detail cannot be dismissed: the execution of the Baptist certainly took place at a meal.

As the narrative closes, the Baptist's disciples bury their master. It is worth noting that these disciples pop up very every now and then in the gospel tradition and in primitive Christian traditions more generally. Certainly they played a greater role than the tradition lets on, since it was after all a Jesus tradition.[8]

The text of Matt 14:3-12 makes sense as a condensation of Mark's version.[9] One distinctive feature in Matthew's version is the fact that the end of it connects directly with Jesus: καὶ ἐλθόντες ἀπήγγειλαν τῷ 'Ιησοῦ. This fits well with the beginning of the next pericope in Matt 14:13: ἀκούσας δὲ ὁ 'Ιησοῦς ἀνεχώρησεν ἐκεῖθεν. Clearly the first evangelist has cobbled together here some stories that were either close to each other (or perhaps even in sequence with each other) in the Gospel of Mark. But Matthew treats the episode of the Baptist's death as a postscript, relocating it to the close of the transition. The aim is to make Mark's narrative of the Baptist's death more consonant with the story of Jesus: Jesus avoids Herod because he murdered the Baptist. Unless Matt 14:3-12 is an addendum, this chronological connection is impossible, and the result is a clear discrepancy in content, since Jesus would have had nothing to fear from Herod's extorted execution of the Baptist. Finally, it is not to be overlooked that there is a small sign of a seam at this point: it is the word ἐκεῖθεν, a characteristically Matthean word that is topographically insignificant, which points to nothing but a seam.

The story of the Baptist's death is missing from Luke. Clearly this kind of interpolation is not consistent with the third evangelist's more pragmatic and chronological style. The reasons behind his passing over the Baptist's death so briefly have already been explained above on pages 22-23. But that is not to say that Luke is chronologically correct here.[10] It does not confirm

---

8. Cf. M. Dibelius, *Die urchristliche Überlieferung von Johannes dem Täufer*, as well as C. A. Bernoulli's epilogue to Overbeck, *Das Johannesevangelium*, 527ff.

9. This point is developed well by Klostermann, *Matthäus*, 260. But J. Weiss (*Das älteste Evangelium*, 202) is of the opinion that: "On the whole it appears to me that the text of Matthew is not a condensation but rather that it must have arisen from a simpler predecessor." Similar judgments are expressed by Merx, *Markus und Lukas*, 228-29. Wellhausen (*Matthew*, 75) rightly holds on to the idea that on this point Matthew is independent of the outline of the Gospel of Mark, but that a trace of the original tradition shines through Mark's highly unworked version. In my view this basic thesis, as it has been expressed by many researchers is not to be taken lightly, i.e., the final narrative still has to present something of the earlier version.

10. So Wellhausen, *Luke*, 40; and also Spitta, *Die synoptische Grundschrift*, 214ff. It is begging the question to say that Luke has the older version because the narrative of the death of the Baptist is a parenthesis in Mark and Matthew.

JESUS OUTSIDE OF GALILEE IN GENTILE TERRITORY   163

the synoptic conception that Jesus began his activity only after the Baptist was imprisoned.

We have not yet answered the question of why the Herod episodes are situated here in Mark, who offers the oldest outline. This question cannot be avoided, because there is no genuine chronological connection between Mark 6:13 and 6:14ff.[11] 6:17-29 (= Matt 14:3-12) marks the disconnection, as this piece is a parenthesis. After the commissioning of the disciples, Mark opens a new section that shows Jesus outside of Galilee among the Gentiles. This period in the story of Jesus is made necessary by the resistance of the people, from whom Jesus now turns away, or rather sends his emissaries in his place. Within this context the Herod episodes are superfluous.[12] But they are still useful at this point, although this fact is not especially evident in Mark. He brings in only one story, to the effect that Herod has given at least some thought to Jesus. But Matthew's redactional work shows that he understood Mark correctly, for he puts that idea out front: Jesus has to flee from Herod. In this way an external motive becomes attached to the internal motive (i.e., the resistance of the people) for Jesus' flight. If we think about the connections we have already noted between Jesus and Herod, and the Herodians, it becomes clear that this is a reliable ancient tradition that goes back to real historical events.[13] The citations mentioned show that Jesus had to be protected from that group. He had to get away from their efforts to trap him. It is abundantly clear in Mark and even more so in Matthew, that Jesus cuts his Galilean activity short because of Herod. Yet this schematization is not historical, and neither is any chronology that builds upon it.

Moreover, the Herod episodes appear to fill in a hole between the withdrawal of the disciples in 6:13 and their return in 6:30. Even if at bottom Herod's condemnation of John and the episode of the death of the Baptist use up some amount of time during this interval, that point of view is not from Mark. A smooth narrator would use supplements to fill up real time. But does 6:30 really pick up where 6:13 leaves off? And even if Mark understood them to be connected in that way, is that connection original?

---

11. A chronological connection is presupposed by Wohlenberg, *Markus*, 185-86, when he expresses the opinion that both events (the death of the Baptist and the commissioning of the disciples) took place at approximately the same time. He argues that the disciples could not have been indifferent to the Baptist's death, if their own activity had also not been disturbed thereby. Wohlenberg inserts a psychological connection into the text that is not really there.

12. Now we can understand why some scholars have searched for an Ur-Mark (J. Weiss) or a pre-synoptic document that did not contain these pericopes.

13. See above, pg. 74.

Mark 6:30

Mark 6:30 reads: καὶ συνάγονται οἱ ἀπόστολοι πρὸς τὸν Ἰησοῦν καὶ ἀπήγγειλαν αὐτῷ πάντα, ὅσα ἐποίησαν καὶ ἐδίδαξαν. As the verse now stands, it belongs with the section that follows: the apostles reassemble with Jesus, and he gives them an opportunity to rest. But we must not underestimate the difficulty of understanding this verse within this context. This fact shows itself not only in the unclear connection with what precedes, but also in the considerable uncertainty of the textual tradition. We have seen that the Herod episodes are an insertion. On that basis 6:30 has to be connected back to 6:13, that is, the apostles come back from their journey and report to Jesus about what they have done and taught. That is how Luke understood the connection, for in 9:10 he uses the word ὑποστρέψαντες instead of συνάγονται. If we keep in mind this progression in the narrative, which Mark probably and Luke certainly picked up, then something is missing from this depiction of the situation. The return of the disciples is not described clearly enough: when did they come back? Where was Jesus in the meantime? There is a gap here, and it is evident in the fact that an even larger insertion could have been made here. What is the explanation for this broken connection?

Does a new pericope begin here, having nothing at all to do with 6:7–13? Or are we looking at redaction here? The first is quite possible: 6:30 could be the beginning of a new pericope, which reports that the apostles gathered with Jesus. Mark put that piece here, because it could represent the return of the apostles from their missionary journey. Luke then re-presented this version by gently recalibrating its slightly vague introduction. We thus arrive at the question of whether 6:30ff is in fact a self-contained pericope. Quite apart from these questions, which have occupied our attention, the textual tradition of 6:30 indicates that we have here a redactional insertion. While ℵ B C D E L Δ 33 it vg cop arm aeth read πάντα ὅσα, the reading πάντα καὶ ὅσα is found in A Γ go, et al. Even if we cannot exclude the possibility that both readings have essentially the same meaning, it is more precise to separate the πάντα from the ὅσα in the second reading. Ὅσα relates to the apostles' journey, while πάντα refers to the death of the Baptist: the apostles find themselves back with Jesus, and they report on the death of the Baptist and their own activities. The καί can be a later insertion by someone who wanted to establish thereby a connection with the death of the Baptist, which immediately precedes. But it could also belong to the original text of Mark. In that case we would have here a trace of redactional activity, in an effort to attach what follows to the commissioning of the apostles on one side and to the death of the Baptist on the other. A trace of that is clearly evident in syr^{sin}, which reads: πάντα ὅσα ἐποίησεν καὶ ἐδίδαξεν. Here the meaning is clear: the apostles come to Jesus and tell him everything that he (i.e., the Baptist) had done and taught. This form of the text cannot be original, for ὅσα ἐποίησαν καὶ ἐδίδαξαν is what needs to be communicated to Jesus, as he hardly needs to be told about the Baptist's activity. In addition, John's ministry is not accurately described by the words ποιεῖν and διδάσκειν. Nor is it possible that 6:30 is a statement about John's disciples. At this point the Syriac uses a word that can be translated as either οἱ ἀπόστολοι or just ἀπόστολοι. The first possibility does not work here, because the disciples of John cannot be called first οἱ μαθηταί and then οἱ ἀπόστολοι in close succession. If the correct reading is ἀπόστολοι, then there was a special mission from the circle of John's disciples, and the following translation suggests itself: "Then messengers came to Jesus and told him everything that he (i.e., the Baptist) had been doing and teaching." But this reading runs aground not only on the contents of the message, but even more so on the fact that it would leave the word αὐτοῖς with no referent.

There is, however, **one** meaning that preserves all the color of the tradition: v. 30 shows itself to be a product of composition. The conclusion of the narrative about the Baptist would have run something like this: they (the disciples of John, or the messengers sent by him) give Jesus the news of their master's death. Mark, who must have created the link to the story of commissioning the disciples, formed the text as we now have it out of that story. That connection was unsuitable to Matthew, because he had placed the commissioning of the disciples in a completely different position, so he had to clean up the Markan outline from that point forward. He brought in a text that may have been part of the original opening of the pericope, even though nothing is certain about the connections of chronology and content between Matt 14:3–12 and Matt 14:13ff. The Herod episodes were now no longer situated within a firm chronological sequence.

What then is the result of our deliberations? Questions about compositional technique are always difficult because the results are not clearly circumscribed. In less complicated settings, exegetes can arrive at decisions with certainty, in spite of varying approaches, because there is still only one continuous sequence of pericopes. Yet in this case no such sequence is evident. Mark put his stories together on the basis of both internal and external factors, and we do not know what they were, although we can sketch their outlines. Pure literary reflection helps in this regard, and the important and informative result is this: the original connection between 6:7ff and 6:30ff, in the sense of a commissioning and return of the disciples, is not secure.

Excursus: The Itinerary of Mark 6:31—8:26

Before we look at the next series of pericopes and their framework, we have to examine the collective framework into which these stories are set. To that end we will take 6:31—8:26 as a whole. Thus far the results of our investigation show that Mark selected individual pericopes out of the tradition and arranged them (along with their introductions and conclusion) for the most part on the basis of their content. There was no continuous chronology or topography, and he often brought together stories on the basis of connections of time and/or place (cf. 1:21ff; 4:35ff). In some cases his compositional technique left behind a clear seam in the itinerary, about which he was indifferent. The sequence of stories engages us very differently now: an entire series of experiences rises before our eyes, and we behold a variety of colorful settings, as Jesus travels from here to there and from place to place, and journeys by land and sea blend into each other. It feels as if we are reading an actual chronological sequence, a continuous travel narrative. Now that we have examined this complex of stories, there are two important results: 1) the geography and the chronology are not merely unclear but also incomplete; and 2) the individual stories are not securely anchored in their contexts. As a result they cannot be clearly marked off from what precedes or from what follows.

Jesus rejoins his disciples and encourages them to withdraw, so he and they together get into a boat in that area. But the people see him coming and begin to hurry in his direction. When they come ashore, Jesus and his disciples are once again set upon by a crowd (6:31-33). He preaches, and later that evening he miraculously feeds all five thousand of them (6:34ff). Then he orders the disciples to get back into the boat and sail for the other side of the lake, to Bethsaida. After dark he appears to them, walking on the water (6:45-52), and then they come ashore at Gennesaret. People stream toward him from all the surrounding area (6:53-56). Scribes and Pharisees start an argument with him (7:1-13), and he tells the people a parable (7:14-16) before going into a house to talk with his disciples about the parable (7:17-23). From there he proceeds into the region of Tyre and Sidon, where he heals the daughter of a Gentile woman (7:24-30). Once again he leaves that area, wandering out of the region of Tyre, through Sidon to the Sea of Galilee in the area of the Decapolis. There he heals a dumb man (7:31-37). During this time he also provides a meal for four (4) thousand people (8:1-9). Next he travels by ship with his disciples to Dalmanutha (8:10), and then the Pharisees argue with him (8:11-12). He leaves them and travel back to the other side of the Sea (8:13). On the way he has a conversation with his disciples, and he heals a blind man (8:22-26).

There is something quite remarkable about this travel narrative. Jesus orders his disciples to sail "to the other side of the lake, to Bethsaida" (6:45), but then does not go there. Instead he seeks out other areas, both on foot and by sea, and does not arrive at Bethsaida until 8:22. As the explication of the details has shown, the inherent difficulty in this itinerary can be rectified by a combination of both eisegesis and exegesis. Nothing is clear, not even the location of the town of Bethsaida. We can start from the end, in 8:22. According to the order of events, Jesus and his disciples have come from the region of Dalmanutha (8:10), and he sails to the other side (8:13), landing in Bethsaida. The phrase "to the other side" refers to the east side of the Sea of Galilee. In an earlier context[14] we found that the expression τὸ πέραν, which is used for κατ' ἐξοχήν, can have this meaning.

Unfortunately it is not possible to fix the location of Dalmanutha, from which Jesus has come. In the manuscripts the tradition varies, with most manuscripts reading Δαλμανουθά. D* offers the reading Μελεγαδά, and D² has Μαγαδά, and the Old Latin manuscripts are similar: *magidan, magedan, magedam, mageda*. Strong support for this tradition comes from syr^sin, which reads "Mount Magadan." The instability in the Markan text coheres with the fact that Matt 15:39 reads Μαγαδάν, but even here the tradition is not consistent. In addition to Μαγαδάν we also find Μαγδαλά(ν); cf. E F L Γ Δ gr arm aeth cop. Thus the place is given three different names: Dalmanutha, Magadan, and Magdala. There are other forms, which we will not discuss here, because they are clearly orthographic deviations. Out of all these place names only one—Magdala, the hometown of Mary Magdalene—is known. With some certainty we can say that Magdala was located in what is today called Migdal, about an hour north of Tiberias on the western shore of the lake.[15] But we cannot de-

---

14. See above, p. 128.

15. Cf. F. Buhl, *Geographie des alten Palästina* (1896), 225. Translator's note: Buhl's estimate presumes the traveler is going from Tiberias to Migdal on foot.

termine whether Μαγδαλά was the original reading, nor can we know whether Μαγδαλά and Μαγαδάν are in fact the same place. For if "Magdala" is the original reading, then the disunity and corruption of the tradition would have no reasonable explanation, yet we can still understand why some manuscripts substituted the well-known name of Magdala for the unknown "Magadan." About Magadan, which possibly ought to be distinguished from Magdala, we have no clear information at all. Eusebius and Jerome are our authorities in such matters, yet in this case their remarks cannot be confirmed. Eusebius[16] speaks of Μαγεδανὴ περὶ τὴν Γερασάν, and Jerome[17] says something quite similar: καί ἐστι νῦν ἡ Μαγαιδανὴ περὶ τὴν Γερασάν. Thus Magadan is not located on the west side of the lake, but in the Decapolis. If Dalmanutha (so Mark) is the same as Magadan (so Matthew)—although we cannot be sure of that[18]—then today's a-Delhemija, located in the Decapolis south of the lake at the confluence of the Yarmuk River in Jordan, might possibly be ancient Dalmanutha.[19]

How then are we to understand εἰς τὸ πέραν (Mark 8:13), if the destination and the point of departure both lie on the east side? Could a journey from the southern end of the east side to a more northerly location on the same side be described as εἰς τὸ πέραν? Instead of crossing the Sea, does Mark 8:13 refer to a journey along the shore? A topographical expression of that sort cannot be ruled out, but it is unlikely. If we stay with the notion of a crossing with its end point on the east side, and if we want to develop a smooth itinerary from 8:11ff, then Dalmanutha cannot have been in the southeast. It has to have been located in the west, somewhere in the area of Gennesaret. Both of the highly uncertain references in Eusebius and Jerome, and the even more uncertain ed-Delhemija hypothesis, are unworkable. Dalmanutha[20] is not mentioned in Eusebius or

16. Eusebius, *Onomasticon* 134 (Klostermann's ed.).

17. Jerome, *de Loc. Hebr*; cf. Tischendorf, *Editio VIII*, Markus 8:10; also Pölzl, *Marcus*, 89.

18. Augustine explicitly says that Dalmanutha and Magadan are the same place (*de Consensu Evangelistarum* II, 51; read likewise by Tischendorf), which only goes to show that on this point there is a great deal of uncertainty.

19. Merx regards that as a "baseless combination," both geographically and etymologically (Merx, *Markus und Lukas*, 79).

20. Cf. the instructive articles on Dalmanutha in *Encyclopedia Biblia* and *Dictionary of the Bible*.

Jerome, or in any early Christian and medieval pilgrim narratives, but it must have been located somewhere on the Sea of Galilee. At this point the hypothetical floodgates swing wide open. Nothing precludes a location on the western shore, but εἰς τὸ πέραν seems to suggest the east side of the Sea, where there is no evidence for a Bethsaida.

According to Josephus (B.J. 3.10.7) and Pliny the Elder (Nat.Hist. V.15), Bethsaida was located on the eastern bank of the Jordan, not far from its mouth at the Sea of Gennesaret. At that location today lie the ruins of et-Tel. Under Philip the tetrarch it was expanded into a city, and it was named for Julia, the daughter of Augustus. That does not cohere especially well with the fact that Mark 8:23 calls Bethsaida a κώμη, but perhaps a compromise is possible here. Perhaps the old community of Bethsaida became a suburb of Julia, or it may mean that it was a village in the area. κώμη evokes the impression of a city, but perhaps it was only a vernacular form of expression. All of these attempts at explanation may be unnecessary, because the reference could be nothing more than an error in the tradition.

To this point our discussion of the topographical connections within Mark 8 has been consistent on one point: after the feeding of the 4000, Jesus repairs to the region of Dalmanutha, which we can place on the east side of the Sea. From there he goes back to the other side of the Sea, to Bethsaida-Julia. The setting throughout is the northern region of the Sea of Gennesaret.

But we still have to take note of Mark 6:45, where Bethsaida is first mentioned. In this passage Jesus invites his disciples to set out with him εἰς τὸ πέραν πρὸς Βηθσαΐδαν (across, toward the east side, to Bethsaida). Where is Jesus when he gives this command? The preceding story about the feeding of the 5000 has no specific location. According to 6:31ff, it seems to have taken place on the eastern shore of the Sea. Certainly all of the commentators read it that way. For the time being I will allow for that possibility, but I will also seek to present the difficulties that accompany it. To begin, a voyage from one place on a seashore to another place on the same seashore simply cannot be described with the words προάγειν εἰς τὸ πέραν. Certainly we might imagine a kind of shore cruise; a journey from Dalmanutha in the south eastward to Bethsaida in the northeast, for example. In that case, the two locations would lie at some distance from each other, so there might be room to speak of εἰς τὸ πέραν. On the other hand, Bethsaida lies very near to the location of the feeding of the 5000, and in that setting the phrase εἰς τὸ πέραν makes no sense. The result of all this is an utterly amazing exegesis of 6:45, which relocates πρὸς βηθσαϊδαν into the same clause as ἕως.[21] It can be paraphrased as follows: the disciples steer for the opposite shore and land at a place in view of Bethsaida, i.e., which lies across from Bethsaida.[22] This reading results in a journey from east to west. Such an interpretation is hard to disqualify, even though it turns a blind eye to the feel of the language. But the journey from east to west has to be brought back into the discussion. A Bethsaida on the western shore of the sea has been postulated.[23] This too cannot be ruled out, as Bethsaida is a name that comes up frequently. There could have been different places on the sea with the name Bethsaida (more on the meaning of the name later!), just as in Germany there are dozens of Neuhausens, Neustadts, and Neukirches. But surely if the evangelist at 8:22 had in mind some other Bethsaida, namely Bethsaida-Julia, he would have referred at some point to the fact that there was also another place by the same name. Yet the fact is that we know nothing of any other Bethsaida, and none has been found in any archaeological excavations. A third possibility can be considered: the words εἰς τὸ πέραν, wherein the heart of the difficulty lies, have not been preserved in all of the traditions. They are missing from syr[sin] and in some manuscripts of the Old Latin. It is therefore possible that εἰς τὸ πέραν appeared difficult and was stricken for that reason.

Our examination of these individual pericopes has shown that the difficulty encountered by these exegetes does not lie in their methods. And I regard it as a methodological obligation to allow them to have their say. But do these exegetes also have a right to an implausible interpretation, to speculative suppositions about an unknown city, to truly hypothetical text criticism? Not in the slightest. If my objections are correct, then only one consequence follows: a seam lies between 6:33 and 6:34. 6:34 begins a narrative that has no clear connection with what precedes it. There cannot be a suture between 6:44 and 6:45, because 6:45 mentions the ὄχλος, picking up the previous reference.

21. So A. Klostermann and Th. Zahn, in Wohlenberg, *Markus*, 194.
22. Wohlenberg, *Markus*, 194.
23. Cf. esp. B. Weiss, *Markus und Lukas*, 103.

We thus arrive at a result that coheres with our previous investigations: the arrangement of the individual pericopes is embedded in an often presumptuous scroll of details that only seem to be chronological and topographical. All of the following pericopes are independent:

7:1ff	dispute over hand-washing
8:14–21	conversation about leaven
7:24–30, 31	the Canaanite woman
7:32–37	healing of a deaf and dumb man
8:22–26	healing of a blind man
8:10–13	the Pharisees' request for a sign
6:53–56	miracles in the area of Genessaret

The boundaries of these individual pericopes deserve further clarification, so let us return once more to close reading.

Jesus, Disciples, and the People
(Mark 6:31–33; Matt 14:13; Luke 9:10–11a)

The first feeding miracle is preceded by Mark 6:30–33, which contains some topographical details. Verse 30 has already been discussed and identified as the work of the evangelist, and it can reasonably be asked whether the following verse might also belong to his composition, or whether it introduces a new pericope with its use of the formula καὶ λέγει:

> ³¹καὶ λέγει αὐτοῖς, δεῦτε ὑμεῖς αὐτοὶ κατ᾿ ἰδίαν εἰς ἔρημον τόπον καὶ ἀναπαύσασθε ὀλίγον. ἦσαν γὰρ οἱ ἐρχόμενοι καὶ οἱ ὑπάγοντες πολλοί, καὶ οὐδὲ φαγεῖν εὐκαίρουν. ³²καὶ ἀπῆλθον εἰς ἔρημον τόπον κατ᾿ ἰδίαν. ³³καὶ εἶδον αὐτοὺς ὑπάγοντας καὶ ἐπέγνωσαν αὐτοὺς πολλοί, καὶ πεζῇ ἀπὸ πασῶν τῶν πόλεων συνέδραμον ἐκεῖ καὶ προσῆλθον αὐτούς.

The tradition is unstable here, which poses several interesting questions about composition. D and some of the Latin versions read ὁ ις after αὐτοῖς, a reading that exposes an incision at the end of v. 30. D offers a remarkable stylistic correction, as do some Old Latin Mss and syr^sin: ὑπάγωμεν and ἀναπαύεσθαι, instead of the command to the disciples in the second person. Since Jesus himself then goes with them, someone made the change to a first-person plural. At the beginning of v. 32 we have the remarkable variant ἀπῆλθεν in E, F, Γ et al. The same manuscripts also have a similar variant in v. 33: αὐτόν after ἐπέγνωσαν instead of αὐτούς. B and D, on the other hand, omit this αὐτούς altogether, and in A and Γ the words καὶ συνῆλθον πρὸς αὐτόν are inserted at the end of the verse. These variants betray a tendency to begin a new pericope at v. 32, without a reference back to v. 31. The addition of οἱ ὄχλοι after ὑπάγοντας in ς and some other manuscripts points in the same direction, but that gets us only half the way, since both αὐτοὺς ὑπάγοντας and προσῆλθον αὐτούς are still there. The result is a nearly inconceivable text: Γ, for example, puts it this way: "And *he* (Jesus) went by sea to a lonely area in that same region. But people saw *them* (the disciples) leaving, and many recognized *him* (Jesus) and ran toward him . . . and they came to *them* (the disciples) and met **him** (Jesus)." Other similar variants are equally difficult, except the text of syr[sin], which Merx regards as the original. The alterations show that there were various flaws in the scenery, and so we have the efforts of Matthew and Luke.

There is strong evidence for a seam between v. 31 and v. 32, for according to the context, it is the disciples who have just been invited to withdraw into a lonely area. What that means, however, is that Jesus and the disciples undertook a journey. The presence of the difficulty is tipped off by the many variants in v. 32, and especially by the reading of D in v. 31.[24] The situation depicted in v. 32–33 is not as difficult as has often been thought. Jesus goes with his disciples to a lonely place, but the people see him, and they come streaming to him from all the surrounding villages. As far as I can tell, all exegetes[25] take this to mean a voyage across the sea from west to east, while the people go along the northern shore of the sea and arrive before the boats. This view entails substantial difficulties with the geography, for it is virtually impossible for people going on foot around the shore to arrive just as fast as a ship sailing directly across the north end of the sea from west to east. The Jordan River would have been a formidable obstacle

---

24. On this basis it is understandable that Wendling (63–64) explains vv. 30–31 as a redactional insertion, with the pericope beginning at v. 32.

25. For example: "Bethsaida must have been located on the western shore" (B. Weiss, *Markus und Lukas*, 103). "The first meal took place on the far side of the sea, that is, on the eastern shore" (J. Weiss, *Das älteste Evangelium*, 205). Wellhausen is of the opinion that the meal played out on the far side of the sea in the wilderness" (Wellhausen, *Mark*, 50); Klostermann speaks of a journey to the other shore (Klostermann, *Markus*, 50); Catholic exegetes follow suit, for reasons of harmonization.

that the walkers would have had to cross.²⁶ But why does that "lonely place" have to be located on the east side of the sea? The interpreters who take it that way read the Lukan text into this part of Mark, as if εἰς ἔρημον τόπον (Mark 6:32) equals εἰς πόλιν καλουμένην Βηθσαϊδά (Luke 9:10). But the location could very well lie on the western shore, either north or south of Tiberias. Since the shoreline is rather straight there, a steadily increasing number of pedestrians, coming out of villages along the shore, could have stayed in step with the ship, keeping it in sight and arriving at the destination at the same time or perhaps even a little earlier. In this way we get a clear and vivid perception of the scene, by placing ourselves on the west side of the sea. Topographical difficulties no longer exist.²⁷

All the same, 6:32-33 did not develop organically with 6:34ff, but was inserted later as an introduction to a new unit (still recognizable on stylistic grounds) that begins with 6:34. As they lay in the tradition, the pericopes did not have a deep scenic background. Thus we can recognize 6:32-33; 6:31; and 6:30 as transitional pieces from the hand of the evangelist. The arrangement is reminiscent of the collections in 1:14-15 and in 3:7ff. There (in 3:7ff) the general account is interspersed with various details taken from what follows, like the πλοιάριον in 3:9, which is not used until much later. It is the same here: a large number of people in an isolated area is presupposed, and a boat is brought near. But as we have seen in 6:30-33, not everything holds together, and it seems to me that tradition and memory have been interwoven here. The expression ἀναπαύσασθε ὀλίγον is comprehensible as a piece of tradition, and the evangelist's use of it here is not clumsy, for a stylistic rigor persists, whether the subject is the disciples (6:31) or Jesus (6:31) and finally the disciples again.²⁸

As yet we have not answered an important question: why did Mark use such a long introductory piece here, when he so often strings together pericope after pericope without any concern at all for topographical and chronological

---

26. Merx offers a good treatment of the topography, based upon his own observations (Merx, *Markus und Lukas*, 61-62), and I agree with him. Other topographers think only about the east side, and do not notice the difficulties of that view.

27. It is important to note that this location cannot be disputed, although some commentators, based on false presuppositions, have exaggerated the difficulty here, arguing that the text gives us only the clumsy work of a later interpreter, not the evangelist.

28. As has been noted, Wendling (63) removes only 6:30-31 as a redactional insertion, because he thinks that 6:6-13 was also inserted by the editor. This argument is not decisive (cf. above on 6:6-13). Still less enlightening are Wendling's remarks on the confusion of two motives in the depiction of Jesus in v. 31. Here he does not see the richness of the tradition, as for example when he says that the editor "fell asleep for a minute" (63) on the saying from Matt 11:28.

connections?[29] He did so because this is the beginning of a new section, which shows Jesus outside of Galilee among the Gentiles, as the narrative came to a stop with the episode about Herod. Once again there was an opportunity for the evangelist to take the threads of the tradition in hand.

The other two Synoptics regard Mark 6:30-33 as merely as a transitional piece. Matthew (14:13) takes it in his typical way, placing only the most necessary chronological and topographical details in a short sequence: ἀκούσας δὲ ὁ Ἰησοῦς ἀνεχώρησεν ἐκεῖθεν ἐν πλοίῳ εἰς ἔρημον τόπον κατ ἰδίαν. καὶ ἀκουσάντες οἱ ὄχλοι ἠκολούθησαν αὐτῷ πεζοὶ ἀπὸ τῶν πόλεων. The close link between this verse and the Herod narrative has already been discussed. As usual, the dependence of Matthew upon Mark is plain to see: Matthew's text sounds rather abrupt.

Luke (9:10-11a) changed Mark in a slightly different way: καὶ ὑποστρέψαντες οἱ ἀπόστολοι διηγήσαντο αὐτῷ, ὅσα ἐποίησαν, καὶ παραλαβὼν αὐτοὺς ὑπεχώρησεν κατ ἰδίαν εἰς πόλιν καλουμένην Βηθσαϊδά. οἱ δὲ ὄχλοι γνόντες ἠκολούθησαν αὐτῷ.

> Some manuscripts have τῷ ιω in place of αὐτῷ. Instead of πόλιν καλουμένην Βηθσαϊδά (B L 33 cop), D has κώμην λεγομένην Βηθσαϊδά; cf. Mark 8:23. ℵ and syr^cur mention no place name at all, but rather ἔρημον τόπον. This truly is a compromise with the Markan text, unless it is a compromise with the subsequent text of Luke, where the feeding takes place in the same region. On this basis syr^sin wants to combine it all into one text: πύλην πόλεως καλουμένης Βηθσαϊδά. ς puts together A C Γ Δ arm eth: τόπον ἔρημον πόλεως καλουμένης Βηθσαϊδά. Finally, some Old Latin manuscripts and the Peshitta identify the entire region as "Bethsaida": *locum desertum qui (quod) est (vocabatur) Bethsaida.*

Luke fills in everything that was missing from Mark's arrangement and context, creating a clear connection with the commission of the disciples. Jesus withdraws with his disciples. His motive, apparently, is to escape from Herod, who (according to Luke 9:9) wants to see Jesus. Luke's style betrays itself in the choice of the word, καλουμένην. Especially striking, in light of the many corrections in the textual tradition, is the explicit naming of Bethsaida. We should not infer that Luke is making any use

---

29. Wellhausen (*Mark*, 50) is not sufficiently attentive when he describes Mark's composition technique as follows: the disciples had to return, since they had to participate in the feeding miracle, and so on. Yet Wellhausen is correct that 6:30-33 is a redactional closure. But it is not the case that this kind of transitional piece has anything to do with psychology; as Wohlenberg (*Markus*, 189) has observed about this passage: "Jesus would have used even the time on the water with his disciples for serious conversation about matters of the soul . . ." and so on.

of special tradition here.[30] The place name is based upon the later text of Mark, which Luke certainly used.

The Feeding of the Five Thousand
(Mark 6:34-44; Matt 14:14-21; Luke 9:11b [10]-17);
The Feeding of the Four Thousand
(Mark 8:1-10; Matt 15:32-39)

The introduction to the first feeding story in Mark 6:34 runs as follows: καὶ ἐξελθὼν εἶδεν πολὺν ὄχλον καί . . .

> D stylizes this introduction a bit. More important is the fact that ς, along with E F Δ et al., reads ὁ ις after εἶδεν, but A puts it *ahead*. This kind of reading, which we have encountered so often before, indicates that 6:34 begins something new.

The textual tradition makes clear that a new pericope begins with 6:34, and not with 6:32. It is stated that Jesus gets out of the boat and encounters the crowd hurrying out toward him. But, as we have demonstrated in all of our investigations into Mark's compositional technique, this connection is not secure. The pericope has been inserted here, even though it is fully comprehensible on its own. As is characteristic of these individual stories, the people in Jesus' entourage (the crowds, the disciples) appear without any special introduction. Thus it becomes clear that 6:30-33 is a separate piece that should be separated from 6:34ff. The course of the narrative is readily apparent: Jesus has mercy on the people. Evening is coming on (καὶ ἤδη ὥρας πολλῆς γινομένης or γενομένης),[31] and the disciples point out the difficulty of caring for a hungry crowd, yet Jesus satisfies them all.

In the mention of "green grass" (ἐν χλωρῷ χόρτῳ) we may have an unconscious clue to the calendar, although this is unfortunately difficult to determine. If one turns to people who know the terrain in Palestine, one receives different answers. Some say that in Galilee, the grass can remain green into the month of July, and in the areas around perennial streams and rivers it does not become thin. Others say that during the dry seasons a

---

30. Many scholars are inclined in that direction. J. Weiss (*Schriften*, 456) is seeing too much in this designation of the place, when he cites a possible agreement with the Gospel of John, even though that possibility has not yet been satisfactorily explained. Loisy gets it right (*Les Évangiles synoptiques*, 1:931).

31. This reference to the time of day, which rises entirely from the development of the scene, cannot be the beginning of a new pericope. Wendling (66) makes this mistake when he suggests that 6:35 begins a special story inserted from the early stratum of Ur-Mark.

green lawn is quite impossible, even with expert watering. The area around the Sea of Galilee produces that kind of growth only in the spring, and only until the first few weeks of the dry season. On this basis our story has to take place around the time of Passover.[32] Typically we do not put much value on these kinds of details, because we presume that they are products of an evangelist's creativity.[33] That is indeed possible here. On the other hand, there are details here that can go back to genuine memories, not of Mark, but of the first narrator of this story. In this case an incidental detail about the calendar has opened up several possible implications that must be taken into account. If both the story of the gleaning (Mark 2:23-28) and our narrative are set in the Passover season, then an entire year has passed between Mark 2 and the end of Mark 6. If the chronology of these two stories can be fixed, then the chronological framework that Mark seems to assert would be blown to bits.

Our delimitation of the pericope of the feeding of the five thousand (i.e., that 6:34 is the beginning) is supported by the parallel narrative of the feeding of the four thousand (8:1ff), where 8:1-2a is parallel to 6:34. The opening words are different: ἐν ἐκείναις ταῖς ἡμέραις πάλιν πολλοῦ ὄχλου ὄντος . . . προσκαλεσάμενος τοὺς μαθητὰς λέγει αὐτοῖς . . .

> D and various other manuscripts try to create a closer connection with what precedes by inserting δέ. That a new excerpt begins here is made clear in ς (E F Γ et al.) by the insertion of ὁ ις after προσκαλεσάμενος. Instead of πάλιν πολλοῦ, ς A E F Γ read παμπόλλου, clearly the result of a redactor who did not understand πάλιν.

Certainly the two feeding stories are doublets. What is not certain is whether there was a split in the tradition, or whether one narrative has arisen from the other.[34] The framework, especially in the second story, indi-

---

32. Cf. Windisch (146) where he cites Homanner (*Die Dauer*, 86-87). This point of view stands strongly in the service of the thesis that Jesus' public ministry lasted for more than one year.

33. Cf. Wellhausen, (*Mark*, 52), where he speaks of "a painterly attribute." "[Mark] was following his propensity for imagination, when he created this 'green' out of whole cloth, which is why we cannot take it as a remark that has any meaning" (Windisch, "Die Dauer der öffentliche Wirksamkeit Jesu nach den vier Evangelisten," ZNW 12 (1911), 147-175).

34. J. Weiss (*Das älteste Evangelium*, 218ff) thinks there is a split in the tradition. Wellhausen (*Mark*, 53) is inclined to see 8:1ff as the older tradition. On the other hand Wendling (69ff) establishes after a thorough investigation that the first feeding story is the older version, from which the second was borrowed rather mechanically. It is a complicated issue, whether there is an historical kernel to be found here, or whether at the end of the day it is merely a matter of taste.

cates that Mark found both narratives in the tradition. πάλιν is one of Mark's favorite transitions, so its appearance here can be credited to his account. ἐν ἐκείναις ταῖς ἡμέραις, by contrast, belongs to the original pericope. For this reason the suture[35] cannot have come from the evangelist, because (with the exception of 1:9) this kind of time determination is not found in his work. How many opportunities there would be, given the dearth of chronological connections in the narrative, to attribute transitional remarks of this sort to the individual scene! Whoever wants to chalk up this caesura, or even the entire narrative, to Mark must answer the impossible question of why the evangelist put this kind of introduction precisely here, while the Gospel of Matthew (for example) often connects individual scenes in just this way.[36] At an earlier stage the pericope may have stood in a different context, from which it has been lifted and placed here. The saying of Jesus in 8:2 indicates that the crowd has already been with him for three days. The course of the narrative as it now stands, however, says nothing at all about such a context. More will be said about 8:10 later.

Neither feeding story includes any indications of time or place. The setting is described only vaguely: we find ourselves near the Sea of Galilee. Not entirely superfluous is the mention of fish, which imparts a certain local color.

Matthew (14:14-21) generally follows the framing of the scene as he received it from Mark. The introduction to the first feeding (14:14) agrees verbatim with Mark: καὶ ἐξελθὼν εἶδεν πολὺν ὄχλον (as in Mark, ς C E F Γ et al. insert ὁ ις after ἐξελθών; L et al. make the insertion after εἶδεν). In the second narrative (Matt 15:32-39), Mark 8:1b is missing. All of this establishes a stronger connection with Matt 15:29-31, which Mark, in spite of his uniqueness, already had.

Luke (9:11b) is the only one of the Synoptics who moves the feeding story back in the narrative in order to give it a close context (Luke does not have the second feeding story, about which more will be said later). The seam between Mark 6:33 and 6:34 is smoothed out. According to Luke, the feeding plays out in the wilderness (despite the reference to Bethsaida in 9:10!).[37]

---

35. Closer determination of the chronology is utterly unproductive, including what πάλιν might refer to.

36. Wendling (7) correctly recognizes the characteristics of a caesura, but does not correctly address the question of the origin of the word.

37. With reference to the close connection between Luke 9:11 and 9:18, Spitta (*Die synoptische Grundschrift*, 221ff) separates the stories, which seems not quite cogent. Interestingly, Spitta has to concede that none of Luke's digressions from Mark and Matthew preserves the oldest form of the text. Thus he has to excise Luke 9:12-17 from the basic synoptic document.

Jesus Walks on the Sea
(Mark 6:45–52: Matt 14:22–33)

⁴⁵Καὶ εὐθὺς ἠνάγκασεν τοὺς μαθητὰς αὐτοῦ ἐμβῆναι εἰς τὸ πλοῖον καὶ προάγειν εἰς τὸ πέραν πρὸς Βηθσαϊδάν, ἕως αὐτὸς ἀπολύει τὸν ὄχλον. ⁴⁶καὶ ἀποταξάμενος αὐτοῖς ἀπῆλθεν εἰς τὸ ὄρος προσεύξασθαι.

> D^gr* reads προσάγειν. D vg arm aeth et al. insert (cf. Mt) a meaningless αὐτόν after προάγειν.

Like the preceding stories, this one is rich in apparent designations of place and time that are closely tied to the feeding stories. A special pericope would not likely have begun with a reference to Jesus separating himself from the crowds. In the same way the statement, "He compelled his disciples," also suggests a somewhat unusual situation, and the explanation lies in the feeding story. In addition, 6:52 establishes a further connection with the miracle. All of this points to the fact that the stories were already connected when the evangelist came upon them. The only alteration is (καὶ) εὐθύς, but even though this is Mark's favorite caesura, it does not necessarily indicate that a new scene, entirely separate from what precedes, begins here. Mark had 6:27 as part of a traditional connection that included (καὶ) εὐθύς. But the mountain location does not figure prominently in this nicely painted scene.[38] A striking image is presented: as in 3:13, Jesus is alone atop the mountain (cf. Matt 14:23: εἰς τὸ ὄρος κατ᾽ ἰδίαν). Scruples based on the indicators of time (here, ὀψίας γενομένης, but in 6:35, ὥρα πολλή) are not convincing.[39]

Matthew 14:22–33 follows Mark in every way, except that he drops the reference to Bethsaida from the introduction. Perhaps he had topographical concerns, because Jesus had not yet arrived at Bethsaida. Matthew does know the location of Bethsaida, for he records the saying of Jesus about it in 11:21 (= Luke 10:13). Here I would like to venture the guess that Matthew

---

38. B. Weiss (*Markus und Lukas*, 104) is obviously right when he remarks that the phrase ἐν μέσῳ τῆς θαλάσσης is not spoken in the geographical sense, but rather more generally in contrast to "on land."

39. In the opinion of Wendling (*Die Enstehung des Marcusevangelium*, 82), it is a secondary feature that Jesus steps out from hiding and seizes the initiative. We must reject that idea, especially in light of the judgments of more recent criticism that sees Mark 6:45ff as a doublet of 4:35ff. (Cf. von Soden in "Das Interesse des apostolischen Zeitalters," 148. Wellhausen, *Mark* 54, calls it "an enhanced variant"). The two feeding stories are certainly a doublet. But it also seems to me that we sometimes resort to this doublet theory too often. In the gospel tradition, many stories and motives are independent from each other, and they are still often interchanged with each other, without being directly dependent upon each other.

has intentionally erased Bethsaida from the saying at this point, because the Lord had previously pronounced a woe over Bethsaida, after which he could not instruct his disciples to return to that town. Chorazin, which also had been cursed, disappears from the Jesus tradition, even though Jesus must have had further contact with the place. Matthew is the only gospel that includes the story of Peter sinking into the water (vv. 28-31).

Jesus' Activity in the Area of Gennesaret
(Mark 6:53-56; Matt 14:34-36)

καὶ διαπεράσαντες ἐπὶ τὴν γῆν ἦλθον εἰς Γεννεσαέρ (Γεννησάρ).

> D and various Itala mss. have ἐκεῖθεν after διαπεράσαντες. In the same mss, as well as in syr^{sin} pesh arm, καὶ προσωρμίσθησαν is missing, and in v. 56 πλατείαις ("streets") appears in place of ἀγοραῖς, since the ἀγροί ("farms") did not have "markets" in the strict sense.

The connection between this passage and what precedes is stylistically good, but in terms of content and topography it is quite difficult. An arrival in Bethsaida is implied by διαπεράσαντες, but in the same breath the landing in Gennesaret takes place. How is this change in course to be explained? We might suppose that the storm may have forced the disciples to make a forced landing, which Jesus had not planned.[40] But now the storm has abated, so that (as in 4:36ff) the journey could come to a successful end after the storm at sea. Or does it perhaps mean that the wind drove the ship off course for a time, and they were tired from the trip (it was already quite late; cf. 6:47), so they headed straight for the shore? The interpreter of these texts will have to draw the right connections, while remaining cognizant of the fact that the text allows for many different interpretations.

How do things stand with this section itself, which plays out in Gennesaret? We are not dealing here with a report about a particular act of Jesus, but rather a collection of reports, with similarities to 3:7ff. Almost no original connections survive, and then only here and there.[41] Is the whole thing just an elaboration on the part of the evangelist? That is possible. The basis for an insertion at this point might be as follows: in the next pericope the Pharisees appear, along with scribes from Jerusalem. Bethsaida, which was located outside of Palestine in the territory of Philip the tetrarch, is not

---

40. This thesis is well developed by J. Weiss (*Das älteste Evangelium*, 207).

41. Cf. Wendling (*Die Entstehung des Marcusevangelium*, 86-87), who once again overstates the difficulty of the situation as depicted.

an apt or suitable location. That would explain 6:53, but not the report itself in 6:54-56.[42] From this point on it is wise to regard 6:53-56 as a piece of tradition that the evangelist has set into a coherent complex (feeding, sea voyage, arrival in Gennesaret). This collection—and in spite of everything these verses must be designated by that term—was either put together in the course of the tradition, or it might go back to a real memory.[43] It is not insignificant that the fourth evangelist, who is generally independent of the Synoptic outline of the story of Jesus, has the same grouping of stories (feeding, sea journey, landing) in John 6.

Matthew (14:34-36) offers a substantially shorter version of Mark, as the first evangelist is generally sparing with topographical details. When he refers to τόπος ἐκεῖνος, he appears to regard the area of Gennesaret as a city.

Controversies over Hand-washing, Purity, and Impurity (Mark 7:1-23; Matt 15:1-20)

καὶ συνάγονται πρὸς αὐτὸν οἱ Φαρισαῖοι καί τινες τῶν γραμματέων ἐλθόντες Ἱεροσολύμων.

The scene that opens with these words is a parade example of an unlocalized pericope that is not fixed in place with any clamps.[44] If there were some clear chronological connection here, we would expect Jesus to set out on an uninterrupted journey to Bethsaida. These stories of controversy between Jesus and his opponents, which clearly were still alive in the earliest Christian community, have in their very nature something timeless and place-less.[45] There are comparable to scenes in 2:18-22; 2:23-28; and 3:1-6. The evidence indicates that the scene is set outside of Jerusalem, and probably outside of Judea, too. This is indicated by the expression ἐλθόντες ἀπὸ Ἱεροσολύμων, which refers to the second group of opponents, the scribes. It is highly likely that we have to think of a location in Galilee,

42. Wellhausen (*Mark*, 55) offers an explanation here that is too easy, which Klostermann follows (*Mark*, 56).

43. In opposition to Wendling, J. Weiss (*Das älteste Evangelium*, 207-8) regards this report of events around Gennesaret as very good tradition, in the form of Matt 14:34-36 (Ur-Mark). It seems to me that Weiss is reading too much psychology into the text.

44. It is noteworthy that Catholic harmonizers (cf. J. Belser, "Zur Evangelienfrage," 365) see a break before 7:1 and conclude: "These links in the arrangement of the report point to the time after the Passover when the hatred of the Jewish opponents toward Jesus was increasing."

45. Wendling's question (68) at this point is very nicely put: "Is it possible that a tendentious piece like the scene with the Pharisees in 7:1ff had a place in the oral pre-tradition?"

and it is significant that a relocation from Jerusalem to Galilee is indicated, even though Mark never mentions it specifically. The tradition provided him with the names of the two groups of opponents, whom he usually describes differently (cf. for example, 2:6, 18, 24; 3:6, 22).

Matthew 15:1-9 is clearly dependent upon Mark 7:1, because it says: τότε προσέρχονται τῷ ᾽Ιησοῦ ἀπὸ ᾽Ιεροσολύμων Φαρισαῖοι καὶ γραμματεῖς.

> Instead of τῷ ᾽Ιησοῦ, D it vg aeth have πρὸς αὐτόν (cf. Mark 7:1); this reading may be original, as τῷ ᾽Ιησοῦ is later pressed into service as a pericope introduction. ς C E F L Γ Δ et al. read οἱ ἀπὸ ᾽Ιεροσολύμων Φαρισαῖοι καὶ γραμματεῖς (cf. Mark 7:1).

The word τότε fills in the seam between Mark 6:53 and 7:1. Both the Pharisees and the scribes come from Jerusalem. προσέρχεσθαι is reminiscent of Matthew's style, who uses that word fifty-two times, while Mark uses it only six times, Luke ten, and John only once.

In Mark the conversation with the opponents about hand-washing actually ends in 7:13. Something new begins in v. 14 (vv. 14-16, perhaps 15), which at this point is arranged on the basis of the content: καὶ προσκαλεσάμενος πάλιν τὸν ὄχλον ἔλεγεν αὐτοῖς. The issue is a saying about purity and impurity in the context of a debate about hand-washing.

The fact that a new and completely independent scene begins here is evident from the appearance of ὁ ᾽Ιησοῦς ahead of πάλιν in some manuscripts.

This kind of unmediated arrangement of sayings from Jesus, which elucidate a common theme, we have previously seen in 4:21-26. The patchword πάλιν comes from Mark. προσκαλεσάμενος is an introductory expression that is also common in sayings of Jesus, so we cannot determine with certainty whether this saying goes back only to Mark or was taken up out of the tradition by him. In his parallel passage, Matthew (15:10-11) follows this same form, although he drops the πάλιν. He also adds an additional item to the series of sayings: vv. 12-14, where the Pharisees are described as "blind guides." This saying is introduced within a scenic framework that has a distinctively Matthean shape. We cannot be certain that this saying of Jesus originally applied to the Pharisees, because Luke 6:39 offers a similar saying that includes no mention of the Pharisees.

Mark 7:17 completes the change of scene: ¹⁷ καὶ ὅτε εἰσῆλθεν εἰς τὸν οἶκον ἀπὸ τοῦ ὄχλου, ἐπηρώτων αὐτὸν οἱ μαθηταὶ αὐτοῦ τὴν παραβολήν. ¹⁸ καὶ λέγει αὐτοῖς . . .

> In place of τὸν οἶκον (so ℵ Δ syr^sin), A B L et al. read simply οἶκον. But that is a distinction without a difference.

As was the case in the parable of the sower (4:10ff), here too a commentary is attached to the saying about purity and impurity. The topography is not as difficult here as it was in that saying, but unfortunately we can do rather little with the mention of a house: is it in Capernaum? the house of Jesus? the house of Peter?

With the words ἔλεγεν δέ, v. 20 begins a new saying (remarkably, D^gr and F read ἔλεγον δέ), which must have been spoken on a different occasion. The repetition of the introductory formula indicates as much. In both cases Matthew (15:15–20) erases the new beginning. Verse 15, like 9:1 (= Mark 2:1), leaves out the house and identifies Peter as the one who asks the question: ἀποκριθεὶς δὲ ὁ Πέτρος εἶπεν αὐτῷ. But his question comes after the same saying in 10–11. Here again it is clear that Mark's outline has brought together vv. 12–14. Verse 18, and its parallel Mark 7:20, extend the saying without inserting the connecting phrase ἔλεγεν δέ.

It has already been pointed out that this assembly of a complex of longer and shorter sayings of Jesus is reminiscent of the "parables chapter," i.e., Mark 4. That allows us to suspect that it was Mark's idea to put these controversy stories here, in order to introduce Jesus' basic outlook on purity and impurity just before he crosses over into Gentile territory. We will engage with that topic in the following pericope.

The Canaanite Woman
(Mark 7:24–30; Matt 15:21–28)

Jesus goes into Gentile territory: ἐκεῖθεν δὲ ἀναστὰς ἀπῆλθεν εἰς τὰ ὅρια Τύρου. καὶ εἰσελθὼν εἰς οἰκίαν οὐδένα ἠθέλησεν γνῶναι.

In ℵ A B et al., Mark has an untypical δέ here, which may be the reason that ς reads καί. The influence here is most likely Matt 15:21, where the words καὶ Σιδῶνος also follow Τύρου. ς also has μεθόρια ("border area"), which is a weaker form of ὅρια ("area"). After ἀναστὰς some manuscripts have ὁ ϊς: the introduction to this pericope has been influenced by the text of Matthew!

After the transition, ἐκεῖθεν refers back to the house mentioned in 7:17. Some interpreters take this word in an exceptional sense, suggesting that ἐκεῖθεν refers all the way back to the plain of Gennesaret. Such questions about geographical references only do harm. Mark uses ἐκεῖθεν only five times, and so it certainly does not appear to be an expletive. But in the text of the pericope that lies before us there is nothing left of its original location. With an introduction like ἐκεῖθεν δὲ ἀναστάς, it may have once stood in another series of stories, and Mark has picked up that pericope along with its introduction. For this reason ἐκεῖθεν δέ is used by this author as a transition. Any and all further questions about geographical details— such as whether the house belonged to a follower of Jesus who lived in Gentile territory, or whether it was the house of a Gentile, or where exactly the scene was set, whether it was in Tyre or Sidon, or in the south or in the north—all these questions are pointless.[46] We need not conceive of any special circumstance or any long journey by Jesus off into the distance, if we keep in mind that the region of Tyre extended right up to the border of northern Galilee. But that is at best a second or third order question. At this point it comes down to the fact that while he is in Gentile territory in the region of Tyre, Jesus wants to remain hidden (the house!), but a Gentile woman extorts a miracle from him.[47] That follows naturally from the location in a Gentile region. Thus the setting is anchored in the narrative: 7:26 is indeed the words of a woman who is Greek (because of her religion) and Syro-Phoenician (because of her origin).[48] [49]

Matthew (15:21-28) follows Mark all the way: καὶ ἐξελθὼν ἐκεῖθεν ὁ Ἰησοῦς ἀνεχώρησεν εἰς τὰ μέρη Τύρου καὶ Σιδῶνος. There follow some characteristically Matthean digressions. Ἀναχωρεῖν is obviously one of Matthew's favorite expressions: he uses it ten times (only once in Mark; not at all in Luke). The woman is described as Χαναναία instead of Συροφοινίκισσα, because that is an older "biblical" expression and the Phoenicians liked to represent themselves as descendants of the ancient Canaanites. In this context it is a sign of the writer's erudition, as we have already seen in Matt 4:12ff. There is no particular significance to the fact that Matthew changes Mark's τὰ ὅρια Τύρου into τὰ μέρη Τύρου καὶ Σιδῶνος. Nothing about the geography is changed thereby. More noteworthy is the fact that in this case the

---

46. For the necessary topography, cf. B. Weiss, *Markus und Lukas*, 115-16; Wohlenberg, *Markus*, 211-12.

47. This conclusion, which has been expounded by some scholars, is on the same level as the legends about the name of the woman. According to the Clementine Homilies (III, 73; IV, 1, 3, 6), her name was Justa and her daughter was Bernike.

48. Spitta, *Jesus und die Heidnischen Mission*, 44ff., overinterprets this situation.

49. Wendling (*Die Entstehen des Markusevangelium*, 79ff) draws upon Wrede's theory of the messianic secret (v. 24b: the house is a symbol of secrecy!) in order to argue that the whole pericope is Mark's elaborate re-working of the Jairus narrative. He finds further evidence for this thesis in the coherence of 7:24, 31 with 3:8 (reference to Tyre and Sidon!). But here is where the matter stands: Mark could refer to Tyre and Sidon in his report (3:7ff), because he knew of this story in the tradition. Thus 3:8 depends upon 7:24, 31, and not the other way around. On a later page in his book (p. 115), Wendling sees the journey to Tyre as a doublet with the journey in 8:27. Equally unconvincing is his derivation of the setting for the Lord's sayings in Matt 11:20ff.

Markan narrative is not shortened but lengthened. I cannot decide whether Matthew is following a special tradition here, or whether he is building a framework for the saying which is known to us from Matt 10:6 (i.e., that the mission should only apply to the lost sheep of the house of Israel).

The Healing of a Deaf and Dumb Man (Mark 7:31–37); The Healing of Several Sick People (Matt 15:29–31)

The connection between these two stories and what precedes appears to be especially strong: ³¹καὶ πάλιν ἐξελθὼν ἐκ τῶν ὁρίων Τύρου ἦλθεν διὰ Σιδῶνος εἰς τὴν θάλασσαν τῆς Γαλιλαίας ἀνὰ μέσον τῶν ὁρίων Δεκαπόλεως. ³²καὶ φέρουσιν αὐτῷ κωφὸν καὶ μογίλαλον.

> F Γ and a long series of other manuscripts have ὁ ις after ἐξελθών. In place of ἐκ τῶν ὁρίων Τύρου ἦλθεν διὰ Σιδῶνος (ℵ B D L 33 Latt cop aeth), A Γ ... syr^sin pesh arm read ἐκ τῶν ὁρίων Τύρου ἦλθεν καὶ Σιδῶνος.

The route that Jesus traverses in this text is quite strange. If we take the route suggested by the best witnesses, we get the following itinerary: Jesus leaves the region of Tyre (somewhere on the northern border of Galilee), wanders toward Sidon—a journey of about 36 km along the Sea—and then turns toward the Decapolis, which is found on the eastern and southeastern side of the Sea of Galilee. For that journey the best route would have been the main road through Lebanon. From there he goes to Caesarea Philippi by way of Bethsaida-Julias, apparently by sea. That is the long way around, which, although it is not totally impossible, it is certainly not very probable. It is significant that important ancient textual witnesses, by way of tiny alterations, produce a text in which this complicated journey disappears: Jesus leaves the region of Tyre *and* Sidon, and goes toward the Decapolis. Perhaps this is what Mark meant. Certainly he never intended for a long journey to separate the two healings in Gentile territory, but due to his lack of familiarity with the geographical relationships, Mark expressed himself awkwardly.

We cannot attribute v. 31 directly to Markan composition.[50] For when someone creates a framework for a narrative, they do not make it as intricate and complicated as this. We arrive therefore at the boundary to

---

50. J. Weiss has a hunch that is quite fine but also quite dubious: "According to Mark, Jesus had an abode in the region of the Decapolis. According to Mark's plan, Jesus could not go into Galilee, so he sent him to the Decapolis by way of Sidon" (J. Weiss, *Schriften*, 139–40).

the story about the healing of a deaf and dumb man. Does it begin with v. 31 or with v. 32? Certainly v. 32 (καὶ φέρουσιν αὐτῷ κωφόν . . .) would be a good introduction to a pericope, as 1:40 and 2:18 can attest. In addition, the narrative itself is readily comprehensible, even though it lacks any connection to any particular place. In the preceding pericope about the Canaanite woman the situation was quite different. How then did this narrative end up in this location? Should we suppose that Mark could not find a better place for it? That might be. But then what about v. 31? Mark himself would have wanted the pericope to begin with v. 31, as is shown by his characteristic use of the word πάλιν, and so did the manuscripts that insert ὁ ις at this point. Yet none of this has any bearing on the content of the tradition as Mark found it. It is easy to regard v. 31 as the conclusion of a pericope about the story of the Canaanite woman, but that would leave unclear the status of the story about the deaf and dumb man. In its current context it is a report about Jesus' miraculous healing of a sick man in Gentile territory. Long before Mark, it had already been located by the tradition in the Decapolis, which was indeed a Gentile area. Either both stories belonged together as a complex from the very beginning, or there was an independent narrative about the Decapolis, to which the evangelist attached v. 31, as both an introduction and a conclusion.[51]

Mark's account has been thoroughly reworked in Matthew's parallel passage, but it still shows through, despite the changes. At one time the word μεταβάς pointed to a specific location (cf. 11:1; 12:9), and in this way v. 31 corresponds to the sentence in Mark 7:37. But Matthew does not specifically mention the Decapolis and leaves Sidon out altogether, thereby avoiding the geographical uncertainties in Mark. Instead of describing particular miracles, Matthew gives only an overview of Jesus' ministry among the sick.

Why is this particular narrative about the deaf and dumb man missing, just as the story of the blind man in Bethsaida will be later on? In chapters 8 and 9, Matthew put together two similar stories, both of which obviously come from his special source. Matthew 9:27-31 is *the healing of two blind men*: v. 27, καὶ παράγοντι ἐκεῖθεν τῷ Ἰησοῦ ἠκολούθησαν αὐτῷ δύο τυφλοί is a truly Matthean pericope introduction, and v. 28 mentions οἰκία, a word already well-known to us; exegetes should know better than to ask about its location. Matthew 9:32-34 is *the healing of a dumb demoniac*: v. 32, αὐτῶν δὲ ἐξερχομένων, ἰδοὺ προσήνεγκαν αὐτῷ differentiates this story from the one that precedes. Indeed it is not certain that there is any connection between

---

51. Wellhausen (*Mark*, 60) accepts just such an arrangement: "Perhaps we have here only one event with two different versions of the setting for the healing of the deaf and dumb man." I cannot verify Wellausen's interesting thesis: "The reference to Sidon is a mistake. צידן means 'Saidan,' and that is Bethsaida."

them at all. Since Matthew now presents the healing of a blind man (20:29ff) and the healing of a deaf and dumb man (12:22ff),[52] he feels obliged to omit two similar stories from Mark.[53]

The description of the location in which Jesus situates himself atop the mountain (v. 29 ἀναβὰς εἰς τὸ ὄρος) is odd, as it seems to assign a special significance to this particular mountain. It is hard to erase the picture, indeed the painting, which Matthew has in mind: Jesus at the top of the mountain, surrounded by the sick. It is reminiscent of another occasion when Jesus was on a mountaintop surround by those who wanted to hear his teaching, and still another time when he was on a mountaintop surrounded by his disciples.

Both evangelists (Mark 8:1-10 = Matt 15:32-39) follow this narrative with the *feeding of the four thousand*, which has already been discussed.

There is, however, something yet to be said about the closing verse Mark 8:10 = Matt 15:39, the geography of which has already occupied our attention. Does this verse belong to what precedes or what follows? Modern editions and interpretations vary. Even in antiquity some interpreters took it as the beginning of a new pericope, as is indicated by the insertion of ὁ ις in ℵ* L and several Latin versions: *Jesus autem ascendens*.

The Pharisees Seek a Sign
(Mark 8:11-12; Matt 16:1-4; Luke 11:29; 11:16; 12:54-56)

The fact that the pericope starts at Mark 8:10 does not change the fact that the original beginning was in v. 11. For like the dispute over handwashing in 7:1ff, the brief account given here about the Pharisees' request for a sign

---

52. The usual explanation for this is that the stories in Matt 9:27-33 are doublets of Matt 20:29-34 (here two blind men, perhaps because Matthew combines the blind man of Bethsaida with Mark 10:46-52?) and Mark 12:22-24. In my judgment this much-loved doublet theory does not get the relationships right. There are features of Matt 9:27-33 that this theory cannot explain. Worst of all, it underestimates what an historical treasure the earliest Christian tradition actually is. Clearly there were doublets, and the same historical event came down in different versions. But the evangelists came upon these doublets; they did not create them. It is not possible to extract any kind of motif (healing of the blind, e.g., or healing of the deaf). The stories in which these motifs appear go back through the evangelist to an unrefined original form. Otherwise we will not correctly appreciate the literary distinctiveness of these narratives, nor of the actual story of Jesus, who could have healed more than one deaf and dumb person.

53. The oft-expressed opinion that Matthew stumbled over the solidity of Mark's two healing stories ("magical healings," because saliva was used) leads to a vicious circle, where one can say that originally Mark worked only with a template, because he had none of these stories (a "younger tradition," according to J. Weiss, *Schriften*, 140).

always lacks a specific setting in place and time. Thus the words ἐξῆλθον οἱ Φαρισαῖοι mark off the original beginning. For this reason certain questions cannot be answered, such as: were the Pharisees on the shore? Or were they in the Decapolis? Indeed, such questions cannot even be debated.[54]

Matthew (16:1-4) follows Mark. The distinctive hand of the evangelist can be recognized in the word προσελθόντες (cf. 15:1). After the Pharisees, the Sadducees are named. In Mark we never find them in combination, but that is not an especially significant problem. Mark certainly knows of the Sadducees. As in 3:7 and 6:11-12, here also Matthew has unintentionally connected the two groups. Perhaps one would not often have had to deal with Sadducees outside of Jerusalem and Judea, and in fact Mark speaks of the Sadducees only in connection with Jerusalem. In that case, our scene must play out somewhere outside of Galilee. That is not impossible but neither is it demonstrable. In contrast to Mark, Matthew has added an extra two verses about a sign from heaven and the signs of the times. The manuscript evidence for vv. 2-3 is uncertain (missing from ℵ B Γ . . . syr^{sin} arm). Luke puts it in a different place (12:54) and gives it a quite different address: ἔλεγεν δὲ καὶ τοῖς ὄχλοις.

What Mark and Matthew have in common can be found in Luke 11:29. But this saying, which is directed toward the ὄχλοι, has its own parallel in Matt 12:38f (from Q), while Matt 16:1-4, which is identical in content, was created from Mark.[55]

The Conversation about Leaven
(Mark 8:13-21; Matt 16:5-12; Luke 12:1)

Once again we face uncertainty about the point at which a pericope begins: is it v. 13 or v. 14? On behalf of v. 13, there is the presence of the word πάλιν; and on behalf of v. 14, there is the fact that ἐν τῷ πλοίῳ signifies the beginning of a sea voyage (εἰς τὸ πέραν; v. 13). The connection between the two stories lies principally in the saying about the leaven of the Pharisees and Herod (v. 15). Yet this saying does not belong to the actual material of 8:14-21. It found its place here alongside an isolated saying of Jesus that was in circulation at that time. In Luke 12:1 that same saying found still another setting.

The sense of the saying is not clear, not even in Matthew, who (as in v. 1) mentions Pharisees and Sadducees and then at the end goes back to a saying that had been mixed in. Thus we will have nothing but bad luck if we

---

54. Cf. B. Weiss, *Markus und Lukas*, 124; Klostermann, *Markus*, 64; Wohlenberg, *Markus*, 223: "It is as if they came out of their hiding places."

55. Cf. above, p. 108.

try to juxtapose Matthew and Mark 8:13 (which is both a conclusion and an introduction at the same time): 1) Conclusion of the preceding narrative: Jesus dismisses the Pharisees; 2) Beginning of a new narrative: the disciples travel across the sea. When we analyze this account, it becomes clear that Jesus goes ahead of the disciples, who make their journey across the sea alone. Thus their conversation takes place not in the boat, but rather on land. ἐλθόντες cannot mean "during the course of the crossing."

Interpretations of these special scenes with the disciples generally come to the conclusion that they are not historical. In fact the withdrawal of Jesus after the miraculous feeding—after two miraculous feedings, of the five thousand and the four thousand—leaves us no other choice. It would be premature, however, to conclude that the conversation has been elaborated by the evangelist. Certainly the narratives of the story of Jesus are arranged as individual pericopes without any consideration for each other.[56] Thus it is noteworthy that 8:17ff. refers to the feeding story. If these two narratives were both well-known, it is conceivable that some sort of connection between them might have developed within the course of the narratives' emergence from the tradition: Jesus is alone with his disciples in a boat; no one has brought any bread; the disciples are worried, but the master rebukes their lack of faith; he is the one who can always help, just as he helped the five thousand and the four thousand in their time of need. This is an entirely plausible scenario, the emergence of which I would attribute to the tradition, i.e., to the people, not to an individual.[57] Mark took this pericope, with its connection to the feeding stories, and (for reasons we can no longer grasp) put it together with a saying of Jesus about leaven. Then he placed the whole thing right after the feeding stories and the arguments with the Pharisees.

---

56. This point has been nicely made by Wendling, *Die Enstehung des Markusevangelium*, 76.

57. Recent critics find the work of the evangelist in the conversation: J. Weiss, *Das älteste Evangelium*, 209; Wellhausen, *Mark*, 63; Wendling 76; Loisy, *Les Évangiles synoptiques*, 1:1005. More reserved is Klostermann, *Markus*, 65. The argument runs as follows: there was one feeding story in the tradition. Mark had a doublet of it, and thereby clamped both narratives together in the tradition. Since both stories were alive in the tradition, there was nothing remarkable about the development that put the two of them together. Wendling (76) points with special energy to the slightly deep and mystical outlook within the scene and recalls what Wrede asserted: "How is it that hardly anyone rightly understands that such things are to be read in our oldest Gospel?" (*Das Messiasgeheimnis*, 105). It is to Wrede's credit that he recognized this characteristic of Mark's gospel, even if he may have stated it in overly sharp terms. But for that reason should we now, like Wendling, even though he wants to follow only literary indices, make the effort to distill out of the gospel a clear concept of miracle, a deeper understanding, which fully corresponds with what we might call pure reason?

The Blind Man of Bethsaida
(Mark 8:22-26)

Καὶ ἔρχονται εἰς Βηθσαϊδάν. καὶ φέρουσιν αὐτῷ τυφλόν...

In our consideration of the geography in the complex 6:45—8:26, we reckoned only with the reading Βηθσαϊδάν. But we now find in D, as well as in a series of Itala manuscripts and in the gothic Bible, a remarkable reading: εἰς Βηθανίαν. Based on the well-known rule that the more difficult reading is to be preferred, we have to stay with Βηθανίαν. We know of a place by this name in the area around Jerusalem, for it is mentioned in the Passion Narrative (cf. Mark 11:1). But Mark's composition technique is typically to arrange stories in sequence with topographical introductions, and on that basis the Bethany in this story cannot possibly have been located in Jerusalem. There are other narratives about the Galilean activity of Jesus that may have originally been located in Judea or Jerusalem, but here we have the only case in the Galilee narratives where a specific location in Jerusalem is named. We might consider Bethany beyond the Jordan, which according to John 1:28 was in the area in which John the Baptist was active, but unfortunately that Bethany cannot be located with any degree of precision. Origen settled upon the reading Βηθαραβά, which appears in a few manuscripts, because he could not find any "Bethany" on the east side of the Jordan River. Betharaba was located on the east side of the Jordan, at about the elevation of Scythopolis, as suggested by some of the narratives about the Baptist (cf. John 3:23). Unfortunately the locations of Aenon and Salim are unidentifiable, but they also appear to have been opposite northern Samaria. It is possible that by the post-apostolic era Bethany had already been destroyed and rebuilt under the name Bethabara. This Bethany/Betharaba comes into view in Mark 8:22. Given the overall plan of the Gospel at this point, we should expect that the next narrative will be a miracle story that takes place in Gentile territory, and indeed Bethany was located in the Gentile Decapolis. Thus we see that it is worthwhile to look deeply into these detailed questions about geography, because we now have a tradition that situates one of Jesus' actions in a city of the Decapolis, where the Gospels say that Jesus was active. Even if this tradition were standing all on its own, it would still make an equally trustworthy impression, and it is precisely because of its rarity that Bethany was replaced by Bethsaida, which was much more common. When these stories are read together, Bethsaida lies near at hand in the circle of vision, since it is located by the sea, and this is a story about a sea journey. It is even possible that this could be a scribal mistake, since the two names are so similar. Over time, Βηθανίαν could have become Βηθσαϊδάν.

Since Bethany is by no means secure, let us take up the question of composition, and how it may have produced the reading Βηθσαϊδάν. The sentence καὶ ἔρχονται εἰς Βηθανίαν cannot be the conclusion of the pericope about the conversation on the topic of leaven. It has to be the beginning of a new pericope, which owes its position at this point in the narrative to its content and perspective. Yet this question about the beginning and end of the pericope is complicated by the fact that the sentence says καὶ ἔρχονται εἰς Βηθανίαν. The story of the journey with the disciples (cf. 8:14: ἐν τῷ πλοίῳ) cannot have ended with that remark. The story about the blind man would begin with καὶ φέρουσιν, and then the same problem would come up again in 7:31 and 7:32. In this case it seems that we have a reference to Bethsaida (which has already been mentioned) in the phrase ἔξω τῆς κώμης. But this link is not strong enough to compel us to connect v. 22a with what follows. The village itself has a certain peculiarity: in v. 23 Jesus brings the sick man out of the village; in v. 26 he sends him home, telling him not to go into the village: μηδὲ (or μὴ) εἰς τὴν κώμην εἰσέλθῃς. Should we conclude that there were two different villages? More likely (as I suspect) it means that Jesus said, "Go straight home and do not wander around in the village."[58]

But where is the beginning of the pericope about the blind man? Here we have to confront the same decision as in 7:31 and 32.[59] Certainly Mark found the place name Bethsaida in the tradition, because the context requires the narration of a healing story about a Gentile, and it is scarcely conceivable that the evangelist independently set the narrative in a location that was not already in the story. The manuscript tradition is especially noteworthy in this regard. On the basis of ℵ^c B C D L 33 cop arm go aeth it (*veniunt*) vg (*venerunt*), the editors of the Greek New Testament give the text as καὶ ἔρχονται. ς reads, along with ℵ* A Γ et al., καὶ ἔρχεται. This second reading is not weakly supported and can therefore be legitimately debated. Usually the plural is regarded as the original reading, for it is the more difficult text, since the singular may have emerged in conformity with the singular αὐτῷ.[60] But this train of thought is too weak to be convincing, since

---

58. At this point the description is uneven, and for that reason various manuscripts have altered the text. D reads: ὕπαγε εἰς τὸν οἶκόν σου καὶ μηδενὶ εἴπῃς εἰς τὴν κώμην. Clearly "the house" is to be found in the village. Various Itala manuscripts print it that way. In ς both readings are combined under the influence of A C Γ Δ . . . pesch aet go. In Wendling's view (79), whether or not, as he says, there was a dearth of perspective on the part of the first narrator of this story, the obvious inelegance of the description is a sign that a redactor's work underlies this text. But I would know better than to state why a redactor, who wanted to put a particular idea into action within a story, would present us with a topographical riddle.

59. Cf. above, p. 180.

60. Cf. B. Weiss, *Markus und Lukas*, 129.

we could equally well regard the singular as the more difficult reading. If we read the conversations about leaven and the healing of the blind man together, then the singular reading cannot possibly be satisfactory, because the conversation is between Jesus and his disciples. Thus the plural stands. Often I have referred to the form of the text, which is anchored in analysis of the introductions to the pericopes. It seems to me that we have here an especially instructive case. καὶ ἔρχεται is the beginning of a new pericope, which, by its nature as a story about Jesus, would naturally use καὶ ἔρχονται less often. The question is whether some pericope picked up ἔρχονται along the way (in the handwritten tradition we see this kind of thing all the time), or whether the Markan text, in which the individual Jesus stories were lined up one after another (ἔρχεται), was later formed into a continuous narrative. The text-critical problem here is certainly more difficult and complicated than text critics appear to realize.

Excursus: The Complex of Mark 6:14—8:26:
The Question of the Arrangement and Setttings
for the Activity of Jesus

How is the construction of the complex 6:14—8:26 to be assessed? The best title for this collection, especially 6:30—8:26, is: "Jesus Outside of Galilee in Gentile Territory."[61] Yet that idea is not well-developed here, as it is encumbered by a complex of stories (feeding, sea voyage, landing) that were already present in the tradition. This complex has been enlisted by scholars in the service of the idea that Jesus wanted to operate outside the land of Israel: almost involuntarily the Galilean soil somehow has an effect upon him, and he becomes more passive than active. Yet the controversy stories that came in have no local settings. In the conversation about purity and impurity we saw that, with regard to content, it belongs with the pericope about the Gentile woman. The case of the narrative about the Pharisees' request for a sign was more difficult, for it hangs together with the discussion about leaven. Perhaps here the arrangement is also the result of a

---

61. This train of thought is widely recognized. Cf. on the one hand J. Weiss, *Schriften*, 127; and on the other Wohlenberg, *Markus*, VIII. The latter makes a separation at 7:1, in order to come up with two sequences of seven stories each: 6:6b–53 = seven stories, and 7:1—8:26 = seven stories, as Jesus and his disciples move back and forth across the northern holy land. Cf. above, pp. 66 and 152.

pre-existing complex of traditions.[62] On the whole the structure of this section (6:30—8:26) produces a picture very similar to that of its predecessor, 3:7—6:13. The Herod episodes (6:14-29) might fit into the account of Jesus' sojourn in Gentile territory, for a suture is evident at 6:30.

As I have tried to demonstrate, this whole complex is made up of individual stories that were handed down to the evangelist.[63] The individual pericopes lend to this framework an aura of topography and chronology, but this is not by design, since the details serve only as connectors of the episodes within the series. If we were to try to read these sequential incidents as if they represent an itinerary, i.e., if we were to try to unravel a series of events and places, we would find that it cannot be done. It is precisely this quality of irregularity that points back to the oral tradition. An author who was working with these stories would have produced a simpler and more successful topography. But the fact is that the evangelist, who was on the whole only a compiler, attached no significance at all to those kinds of things as he took them up. The geography in this section, every bit of it, is only a framework, and it has to be evaluated accordingly. Yet it is precisely those indications of place, to which the collector (and perhaps even the tradition itself) paid no mind, which were

---

62. Cf. J. Weiss, *Das älteste Evangelium*, 209. Mark found the story of the request for a sign already located after the feeding (of the 5,000, not the 4,000).

63. J. Weiss, *Das älteste Evangelium*, 204ff, finds two parallel series of narratives in 6:30-8:26, and peels them down to one original series: first feeding, sea crossing, landing, and a request for a sign. According to Wellhausen (*Mark*, 61), 6:32-52, 7:31-37, and 8:1-26 are "groups of variants" that could have been in the oral tradition, but 6:53-7:30 is a "transitional piece." Wendling (68ff) regards the whole series 6:45-8:26 as an elaboration on the part of the evangelist, and, in a very sharp-eyed investigation, makes some pointed remarks about the characteristics of these stories. I have three (3) criticisms of his work: 1) his theory of doublets is too strong, for it presumes that the evangelist must have developed a story himself out of its parallel; 2) even stories like those that underlie 6:45-826 could not have been formed *ad hoc* by the evangelists, whether they are historical or not. They have their origins instead in a circle of storytellers whom we can no longer recover; and 3) topographical indicators, as we find them in the context of the individual stories, cannot have been invented by the evangelists. Wendling (94-95) holds fast to one place name: Bethsaida, in order to use the sentence from 8:22 (καὶ ἔρχονται εἰς Βηθσαϊδάν) as the conclusion to the story of the feeding of the five thousand (6:30-44) and perhaps even to locate the story in Bethsaida. Wendling makes use of only this one local detail within a longer report because he views it as the necessary starting point for 8:27 (ἐξελθών). But the pericope does not provide that kind of support. What might be the implications of this fact for place names like Dalmanutha, Tyre, Sidon, and the Decapolis?

JESUS OUTSIDE OF GALILEE IN GENTILE TERRITORY   193

included with no objective or aim, whose preservation is basically just a coincidence, to which historians then attribute a special value. But I regard as historically worthless, for example, that Jesus' debut sermon was located in Nazareth (Luke 4:16ff), because I see it as an expression of Luke's idea that Jesus has to begin his public ministry in his hometown. On the other hand, what kind of theological purpose could there possibly have been in the naming of Bethsaida (Bethany), Dalmanutha, or Magadan? The evangelist cannot have invented these names, because their mention is basically a matter of indifference and insignificance. These observations result in a point of view that destroys the so-called "synoptic outline." Jesus must have somehow had something to do with the places that are named, even as far away as Tyre and Sidon, and he was also active in the Decapolis. We can suspect all of this with a high degree of confidence, on the basis of these stray surviving remarks in this text. Perhaps the last weak rays of an earlier and much richer tradition shimmer in these texts.

Excursus: Special Perspectives on the Location of Jesus' Activities:
Woes Pronounced upon Galilean Towns
(Matt 11:20–24; Luke 10:13–15)

The fact that our study does not cast baseless aspersions will be evident in my treatment of the famous "woes" over the Galilean towns from the Sayings Source Q, as they appear in Matt 11:20–24 and Luke 10:13–15. Matthew offers an historical introduction, which can easily be separated from the following text and therefore must be regarded as a work of ornamentation on the part of the evangelist: τότε ἤρξατο ὀνειδίζειν τὰς πόλεις, ἐν αἷς ἐγένετο αἱ πλεῖσται δυνάμεις αὐτοῦ, ὅτι οὐ μετενόησαν.[64] Luke puts this saying without any introduction at the conclusion of the instructions to the seventy disciples. The words do fit better there, especially when we recall Matt 10:15 (the commissioning of the disciples). As to the authenticity of these sayings, however, nothing definite can be said. What interests us here is the content

---

64. An abundance of manuscripts, such as C L syr[sin] aeth and the Gospel lectionaries, have a clearly marked addendum to the introduction for this pericope: ὁ Ἰς after, or sometimes before ἤρξατο. Merx (*Markus und Lukas*, 1:94) sees the beginning of a special saying of Jesus in 11:20. Thus the introduction to the pericope holds no interest for him.

of the saying: a "woe" over the towns of Chorazin and Bethsaida, which are worse than Tyre and Sidon. For if the things that have been done in Chorazin and Bethsaida had also been done in Tyre and Sidon, then those Gentile cities would have repented long ago. How did these cities come into Jesus' field of vision? For places as famous as Tyre and Sidon, direct personal experience was not necessary, and as we noted earlier with reference to Sodom and Gomorrah (Sodom is also named in an adjoining saying), their mention is a reflection of Jesus' knowledge of the Bible. But he must have had personal knowledge of Chorazin and Bethsaida, as is evident from the reports about the powerful actions of Jesus that took place there. In this way the perspective, which Mark's explicit mention of Bethsaida opened for us, is now expanded further: Jesus was active in this city. When and how? Those memories have been buried. About the blind man of Bethsaida nothing much was preserved. But was Jesus active, however sporadically, only in those locations that appear in the Synoptic tradition, or was he also active in other cities where the tradition has simply been lost? Nowhere in the New Testament is there any report of Jesus' activity in Chorazin. Once again we come to the same result: the evidence blows up the outline of the story of Jesus, as it is generally conceived.[65]

Excursus: Allegorical Place Names?

It is widely accepted that place names such as Bethsaida, Chorazin, etc., are in fact the names of real places. On the other hand, there also remains the possibility that folk etymologies may have had an influence on (and may have even created) the names in these narratives. The concept of folk etymology would lead us to expect that we have before us a collection of narratives that were formed by popular voices, rather than the product of an evangelist, who could not have made use of these cultured etymologies and implications. Bethsaida, for example, combines

---

65. Wellhausen says: "In Mark the talk is not only about his (Jesus') mistreatment in Nazareth, but also about his great success in Capernaum, so that Antipas became suspicious. Q is no match for that. Perhaps during the apostolic era Christianity lost its roots in Capernaum, as Peter and the disciples relocated from there to Jerusalem" (*Matthew*, 56). This is a parade example of carelessness about the perspectives that have been productive in Mark, as well as of an exaggerated emphasis on the historical reliability of Mark's gospel alone.

the words בית and ציד. ציד means "hunt," so that Bethsaida would mean "hunting house" or "travel provisions," or "stores," and thus "storehouse" or something like "eating house." Nestle thinks of the word צידה, which is often translated in the LXX as ἐπισιτισμός. This Greek word appears in the feeding story at Luke 9:12, which reads: ἵνα εὕρωσιν ... ἐπισιτισμόν. Thus a symbolic translation of the meaning of Bethsaida is οἶκος τοῦ ἐπισιτισμοῦ. This translation leads to a two possibilities for the meaning of the story: 1) as the story of the feeding was told and retold, and the location of Bethsaida ("dining-house") was introduced, for it was reminiscent of an already well-known location, namely, Bethsaida-Julias. In this case the etymology would have shaped the form of the story, providing it with a specific location. 2) the meaning of the place-name "Bethsaida" was already well-known, and the feeding story narrated the origins of the name. In this case the eytomology would have risen from a legend.

Nestle made a similar effort with regard to the origin of the place name "Chorazin": this word may be a transposition of the Arabic word *chinzir* (which means "pig"), and more specifically, it may come from the phrase *ras el chinzir* ("pig's head"). Nestle thinks the name may be connected to the narrative about the two thousand swine at Gadara.[66]

In my judgment it may be that a certain kind of place-name symbolism, which we can no longer understand, played a role in the stories of the two thousand pigs and the feeding of the five thousand. On the whole, however, caution is called for here. There was a time when scholars also found allegories in New Testament place names, including Nain,[67] Βηθανία = בית עניה = "house of torment";[68] Salim = שלים = "peace" (John 3:23); Αἰνών = עין = "spring" (John 3:23). This kind of symbolic interpretation may be called for when the topography is too vague, or if the places are otherwise unknown. The situation is different with well-known place names like Bethsaida. To resort to allegory in that case would lead us toward a method that would eventually explain everything as an allegory, reducing the story of Jesus to nothing more than a myth about a cult god within a

---

66. Cf. above, p. 125.
67. Cf. above, p. 101.
68. Cf. Nestle in "Chorazin, Bethsaida," 185.

sect of Jewish religion.⁶⁹ Jesus = helper and healer, and no one would notice that Jesus was a common name in that world at that time.

If these remarks about place-name symbolism had nothing to do with Jesus' pronouncement of woes over Chorazin and Bethsaida, then we would have to regard those sayings as unhistorical, a hypothesis that I regard as impossible.⁷⁰ For in that saying Jesus specifically refers to his miracles in those towns, requiring us to think of Chorazin and Bethsaida as places that actually exist. There remains here the viewpoint of a piece of tradition that was not firmly rooted in the story of Jesus, and so is no longer fully known to us. Place names like Magadan, Dalmanutha, which are mentioned in the same context, put the lie to that tendency toward symbolism.

Excursus: The Complex Mark 6:14—8:26 in Matthew

There is not much to say about the form of the complex Mark 6:14—8:26 as it has been collected in Matt 14:1—16:12. Our detailed discussion has shown that Matthew is thoroughly dependent upon Mark. The first evangelist was casual about circumstantial details, as is shown by the fact that Bethsaida and the Decapolis go unmentioned (Mark 6:45; 7:31). Matthew slices up the abundant framework of Mark. That process is understandable, for (as we have seen) it is built into the process of the disappearance of place names in the Jesus tradition. Sometimes traditional (and therefore historical) topographical information is accidentally lost. On the other hand, place names are sometimes added to traditions that lacked them, and there may be a certain tendency toward that kind of supplementation. This double-edged sword must be handled with care. The details of the framework of the story of Jesus must be tested through individual examination on a case-by-case basis.

---

69. See A. Drews, *Die Christusmythe*, 17.

70. Nestle appears to do this when he concludes his discussion of the symbolic character of the name Bethsaida with these words: "Woe to you, Bethsaida!" (Nestle, loc. cit.).

Excursus: The Complex Mark 6:14—8:26 in Luke:
Critique of Mark's Arrangement and Content

Luke substantially abbreviates the Markan text by creating a collection of stories that begins with the feeding of the five thousand, i.e., from Mark 6:45 to Mark 8:26. Whenever Luke does not have a parallel to something in Mark or Matthew, we can conclude that Luke did not know that passage, although most of the time we can deduce rather quickly the reason for the omission. In this case, however, the matter is more difficult. It is not hard to understand why some stories are missing: Luke regarded the feeding of the four thousand, for example, as a doublet for the feeding of the five thousand. The Pharisees' request for a sign looks like a doublet from Q (11:29), as does the saying about leaven in 12:1, although Mark records that saying. Luke drops the conversation about bread with the disciples in the boat, because it comes from the feedings of the five thousand and the four thousand. For the healing of the deaf and dumb man, there is a parallel in the healing of a blind man at 18:35ff. Mark and Matthew both collect various miracle stories of this sort. It is the same with the story of walking on the water, a story that is an analogy for the calming of the storm (in Luke at 8:22–23). This collection of stories about Jesus' activity in the region of Gennesaret can be dropped, because it contains no concrete detailed content. But what of the controversy sayings about purity and impurity, and the story of the Canaanite woman? This material, one would think, must have had an especially strong attraction for a Gentile Christian like Luke. On the other hand, perhaps a Gentile Christian might have found precisely these stories most offensive? The story about the believing Gentiles, for example, shows Jesus caught in a particularistic outlook, and the sayings about pure and impure are interlaced with choice examples of Jewish concerns, from which Gentile Christianity was already moving away.

Substantial gaps in Luke can be explained in this way, or in similar ways. Obviously the third evangelist carried out a thorough critique of the arrangement and content of Mark's account. Out of all that has been said so far, however, I would like to emphasize just one point, a point that Luke has made quite well, in spite of all that he left out. It has often been observed that the third evangelist strove for a sequential and practical biographical presentation of the outline of the story of Jesus. The difficulty of the two feeding stories, standing so close to each other, posed serious difficulties for an author working toward that goal. Perhaps Luke's critique began at this point. It seems to me that dropping the doublet of the feeding story came first, and despite the noteworthy comments made above, the material embedded between the two feeding stories appears to be secondary.[71]

---

71. Other explanations, which suggest either an external accident or a mistake on Luke's part, betray a surrender of the effort to find an explanation. On one hand, we hear about a defective text of Mark, and on the other about a defective text of Luke. Cf. in this regard B. Weiss, *Markus und Lukas*, 422-23. Hoffmann, *Das Marcusevangelium und seine Quellen*, 277, thinks the most plausible explanation is that "Luke knew these sections, but the narrative of the feeding of the five thousand was accidentally interchanged with the feeding of the four thousand, which had stood at the end of this series of stories, and in this way both the last story and the ones in between were lost." J. Weiss (*Schriften*, 456) says: "Here is a point at which we can only admit our ignorance." Wellhausen (*Luke*, 40) expresses a rather complicated outlook: "What lies in the middle of Mark (6:45-8:26) is a later compilation. No doubt, however, Luke does not give us the kernel that lies at the base." Spitta (*Die synoptische Grundschrift*, 218ff) also regards the feeding of the five thousand as an excerpt from the foundational document of the Synoptic tradition, and thus sees our text as only "a *supposed* gap in Luke."

6

Jesus and His Disciples, The Approaching Passion

(Mark 8:27—10:45par.)

Peter's Confession at Caesarea Philippi
(Mark 8:27-30; Matt 16:13-23; Luke 9:18-22)

Καὶ ἐξῆλθεν ὁ Ἰησοῦς καὶ οἱ μαθηταὶ αὐτοῦ εἰς τὰς κώμας Καισαρίας τῆς Φιλίππου. Καὶ ἐν τῷ ὁδῷ ἐπηρώτα τοὺς μαθητὰς αὐτοῦ.

D and some Itala-mss. read simply εἰς Καισαρίαν.

The preceding narrative mentions Bethsaida-Julia but not Bethany, so the identification of this new location is quite specific. From Bethsaida-Julia to Caesarea Philippi is a distance of about 40 km as the crow flies. The villages mentioned here could have been located to the south of the city, or they may have been strung out through the region of Bethsaida, but Bethsaida itself belonged to the territory governed by Philip the tetrarch.[1] Thus ἐξῆλθεν takes its meaning from the immediate context: he goes out of and away from Bethsaida and toward the villages of Caesarea Philippi. On the basis of what we have already demonstrated about the construction of the Gospel of Mark, this topographical connection cannot be regarded as secure. It is possible that the healing of the blind man at Bethsaida belongs to this setting in the tradition or even in historical reality, but it might just as well have been the case that the pericope in 8:27ff was originally located in a different context. It is important to remember that the word ἐξῆλθεν says

---

1. In my opinion there is no basis for J. Weiss' claim that there are difficulties with this location, and that Luke confuses here the area around the Sea of Gennesaret with the villages in the territory of Philip (J. Weiss, *Schriften*, 145). B. Weiss (*Markus und Lukas*, 131) has similar ideas, when he suspects that Jesus' rejection of Tyre and Sidon took place during the trip through the area of Tyre and Sidon (7:31). If these sorts of difficulties are present here, then they merely show that there is a gap between 8:26 and 8:27. They do not justify complicated relocations that supposedly improve the geography.

nothing at all about wherefrom or whereto: it is simply the introduction to an independent pericope. It does point beyond itself to a wider context, by making it clear that the disciples are assessing the mood of the public more accurately than Jesus does. Over the course of time Jesus may have lost touch with his disciples, and they may have drawn away from him toward the people. In Mark's narrative the motivation for this development, which we can infer from the text, is not explained. Should we think that the disciples were sent out? But that event already lies in the past, and in the stories in the previous section we find Jesus still together with his disciples.[2] We see, therefore, that in spite of the smooth topographical connection with 8:22ff and 8:27ff, there is a gap between 8:26 and 8:27. Once again the contents of the individual narratives explode the framework of the story of Jesus, as it has come down to us in the Gospel of Mark.

The designation of place that occupies our interest right now belongs, however, to the beginning of the individual narrative about Peter's confession. Two consequences follow from this fact: 1) the region of Caesarea Philippi has not come up in the gospel tradition before. It does not appear here as part of a route inserted by Mark. On the contrary, this detail is specific and not at all schematic. Mark found it in the tradition, but the tradition did not invent this place name, for it has no didactic or symbolic meaning. We stand here on the ground of the oldest tradition, where a true memory of fact is preserved and survives. 2) In the phrase ἐν τῷ ὁδῷ there is a secure anchor to an historical setting. We have already seen similar links between place names and settings at 6:45ff; 7:24, 26; 8:10, 13; 8:22, 23. It indicates that an accurate memory is also at work here, when Jesus does not enter the town of Caesarea Philippi, just as he did not enter Tiberias, the residence of Herod Antipas. We cannot determine with certainty why Jesus would take himself north from Bethsaida into this region. Did he want to get away from the authority of Herod Antipas, or did Mark insert the Herod episode into this part of the journey as a motif? In such matters clarity is not to be found, for the account itself is unclear on this point.

Verse 30 is rather loosely attached, which means that he threatened all of them (i.e., all the disciples) even though only Peter was referred to earlier. Matthew, who made an insertion between Mark 8:29 and 8:30, has τότε here, thereby marks an almost new beginning. Luke 9:21 is similar to Mark, except that by using δέ instead of καί a stronger connection is

---

2. J. Weiss (*Das älteste Evangelium*, 235) correctly evaluates the obvious uncertainty here (although his remarks in *Schriften*, 146, are different), arguing that it must have been better explained in the older tradition. In my opinion that postulate carries no weight, since in the original tradition the individual stories circulated without any connections and not in any series.

established. Even in Mark there does not appear to be a genuine seam between 8:29 and 8:30.

Matthew (16:13-23) completely loses touch with Mark's vivid description of local details, mentioning instead only what is necessary. 16:13 is stated in abbreviated form: ἐλθὼν δὲ ὁ Ἰησοῦς εἰς τὰ μέρη Καισαρίας τῆς Φιλίππου. After Peter's answer there follows the famous passage about the keys given to Peter: vv. 17-19. These verses go back to tradition and have been inserted here by Matthew, while the historicity of that tradition is a problem that is of no concern to our investigation.

Luke (9:18-22) offers a text that connects very closely with the preceding pericope, i.e., the feeding of the five thousand. The omission of Mark 6:45—8:2 means that Caesarea Philippi is not mentioned at all. Shortly before this section, at 9:10, reference is made to Bethsaida. A brief mention of this locality, which lay so near to Caesarea Philippi, was enough for the third evangelist.[3]

Three Predictions of Jesus' Suffering
(Mark 8:31-31; Matt 16:21; Luke 9:22; Mark 9:30-32; Matt 17:22-23; Luke 9:43b-45; Mark 10:32-34; Matt 20:17-19; Luke 18:31-34)

Verses 31 and 32 are a special piece, introduced by καὶ ἤρξατο. In Mark 26:21 this new beginning is even more clearly marked: ἀπὸ τότε ἤρξατο ὁ Ἰησοῦς. Luke 9:22, by contrast, uses a participle εἰπών to create an even closer connection with what precedes. Of course that is an authorial gloss. Mark's version of the scene is determinative, especially in vv. 31-32, which slides smoothly out of its narrative context. Given Mark's paratactic style, however, this observation is less conclusive than it might be otherwise. It is the content of the scene that is most important here, as it reports the first of Jesus' passion predictions to his disciples.

There are two more of these references to Jesus' upcoming suffering in Mark, at 9:30-32 and 10:32-34, and all three texts agree as to the content of the prediction: Jesus will be put to death by the elders of the people in Jerusalem, and after three days he will rise. 10:32ff presents this information somewhat more clearly and thoroughly than the other two texts. None of the three sayings are closely connected with their immediate context. At the end of the day our literary assessment here is entirely

---

3. In keeping with his point of view, Spitta (*Die synoptische Grundschrift*, 225) finds here the text of the basic synoptic document, and he rightly points out that Mark's distinctive descriptions of places do not change the setting. But we might also point out that on this point Luke is not much different from Mark.

separate from any evaluative judgment about the content of the passion predictions. Can Jesus have said these words, or are they an expression of the viewpoint of the community, including the evangelists? The prediction of resurrection after three days speaks strongly against the former. Even if we understand the amount of time in a more colloquial sense than exactly three days, but simply as a brief period of time, there remains the problem of finding a psychological explanation for the conduct of the disciples and the women in 16:1. On the other hand, the second interpretation is supported by the fact that the statements made here directly confess the faith of the earliest community as we know it from sermons in the book of Acts. It is therefore not necessary to trace the predictions of the passion to a special tradition that preceded the evangelists. I do not believe that individual evangelists made up individual stories. Such pericopes are either real stories, or they have arisen from a tradition over which we can no longer exert any control. In this case it is a matter of a confession of faith that could easily have been built upon the foundation of strongly imprinted community formulas. The overall form, especially as it is repeated three times in the course of a longer complex of stories, looks very much like an expression of an author's point of view.

The second and third passion predictions add new details to the setting. Mark 9:30–31 reads: κακεῖθεν ἐξελθόντες παρεπορεύοντο διὰ τῆς Γαλιλαίας ... ἐδίδασκεν γὰρ τοὺς μαθητὰς αὐτοῦ. The words ἐκεῖθεν and ἐξέρχεσθαι are immediately recognizable as patch words. It is better not to ask where these episodes took place, whether in the area around Caesarea Philippi (8:27) or in a house (9:28). The word παραπορεύεσθαι is not especially vivid and does not seem to be anchored in any particular situation. The literal meaning of "pass by," with its implication of a fleeting sojourn, should not be pressed, since παραπορεύεσθαι is the same as πορεύεσθαι in the Koiné, which often used the complex form of a verb in place of the simplex (from the standpoint of Atticization, the reading of B* D Itala, ἐπορεύοντο, is quite correct). We must also note that the place designation (διὰ τῆς Γαλιλαίας) gives no specific indication of a particular location, but coheres with the typical style of a general report formed by the evangelist (cf. 1:14: εἰς τὴν Γαλιλαίαν; 3:7: πολὺ πλῆθος ἀπὸ τῆς Γαλιλαίας). A location like Dalmanutha (8:10) cannot have been created by the evangelist, but referring to Galilee in this general way would have required no special tradition.

The third occurrence (10:32–33) is similar: ἦσαν δὲ ἐν τῷ ὁδῷ ἀναβαίνοντες εἰς Ἱεροσόλυμα, καὶ ἦν προάγων αὐτοὺς ὁ Ἰησοῦς. καὶ ἐθαμβοῦντο, οἱ δὲ ἀκολουθοῦντες ἐφοβοῦντο, καὶ παραλαβὼν πάλιν τοὺς δώδεκα ... Here again the local details are all general, inspired by the evangelist's plan to use this third prediction of suffering to bring Jesus closer to the holy city.

The depiction itself is, from the start, trans-historical: crowds of astonished people line the way, which looks like a pilgrimage route, as Jesus moves on toward Jerusalem. (D^gr did not understand this and therefore spoiled it by changing προάγων to προσάγων).

What we have been able to observe in the parallels between Matthew and Luke important, and it is also fully consistent with our other investigations to this point. Matthew 17:22 (the second prediction) and 20:17 (the third prediction) offer an abridged version of Mark, while Luke's account (9:43b and 18:31) leaves out all the indicators of location. The third evangelist has a good feel for the gaps in the narrative, which only serve to slow down the ongoing presentation he is trying to make.

Satan and Peter
(Mark 8:32b-33; Matt 16:22-23)

A very brief scene is introduced here with the words:

³²ᵇ Καὶ προσλαβόμενος ὁ Πέτρος αὐτὸν ἤρξατο ἐπιτιμᾶν αὐτῷ. ³³ ὁ δὲ ἐπιστραφεὶς καὶ ἰδὼν τοὺς μαθητὰς αὐτοῦ ἐπετίμησεν Πέτρῳ καὶ λέγει...

Instead of ὁ δὲ, A and several other sources read ὁ δὲ ις. The introduction to the pericope cannot have begun with v. 33, and that is proven by the reading ὁ δὲ ις.

This saying of Jesus introduces a very specific situation, although this fact is not clearly evident in v. 32b. We will get the sense of it if we connect it to the passion prediction: Peter wants to pull Jesus away from the path of suffering, and to that end he approaches the Lord and delivers a strong reprimand. If we are right that these passion predictions are a product of Mark, must we also attribute this scene to him? This assumption is possible, as it extends the framework of the narrative. But Jesus' words to Peter may also have been handed down as an isolated saying, and it may have been the evangelist who connected that saying with the passion prediction, making it refer not only to Peter but to all the disciples. Perhaps this little story in vv. 32b-33 is an older narrative that the evangelist believed would fit nicely here.[4]

---

4. Wendling (114ff) believes that "facts connect with facts," and so he thinks he can reconstruct the original connection: v. 27 + 28 + 29 + 30 καὶ ἐπετίμησεν + 33 Πέτρῳ καὶ λέγει... (cf. also *Ur-Markus*, 49-50). Later J. Weiss (*Das älteste Evangelium*, 238ff) adduced a similar connection, which he later rejected. Wendling's reconstruction follows the same lines as Wrede's, which raised doubts about the entire pericope 8:27ff. He argued that v. 30 precedes the messianic secret of Mark (cf. on the other hand J.

Matthew (16:22-23), who generally agrees with Mark, has the same introduction here. But in v. 22b the word τοῦτο clearly announces the beginning of the Passion Narrative.

Luke passes over this scene in silence, for obvious reasons, a decision obviously the result of Luke's attitude toward Peter, leader of the apostles, and the fact that in this episode, Peter is rebuffed by Jesus.

Sayings about the Sufferings of Disciples
(Mark 8:34-9:1; Matt 16:24-28; Luke 9:23-27)

Just as these sayings present Jesus as the suffering messiah, they also present the Christian, i.e., the disciple of Jesus, as one who suffers with Jesus. Clearly this is the trajectory of the thought. But the individual sayings that are now arranged in this context are no longer in their original settings, and there is little or no coherence in the series. On the contrary, v. 34, 35, 36, 37, and 38 all have their clearest meanings as individual sayings. Here they have simply been strung together, with γάρ functioning as a very loose clip. Mark 9:1 uses one of the most primitive introductory formulas to begin a new saying of Jesus: καὶ ἔλεγεν αὐτούς.

Matthew and Luke follow the same method of composition. Only once (16:26b) does Matthew say ἤ instead of γάρ, and both Matthew and Luke leave out the connecting piece καὶ ἔλεγεν αὐτοῖς. Versions of the sayings in Mark 8:34, 35, and 38 are found elsewhere in Matthew and Luke, where they are similar even though the context is different. That the links in the series are loose is quite clear (cf. Matt 10:33, 38, 39; Luke 12:9, 14:27; 17:33).[5]

The complex is introduced with the following setting for the scene: καὶ προσκαλεσάμενος τὸν ὄχλον σὺν τοῖς μαθηταῖς αὐτοῦ εἶπεν αὐτοῖς. The mention of the crowd is striking, because it indicates that we are now in a situation that applies to the disciples of Jesus. It is understandable, then, that Matt 16:24 refers only to the disciples (τότε ὁ Ἰησοῦς εἶπεν τοῖς μαθηταῖς αὐτοῦ). Luke 9:23, by contrast, includes the words ἔλεγεν δὲ πρὸς πάντας and

---

Weiss (*Das älteste Evangelium*, 236), who argues that v. 30 is supported by first-rate psychology). Wendling goes on to argue that ἐπιτιμᾶν in v. 32 may be coincidental with ἐπετίμησεν in v. 33. The point of the resulting scene is very sharp-edged. But at that point we are no longer hearing the voice of a stylistic critic, for in spite of his contrary attitude, Wendling still counts on the historicity of the messianic consciousness of Jesus.

5. Wendling (109ff) and J. Weiss (*Das älteste Evangelium*, 241-42) wonder about the possible dependence of Mark's editors upon the editors of the sayings source Q. In my view both scholars do not sufficiently understand that these sayings could have been alive in the tradition in various forms. The idea that vv. 36 and 37 were originally directed against Peter, and that they thus extend upon v. 33, is nothing more than a suspicion.

in so doing leaves unresolved the uncertainty about whether members of the general public are present in the story. Obviously Mark has the original text, which helps us understand how he picked up what had been a small pericope. The introduction is in v. 34, but the actual length of the original pericope can no longer be determined. Mark basically wants to recount some instructions given to the disciples. I suspect that in this case the original form of the story only had the crowd in view, and it was Mark who then expanded upon it and brought in the disciples, in order to make sufficient room for the connection. At a certain point in the history of Jesus, the whole thing was put to use in the text that we now have before us. When and where these words were actually spoken, whether at the beginning or the end of the activity of Jesus, cannot be determined.[6]

Jesus' Transfiguration
(Mark 9:2-8; Matt 17:1-8; Luke 9:28-36)

Καὶ μετὰ ἡμέρας ἓξ παραλαμβάνει ὁ Ἰησοῦς τὸν Πέτρον καὶ τὸν Ἰάκωβον καὶ τὸν Ἰωάννην, καὶ ἀναφέρει αὐτοὺς εἰς ὄρος ὑψηλὸν κατ' ἰδίαν μόνους. (‍א reads λίαν after ὑψηλὸν).

It is noteworthy that this is the only place in Mark (outside of the Passion Narrative) in which the interval in time between two narratives is noted with precision. Because Mark usually arranges the individual occurrences with hardly any indicators of time, we can be certain that the reference to "six days" comes not from Mark, but from the tradition. This chronological indicator has the effect of connecting our pericope very well with the one that precedes. It is often argued that the stories of the Transfiguration and the suffering of the disciples, including Peter's confession, came together prior to this narrative context. It is said that Peter's confession depends upon the Transfiguration, and in the oldest traditions these stories were already closely bound together.[7] But that conclusion is premature. If Mark had

---

6. Wendling (110) rightly comments upon the unusual introduction in 8:34. In fact the presence of the crowd is not convincing. But Wendling's idea that this reference to the crowd, coming as it does right after the secret scene of the messianic confession, can establish the public nature of that event, well, that is a hair-splitting impossibility.

7. This is the argument of J. Weiss (*Das älteste Evangelium*, 238ff), who more than any other scholar has drawn attention to the indications of time in this context. On the other hand Wendling (138-39) regards 9:2-8 as the younger layer of the original report and sees the "six days" as one of those temporal connections that are often inserted as external connections between passages in the older and earlier layers. In my opinion such simple schemes will never lead us to a correct understanding of Mark's composition techniques.

found the Transfiguration story and its designation of time in some other context, or as an isolated pericope, then he would have simply inserted it here in this form. We already know that he paid no attention to chronology. For him, the words "after six days" were nothing more than a linking phrase, and in that regard he was more perceptive than many modern interpreters who take it at face value as an indicator of time. In no way is this reference as specific as it appears. Granted, the number six is certainly not as schematic as the numbers three or seven, but here and there its schematic character, its not-too-specific generality, is clearly evident. We can note, for example, the enumerations of six months, six brothers (Acts 11:12), six jars (John 2:6), six wings (Rev 4:8), and the number 606/666 (Rev 13:18). Such citations are, of course, not necessarily conclusive. One thing, however, is certain: the number six hangs together with the number seven as the six weekdays in a seven-day week. In Jewish culture the weekdays are simply counted from the beginning: from the first to the sixth day, and then the Sabbath on the seventh day. This type of enumeration was also the rule in rabbinic literature (Mishnah, Midrash, Targumim), so we can be sure that the number six was quite common. "After six days" meant the same thing as "a week later." It is possible that the tradition could use this terminology to refer to God, who established the Sabbath after six days, or to Moses, who (according to Exod. 24) waited on God for six days, and on the seventh day God spoke out of the cloud. Of course Mark would scarcely have given a thought to this kind of symbolism, and for him there was nothing at all unusual about the expression "six days." Whatever we may or may not think about that kind of symbolism, Mark's reference to "six days" is not a specific designation of time, nor is it based upon any particular memory.

But how are we to explain the fact that in the parallel passage (Luke 9:28), Luke refers not to "six days" but to "about eight days" (ὡσεὶ ἡμέραι ὀκτώ)? I cannot find a satisfactory explanation for the process by which Luke's choice of words could have emerged from Mark's.[8] Luke's purpose is just as precise as Mark's, and just as imprecise. Both of them are thinking of a time-span of about one week. But where do these differing expressions come from? We can get on the right track by following an early Christian interpretation that argues that the two designations of time are basically the same, because Luke has added both the day of the passion prediction (8:31) and the day of its explanation to the original six days: αὐτὴν τὴν ἡμέραν καθ'

---

8. The usual explanation is that Luke's designation of time is simply more of an approximation than Mark's or Matthew's. A logical rebuttal has already been given by Spitta (*Die synoptische Grundschrift*, 235): "It is easier to explain how a precise number developed out of an approximate one, rather than the other way around."

ἣν ἐφθέξατο κἀκείνην καθ' ἣν ἀνήγαγεν.⁹ It seems to me that Luke is probably not correct on that score. But one thing is certain: he counts the days of the week differently than Mark. Unfortunately we have no evidence about how people in antiquity reckoned the days of the week. It appears that Christians largely followed the Jewish terminology, which laid out a seven-day week, but on the other hand we also know that the imperial calendar was not governed by a seven-day week: the Romans counted a week as eight days.¹⁰ Did Luke follow that custom? If so, Mark would be working with the Jewish calendar, while Luke would be using a Roman one. Be that as it may, it seems to me that a degree of uncertainty, unclarity, approximation, or whatever you want to call it, must have prevailed in matters of the calendar, just as today we can speak of eight days as "a week," or fourteen days as "two weeks." Thus when John 20:26 says "and after eight days (μεθ' ἡμέρας ὀκτώ) his disciples were together again," surely this meeting took place on a Sunday, as had the previous one. In fact one manuscript, syr^sin, makes this explicit: "and after eight days, on the next Sunday." This offers a very good parallel to the text of Luke: the third evangelist thought in terms of eight days, and whether it was by habit, or out of respect for Roman custom, and just like that he changed the text of Mark. It happened in the same way that today a German from the south would change the northern expression "Sonnenabend" into the southern term "Samstag."¹¹

Thus Luke made a conscious effort to improve the text of Mark. The beginning of this pericope, for example, inserts the words μετὰ τοὺς λόγους τούτους (9:28), firmly clamping this narrative to the words previously spoken by Jesus. At the end of the story it is said that the disciples then (ἐν ἐκείναις ταῖς ἡμέραις) fell silent, a sequencing remark from the author, who wants to set this individual narrative into a wider context. It is thus quite fitting that a distinctly psychological phenomenon is now introduced into the story: the disciples fall asleep! While in Mark 9:2 = Matt 17:1, the scene

9. Cf. Catene 352 (in Klostermann, *Markus*, 72). Hoffmann, *Das Markusevangelium und seine Quellen*, 350, offers an explanation based upon the Aramaic text: in Luke's source there was a scribal error, and a poorly written ו was misread as ה. Unfortunately the Aramaic text is not legible at this point.

10. This eight-day calendar is known from numerous calendar inscriptions from the early Roman Empire; cf. *CIL*, I, 2. 220. Also Th. Mommsen, *Die Römische Chronologie bis auf Cäsar*. I found these references in an unusually rich article: Schürer, "Die siebentägige Woche im Gebrauche der christlichen Kirche der ersten Jahrhunderte." Unfortunately, this research still does not produce total clarity about our passage.

11. To me this characteristic of Luke is especially important, because some researchers incorrectly evaluate Luke's distinctive style, and on the basis of texts like this one, which come from Mark, they are inclined to look for a written source for Lukan special tradition.

plays out on a mountaintop (ὄρος ὑψηλόν), Luke says only that "they went up to the mountain" (Luke 9:28). He conforms this scene to another one in a similar setting (cf. Luke 6:12ff), and in this way all of the vividness evoked by the word ὑψηλόν is lost.

But even the "high mountain" turns out to be a mountain that has nothing at all to do with geography,[12] notwithstanding the old tradition about Mt. Tabor. The old chestnut—that Mt. Tabor lies too far from Caesarea Philippi, three days' journey in fact, so we should rather think of Lebanon—accomplishes nothing, because the resulting chronology does not hold up at all.[13] The only conclusion that matters, therefore, is that, although the tradition about Mt. Tabor is quite old, it is in fact a later addition to the scene, a scene that has no links at all to any geography. This story seeks only to evoke a picture of a high mountain.

Conversation on the Way Down from the Mount of Transfiguration (Mark 9:9–13; Matt 17:9–13)

This story is closely connected to the transfiguration scene by a participial construction that is highly unusual for Mark: καταβαινόντων δὲ αὐτῶν ἀπὸ του ὄρους. The reading in ς seems to me to be the original, not καὶ καταβαινόντων, which is found in the best witnesses (א A B C D L Δ 33 vg cop aeth). That καὶ reflects a later effort to conform either to what was regarded as typical Markan narrative style, or to Matt 17:9.

Jesus' command for silence plainly conforms to the transfiguration scene, and the evangelist did not insert it here as an introductory remark.[14] It appears that it was Luke who attached this statement to the transfiguration scene. Obviously the conclusion of his narrative (Luke 9:36) resonates from the command for silence, which apparently offended Luke, who never specifically mentions it, although he does describe its aftereffects. In any case, the disciples

---

12. Wendling (139) regards it as significant that the text does not refer to a typical mountain (τὸ ὄρος), but rather to a real mountain (ὑψηλόν ὄρος) with clouds and the presence of God. Spitta (*Die synoptische Grundschrift*, 235) argues that instead of Luke's simple εἰς τὸ ὄρος, Mark and Matthew call it a ὑψηλόν ὄρος, which may be a setting totally withdrawn from the world.

13. For a thorough discussion of Mt. Tabor, cf. Pölzl, *Marcus*, 207ff.

14. Wendling (122–23) attributes Mark 9:9–13 to the redactor, and in so doing misinterprets what is actually an introduction to a specific situation. As usual, Wendling's interpretation of this verse (he regards it as a "hanging together" transitional piece) leans too heavily on Wrede's outlook on Jesus' messianic mission.

keep their silence. For his part Matthew stays close to Mark, although he does signify the beginning of a new episode with ὁ Ἰησοῦς.

Mark 9:11 opens a new section totally disconnected from what has preceded: καὶ ἐπηρώτων αὐτὸν λέγοντες. They ask Jesus about the teaching of the scribes and Pharisees to the effect that Elijah must come first. It is possible that in the original form of this story, the disciples were not the ones asking the question, but rather other people who were following Jesus, but Matt 17:10 makes it explicit that it is the disciples who inquire. The Pharisees (Mark 9:10) are missing in ℵ and L, but total clarity on this point cannot be reached, since the opponents of Jesus are sometimes characterized one way, sometimes another. Compare for example Matt 17:10, where the Pharisees are not mentioned. Along with this lack of clarity about who was present, there is also the notably difficult style of v. 11: ὅτι λέγουσιν οἱ Φ., καὶ οἱ γὰρ ... ὅτι ... As I have already pointed out, the original form of the story began with a general designation such as "people are asking ..." The pericope opened with something like this: καὶ ἐπηρώτων αὐτὸν λέγοντες ὅτι Ἠλείαν δεῖ ἐλθεῖν πρῶτον = "and someone asked him: doesn't Elijah have to come first?" In this context in the Gospel of Mark, however, the question has to be asked by a disciple; otherwise he would not dare to put the statement about Elijah directly on the lips of Jesus. Thus the opponents of Jesus are represented here as advocates for that view. But there is yet another possibility. Originally the scribes and Pharisees were named as the ones who asked the question: καὶ ἐπηρώτων αὐτὸν οἱ Φαρισαῖοι καὶ οἱ γραμματεῖς λέγοντες, ὅτι ... Mark has changed that, because in this context a disciple has to ask the question.[15] A parade example of this kind of short pericope about the Pharisees has been handed down in Luke 17:20-21.

Matthew 17:13, introduced by τότε, has been appended by the evangelist, who wanted to reduce the amount of misunderstanding on the part of the disciples. For similar reasons, Luke leaves out this scene altogether.

The Healing of an Epileptic Boy
(Mark 9:14-29; Matt 17:14-21; Luke 9:37-43a)

Here we encounter an unusually vivid situation: they (Jesus and the three chosen disciples who were with him at the transfiguration) return to the other disciples to find that they are engaged in a debate with the scribes, surrounded by a great crowd. The crowd sees Jesus and greets him with surprise. He asks what the debate is about, and then a man steps forward

15. Wendling (123) rightly sees the problem here, but I have resolved it in a way that does not require us to regard the entire passage in bulk as the work of the evangelist.

who had brought his epileptic son to the disciples, but they had not been able to heal him. This scene, which I have just described in keeping with the word order in the Greek text, can only come from oral tradition. In fact we may go further and say that it goes back to real memory and history.[16] Even its attachment to what precedes is pure. It appears that the memory of the ancient narrator has not lost its hold on the original circumstances, i.e., that the healing took place at the foot of the Mount of Transfiguration after Jesus had come back down with the three disciples. And the most important fact of all is that there is no reason for Mark to have brought this story here from some other location. For it has nothing to do with the most basic themes of this part of Mark's gospel, particularly the transfiguration and the passion predictions. At this point Mark was bound by the arrangement of the stories in the tradition. Yet it is not easy as some think to demonstrate that the context in the tradition is original. Yes, the story can be connected with what precedes, but it does not have to be. There are no strong topographical or chronological links. Obviously the sharp-eyed author of Luke (9:37) spotted a gap here, when he explicitly said that they had "come down" from the mountain (κατελθόντων αὐτῶν), and that this happened on the next day (τῇ ἑξῆς ἡμέρᾳ). In this context, the reading of ς in Mark 9:14, which has been rejected by recent editors and exegetes (except for von Soden), gains new significance. Instead of ἐλθόντες . . . εἶδον, ς reads along with A C D Γ it vg cop go aeth: ἐλθών . . . εἶδεν. The text of syr[sin] stands in the middle between the usual reading and ς: "as he came, they saw . . ."[17] If the singular, which is well attested,[18] preserves the original reading, then there remains no significant connection with what precedes. Only Jesus is spoken of, and his disciples drop out of sight, reappearing later for the explanation. It is the same problem that we have encountered in the double reading ἔρχονται and ἔρχεται in Mark 8:22. Once again we have to consider two possibilities: 1) at a later time a Jesus pericope was picked up and the singular was inserted; or 2) the singular was the original reading, but it was

---

16. Spitta (*Die synoptische Grundschrift*, 249ff) regards this passage as a later addition to Mark. But that does not get around the problem. He cannot produce any evidence that the location of the story is secondary.

17. Merx (*Markus und Lukas*, 101) looks for the original reading in syr[sin]: "Attempts to adjust the text to either singular or plural arose from the text of syr[sin]."

18. B. Weiss (*Markus und Lukas*, 143) offers the explanation that it should be singular because of the following αὐτόν, but that is insufficient. Others, like Wohlenberg, do not take the singular reading into consideration. Klostermann (*Mark*, 74) incorrectly reads the variant in syr[sin] and concludes that the singular looks like a correction, but considers it original without being able to explain why. On internal evidence Wellhausen (*Mark*, 78) regards the singular reading as correct: "The subject of the scene is Jesus, not Jesus and his three disciples."

later changed to the plural in order to provide a link with what preceded. In either case we still have before us a thoroughly independent Jesus pericope from the oldest tradition, one that does not quite fit into its current setting. Very strong manuscript evidence speaks for the second possibility. The vivid setting of the scene loses nothing from this observation. We simply do not know what its original context might have been. We can outline it this way: at one point Jesus withdrew from his disciples (that this often happened is confirmed by 6:12; 6:45; and 8:29), and when he came back to them he was greeted with joy by the crowd. Over the course of time this narrative was joined in the tradition to the transfiguration scene. But the old introduction to the pericope survived, for no one noticed that Jesus was not alone, but had three disciples with him. Later on, this lack of clarity was removed when the verb was changed into the plural.

Each of the other two Synoptics has re-formed Mark's version in its own distinctive way. Matthew (17:14–21) omits the broad-brush depiction of the introduction, since in his judgment the focus should be upon the miracle. Luke (9:37–43) is similar, although (as we have already noticed) he does give the scene a precise connection with what precedes.

Mark 9:28 is an addendum that alters the scene: Jesus is alone in a house with his disciples. In Matthew (17:19) the word τότε signifies that the setting for the narrative has changed. I will not venture a guess as to whether this addendum originally belonged to the pericope, or whether it was attached later, during the course of the tradition, or whether it was first inserted here by Mark.[19] The fact that Luke does not have this conclusion is not evidence against Mark. The third evangelist was trying to put together a smooth-flowing narrative, an effort that would have been disrupted by a transition to a new narrative at this point. He brings in a parallel on this same topic (i.e., answers to prayer) in a different context, at Luke 17:6. Matthew linked that saying from Q with our current context.

The Disciples Argue over Status
(Mark 9:33–37; Matt 18:1–5; Luke 9:46–48)

Καὶ ἦλθεν εἰς Καφαρναούμ. καὶ ἐν τῇ οἰκίᾳ γενόμενος ἐπηρώτα αὐτούς, τί ἐν τῷ ὁδῷ διελογίζεσθε; οἱ δὲ ἐσιώπων.

The singular ἦλθεν is read by ς A C L Γ Δ syr[sin] cop go aeth.
A B Itala vg read ἦλθον, and D has ἦλθοσαν. The singular here

---
19. I cannot find any convincing stylistic evidence on this point. Wendling (123) calls this "a stereotypical change of scene for esoteric teaching," but it sounds to me like Wrede's theory of the messianic secret is doing the talking there.

(as in the Mark 8:22 and 9:14) may reflect the narrative style of a pericope, as Tischendorf has remarked: "ὁ ις was added as the text began to become an ecclesiastical text." But the singular may well have been the original Markan text, especially in light of the role of pericopes in the stages of the oldest tradition. Certainly we can conclude that the individual narrative that Mark had before him used the singular.

The scene is set in a house in Capernaum that is already known to us, i.e., in the house of Peter. ἐν τῇ ὁδῷ points back toward the previous excursion. And in this context Capernaum is noteworthy, because the phrase διὰ τῆς Γαλιλαίας in 9:30 makes us think that Jesus could have traveled farther to the south, on the way to Jerusalem, or else to the east, toward the Transjordan. Certainly 9:30 cannot be decisive, for it has been inserted here by the evangelist. Yet if we accept the broad strokes of the Markan outline, then Jesus really was an itinerant, and this narrative may have circulated earlier in a different context than the one in which we now have it. It might even have been handed down as a completely independent story. Mark is the one who put it into the setting where we now find it, because it fit well into this series of stories about Jesus and the disciples. We can tell that Mark has taken up pre-existing tradition here, because the situational details (including the specific indicators of place) do not cohere with what has preceded. It is possible that in an earlier phase, this narrative had no indicators of time or place. The specific reference to Capernaum was added later, because the "house" was taken to mean the house of Peter.[20]

A new beginning appears in v. 35. Jesus has been together with his disciples since v. 33b, which makes it difficult to understand the sentence καὶ καθίσας ἐφώνησεν τοὺς δώδεκα. Why would Jesus need to call his disciples together again? Of course it is possible that we have here the work of a rather unpolished writer who is trying to sound ceremonious. It is noteworthy, for example, that v. 35 is missing from Matthew and in Luke this saying is found at 9:48b. In D the text preserves the impression of καθίσας ἐφώνησεν, even though those words do not actually appear. Perhaps a new addendum begins in v. 36. Indeed it may be that the whole pericope about the disciples striving for status is built upon a few originally individual sayings of Jesus that were collected, and to which an introduction was added. It is important to recall

---

20. In one of the most recent commentaries on Mark, Wohlenberg (*Markus*, 255) offers some stern psychological reflections based upon the place names in this text: Jesus went to Capernaum for the last time (he says) in order to take care of all that would be necessary before his death, and to avoid upsetting or offending anyone by neglecting his earthly human responsibilities. Of course the historicity of such designations of place is highly uncertain, even within the traditional chronological outline.

that similar sayings are found in a different context.[21] We cannot determine with certainty whether Mark put this arrangement together, or whether he found the pericopes already collected in the tradition.[22]

Luke (9:46–48) made two alterations in Mark's report. He leaves out the place name of Capernaum, which struck him as an interruption to the flow of the story. On his view, Jesus has already been on the road for some time, so the activities in Capernaum are left out. This coheres with the fact that Luke takes liberties with Mark, dropping the setting inside a house and giving only a brief description of the situation. A second point follows: Mark's collection of individual episodes has been pressed into one completed whole. Mark 9:35, stripped of its individual setting and buttoned up by γάρ, becomes an isolated verse located at the end of the report.[23]

With the phrase ἐν ἐκείνῃ τῇ ὥρᾳ, Matthew (18:1–5) attaches the argument about status to what precedes it, thereby offering a text that in its structure partly resembles Mark and partly Luke. The disciples' dispute about rank and privilege is somewhat de-emphasized, to be replaced by the question of first place in the kingdom of heaven. The saying about children and the kingdom of heaven in vv. 3–4 appears later in Mark's version of the pericope about the blessing of children (Mark 10:15). Obviously both narratives have been involved in an exchange.

> The textual tradition displays several variations in the framework. B and cop, trying to offer a smooth and flowing account, want the word δέ after ἐκείνῃ. 33 it syr[sin] arm read the more typical ἡμέρᾳ in place of ὥρᾳ. Origen explicitly records the double tradition (cf. the text-critical apparatus in Tischendorf). But there is no real difference in content, since both alterations constitute merely a transitional remark. In v. 2, ς D E Γ Δ vg syr[sin] arm place ὁ ις after προσκαλεσάμενος, and some Latin versions put ὁ ις before προσκαλεσάμενος, while others put it after. A new

---

21. An overview can be found in *Huck's Synopsis of the First Three Gospels*.

22. Several recent critics have correctly observed that Mark's narrative is not unified. But we should be on our guard against exaggerating the problems with the details as they are described. Wendling (98f and 101) and Wrede both ask where Jesus found the child, and they settle upon a literary answer: from the scene in Mark 10:13ff. Once again, however, we must not go too far with our theories of doublets. There is something to be said for how effective the presentation of this report really is, even though it makes a slightly awkward impression.

23. Spitta (*Die synoptische Grundschrift*, 257ff) devotes a long exegesis to Luke's arrangement, and his descriptions of its characteristics are on point. But I cannot regard it as possible that the conglomeration of scenes in Mark could have originated from Luke's smooth arrangement.

pericope could have begun at v. 2 rather than v. 1, and vv. 2–5 (= Mark 9:36–37) may once have been an independent story.

No location is indicated, but it appears that the scene is presumed to be set in Capernaum, which was named in the preceding narrative about the Temple tax.

The Temple Tax
(Matt 17:24–27)

Matthew 17:24–27 presents a tradition that is distinctive to Matthew, which concerns the conduct of Jesus with regard to the temple tax. In typical Matthean form, it begins with a participial construction: ἐλθόντων δὲ αὐτῶν εἰς Καφαραούμ.

> At v. 25 syr[sin] has "into his house" instead of εἰς τὴν οἰκίαν. It evokes a house that serves as a refuge when Jesus speaks to his disciples alone. And except for the reading of syr[sin], it could be referring to the house of Peter, which was viewed as also the house of Jesus. Merx is too sharp-eyed when he says, "With regard to the question about which of the disciples owned the house, the word 'his' eventually was allowed to drop out" (Merx, *Markus und Lukas*, 260).

The designation of place may have been applied later, perhaps first by Matthew, but it has some significance, since the house of Peter is mentioned here, and the story plays out beside the Sea of Galilee. The "didrachma" mentioned in v. 24 is the tax that every Jew over the age of twenty had to pay each year at the end of the month of Adar, i.e., before Easter, in February (cf. Exod 30:13–14; for specifics of the accounting, cf. Josephus, *Ant.* 18.9.1).[24] This calendrical detail[25] fits nicely with the setting of our story in the framework that underlies the Gospel of Matthew, but it is not significant that the story is set in the month of the Passover when Jesus died. Is it important that Peter answers Jesus' question about paying the temple tax in the affirmative? Should we infer that Jesus had paid the tax previously, perhaps once or twice? If so, this apparently off-hand remark might provide the foundation upon which the generally accepted idea of a one-year ministry of Jesus could rest: Peter has already known Jesus for at least a year, so he was not called to be a disciple during the year in which Jesus died. Yet this chronology is unconvincing. Peter would already have been aware of Jesus' conservative

---

24. Cf. Schürer, *History of the Jewish People*, 2:258–59. Meyer, *Griechische Texte aus Ägypten*, 149ff; cf. also the remarks of Deissman on p. 150.

25. Cf. Windisch, "Die Dauer," 158.

positions with regard to the Law, so he could have easily deduced that Jesus would pay the temple tax. Or perhaps the prince of the apostles just had miraculous knowledge independent of any evidence.

It may be that we are overestimating the extent to which this narrative can help us solve the problem of the framework of the story of Jesus. In view of the fact that it emphasizes the distinctive role of Peter, behind whom all the other disciples recede, and because of the legendary saying at the end, which most scholars have watered down,[26] this pericope has been regarded as of very late origin and of no historical value. At bottom, this pericope seeks to resolve the question of whether the Palestinian Christians, who had previously been Jews, continued to pay the temple tax. Matthew put the story here because it is a story about Peter, in the same way that he had already highlighted two other stories about Peter, i.e., the confession at Caesarea Philippi and the transfiguration.

Further Sayings with the Disciples
(Mark 9:38–50, Matt 18:6–35 et al; Luke 9:49–50 et al.)

The overview in the table below makes it abundantly clear that the discourse between Jesus and the disciples has been constructed very loosely. It begins with the saying we have already discussed, i.e., the dispute over status, followed by a series of three pericopes (II–IV in the table) that seem to presume a situation after Jesus' departure from the world. Jesus gives reminders to his disciples. There is no unifying train of thought. The narrative about *outsiders performing exorcisms* somehow came in from somewhere. There is only one catchword, in vv. 37 and 38: ἐπὶ τὸν ὀνόματί μου and ἐν τῷ ὀνόματί σου. The saying about *stumbling blocks* is probably connected to μὴ κωλύετε in v. 39; i.e., the act of putting an obstacle in the way of an exorcist—even an exorcist who is a child (μικρός) in the faith—is itself a stumbling block. At the same time this saying also seems to have in mind the children of v. 37, who certainly are μικροί. The saying about *salt* has a highly unusual connection: it is directly adjoined to the saying about πῦρ in v. 48.

	Mark	Matthew	Luke
A.			
I. Dispute about Status	9:33–37	18:1–5	9:46–48
II. Outsider Exorcist	9:33–41		9:49–50
III. About Disputes	9:42–48	18:6–9	17:1–2

26. Cf. Klostermann, *Matthäus*, 278–79.

	Mark	Matthew	Luke
IV. About Salt	9:49-50	**5:13**	**14:34-35**
V. Salvation of the Lost		*18:10-14*	**15:3-7**
VI. Obligations to Brethren		*18:15-20*	**17:3**
VII. Forgiveness		*18:21-22*	**17:4**
VIII. Unforgiving Servant		*18:23-35*	

B.

	Mark	Matthew	Luke
Against Me, for Me	9:40	**12:30**	**9:50b; 11:23a**
A Glass of Water	9:41	**10:42**	
Disputes (a)	9:42	18:6	
Disputes (b)		18:7	
Disputes (c)	9:43-48	18:7	17:1
		(18:8 = 5:30)	
		(18:9 = 5:29)	
Fire	9:49		
Salt	9:50a	**5:13**	**14:34-35**
Peace	9:50b		
Insignificance		*18:10*	
Obligations (a)		*18:15a*	**17:3**
Obligations (b)		*18:15b-20*	
		(boldface = Q; italics = M)	

The fact that I–IV have no close connections is made even clearer by the treatment of those complexes in Matthew and Luke. II is missing from Matthew, without any interruption in the train of thought. On the other hand, the saying about disputes fits better with I than with II. Yet we should not necessarily conclude that the exorcist episode was therefore inserted by a later editor of Mark.[27] Even if such an operation had been attempted, there is unfortunately no reasonable likelihood that it would have resulted in the smooth connection between Mark 9:37 and 9:42. Obviously the insertion would have had to be made *after* that pericope. Matthew did not include the

27. Cf. the very subtle exegesis in J. Weiss, *Das älteste Evangelium*, 258-59.

saying about salt at this point, because he had already put something similar in the Sermon on the Mount at 5:13. Luke, by contrast, included (as Mark did) the exorcism stories and the sayings about disputes, but he put them in a later context, just as he did with the saying about salt.

Not only are stories I–IV loosely connected, even in their edited forms, but in addition the individual pericopes are not internally coherent. What we have already found in our close examination of I repeats itself when we take a look at Part B of the table. Consider the following excerpts: the saying in Mark 9:40, which hangs loosely on γάρ, appears in Matt 12:30 in Jesus' defense against the Pharisees, and the saying in Mark 9:41, which is also loosely attached, appears in Matt 10:42 at the end of Jesus' commissioning speech to the disciples. Even within the pericopes that follow, we find that the connections are based solely upon catchwords. Thus Mark 9:43–48, which is missing from Luke, is strung together on the basis of the word σκανδαλίζειν in vv. 41 and 43. Verse 50a, which appears in the other two Synoptics in a different, thoroughly revised form, is locked into place by means of the words τὸ ἅλα and ἁλίζεσθαι. Verse 50b gives a strong conclusion to Mark's account, but it is missing from both Matthew and Luke.

The takeaway from our investigation of these complicated literary relationships is that the words of Jesus that underlie the gospel tradition have come to rest in a variety of chronological settings and at different home addresses. On the whole, words are shared here that (according to the three evangelists) were spoken to the disciples at the end of Jesus' activity in Galilee. But some of them originated in other contexts, whether in the Sermon on the Mount or in an argument Jesus had with his opponents. For there are other groups, not just the disciples. Aside from the dispute about status, only one other pericope has a definite framework: the narrative about *outsiders performing exorcisms*. In Mark 9:38 it is introduced with the words ἔφη αὐτῷ ὁ Ἰωάννης. This rather abrupt beginning is in fact the introduction to a pericope from the oldest tradition, which goes back to a genuine memory, so it is not to be examined as if it were the product of artistic creative thinking about John.[28] The later gospels, especially Luke 9:49 (ἀποκριθεὶς δὲ ὁ Ἰωάννης εἶπεν), have substantially altered the course of the narrative here, and they clearly wanted to smooth out somewhat the transition from what precedes. Thus A D Γ and the Itala mss have a reading similar to Luke: ἀπεκρίθη (δέ).

---

28. It often said that John is presented in the gospels as a paradigm of impatience; cf. Mark 3:17 and Luke 9:54. But that hypothesis is uncertain. We can easily fall into a vicious circle here, because the story could just as well have developed the other way around: Mark 3:17 and Luke 9:54 could be the after-effects of exorcism stories. Wendling (103) finds here a reflection on Mark 10:35ff.

The narratives that follow have nothing in the way of introductory framing matter. They are oriented in each case toward the disciples, which Luke makes explicitly clear in another context at 17:1: εἶπεν δὲ πρὸς τοὺς μαθητὰς αὐτοῦ. We can no longer determine to whom these individual sayings were spoken. A particular saying, especially in the Q tradition, may have originally been addressed not only to the disciples but also to others as well. The sayings, which in all three Synoptics are now addressed to the disciples, might originally been addressed to someone else.

Matthew drew upon Q and special tradition to expand upon the Markan material so as to add Jesus' explanations of the sayings to the disciples. At this point familiar observations about chronology and addressees once again apply. The saying about forgiveness is the only one with a distinct framework, for it is occasioned by a question from Peter: τότε προσελθὼν ὁ Πέτρος εἶπεν (Matt 18:21). Peter's questions are a familiar characteristic of the first evangelist (cf. 14:28 and 15:15), although Mark and Luke also know of his special prominence, as we can see in the stories of the confession at Caesarea Philippi and the transfiguration. Yet Peter's position in the first Gospel is unusually prominent (cf. also Matt 17:24–27), which may go back to special traditions, the historicity of which would have to be argued on a case-by-case basis. It is noteworthy that even in the Gospel of the Hebrews this pericope is connected with Peter.[29] The fact that Luke makes no mention of the apostle Peter when he passes along the saying about forgiveness (17:4) does not alter the fact that the original tradition *did* include Peter.

At Matt 18:10 a special saying, distinctive to Matthew, is attached to the saying about the *lost sheep*. Verse 11, which ought to provide a bridge between v. 10 and v. 23, is missing from ℵ B L 33 Itala syr^sin cop. It is certainly not authentic in this location, even if the content might seem to fit. It appears in Luke 19:10. Luke 15:3–7 puts a special introduction on the sayings about finding lost things: εἶπεν δὲ πρὸς αὐτοὺς τὴν παραβολὴν ταύτην λέγων. Luke had already given an historical introduction to the setting (Luke 15:1–2, which is reminiscent of Mark 2:15–16), and he also connects the parable of the lost sheep with those of the lost coin (Luke 15:8–10) and the lost son (Luke 15:11–32). In this context the sayings are not directed to the disciples alone, but to the crowds as well, and especially to the Pharisees and scribes, whom Jesus seeks to refute with these parables.

The most remarkable feature about the structure of these sayings is how inconsistently the frameworks of the individual narratives are treated: they are here today, gone tomorrow. Yet it is precisely at times like these,

---

29. *Gospel of the Hebrews*, Fragment 10. Translated by Jerome in *Contra Pelagium* III.2. Cf. Preuschen, *Antilegomena*, 6. Perhaps the original form of the tradition lies here (cf. Klostermann, *Matthäus*, 282).

when we cannot determine how the framework of each evangelist was formed, that we know we are looking at old tradition. For if each evangelist had wanted to provide the disconnected sayings of Jesus with situational settings, then the result would have been an unevenly greater elaboration of that framework. But none of them had any interest in such peripheral matters, and thus the narratives were simply repeated and passed on as they had been received. The result, often by pure coincidence, was that all sorts of things came in and stayed.[30]

Marriage and Divorce
(Mark 10:1–12; Matt 19:1–12)

This pericope is introduced by a detailed description of an itinerary:

καὶ ἐκεῖθεν ἀναστάς ἔρχεται εἰς τὰ ὅρια τῆς Ἰουδαίας καὶ πέραν τοῦ Ἰορδάνου, καὶ συνπορεύονται πάλιν ὄχλοι πρὸς αὐτόν, καὶ ὡς εἰώθει πάλιν ἐδίδασκεν αὐτούς.

א B C* L cop read καὶ πέραν; C² D Δ it vg syr^{sin} go arm aeth read πέραν (without καὶ; cf. Matt 19:1); ς A Γ et al. read διὰ τοῦ πέραν. For Mark's somewhat unusual ὄχλοι, D and some Itala mss have ὁ ὄχλος (similarly, they have συνπορεύεται in place of συνπορεύονται), and by an alteration of ὡς εἰώθει καί, they translate this phrase, "as was his custom," connecting it not to Jesus but to ὁ ὄχλος.

As in other pericopes, here too the question arises: with which verse does the narrative about marriage and divorce begin? As far as we can tell, this controversy story has no roots at all in the setting given here. We have seen this situation in other narratives (1:39–40; 6:6–7; 7:31–32; 8:9–10; 10:8; 13:14), and in such cases we have generally decided that the introductions to pericopes, along with any specific details they might contain, are nothing more than transitional pieces. This means that the content of a pericope like

---

30. In his thorough examination of Mark 9:33–50, Wendling (98ff) refers to "the elaborate construction of the redactor" (109). Based on my examination of the uneven framework of this excerpt, I have to register here the same objection that I did with regard to Mark 6:14–8:26. A "coherent elaboration" does not bring together something like four different pericopes with no precise designation of place, and with no introduction to the situation, nor any personal details, nothing like that. What we have here is the work of an editor who is collecting otherwise incompatible traditions for his purpose. A synoptic treatment of the question would be very productive. It is too bad that Wendling focuses his close reading only on Matthew and Luke, who are still, as ever, the earliest interpreters of Mark.

this one, which includes a controversy story, is not bound to any particular location. Several such scenes in chapters 2 and 7 are not localized either. On this basis we can reasonably infer that there is an incision after v. 1, and that 20:1 can just as well be the introduction to what follows as the conclusion to the preceding conversations with the disciples (9:33–50). The most satisfactory solution is to isolate the entire verse as a collected report. The content suggests as much, since it is limited to general descriptions of place and vague references to Jesus' activities. We find ourselves in that part of Mark's Gospel that forms, to a certain extent, the bridge between the activity of Jesus in Galilee and in Jerusalem. With the series of passion predictions serving as a motif, the evangelist increasingly strives on toward that end, with designations of place bringing us closer and closer to Jerusalem. Twice the word πάλιν is inserted by the evangelist, just as the expression ὡς εἰώθει in this context directs attention to Jesus' impact. It is precisely this last feature of the collection that most betrays the hand of the evangelist, which looms over the entire series of stories. From this point forward, questions about topography—does ἐκεῖθεν refer to Capernaum in general or to the specific house mentioned in 9:33?—are no longer justified, and the goal of the journey (which is unclear) has no real meaning. The designations of place cannot be fixed any more precisely. What does this mean: did he come into the region of Judea *and* the Transjordan? At this point in the narrative the itinerary becomes meaningless. First Judea and then Perea? The written tradition shows that some things have been changed and others have been improved, but it should be generally clear that Jesus is traveling through the Transjordan toward Judea.[31]

---

31. Wohlenberg (*Markus*, 265–66) offers a precise discussion about the possible location, based upon the rich and colorful scenery in Mark 10:1. But this is a waste of time. Wellhausen, on the other hand, is right on point when he argues (*Einleitung in die drei ersten Evangelien* (12) that the subject is Judea, so far as it lay east of the Jordan (ἡ Ἰουδαία ἡ περαία). But even this explanation runs into difficulty, because the uncertainty about the geography cannot resolve the uncertainty in the textual tradition.—I find myself diametrically opposed to Wendling (125): "If we assume that the original text of the Gospel offered a continuous narrative—an assumption that is justified by our results so far—then a transition (like 10:1) from the northern journey to the southern journey is necessary. Thus 10:1 belongs to the original report, and indeed to its earliest layer." Here we can see that Wendling's "philological investigations" still depend upon a postulate that breaks down time after time, even in the work of defenders of the Markan hypothesis. This is of course the idea that somehow, some kind of continuous narrative of the story of Jesus, a little biography of Jesus, can be uncovered. Wendling, like some others, neglects the fact the individual narratives wandered, with or without topographical or chronological frameworks, and that here and there some narratives were put together into a collection.

Loisy (*Les Évangiles synoptiques*, 2:195) takes Mark 10:1 as "a division in the narrative."

There is only one point to make about the parallel passage in Matt 19:1–2: we find here a distinct echo of the Markan text, with a typical Matthean formula that we have already seen in 7:28; 11:1; and 26:1.

The pericope itself has to do with marriage and divorce, and it is introduced as follows: καὶ προσελθόντες οἱ Φαρισαῖοι ἐπηρώτων αὐτόν (Mark 10:2) = καὶ προσῆλθον αὐτῷ οἱ Φαρισαῖοι πειράζοντες αὐτόν (Matt 19:3). The article οἱ is missing from some manuscripts of both gospels, but that is a stylistic gloss. The old pericope spoke of the Pharisees, both as they were known and as they were presumed to have actually been. What is more important is the fact that some witnesses do not mention the Pharisees. Among the manuscripts of the Gospel of Mark, προσελθόντες οἱ Φαρισαῖοι is missing from D, the Latin versions and syr^{sin}. We cannot know with certainty whether the historical Pharisees (or other lesser-known people) actually carried on these disputes with Jesus. Stories were swapped into and out of the tradition, and at this point we cannot control for those factors. On the other hand, it is certain that Mark found the Pharisees in the tradition and let them remain there, since there was no apparent reason for inserting them here after the fact. That they might have disappeared later is understandable, since if the pericope began with v. 1, or if it was part of a running narrative, then the sudden appearance of the Pharisees would make no sense. They were simply stricken, and their words were put into the mouths of the ὄχλοι from v. 1. That this hypothesis is reasonable is shown by Luke, who wants the Pharisees (or any other opponents of Jesus) to disappear from the narrative at this point. An especially illustrative case is Luke 5:33, in contrast with Mark 2:18 and Matt 9:14.[32]

On the other hand, we cannot give a good reason for Mark's decision to put the pericope on marriage and divorce in this location, for it does not fit with what precedes in 8:27—10:45, where the theme is Jesus and his disciples. Yet it appears that Mark did want to use our scene in the service of this broader theme: for it is precisely the disciples who face the question of whether one should separate oneself from the most tender relationship a human being can have. In this text Jesus is in a house with his disciples (v. 10, which is missing from Matthew), and he gives them a forceful answer. In an additional saying, attached with the introductory formula καὶ λέγει αὐτοῖς, the quintessence of the matter emerges clearly, as the evangelists may have recollected it. We have here a saying from a special tradition, as is evident not only from the insertion of a second introduction to the

---

32. On the basis of his understanding of Mark's compositional technique, Merx (*Markus und Lukas*, 113) correctly sees that "the Pharisees' questions are totally out of place."

saying, but also from the content itself, which is virtually identical with Matt 5:32 = Luke 16:18.³³

Matthew (19:10-12) also sets this saying in a special scene, in the middle of which there also appears the saying about eunuchs and the kingdom of heaven. At this point in its narrative, the Gospel of Luke is generally following the Markan outline, but not in the case of this detailed pericope about marriage and divorce. For him it was enough that 16:18 sheds light on this issue.

The Blessing of Children
(Mark 10:13-16; Matt 19:13-15; Luke 18:15-17)

There follows a pericope without any framework at all: καὶ προσέφερον αὐτῷ παιδία. At this point, at the end of his long Travel Narrative, Luke picks up the Markan outline again, though with some stylistic alterations. Once again Matthew uses his characteristic clamp, τότε. One can make of the setting for this scene what one will, perhaps it was even out in the open, although earlier a house has been mentioned (at 10:10). Imagination can be given free play here, so far as the context allows, as long as we hold firm to the main element in the picture: Jesus blessing the children.³⁴ Originally, of course, this pericope had nothing to do with any instruction to the disciples about the need for renunciation and suffering. All the same, Mark located it (along with the preceding narrative) under the same heading: certainly v. 15 presents us with a teachable moment.

On the Danger of Riches
(Mark 10:17-31; Matt 19:16-30; Luke 18:18-30)

The scene opens with a designation of place, forlorn but still surviving: καὶ ἐκπορευομένου αὐτοῦ εἰς ὁδόν. This detail lives on, and as such it awakens our interest, even though under closer examination it shows itself to be rather

---

33. Wendling (128) attributes the insertion of this pericope to "the practical interest of the community." That is quite correct, but it does not mean that 10:2-12 cannot go back to any specific tradition, and that they are therefore the work of the evangelist.

34. At this point, Wohlenberg (*Markus*, 270-71) is offering a "scientifically" based examination of the setting, when he writes: "An attentive reader will find no lack of clarity even when it comes to the setting . . . it is the house mentioned in v. 10." Then he offers reflections on the mother, and on the age of the children. According to Spitta (*Die synoptische Grundschrift*, 275), the narrative takes place in the "other villages" mentioned in Luke 9:56.

unproductive. At one time there may have been lively details of local color behind this place designation, but in its current context, in which it is not deeply anchored, it suggests a connection with what precedes, to clarify (but not interpret) the words ἐκπορεύεσθαι εἰς ὁδόν.[35] If we regard the story as an individual story, scenic details like this do not matter. If we read these stories in sequence, we will put even less value on these kinds of details. Only a trained exegete loaded down by commentaries would ever conclude that the story is set in the same house mentioned in 10:10. Matthew and Luke have let that designation of place fall away, with good reason. Matthew (19:16) closes up with καὶ ἰδού, after which he artfully uses part of Mark's account to conclude the preceding pericope (19:15). Luke (18:18) uses a simple conjunction to attach this narrative to the preceding one.[36]

The rich man who asks Jesus a question is variously described: Mark and Matt both say εἷς, which is about the same as τίς. Luke, by contrast, has τις ἄρχων, i.e., someone important. This detail is developed in the following report (v. 22), and the phrase τὶς πλούσιος appears in Codex A at Mark 10:17. Luke's authorial efforts here are typical of the way in which he consistently presents himself as a personality—we have already noted numerous similar cases—and for this he needs no special tradition; his purpose can reach its goal with the traditional report alone. The older, more naive tradition allowed the voice of an individual person only gradually at first, as it does in the stories we have before us. Only when the man rejects Jesus' call do we realize what is at stake. The Kingdom is the basis for his movement. That will have to suffice for our characterization of the man. Matthew's report has something special in it, i.e., that it characterizes the one who asks the question as a youth (v. 20, 22: νεανίσκος), in keeping with the way the text is commonly described: "the story of the rich young man." Does that connection point to a special tradition? Yet Matthew leaves out this part of the description, and emphasizes instead the fourth commandment (Matt 19:19). The phrase ἐκ νεότητός μου (Mark 10:20) does not appear in all Mss., and so also may be a later elaboration upon the notion of a rich young man. The expression could apply to a youth, but it would work just as well with a mature man.

35. Wellhausen (*Mark*, 86) may regard this as "a lively and interesting detail," but that remark does not help us understand the evangelists.

36. Most remarkably, the introductory designation of place belongs to Wendling's "Ur-Mark" (Wendling, *Urmarkus*, 51). After excluding various possibilities, he considers what the phrase ἐκπορεύεσθαι εἰς ὁδόν refers to: not to a house, as the evangelist wanted, but "rather some sort of inn or rest stop (cf. 10:46), where the teaching scene in 10:1 takes place" (Wendling, 128n4). From my point of view, a scenic detail of this sort, lost as it is within an imperious text, must be studied as a piece of the framework of the story of Jesus.

The form of our pericope in the Gospel of the Hebrews, as Origen quotes it in his commentary on Matthew, is noteworthy: *dixit ad eum alter divitum*.[37] The fact that two rich people are mentioned in this Gospel is not likely to be the result of a process of harmonization between two different traditions, such as Matthew and Luke. As we have already seen, in the oldest Jesus tradition there was a propensity toward doublets (cf. Matt 8:28; 26:30). The Gospel of the Hebrews conveys no information about the rich man's personal characteristics. Such details are peripheral, and the tradition does not allow us to reckon with personal information, nor about chronology and topography. Something is included because it was somehow of interest, something else comes in by coincidence, and something else grows up somewhere along the line. We cannot recover the motives for these developments, because they long ago disappeared along the way.[38]

The narrative of the rich man ends at Mark 10:22, and v. 23 sets out something new: καὶ περιβλεψάμενος ὁ Ἰησοῦς λέγει τοῖς μαθηταῖς. Matt 19:23 reads: ὁ δὲ Ἰησοῦς εἶπεν τοῖς μαθηταῖς. The ensuing conversation between Jesus and his disciples fits very well into the context of the preceding situation, in which the rich man walked away from Jesus, but 23ff can also be isolated as a conversation between only Jesus and his disciples, which is understandable on it own terms. Luke obviously found a seam between Mark 10:22 and 10:23, and he smoothed it over in a very fine way: while Mark and Matthew have the rich man walk away in sadness, after which Jesus talks with his disciples, Luke has the rich man stay around, while Jesus warns him (i.e., him *and* everyone else who is there) about the dangers of wealth. In this way Luke sets up a stronger connection between the pericope and Jesus' warnings about wealth.[39]

---

37. Origen, *Comm. on Matthew XV*, 14. Cf. Preuschen, *Antilegomena*, 6. Cf. also Hennecke, *Handbuch zu den neutestamentlichen Apokryphen* (1904), 30. Translator's note: *dixit ad eum alter divitum* means "a rich old man said to him."

38. Spitta (*Die synoptische Grundschrift*, 275) does not reflect on the literary distinctiveness of Luke, as I have described it here. Instead he turns it around: τὶς ἄρχων may be original, just as John 3:1 can speak of an ἄρχων τῶν Ἰουδαίων. If Mark does not use the word ἄρχων, perhaps it is because that word may not have been in his vocabulary. On internal grounds Spitta does not consider this possibility worthy of consideration. For "on the one hand, it is characteristic of an older disciple not to cling to earthly possessions, but to be rather casual and prodigal. On the other hand . . . the contrast between wealthy people and children (cf. the preceding pericope) is directed not toward the youth, but rather toward mature adults." As we can see, Spitta must resort to extreme explanations in order to maintain this thesis.

39. As far as I can see, most exegetes pass over this material without comment. But Spitta (*Die synoptische Grundschrift*, 283) reads the differences in Luke's presentation very closely. One notes in particular his strained argument that Mark and Matthew are later versions of the story: in those Gospels, the closing words of Jesus about the

The conversation between Jesus and his disciples about wealth puts together two separate sayings, whose originality and relationship are not at all secure. In particular it appears that Mark 10:24 is a piece of special tradition. It is missing from both Matthew and Luke, and a new beginning clearly occurs at 10:28: ἤρξατο λέγειν ὁ Πέτρος. The topic of rewards is also dealt with in the context of Peter's question. Matthew (19:27) also sets forth a new topic at this point with τότε ἀποκριθείς, while Luke (18:22) eludes the caesura by using a simpler phrase that makes a better connection: εἶπεν δὲ ὁ Πέτρος. Matthew widens the discussion by including a discourse of Jesus from Q, which Luke locates at a different point in the narrative (22:28-30). Mark and Matt both include the saying about "the first and the last, although for Mark it is something of a leftover (Mark 10:31 = Matt 19:30), while Luke puts it in a different location (13:30).

The entire complex of Mark 10:17-31, which begins with a complete pericope and then brings in various related material at the end, has a great deal of similarity with the parables chapter in Mark 4 and the conversation about pure and impure in Mark 7.

In view of the fact that Matthew (20:1-16) brought in the parable of the workers in the vineyard from special tradition, and that all three evangelists included the third passion prediction, the pericope finds a parallel in Matt and Mark in the pericope of Jesus and the sons of Zebedee.

Jesus and the Sons of Zebedee
(Mark 10:35-45; Matt 20:20-28)

This pericope, which contains no indicators of time or place, stretches through v. 40 and is thoroughly clear in and of itself. The second phase of the narrative (vv. 41-45) recounts an argument between the sons of Zebedee and Jesus' words to the circle of his disciples. Luke (22:24-27) sets this second act off and gives it its own introduction: an argument breaks out among them (the disciples) over which of them is the greatest. This variation by Luke suggests that Mark 10:42-45 can be regarded as a special piece, which (on the basis of its introduction προσκαλεσάμενος αὐτοὺς ὁ Ἰησοῦς λέγει αὐτοῖς) may constitute an exceptional and independent piece of tradition. 10:41 would then be connected with what precedes (10:35-41), or it might be a transitional piece that linked the scene about the sons of Zebedee with additional sayings of Jesus. On the other hand, it might be possible to disconnect vv. 38-40, since (quite apart from the sons of Zebedee) this scene could work in a different context: if vv. 37 and 41 were

---

difficulty of rich people entering the kingdom of God spare the rich. (!!)

connected, then 10:35-37 and 41-45 would constitute a striking and complete scene.[40] 10:45 is only loosely related, and its internal characteristics suggests that it might be isolated.

Matthew (20:20-28) opens the pericope with τότε προσῆλθεν αὐτῷ: the supplicant is the mother of the sons of Zebedee, who comes with her two sons. But the answer that follows is given here, as it is in Mark, to the two sons. Obviously this reflects a later attempt to reduce the offense that is given and to rescue the honor of the two disciples.

Excursus: Summary:
Mark 8:27—10:45 and Matt 16:13-20, 28

A major section of the Gospel of Mark, which began at 8:27, comes to its end at 10:45. The section that had described Jesus' activity in Gentile territory came to its end at 8:26. The pericope about blind Bartimaeus (10:46ff), situated in the neighborhood of Jericho, introduces the narrative about the last days of Jesus. It is clear that everything in between is consistently presented from the same point of view: Jesus is devoting himself solely to his disciples. The individual stories are pressed into the service of this idea, loosely strung together because they have originated in very different contexts. The resulting collections of narratives contain no real itinerary, although topographical indicators are strewn about here and there, serving to depict Jesus on the way to Jerusalem, and as such they stand in a clear relation to the three Passion Narratives. They prepare for the goal of the entire story: "the suffering of Jesus in Jerusalem."[41]

---

40. If we pay attention to the framework that is evident in Mark, we can highlight the different forms of the story of the sons of Zebedee. Wendling (133ff) considers only the second, and I cannot choose between the two. It is methodologically interesting that we can easily lift Mark's paratactic accounts out of their contexts, either by verses or by verse-groups, but only at the risk of killing them dead. In this case it remains clear that there must have been some kind of separation between the sons of Zebedee and their question (either from 38-41 or 41-45). Either of these two pieces can be removed, but not both of them.

41. Specific indications about the length of the journey occasionally appear. The usual route from Galilee to Jerusalem took about three (3) days. Going through Perea would perhaps double that, or at least another two days. Could Jesus have undertaken this journey without places to stay? The various stories say nothing about this, because they are not thinking of any long period of time. Or perhaps Jesus approached the city of Jerusalem slowly, stopping along the way? We cannot know. Windisch (151) poses an important question, which is the right one: "It is only due to the preference

Matthew follows with a comprehensive section (16:13–20, 28) that runs parallel to the Markan outline, although he does introduce some new material into the existing framework.

---

of the evangelists that we are told about any experiences on the trip to Jerusalem . . . They could hardly have imagined a trip through Perea; they were more at home in Capernaum or Jerusalem."

7

Luke's Travel Narrative

Luke 9:51—19:27 (9:51—18:14 = Insertion in the Markan Outline)

Introductory Issues

General Characteristics

IN HIS OWN DISTINCTIVE way, Luke inserted into the plan of the Gospel of Mark as he found it a journey by Jesus from Galilee to Jerusalem. For the most part, Luke's version of the story runs almost exactly parallel to Mark's. Thus Luke 9:18-50 encompasses Jesus' last experiences and conversations in Galilee, but at that point there begins a large section with no parallels with Mark in either its outline or its material. Matthew was not obligated to take up what we now call this "Lukan Travel Narrative," the whole of which unfolds in a continuous storyline running from 9:51 to 19:27, reconnecting with the Markan outline at its conclusion. Most of what is in the Gospels of Mark and Matthew stands under a shadow of preparation for Jesus' eventual suffering, and the approach of this suffering is interwoven with his approach toward the city of Jerusalem. In Luke, however, it is the geography that stands in the foreground throughout, and he preserves a special section about instructions to the disciples. In this way the evangelist groups the material together in his own distinctive way, even though there continue to be many parallels with the other Synoptics. The best illustration of this point is to consider the following table, the results of which (as we have already explained) are as follows: there is a break after Mark 10:45 (= Matt 20:28). This verse brings the disciples' part to an end, and afterward the activity in Jerusalem begins. So even though Mark 10:46 (= Matt 20:29) corresponds to Luke 18:35, and Luke 18:35—21:38 is parallel to the section in Mark 10:46—13:37 (= Matt 20:29), the internal structure of the Gospel of Luke requires us to make an insertion after 19:27, and therefore to regard

9:51—19:27 as a coherent section. Only in this way can we correctly understand Luke's geographical layout.

	Mark	Matt	Luke	
Preparing the Disciples for Jesus' Suffering	8:27—10:45	16:13—20:28	9:18—18:34	Final Events
			9:18-50	in Galilee
			9:51—19:27	Journey to Jerusalem
Last Days in Jerusalem	10:46—13:37	20:29—25:46	18:35—21:38	
			19:28—21—38	Jerusalem

Overview of the Parts of the Framework

Can this plan be worked out thoroughly and in detail? To what extent is Luke 9:51ff a "travel narrative"? In a variety of remarks strewn through the narrative, most of which are located in the introductions to pericopes, we find indications that Jesus is traveling toward Jerusalem:

1. I. It is especially significant that, at the very beginning of the Travel Narrative, 9:51 stands out in this regard: he sets his face directly toward Jerusalem, to go there (τὸ πρόσωπον αὐτοῦ ἐστήρισεν τοῦ πορεύεσθαι εἰς Ἰερουσαλήμ).

    II. The same can be said about 9:53.

2. III. A similar statement appears at 13:22: he sets out on a journey toward Jerusalem (πορείαν ποιούμενους εἰς Ἱεροσόλυμα).

    IV. In 13:33 Jesus himself says that he is going to Jerusalem, since a prophet must die in that city (οὐχ ἐνδέχεται προφήτην ἀπολέσθαι ἔξω Ἰερουσαλήμ).

3. V. A specific scene begins in 17:11 and plays out on the way to Jerusalem (ἐν τῷ πορεύεσθαι εἰς Ἰερουσαλήμ).

4. VI. At 18:35 Jesus is in the vicinity of Jericho (ἐν τῷ ἐγγίζειν αὐτὸν εἰς Ἰερειχώ).

5. VII. In 19:1 Jesus passes through Jericho, where he meets Zacchaeus (διήρχετο τὴν Ἰερειχώ).

6. VIII. At 19:11 Jesus tells them a parable "because they were coming near to Jerusalem" (διὰ τὸ ἐγγὺς εἶναι Ἰερουσαλήμ αὐτόν).

Two of these indicators are attached to statements to the effect that Jesus chose a route from Galilee to Jerusalem that went *through Samaria*:

I. 9:52 They enter a Samaritan city (εἰσῆλθον εἰς πόλιν Σαμαρειτῶν).

II. 17:11 He passes through the middle of Samaria and Galilee (αὐτὸς διήρχετο διὰ μέσον Σαμαρίας καὶ Γαλιλαίας).

Moreover, there are additional stray remarks, which do not speak specifically of a journey to Jerusalem but which do indicate that Jesus is *on a journey*:

7. I. 9:57 "as they were traveling on the road" (πορευομένων αὐτῶν ἐν τῷ ὁδῷ).

8. II. 10:1 Jesus sent seventy disciples into every city and every village, into which he wants to go (ἀπέστειλεν ... εἰς πᾶσαν πόλιν καὶ τόπον, οἱ ἤμελλεν ἔρχεσθαι).

9. III. 10:17 the seventy return (ὑπέστρεψεν ... οἱ ἑβδομήκοντα).

10. IV. 10:38 as they continued their journey, Jesus entered a village (ἐγένετο ... ἐν τῷ πορευομέσθαι αὐτοὺς καὶ αὐτὸς εἰσῆλθεν εἰς κώμην τινά).

11. V. 11:1 he prayed at an unspecified location (ἐγένετο ἐν τῷ εἶναι αὐτὸν ἐν τόπῳ τινὶ προσευχόμενον).

12. VI. 13:10 he is in a synagogue (ἐν μιᾷ τῶν συναγωγῶν).

13. VII. 14:1 he enters the house of one of the leaders of the Pharisees (ἐγένετο ἐν τῷ ἐλθεῖν αὐτὸν εἰς οἶκόν τινος τῶν ἀρχόντων τῶν Φαρισαίων).

14. VIII. 14:25 many people are traveling with him (συνεπορεύοντο ... αὐτῷ ὄχλοι πολλοί). Even when topographical details are lacking, there are other transitions, some of *a chronological nature*:

(8). I. 10:1 (here too a local detail) "after that" (μετὰ ... ταῦτα).

15. II. 10:21 "at the same time" (ἐν αὐτῇ τῇ ὥρᾳ).

16. III. 10:25 "and behold" (καὶ ἰδού).

17. IV. 13:1 "at that very moment" (ἐν αὐτῷ τῷ καιρῷ).

18. V. 13:31 "at that same hour" (ἐν αὐτῇ τῇ ὥρᾳ).

Or there are short situational introductions, which *establish a connection with the preceding content*:

19. I. 10:29 introduction to the parable of the good Samaritan.

20. II. 11:27 "while he was saying *this* . . ." (ἐγένετο δὲ ἐν τῷ λέγειν αὐτὸν ταῦτα).

21. III. 11:37 but while he was speaking (ἐν δὲ τῷ λαλῆσαι).

22. IV. 14:7 he spoke to the invited guests (ἔλεγεν δὲ πρὸς τοὺς κεκλημένους).

23. V. 14:15 but when one of them at the table heard this (ἀκούσας δέ τις τῶν συνανακειμένων ταῦτα).

24. VI. 16:14 the Pharisees heard about *all of this* (ἤκουον δὲ ταῦτα πάντα οἱ Φαρισαῖοι).

(6). VII. 19:11 (here another local detail) "but when they heard this" (ἀκουόντων δὲ αὐτῶν ταῦτα).

Many pericopes lack both topographical and chronological connections and have no connection in content with what precedes. Instead they quickly sketch out a completely new situation, so that the individual narratives hang disconnected from what precedes. Situational details were formed in various ways. Next we review the *scenes with the disciples*:

I. 10:22 "and he turned to his disciples and said" (καὶ στραφεὶς πρὸς τοὺς μαθητὰς εἶπεν), followed by the second half of the so-called "exclamation of joy."

25. II. 10:23 "and he turned specifically to his disciples and said" (καὶ στραφεὶς πρὸς τοὺς μαθητὰς κατ' ἰδίαν εἶπεν), followed by blessings upon eyewitnesses.

III. 12:1 "while the thousands in the crowd were gathering . . . he began to say to his disciples" (ἐν οἷς ἐπισυναχθεισῶν τῶν μυριάδων τοῦ ὄχλου . . . ἤρξατο λέγειν πρὸς τοὺς μαθητὰς πρῶτον), followed by the teaching about yeast.

26. 12:2–3 **Warnings about Honest Confession.**

27. IV. 12:22 he speaks with his disciples (εἶπεν δὲ πρὸς τοὺς μαθητὰς αὐτὸ) about cares and storing up treasure.

28. 12:35 about vigilance and faithfulness.

29. 12:47 about a servant's reward.

30. 12:49 about the seriousness of the times.

31. V. 16:1 he tells his disciples (ἔλεγεν δὲ καὶ πρὸς τοὺς μαθητὰς) the parable of the dishonest servant.

32. VI. 17:1 he speaks to his disciples (εἶπεν δὲ πρὸς τοὺς μαθητὰς αὐτοῦ) about anger.

33. 17:3 about forgiveness.

34. VII. 17:5 the apostles speak to the Lord (καὶ εἶπον οἱ ἀπόστολοι τῷ κυρίῳ), and the Lord replies (εἶπεν δὲ ὁ κύριος) about faith.

35. 17:7 about a servant's reward.

36. VIII. 17:22 he speaks to his disciples (εἶπεν δὲ πρὸς τοὺς μαθητάς) about the Day of the Lord.

37. IX. 18:15 the people were bringing children to him ... but his disciples ... Jesus called the children to him and said (προσέφερον δὲ αὐτῷ καὶ τὰ βρέφη ... δὲ οἱ μαθηταὶ ... ὁ δὲ Ἰησοῦς προσεκαλέσατο αὐτὰ λέγων), and he blesses the children.

38. X. 18:31 he takes the Twelve and speaks with them (παραλαβὼν δὲ τοὺς δώδεκα εἶπεν πρὸς αὐτούς), the third prediction of the passion.

The following scenes with the disciples are noteworthy because the pericopes have a distinctive introduction:

(8). XI. 10:1 the Lord appoints the seventy and sends them out (ἀνέδειξεν ὁ κύριος καὶ ἑτέρους ἑβδομήκοντα ... ἔλεγεν δὲ πρὸς αὐτούς).

(9). XII. 10:17 the seventy return ... and he speaks to them (ὑπέστρεφαν δὲ οἱ ἑβδομήκοντα ... εἶπεν δὲ αὐτοῖς).

(15). XIII. 10:21 he rejoices in the Holy Spirit and speaks the first half of the cry of joy (ἠγαλλιάσατο ἐν τῷ πνεύματι ἁγίῳ καὶ εἶπεν).

(11). XIV. 11:1 after he finishes praying, one of the disciples speaks to him (ὡς ἐπαύσατο, εἶπεν τις τῶν μαθητῶν αὐτοῦ πρὸς αὐτόν), and he teaches them the Lord's Prayer.

In addition to the scenes with the disciples, there are *scenes with his opponents*:

39. I. 11:14 he drove out a demon, and the crowds were amazed, but some said that he drove out demons by the power of Beelzebul (καὶ ἦν ἐκβάλλων δαιμόνιον ... καὶ ἐθαύμασαν οἱ ὄχλοι· τινὲς δὲ ἐξ αὐτῶν εἶπον· ἐν βεελζεβοὺλ ἐκβάλλει), and Jesus defended himself against this accusation.

40. 11:24 on backsliding.

41. II. 15:1 tax collectors and sinners come to hear him, and the Pharisees and Sadducees murmur about it . . . but he tells them this parable (ἦσαν δὲ αὐτῷ ἐγγίζοντες πάντες οἱ τελῶναι καὶ οἱ ἁμαρτωλοὶ ἀκούειν αὐτοῦ. καὶ διεγόγγυζον οἵ τε Φαρισαῖοι καὶ οἱ γραμματεῖς . . .) (εἶπεν δὲ πρὸς αὐτοὺς τὴν παραβολὴν ταύτην λέγων), i.e., the parables of the lost sheep and the lost coin.

42. 15:11 the parable of the prodigal son.

43. III. 17:20 as he was questioned by the Pharisees . . . he answered and spoke about the kingdom of God (ἐπερωτηθεὶς δὲ ὑπὸ τῶν Φαρισαίων . . . ἀπεκρίθη αὐτοῖς καὶ εἶπεν)

On the other hand there are a number of other stories, which have already been mentioned because they have a distinctive introduction to the pericope:

(16) IV. 10:25ff. a teacher of the Law stands up (. . . νομικός τις ἀνέστη), and asks about the greatest commandment.

(19) 10:29ff. the parable of the Good Samaritan

(21) V. 11:37ff. a Pharisee invites him (ἐρωτᾷ αὐτὸν Φαρισαῖος), and he speaks against Pharisaism.

(12) VI. 13:10ff. the healing of a crippled woman.

(18) VII. 13:31ff. some Pharisees came up to him (. . . προσῆλθάν τινες Φαρισαῖοι), and he departs from Galilee.

44. 13:34–35 he laments over Jerusalem.

(13) VIII. 14:1ff. into the house of a leading Pharisee (εἰς οἶκόν τινος τῶν ἀρχόντων τῶν Φαρισαίων), where he heals a man with dropsy.

(22) 14:7ff. conversation around the table.

(23) 14:55ff. the parable of the feast.

(24) IX. 16:14–15 the Pharisees turn up their noses at him (οἱ Φαρισαῖοι . . . ἐξεμυκτήριζον αὐτόν), and he condemns Pharisaic pride.

45. 16:16ff. the Law and divorce.

46. 16:19ff. the parable of the rich man and Lazarus.

There is a third group, made up of *scenes with the people*:

47. I. 11:29ff. but as the people were gathering he began to speak (τῶν δὲ ὄχλων ἐπαθροιζομένων ἤρξατο λέγειν) against the desire for miracles.

48. 11:33ff. about light.

49. II. 12:13ff. someone in the crowd spoke to him (εἶπεν δέ τις ἐκ τοῦ ὄχλου αὐτῷ) ... but he told him (ὁ δὲ εἶπεν αὐτῷ) the parable of the foolish rich man.

(30) III. 12:54ff. he tells the crowds (ἔλεγεν δὲ καὶ τοῖς ὄχλοις) the second part of the saying about discerning the time.

50. 12:57ff. the parable about settling with your accuser.

51. IV. 18:9ff. to those who are confident that they are righteous (εἶπεν δὲ καὶ πρός τινας τοὺς πεποιθότας ἐφ ἑαυτοῖς, ὅτι εἰσὶν δίκαιοι ... τὴν παραβολὴν ταύτην), he tells the parable of the tax collector and the Pharisee.

52. V. 18:18ff. in response to a rich man's question (καὶ ἐπηρώτησέν τις αὐτὸν ἄρχων) about the danger of wealth, he spoke about the danger of riches.

(7) VI. 9:57ff. he spoke to various disciples (εἶπέν τις πρὸς αὐτόν).

(20) VII. 11:27-28 a woman in the crowd speaks to him (γυνὴ ἐκ τοῦ ὄχλου εἶπεν αὐτῷ) and blesses his mother.

(17) VIII. 13:1ff. (he is told about the Galileans whom Pilate killed) and he calls them (εἶπεν αὐτοῖς) to repentance.

13:6ff. he tells the parable about the fig tree (ἔλεγεν δὲ ταύτην τὴν παραβολήν).

(2) IX. 13:22ff. a man spoke to him (εἶπεν δέ τις αὐτῷ) but he told them (ὁ δὲ εἶπεν πρὸς αὐτούς) about the threat to Israel with the coming of the kingdom of God.

(14) X. 14:25ff. many people were coming to him, and he turned to them and told them (... ὄχλοι πολλοί, καὶ στραφεὶς εἶπεν πρὸς αὐτούς) the conditions of discipleship.

(6) XI. 19:11ff. he told the parable (εἶπεν παραβολήν) of the talents.

As folk-scenes, the following sayings have no further introduction than the general comment that Jesus spoke them:

53. XII. 11:5ff. then he spoke to them (καὶ εἶπεν πρὸς αὐτούς); we should understand αὐτούς to mean the disciples, who were the subject of the

preceding pericope, 11:1-4. There follows the parable of the friend who asks for help.

54. XIII. 11:9ff. "And I tell you" (κἀγὼ λέγω ὑμῖν), that God hears your prayers.

55. XIV. 13:18-19 "And then he said" (ἔλεγεν οὖν) the parable of the mustard seed.

  13:20-21 "And he also said" (καὶ πάλιν εἶπεν) the parable of the yeast.

56. XV. 18:1ff. "He told them a parable" (ἔλεγεν δὲ παραβολὴν αὐτοῖς), the parable of the unrighteous judge.

In this section there are also several episodes with disciples, opponents, and the people that are not easy to categorize. They include:

9:51ff	a Samaritan village refuses to welcome Jesus (1)
10:38ff	Mary and Martha (10)
17:11ff	the healing of ten lepers (3)
18:35ff	the healing of Bartimaeus (6)
19:1ff	Zacchaeus (7)

The sequential enumeration of the pericopes on the left side comes from Huck's *Synopsis* (4th ed.), which isolates fifty-six individual stories in Luke 9:51—19:27. In that tabulation, these stories include Nrs. 137-186, 188, 189, 191, 193-195. The table makes clear that in several cases there is a better way to enumerate the stories. 10:22, for example, which Huck regards as the second part of the cry of joy, is better regarded as a short but independent pericope because of its newly constituted introduction. This introduction lays out a new situation, so we should leave the transition from chapter 11 to chapter 12 where it is, and we should not connect 12:1 with the great discourse about Pharisaism. In addition, a new situation is introduced in 12:54, so the sayings in 12:49-53 and 12:54-56 should be grouped together under the heading "The Seriousness of the Time." The content of these verses points in the same direction: the first part concerns conflict with others, and the second part deals with signs from heaven and signs of the times. In a similar way it would be a good idea to isolate the parable of the fig tree (13:6-8), which also opens with a distinctive introduction.

The Textual History of the Framing Pieces

The textual history shows that repeated efforts were made to improve upon these introductions. Basically there was a recurrent tendency to strengthen the connections between the individual stories, usually by inserting a particle or by rearranging an existing particle to make it more evocative. δέ is frequently inserted. In 9:57, for example, ς reads ἐγένετο δέ instead of καί (without ἐγένετο), on the basis of C D Γ Δ Itala vg go. In 10:21, D Λ cop et al. also reads δέ after ἐν αὐτῇ, just as in some manuscripts we find this particle after ἐν αὐτῇ at 13:31. At 10:25, the beginning of the pericope about the greatest commandment, D drops καὶ ἰδου and says ἀνέστη δέ. There certainly ought to be a closer connection at this point with what precedes, as is the case again only a few verses later in the introduction to the parable of the good Samaritan, where A D et al. insert a δέ after ὑπολαβών. 11:33 begins a new saying (about light): at the beginning stands οὐδείς, after which ς puts δέ (based on A L Δ Λ Itala cop aeth).

In the texts cited above, an introduction with δέ is often preferred for its asyndetic character, but there are cases in which an earlier version of the text, which used more suggestive words like καί or οὖν, was later amended to δέ. In 18:18, for example, the introduction to the parable of the mustard seed, ς prefers ἔλεγεν δέ (the reading of A D Γ Δ Λ) to ἔλεγεν οὖν. In 12:41-42, a conversation between Jesus and Peter, the tradition swings back and forth between καί and δέ (εἶπεν δέ, καὶ εἶπεν). Unfortunately we can no longer unravel that complex process. On the other hand, there is an entire series of texts in which δέ is replaced by οὖν or καί. A good example is the introduction to the sermon to the seventy disciples in 10:2, where the text reads ἔλεγεν δέ. But at this point ς follows the reading of A Γ Δ Λ, ἔλεγεν οὖν. The Latin manuscripts read *et dicebat*. While in 13:18, ς replaces οὖν with δέ, at 13:15 that exchange is reversed in A Γ Δ Λ. In all these cases the alteration of the text aims to produce a more precise connection or a smoother flow in the narrative, even though we cannot always identify the exegetical interests served by the emendation. Certainly this is the case at 12:2 (the beginning of the exhortation to honest confession), where D syr[cur] syr[sin] arm all read γάρ in place of δέ.

In virtually all of these cases there are manuscripts that lack any kind of connecting particle: at 10:2, syr[cur] and syr[sin]; at 12:2, ℵ; at 12:41-42, syr[cur] syr[sin] arm; and at 16:19 Itala vg arm aeth. The basis for such emendations is hardly to be found in stylistic considerations. They arise instead from the usage that was customary in pericopes, where it was simply not correct to begin with the word δέ. It seems to me that in these manuscripts we have before us the precipitate of two tendencies. On the one hand there is an effort to smooth out the connections. To that end many kinds of Atticisms are pressed into service, in an attempt to polish the text into correct Attic Greek. Certain manuscripts consistently incline toward the more literary δέ than the folksy καί (the most frequent is D, which has been freely reformed at 11:37, 11:53, and 12:1). But this trend is diametrically opposed by one which pays no attention at all to the connection of the pericopes in a series. These texts lift out καί or δέ, which is deemed to be too precise, replacing it either with καί or with a totally asyndetic link.[1]

The fact that the text has been influenced by the use of pericopes shows up in the insertion of ὁ ις, which was added—sooner here, later there—to almost all of the introductory phrases that spoke of Jesus only as "he" (cf. among others, 10:21; 11:5; 11:14; 11:37; 13:10—especially in the lectionaries—13:22; 15:1). More substantial changes took place as well. A typical case is 16:9, where the best-attested text uses a simple δέ to transition from the introduction (16:16-18) to the parable of the rich man and poor Lazarus. Yet D reads εἶπεν δὲ καὶ ἑτέραν παραβολήν, while in the lectionaries we find the text as follows: εἶπεν ὁ κύριος τὴν παραβολήν ταύτην. If on the other hand 10:22a, καὶ στραφεὶς πρὸς τοὺς μαθητὰς εἶπεν is missing from ς (based upon ℵ B D L), this absence can be explained by the fact that the sentence was regarded as an interruption, since 10:21-22 was taken to be a separate pericope (as it is in Huck). The same goes for the removal of

1. A. Deissmann once said in a New Testament seminar that he suspected a study of the Atticisms in the textual history of the New Testament could lead to a clearer grouping and sharper characterization of the manuscripts. Here I have limited myself to the introductory pieces, the framework of the pericopes. It would be necessary to follow the use of particles in the Atticizing alterations, especially in inflections. Much that is necessary for this discussion does not yet appear in the critical apparatus of editions of the New Testament by Tischendorf and von Soden. In his *Untersuchungen zu den Evangelien*, which is both literate and generally seeks to defend the honor of syr^{sin}, Merx often restores Greek textual readings that belong to the Atticizing movement, but at that point he does not make anything of them. The current situation has to be chalked up to von Soden, or even more to Tischendorf. B. Weiss discusses much of the material, but his commentary and text-critical studies do not correctly understand the linguistic distinctiveness of the New Testament. He does not appreciate the grammar of the Koine thoroughly enough, if in fact it can be appreciated. Figuring out the Koine has only recently begun in earnest (cf. especially the studies of A. Deissmann, J. H. Moulton, A. Thumb).

In the present study we are occupied with the linguistic distinctiveness of the introductory pieces, and thereby also with the related question of the form of the composition technique of the evangelists. These issues have hardly been considered in gospel commentaries. A notable exception is Merx (*Markus und Lukas*, 269) who seeks to determine whether "the connection, which did not exist for long, has been recreated by the insertion of the particles." This comment grasps only part of the problem. For it was the use of pericopes that set off the process by which the pericopes were picked up and isolated.

κατ ἰδίαν from 10:23 in D latt 33 syr^sin cop arm. This κατ ἰδίαν is not typical of introductions to scenes about the disciples, and thus would have been regarded as superfluous.

In two places Luke introduces a new pericope with the phrase ἐν αὐτῇ τῇ ὥρᾳ. In both cases the text is somewhat improved thereby. At 10:21 A Δ cop go read ἐν ταύτῃ τῇ ὥρᾳ, and e changes it even more profoundly: *in illa die*. And at 13:31 this alteration appears yet again in many manuscripts: D reads ἐν ταύτῃ τῇ ὥρᾳ, but ς (supported by B³ Γ Δ Λ it vg cop arm aeth) has not ἐν αὐτῇ τῇ ὥρᾳ but ἐν ταύτῃ τῇ ἡμέρᾳ, which is similar to the reading of syr^cur and syr^sin, "and in those days." In place of a specific designation of the time, only the day is mentioned, since this form of expression is better suited to the introduction to a pericope. In a similar way at 9:57 C³ has *initium sic dat* = τῷ καιρῷ ἐκείνῳ ἐγενέτω (obviously an unrefined expression!). "At that time" or "on that day" are also favorite introductions to pericopes.[2]

Pericope Introductions Adopted by Luke

Based upon the many and varied introductions to the pericopes in Luke's Travel Narrative, the number of which increases over the course of the textual tradition, we would like to be able to conclude that individual pericopes nonetheless lie before us here, as Luke took them up and arranged them, with their introductions and framework. But that conclusion would be premature. We know that the third evangelist was an author who took care to spin out a continuous thread of narrative as far as he could. Yet when he took up these individual stories, his efforts in that regard were not completely successful. The history of the text shows that at many points, in order to produce a running account, certain things had to be changed, and Luke was not able to get very far along the track he had laid down. The textual history also shows that the connections within Luke's arrangement of the material now make it rather difficult to delineate the individual pericopes with precision. At this point the manuscript tradition becomes indispensable for getting to know our distinctive third evangelist. As an author, he stood before a profusion of individual stories, which he wanted to assemble and arrange, but there would be resistance in the early process of editing, and for some time to

---

2. Merx (*Markus und Lukas*, 313) comes to a conclusion that is exactly backward, because he does not pay enough attention to the way pericopes were used, and because he wants to regard syr^sin as the oldest text: "But the original lies in Syr^sin and Syr^crt, which still do not point to a close connection between the scenes, but rather a loose assemblage." Granted, in the old tradition there were no close connections between the scenes, but that does not allow us to ignore the fact that the author of Luke reworked those discrete pieces.

come. Some stories would be left largely untouched even by repeated efforts to put them to practical use, and old pericopes would continue to circulate *with* their respective introductions. We can see it in the first lines of stories with very simple introductory notices: καὶ εἶπεν πρὸς αὐτούς (11:5); κἀγὼ ὑμῖν λέγω (11:9); ἔλεγεν οὖν (13:18); perhaps also καὶ πάλιν εἶπεν (13:20); ἔλεγεν δὲ παραβολὴν αὐτοῖς (18:1).[3] We cannot be fully certain about why any particular opening formula was chosen. In order to handle the tradition responsibly, we must face the fact that Luke intentionally changed it. Matthew, by contrast, appears to have intentionally and consistently brought in various formulaic transitions (cf. Matt 13:31 ἄλλην παραβολήν; the same at 13:33; ἐν παραβολαῖς αὐτοὺς λέγων 22:1). Similarly the addressees in the individual sayings of Jesus are variously called "the people" or "the disciples, and this too was determined by the tradition. We cannot see through to be able to know why he picked them up as he did, as they lay before him in the tradition. We can only see the differences in the introductions to the scenes with the people[4] and to the scenes with the disciples.[5] That is true of his encounters with opponents as well,[6] in which the truth of Jesus' reply is confirmed by the associated saying. It appears to me that the parade example for this kind of pericope is 17:20–21, which was taken up without alteration by Luke. Here a saying of Jesus about the kingdom of God is occasioned by a question from a Pharisee. When Matthew makes use of these parallel passages, he does not include the introductions, but that does not speak against the originality of the tradition that Luke was using. For the third evangelist left the isolated sayings in the Q material alone, while the first evangelist brought them together in large numbers, dropping out all the introductory remarks in the process. That Luke depended upon pre-existing introductory remarks is obvious at 10:22 and 10:23, where several sayings of Jesus to the disciples are arranged in sequence one after the other. In this context v. 23 is utterly superfluous, and we can see why someone tried to help by cutting out v. 22a. As a matter of history, however, we cannot always ascertain whether a saying was directed to the people, or to the disciples, or to the opponents. It all depends upon whether that saying is anchored in a specific situation. That this is so frequently not the case tells us that the various sayings of Jesus in the tradition were experienced in different contexts. In this regard Matthew is very different from Luke.

---

3. Cf. the table on p. 228.
4. Cf. the table on p. 227.
5. Cf. the table on p. 227.
6. Cf. the table on p. 226–27.

Pericope Introductions Formed and Reformed by Luke: Chronological and Topographical

Even if Luke did lean heavily upon the tradition, which presented each individual story with a short introduction, nevertheless on occasion he managed to improve the connections and to introduce a more vivid dramatization of the individual accounts. This was the only way he could interpret the richness of the individual pieces. In this section we want to highlight various qualities that are typical of Luke. We begin with the short situational introductions, by which he created a direct attachment in content between a scene and the one that preceded.[7] That kind of link was not characteristic of the gospel tradition, which simply arranged the scenes alongside each other, at least until Luke, as we know from earlier case studies (cf. for example, 5:27, 29, and 33). Here and there he expands the setting somewhat more broadly than in the tradition, as for example at 10:1, where the commission of the seventy disciples begins with a vivid introduction. To introduce the sayings against the Pharisees (11:39ff), which are also handed down in Matt 23, Luke creates a specific setting: a Pharisee invites Jesus to dinner and marvels that he does not complete the ritual of washing before the meal. In these introductory pieces we often find the construction ἐγένετο followed by καί with a finite verb: 9:51; 10:38; 14:1; 17:1. Or it might be followed only by a finite verb, without καί: 11:1; 11:14; 11:27; 18:35. Almost all of these constructions are temporal clauses beginning with ἐν. In the entire New Testament this construction is found almost exclusively in Luke.[8]

The chronological transitions[9] also go back to Luke. About καὶ ἰδού we cannot be confident, but μετὰ ταῦτα (10:1) is Lukan, because the entire setting of the situation in 10:1 comes from him. The same applies to ἐν αὐτῷ τῷ καιρῷ in 13:1, and the twice repeated formula ἐν αὐτῇ τῇ ὥρᾳ in 10:21 and 13:31 is probably Luke's formulation, because he uses it in these contexts: 2:38; 20:19 (with no parallel in Mark and Matthew); 34:33; cf. also 12:12. Also noteworthy is the fact that Matt 11:25, the cry of joy, begins with the general pericope introduction ἐν ἐκείνῳ τῷ καιρῷ ἀποκριθείς.

Assessing the general topographical details is a more difficult task.[10] The specifications in 10:1 and 10:17 come from Luke; indeed the entire composition of the pericope about the seventy disciples goes back to him.

---

7. Cf. the table on pg. 227.

8. See the instructive explication in the German edition of Moulton, *Introduction to the Language of the New Testament* (1911), 21ff.

9. Cf. the table on pg. 227.

10. Cf. the table on pg. 222.

The detail in 10:38, "he came into a village," is plainly anchored in the ensuing situation, as are "he was praying in a certain place" (11:1) and "he was teaching in one of their synagogues" (13:10). In this last case the introductory formula ἐν μιᾷ τῶν συναγωγῶν traces back to Luke (cf. in this regard 5:12, ἐν μιᾷ τῶν πόλεων, and 5:17, ἐν μιᾷ τῶν ἡμερῶν. It is the same with the introduction to 14:1, "he went into to the house of a leader of the Pharisees." The remarks about his travels, such as 9:57; 10:1; 10:38; and 14:25 also come from the evangelist, who occasionally wants to remind us that Jesus is on the road. But the pericopes in 9:57 (about the different kinds of disciples) and 14:25 (about the conditions for discipleship) are not travel stories in any way, shape, or form.

There remain only the specific designations of place.[11] Four of these cases are found in pericope introductions that Luke has created, as is particularly obvious in 9:51, ἐγένετο δὲ ἐν τῷ συμπληροῦσαι τὰς ἡμέρας τῆς ἀναλήμψεως αὐτοῦ καὶ αὐτὸς τὸ πρόσωπον αὐτοῦ ἐστήρισεν τοῦ πορεύεσθαι εἰς Ἰερουσαλήμ. This sentence fits the form of a Lukan introduction. With v. 52 or perhaps 52b the narrative of the Good Samaritan begins. This story lacks a specific setting in time, but Luke puts it in a place of considerable significance, because it makes explicit the point of the phrase τὸ πρόσωπον αὐτοῦ ἦν πορευόμενον εἰς Ἰερουσαλήμ. Luke regards this story as the prelude to Jesus' suffering, death, and resurrection, which are gathered together here under the heading ἀνάλημψις. It is not entirely clear whether the phrase "when the days were fulfilled" is spoken by the narrator, or whether it should be attributed to Jesus, as if he recognized the significance of the moment, but the latter is more likely. Luke wants to make Jesus understandable from a psychological perspective, and in this verse Jesus sees that a new period in his life is beginning. In this way Luke sequences and psychologizes Jesus, as we have already seen several times.[12] His distinctive style is clear when we compare Mark 10:1 (perhaps also 10:32) and Matt 19:1 (cf. also 20:17), texts that speak of Jesus' departure from Galilee, but without Luke's distinctive accent. In this case Luke puts that accent down very strongly.

A similar pericope introduction is found in 13:22: καὶ διεπορεύετο κατὰ πόλεις καὶ κώμας διδάσκων καὶ πορείαν ποιούμενος εἰς Ἱεροσόλυμα. This notice will not be fully developed in the story, but it does look like it is a collective report or a pericope introduction from the hand of the evangelist. Within the wider context of the Lukan Travel Narrative, it reminds the reader once again that Jesus considers himself to be on the way to Jerusalem.

---

11. Cf. the table on pg. 222ff.
12. At the same time, this case is also illustrative of the liturgical and cultic style.

The same goes for the additional topographical details in 17:11, which also help to introduce a specific individual scene: καὶ ἐγένετο ἐν τῷ πορεύεσθαι εἰς' Ἰερουσαλήμ καὶ αὐτὸς διήρχετο διὰ μέσον Σαμαρίας καὶ Γαλιλαίας. The pericope itself begins with v. 12, and perhaps the statement εἰσερχομένου αὐτοῦ εἴς τινα κώμην can be credited to Luke's account. In that case the original pericope would have begun with καὶ ὑπήντησαν αὐτῷ δέκα ... The purpose of the location is clear: it reaffirms the beginning of the Travel Narrative. But the description of that location is *not* clear. Based on what has been depicted so far, Jesus is already in Samaria in 9:52, but in 13:31, he is back in Galilee, and here it says: "he went through Samaria and Galilee." Where are we, anyway? "Between Samaria and Galilee" more likely suggests that he is on his way north rather than south (Jerusalem). The difficulty of the reading shows up in the degree of uncertainty in the manuscript evidence: ℵ B L read διὰ μέσον, which the Latin manuscripts render as *per medium*. D, along with several other manuscripts, reads simply μέσον. ς A Γ Δ Λ, have διὰ μέσου. Individual manuscripts here and there have διὰ μέσης, διὰ τῆς, or simply διά. The topographical muddle is further complicated by the reading *et Hiericho* in various Itala manuscripts, and in one of those manuscripts we find this highly unusual reading: διήρχετο τὴν Ἰερειχὼ καὶ διὰ μέσον Σ . . . This tangled nest of textual variants shows that even in antiquity the topography of 17:11 remained unclear. Modern efforts to understand the variants from a geographical point of view are equally unsatisfying. Over and over again, attempts have repeatedly been made to conceive the route as running along the boundary between the two regions, from west to east. It appears that D was thinking of it that way when it dropped out the word διά. It is striking that Samaria is mentioned in all of the descriptions, perhaps in order to prepare for the appearance of the Samaritan in v. 16. But even this explanation of διὰ μέσον (μέσου) is highly uncertain, and some other scholars prefer to think of a journey across Samaria into Galilee, thereby artfully harmonizing the topography with other citations from the Gospels. "The facts suggest the translation 'through the middle of.' The point of departure is given in John 11:54, and the parallels in Matt 19:1ff and Mark 10:1ff describe a stop in Galilee. Thus the Lord took the long way around through Samaria and Galilee, and then at the eastern bank of the Jordan headed south through Perea (Matt 19:1; Mark 10:1), coming to Jerusalem by way of Jericho."[13] It is not just that this explanation is a fuzzy and tangled web, but that it also locates the story on the basis of specific

---

13. See Pölzl, *Lukas*, 359. Others who offer rather complicated explanations of the geography include B. Weiss, *Markus und Lukas*, 561–62: "Only by going all the way through (διήρχ. διά, as in 4:30; 11:24) the regions of Samaria and Galilee could Jesus have met a Samaritan (v. 16) in the company of Galileans."

details in the text. Those who had been healed were required to show themselves to the priests. The plural noun "priests" would have had no particular significance, except that neither the healing of a leper in Mark 1:40ff nor its parallels speak of only one priest. Otherwise we would have to accept that the story intends for each leper to present himself to a priest in his own hometown, so that the Samaritan has to present himself to a Samaritan priest. That way the story could have played out in either Samaria or Galilee. The fact that the victim is required to present himself to the priests, and that this could not take place anywhere outside of the Temple in Jerusalem, does not speak against this location. We have already encountered a situation like this in the narrative of the leper in Mark 1:40-41, where we decided that the healed man would have made his way to Jerusalem. But in this case when Jesus pronounces the man clean, they are still in the same place. Therefore we will be inclined toward Jerusalem, or toward a village near that city. There is nothing remarkable about a Samaritan going to Jerusalem, but obviously in this story Luke was paying no attention to such "realistic" details.[14] He makes use of this narrative with the Samaritan because it enhances the story of Jesus' journey through Samaria. He locates it there, but he is not thinking of the nine Jewish lepers, who would not fit in that setting.[15] He chooses the setting on the basis of his own purposes, and the specifics of the topography remain unclear.

The fourth "topographical" pericope introduction that comes from the authorial work of Luke is found in 19:11, which reads: ἀκουόντων δὲ αὐτῶν ταῦτα προσθεὶς εἶπεν παραβολὴν διὰ ἐγγὺς εἶναι Ἰερουσαλὴμ αὐτὸν καὶ δοκεῖν αὐτοὺς ὅτι παραχρῆμα μέλλει ἡ βασιλεία τοῦ θεοῦ ἀναφαίνεσθαι. The pericope itself begins with v. 12: εἶπεν οὖν. That is the same introduction that apparently underlies 13:18. The reason for this similarity at this particular point is significant: in the immediately preceding narrative (Zacchaeus) Jesus declares his calling: "The Son of Man has come to seek and to save that which was lost." This now leads into a parable that further clarifies the details of his call, and which also defines more precisely what his call will not include. The crowds expected that the messianic crown would be placed on Jesus' head in Jerusalem. Jesus' parable speaks against these popular expectations: it will not be long until the messianic king appears, but until

---

14. Wellhausen, *Luke*, 94 remarks: "We should not ask such realistic questions of our stories." In this regard his judgment is correct, for we are not allowed to burden Luke's outlook with such things. But why should we not take advantage of the opportunity, when we can, to set a story that has no location at all into its actual historical framework?

15. Windisch, 163n2: "Apparently Luke wrote from the point of view of the Samaritan, the main character in the story."

then we must prove ourselves diligent and true. This subtle connection with what precedes is a creation of the third evangelist, who gave this story a special framework that it does not have in Matthew, where it appears within a series of parables at 25:14–30. All the same, there is a commonality between them at one point: in both cases the parable has to do with the parousia. In the synoptic outline the problem of the parousia is relegated to the back of the train, a chronological arrangement that is not likely to be historically accurate. Luke resolutely situates this idea in the context of Jesus' journey to Jerusalem, introducing in this way a messianic element, and that is exactly the way people understood it. Matthew's version had to be interpreted allegorically, thereby pushing the kingdom far into the distance. Generally one thinks that we have here a reference to one of the Herodians, who had to go to Rome to be confirmed as governor. If we could determine which governor is being referred to, then we would gain a starting point for an absolute chronology. There is some reason to think that the reference might be to Archelaus, whose story played out in Jericho, a city that had been significantly beautified and decorated with splendid new buildings. But it could equally well refer to some other Herodian, perhaps Antipas, who sent his daughter Herodias to Rome. But these events were taking place in a time of considerable political disruption: every eastern client king had to betake himself to Rome before assuming power. Our effort to deduce a chronology here is unfortunately not likely to be productive.[16]

Two Jericho Stories:
Luke 18:35–43par; 19:1–10

Two Jericho pericopes are different from the four Lukan stories just discussed (9:51; 13:22; 17:11; and 19:11). 18:35 opens the narrative about the healing of a blind man with the words: ἐγένετο δὲ ἐν τῷ ἐγγίζειν αὐτὸν εἰς Ἰερειχώ. This detail, even though it is expressed in a Lukan form (ἐγένετο δὲ, etc.), does not therefore come from Luke, because at this point the third evangelist is following Mark, who situates the pericope 10:46–52 in Jericho. There is a difference between Luke and Mark, but it extends only so far as the fact that in Luke the narrative does not take place behind Jericho, as Jesus is leaving, but rather in front of the city, as he is approaching it. In this regard it coheres with another Jericho story that Luke found in his special tradition, namely, the story of Zacchaeus (Luke 19:1–10), which does play out in Jericho itself. The introduction to that story reads: καὶ εἰσελθὼν διήρχετο τὴν Ἰερειχώ, καὶ ἰδοὺ

---

16. An especially thorough discussion of the Herodian dynasty, based upon the appropriate passages in Josephus, is give by Pölzl, *Lukas*, 93ff; cf. also pp. 381 and 387ff.

ἀνὴρ ὀνόματι καλούμενος Ζακχαῖος. Lukan coinage is evident in the formulation of that sentence, literally, "a man with a name, called Zacchaeus." But the designation of the place does belong to the traditional material, which knew about a tax collector named Zacchaeus in Jericho. A later attribution of this story to Jericho is inconceivable.[17] On the other hand it is not certain that the Zacchaeus story has any historical connection with the stories that precede it. It is more likely that two Jericho stories were brought together on the basis of their common location.

Two Notes from the Journey to Jerusalem: Luke 9:53; 13:33

The Good Samaritan
(Luke 9:51, 52–55)

The pericopes discussed to this point all mention locations along Jesus' itinerary between Galilee and Jerusalem. By taking the introductions to all these pericopes together, we can identify two that explicitly refer to a journey to Jerusalem: 9:53 and 13:33. Let us begin with the second of them, which is set within a little story in 13:31–33: some Pharisees encounter Jesus and tell him he should leave Galilee because Herod wants to kill him. Jesus says to these opponents: "Go tell that fox: 'Look, I am driving out demons and performing miracles day and night, and on the third day I will be perfected. But today and tomorrow and on the following day I must go, since it is not fitting for a prophet to die anywhere but in Jerusalem." While the main idea is clear, the details are rather difficult. "Today and tomorrow" is easy to understand: it means that in a short time Jesus will get to work. But what does he mean by "on the third day I will be perfected?" We could take the meaning from the context and paraphrase it something like this: "On the third day I will come to the end, i.e., I will be finished with my work

---

17. Wellhausen, *Luke*, 103 expresses this opinion: "19:1 contradicts what follows. Jesus is still outside the city, not inside it. Otherwise Zacchaeus would be up on a roof rather than up in a tree. And Jesus could not have been leaving the city, because he is looking for a house in the city where he can spend the night." Here Wellhausen goes too far. I can imagine a tree in a garden or in front of a house (cf. Loisy, *Les Évangiles synoptiques*, 2:254). If Zacchaeus is not up on a roof, it may be because his house was not along the street that Jesus came down, and he certainly would not want to climb onto the roof of a stranger's house (besides, tax collectors did not have good reputations). By the way, Wellhausen refers to a specific itinerary, as part of which Jesus wants to spend a night in Jericho. But this story does not have to be connected with any itinerary, including the great journey from Galilee to Jerusalem.

here."[18] But the word "end" seems to have a deeper meaning here, pointing to the end of Jesus, to his death and exaltation. In that event an idea that Luke has already mentioned in 9:51 would once again be evoked. The precision of the expression is striking. We can sense here a certain kinship with Jesus' three predictions of his passion, the formulaic properties of which set forth the confession of the Christian community: Jesus suffered, died, and after three days rose again. I suspect that an ancient Easter confession lies behind the words "on the third day I will be perfected." Luke has refracted the meaning, for he is plainly thinking of "three days" with reference to Jesus' upcoming three-day journey to Jerusalem. The "perfecting" thus has to do not with the resurrection, but with the beginning of the passion. For the primitive Christian community there was not a great difference between the two. Suffering, death, and resurrection were basically one great complex of assurance, which followed from one certainty: Jesus is the Victor, the Lord, and the Savior. There is, however, something rather secretive about the expression "Today and tomorrow, and on the following day I must go." If at this point we try to conceive of him wandering here and there around Galilee, then the saying is merely tautological, repeating exactly what had already been said in the preceding statement. Nor can it refer to his departure, since in that case the words "today and tomorrow" would make no sense. Plainly Luke is thinking here about the journey to Jerusalem, which encompasses today and tomorrow and a third day. Thus the meaning of Jesus' reply to Herod is: "I am going to continue to be active for some time, and my activity includes a trip to Jerusalem." On this interpretation the "third day" does not precisely refer to the day after tomorrow. The consummation will take place after a three-day journey, i.e., on the fourth day, although the stereotypical expression, "the third day," allows for a certain indeterminacy between two and three days of running time. It appears as if Luke is using a passion prediction of Jesus that was joined to a confession of the Christian community, in order to supply a motivation for Jesus' last journey to Jerusalem. History, tradition, and ornamentation by the evangelist are all woven together here. It will be very difficult to determine what is actually historical. Jesus' distinctive answer to the Pharisees seems to be historically inconceivable: with biting irony Jesus rejects their demand to leave Galilee. No, he will instead be active for today and tomorrow, and that means for awhile. Luke uses this situation in order to show that Jesus, who must go to Jerusalem, will be working along the way. The original pericope may have ended with v. 32 (up to and including αὔριον). The conclusion of v. 32 and v. 33 are the work of the evangelist, who expanded and revised an

---

18. So B. Weiss, *Markus und Lukas*, 514.

old pericope. Nothing authentic is reported here about Jesus' last journey to Jerusalem or about the itinerary.[19]

The clearest reference to a journey by Jesus to Jerusalem, and Samaria as well, is found at the beginning of the so-called Lukan Travel Narrative: 9:52-53: Jesus sends messengers ahead, and they enter a Samaritan village,[20] looking for a place to stay. But the people in the village refuse this request, since Jesus intends to go on to Jerusalem. James and John pronounce divine punishment upon the Samaritans, but Jesus scolds them, and they move on to a different village. The situation here is clear: the Samaritans reject Jesus and his disciples, most likely because they have the look of pilgrims who are on their way to Jerusalem. To the Samaritans, Jewish pilgrims are unsympathetic (cf. John 4:9-20), and an old hatred flares up here, expressing itself in the denial of hospitality. But Jesus does not break with these people; he simply goes on to another village.[21] There he appears to have found an exception. It should be made clear that in this narrative Jesus is not totally rejected by the Samaritans, but we do have to admit that the narrative has enough color to make an historical impression. The only difficulty is the remarkable isolation of this story within the gospel tradition. Shouldn't the well-known tendency toward story formation have influenced this pericope? When he sent them out (Matt 10:5), Jesus had specifically forbidden his disciples to enter any Samaritan streets or towns. It must have been difficult for the earliest Christian missionaries to understand why Jesus prohibited any work among the Samaritans. This narrative, which in fact agrees with common opinions about Samaritans at that time, tries to provide an answer: Jesus attempted to establish a compassionate relationship with them, but was rebuffed. In this story the Samaritans do not cut off relations quite that sharply. The only thing described in the report is what they did. Each side rendered a harsh judgment, but Jesus himself

---

19. Here we can understand the sense of the pericope as Luke took it up. From my point of view, recent exegetes, who regard the pericope as a non-historical formation, have abandoned the effort to make Luke's setting comprehensible. They regard the following text as original: "Look, I drive out demons and perform healings today and tomorrow; but on the following day I have to go, because it will not do for a prophet to die outside of Jerusalem." Cf. Wellhausen, *Luke*, 76; J. Weiss, *Schriften*, 477; Windisch, 163. Loisy offers a different explanation that is closer to mine: "The three-days should not be interpreted strictly, as if they contain any chronological information" (Loisy, *Les Évangiles synoptiques*, 2:127).

20. The readings in v. 52, πόλιν Σαμαρειτῶν (ℵ* Γ Λ Lat syr^{sin}) and κώμην Σαμ. (A B D L cop go) are obviously reminiscent of Matt 10:5. In v. 56, the reading εἰς ἑτέραν κώμην strongly supports the reading κώμην in v. 52.

21. We will misunderstand the tenor of this narrative, if we think of the other village (v. 56) as a non-Samaritan, Galilean place, somewhere on the boundary with Samaria.

remained neutral. This kind of mild reaction toward opponents is a striking characteristic of Jesus, and it may have been motivated by his missionary interests. He does not want to get into a quarrel with the Samaritans, because soon enough there would be good relations with these people: many Samaritans would become Christians (cf. Acts 8). We must reckon with the possibility that the harsh judgment expressed by the disciples James and John is related to missionary problems within the earliest community. Perhaps these two disciples, the "sons of thunder," adopted a rejectionist attitude toward the Samaritan mission. We know nothing further about the role of James in the history of mission in the earliest community, but we do know a bit about his brother John, who plays a key role alongside Peter in the oldest stories. And there is a remarkable consistency in the tradition about the fact that this same John, who in our passage calls down judgment upon inhospitable Samaritans, later went back to the Samaritans with Peter and bestowed the Holy Spirit upon them (cf. Acts 8:14ff). If this saying of Jesus about not entering Samaritan towns was present in the tradition— and there is no doubt that it is a genuine saying—then the Samaritan mission was certainly a problem for the first Christians. A gap yawns open between Jesus' appearance and the events narrated in Acts 8. Within this gap belongs, it seems to me, the narrative of the inhospitable Samaritans and the fanaticism of James and John, who must have experienced a change of heart about Samaritans at a later time.[22]

Luke did not create the pericope we have been discussing here. It is simply not conceivable that he, all by himself, could have put this story into circulation. More likely, he attached here a tradition that was already in existence, using it to give shape to his own report about Jesus' final journey to Jerusalem. Certainly the entire Lukan Travel Narrative does not depend upon this story about the Samaritans, so Luke pressed into service a tradition about Jesus' activity in Samaria—or about Jesus' *attempted* activity in Samaria—which could serve as a source of reflection on Jesus' missionary activity. The Gospel of John points in the same direction. A lengthy section in John 4:1ff reports on Jesus' relations with Samaritans. In that passage, Samaritans, who are half-Jewish but who listen to Jesus with interest, are sharply contrasted against Jews, who seem to exalt themselves above Samaritans.[23] Luke took that tradition into account, and in keeping with the

---

22. As far as I can see, the problems that we have been discussing here are not actually present in the pericope about Samaritan inhospitality. Confident judgments to that end run aground on the miserable state of the earliest material about early Christian mission.

23. We can reckon here with the possibility that there was a document from the history of the earliest missions. The Jewish Christians in Jerusalem preferred to keep

outline of his gospel, he included a Samaritan story about the last journey of Jesus toward Jerusalem.

Excursus: Literary and Historical Evaluation of the Lukan Travel Narrative

Given the poor condition of the material, Luke never had a chance to create a proper travel narrative. As surprising as it may be to read that Jesus is traveling to Jerusalem, it is even more surprising that nothing much really happens on that journey, because Luke could no longer recover what had actually happened. The sum total of what he had to work with was one Samaritan story and two Jericho stories. No other scenes are set in specific locations. If these few stories had ever been part of a travel narrative, then that narrative recounted a trip through Perea (so Mark and Matthew) rather than Samaria. Vague generalities betray a substantial lack of familiarity, or even ignorance, about matters related to the geography of Palestine. Most of the narratives in Q and Luke's special source give no hint at all about the location in which they take place. Since the locations could be altered at will, Luke gave them all a home together here.[24] We can no longer determine what the original connections between and among the individual stories might have been. For it is a basic characteristic of this tradition that it puts forward individual pericopes, which are not only place-less but also time-less. In one story, the healing of the ten lepers (Luke 17:11ff), we were able to fix the location more closely, but in most pericopes that kind of effort will

---

their distance from Samaritans, a practice that was opposed by John.

24. Attempts have been made to explain the difficulties with the whole Travel Narrative by stipulating that it is a collection of reports from several different journeys to Jerusalem; cf. B. Weiss, *Markus und Lukas*, 436. These attempts mark the end of the road for efforts to harmonize the Gospels, especially for Catholic scholars. The following comparisons repeatedly appear: Luke 9:51ff = Jesus' journey to the Feast of Tabernacles in John 7:2; Luke 13:22ff = temple consecration in John 10:22; Luke 17:11 = journey to the Passover festival in John 12:1; cf. also 11:54. Taking a totally different tack, Spitta has tried to arrange them all into a logical sequence. This he attains in the following series of pericopes: Luke 9:49-50 (the unauthorized exorcist), Luke 9:51-56 (the unfriendly Samaritans), and Luke 18:15-17 (blessing upon the children). But in these and all the preceding pericopes, the real subject matter is Jesus' correction of the disciples. That is why Luke re-inserted 9:57—18:14, which Spitta calls "the book of the sayings of Jesus," into the Synoptic *Grundschrift*.

inevitably run aground.[25] Above all we must remember that the saying about the lilies (Luke 12:27-28 = Matt 6:28-29) belongs in the springtime and not in the rainy season, which—if Luke's outline can be taken seriously—is the setting for that saying. On the whole, then, Luke arranges the stories on the basis of their content, even though he also wants to arouse the impression of a journey, and more specifically of stories that take place along that journey. We can arrange two large sections under these headings: 1) the special preparations for the disciples (9:51-13:17); and 2) the teachings about the kingdom of God (13:18ff), but these connections do not explain very much. The story that concludes the first part, i.e., 13:1-17, does not fit well in its context, and in the tradition it might have previously been set either earlier or later. In the second part, Luke appears to be depending upon the tradition for his arrangement of the individual sayings of Jesus: the three parables about the lost appear to form a unit, for they all relate to the Pharisees, so the following parable of the dishonest steward (16:1-13) was apparently spoken to the disciples. If we do not notice this change in the audience, we will necessarily be reduced to dependence upon the tradition, unable to see what stands behind the three connected sayings in Q 16:16 and 17:18. Certainly small groups of pericopes had already been collected in the tradition. In addition we must be aware of the fact that at times Luke obviously grew weary at the task of arranging the individual stories. He could not always put each and every pericope into a clear train of thought. He did it as well as he could, following both internal and external criteria, which we can no longer recover.

Excursus: A Perspective on the Question about the Length and Location of the Ministry of Jesus

The Prophecy over Jerusalem

One saying, Mark 13:34-35, utterly destroys the framework of a short, several-month, or even one-year ministry of Jesus as

---

25. When Luke 10:38 omits the name of the village, it should serve as a reminder that the later tradition about the widow of Bethany, who anoints Jesus, was juxtaposed with the Mary in our story. Cf. in this regard Pölzl, *Lukas*, 246: "Perhaps Luke did not give the name of the village out of consideration to the woman, who was still living . . ."

depicted in the Synoptics. An almost exact parallel to that saying appears in Matt 23:37-39. This lament does not fit the setting of the journey to Jerusalem, since (according to Luke) Jesus has not entered Jerusalem yet; nor does it fit the beginning of the Passion Narrative, which says that Jesus first spent a few days in Jerusalem (according to Matthew). The wording would fit better and would be easier to understand if Jesus had perhaps already spent a relatively long period of time in the Holy City, or more often, or had been more active there. The word ποσάκις = "how often" (Luke 13:34 = Matt 23:37) leaves us no other choice. The fact that both evangelists, like the entire synoptic tradition, report nothing about an earlier, more frequent, or longer ministry by Jesus in Jerusalem, does not settle the issue. We encountered a similar case in the lament over the Galilean towns, in which Jesus must have been active, although the Gospels tell us nothing about Chorazin. Luke attached this saying *ad vocem* to 13:33. Matthew put it into the context of a long series of woes over the cities and their inhabitants who had rejected Jesus. Matthew's setting is thus more believable than Luke's, since we regard the passion as basically the farewell of a distinctive prophet from a blinded city. We also have the saying of Jesus about the Parousia, which points to his eventual death and return after all of his futile attempts with regard to Jerusalem.[26] [27]

26. Only an eschatological interpretation makes sense of the tenor of this saying. It will not do to think of some earlier departure from Jerusalem (cf. John 10:22-39) anticipating his later return in Matt 21:9 (John 13:13). This interpretation is especially popular among Catholic scholars (J. Belser, e.g.); cf. also Pölzl, *Lukas*, 310; Klostermann, *Matthäus*, 318.

27. The implications of this text for our evaluation of the framework of the story of Jesus are widely recognized. But many interpretations are incorrect, and the text is misunderstood in many ways. Researchers who think that the text has value for chronology tend to express themselves reservedly. J. Weiss (*Schriften*, 377) is unnecessarily careful: "This saying appears to confirm a connection to the Johannine presentation." Wellhausen is similarly quiet (*Matthew*, 121; *Luke*, 76), as is Klostermann, *Matthäus*, 318-19. H. J. Holtzmann skips over this passage too quickly; cf. *Die Synoptiker. Die Apostelgeschichte*, 255. Some, on the other hand, have stepped out openly and tried to invalidate in various ways the evidential value of our text, especially its implications against the idea of a shorter ministry of Jesus, i.e., against the synoptic framework. On the whole these efforts operate along two lines:

1) The entire passage can be regarded as unhistorical, i.e., it was not spoken by Jesus, and it therefore has to be accounted for in various ways:

a) The words that this text places in the mouth of Jesus actually belong to the time of the destruction of Jerusalem (so Wellhausen, *Matthew*, 121). Certainly it is possible that the text was revised or expanded on the basis of the situation after 70 CE. Thus the sentence, "your house (i.e., the city of Jerusalem) shall be laid waste" was spoken from the perspective of a later time. In these interpretations, the word ἔρημος is not usually taken literally. But to deny that Jesus ever said any of this depends upon the widespread and incorrect view that Jesus could not have spoken words so explicitly eschatological.

b) It is not Jesus who is speaking here, but an older expression originally associated with the wisdom tradition (cf. Matt 23:34 = Luke 11:49: διὰ τοῦτο καὶ ἡ σοφία τοῦ θεοῦ εἶπεν) and its reintroduction into Jerusalem along with messianism. For this view, cf. Strauss, *Das Leben Jesu*, 127; and Merx, *Markus und Lukas*, 336–37. Merx rightly takes up the word ποσάκις, and argues that it would be unnatural for a man to tell a parable about a hen, under whose wings chicks crawl for refuge. In my judgment this interpretation is too clever by half, for it places too much value upon the Sophia citation, which in my view is secondary.

c) A middle path has been suggested by Margarete Plath, "Die Neutestamentlichen Weherufe über Jerusalem," 455–56. She argues that there are echoes here of ancient prophetic woes over Jerusalem: "The piece can be understood as a poetic form of actual calls to repentance that were heard in Jerusalem, or as an artistic expression of the mood of a lonely prophet who looks back at the city one last time." Such reminiscences are indeed preserved in old expressions preserved by the tradition. But if so, why could Jesus himself not have made use of such formulations? Compare, for example, Harnack, *Sprüche und Reden Jesu*, 119, according to which Jesus *cited* the sayings in 23:34–38. Despite the possibility of a citation here, the word ποσάκις must be understood as a concise expression on Jesus' part. It will not do to interpret it in the light of prophetic texts that include the words "how often."

2) Less complicated, but equally unenlightening, are efforts to reinterpret the meaning of "Jerusalem." Following the Tübingen school of F. C. Baur and A. Hilgenfeld, some interpreters—e.g., Keim, *Geschichte Jesu von Nazara*, 3:186; and Holtzmann, *Die Synoptiker. Die Apostelgeschichte*, 255—understand "Jerusalem" and "his children" to mean the entire Jewish people, rather than the city of Jerusalem and its inhabitants. Holtzmann calls for this interpretation in Gal 4:25 as well, where he regards "Jerusalem" as a reference to the Jewish people. But these parallels do not support that thesis. The topic in Gal 4:25 is an allegory about a present ("earthly") Jerusalem and a future ("heavenly") Jerusalem. Everyone understands that to mean Christ, who was at home in apocalyptic discourse. Thus the expression "Jerusalem" in Gal 4:25–26 appears to be part of some sort of numbers game; cf. Lietzmann, *Die Vier Hauptbriefe*, 252.

All of these efforts basically serve the thesis that Jesus could not have been in Jerusalem longer and more often. I conclude with a well-formulated sentence from D.F. Strauss, who sees our text as the only meaningful instance against the synoptic account, even though he does not regard the words as authentic: "In this case every excuse comes up empty, and we have to recognize that, if these are the words of Jesus, then he must have actually been in Jerusalem longer and more often than it appears in the synoptic accounts" (Strauss, *Das Leben Jesu*, 127).

8

Jesus' Final Activity in Jerusalem

Mark 10:46—13:37 par

Introduction

The Topography and Chronology of the Sections

AT THIS POINT WE begin the treatment of a longer section of the Gospel of Mark, which reaches from 10:46 to 13:37, with parallels in Matt 20:29—25:46 and Luke 18:35—21:38. Of course, in the case of Luke we cut out the Travel Narrative (9:51—19:27), including 9:28—21:38. The theme of this complex is obvious: it presents experiences, words, and actions of Jesus during his last few days in Jerusalem. We should make clear that the framework of the story of Jesus is quite simple here, because it dissolves away at the outset. What we would call a report about "the last days of Jesus" would have to be built upon chronological and topographical viewpoints, and that is what we initially appear to have here: on his journey Jesus comes nearer to Jerusalem, enters the city, leaves it again, goes back in again, and so on until he is arrested. There is no lack of details about his itinerary, nor of chronological sequence. According to Mark, Jesus comes near to Jericho with his disciples (10:46a); as he leaves the city he is met by the blind man, Bartimaeus (10:46b-52). He approaches Jerusalem at Bethany on the Mount of Olives and sends two of his disciples into a nearby village (is it Bethany, or some other village with a different name?), with instructions to steal a donkey, upon which he will enter the holy city (11:1-10). In Jerusalem he goes into the Temple, looks around, and since it is late, he goes back to Bethany with his disciples (11:1) The next morning they leave Bethany, and Jesus curses a fig tree (11:12-14). They come to Jerusalem, where Jesus drives the moneychangers and the sellers out of the Temple. His opponents come up with a plan. Since it is late, Jesus leaves the city (11:15-19). Early the next morning Jesus and his disciples arrive at the fig tree, which has dried up, and

Jesus talks about what happened (11:20-25, 26). They come into Jerusalem again, where Jesus' opponents question his authority. Jesus answers their questions (11:27-33), and then he tells the parable of the evil tenants in the vineyard (12:1-12). His opponents send some Pharisees and Herodians, to ask him whether the tax tributes are justified (12:13-17). Sadducees come and confront him with the problem of the resurrection (12:18-27). A scribe steps forward and asks about the greatest commandment 912:28_34). Jesus himself poses a question, about the Son of David (12:35-37), and then he gives a speech against Pharisaism (12:38-40). As he sits by the treasury of the Temple he watches those who bring large gifts, and he speaks of the widow's mite (12:41-44). As they leave the Temple he responds to a question from a disciple by predicting the destruction of the Temple (13:1-2). Sitting on the Mount of Olives, Peter, James, John, and Andrew ask him about future events, and Jesus delivers a long discourse (13:3-37).

This whole report represents itself as an ongoing string of daily events over the course of three days (11:11 = evening; 11:12 = morning; 11:19 = evening; 11:20 = morning). The third day is depicted very richly, encompassing the large complex 11:20—13:37. By contrast, the first day covers only 10:46—11:11, and the second only 11:12-19. We cannot help but notice that there is clear lack of proportion in this distribution of the material. If we try to view the section as an authentic report about the last three days of Jesus, before the beginning of his passion, we are going to be hopelessly misled about the chronology. It is just this kind of singular viewpoint that can expose how brittle the connections actually are, although that will not necessarily always be convincing. The most important task is to investigate the framework of the excerpts, to measure the extent to which the individual pieces in the framework amount to a coherent array, in the sense of an ongoing description.

The Text History of the Framing Pieces

Once again I begin with the manuscript tradition, which offers the most highly instructive observations. Just as with the Lukan tradition, here too there are three groups of variants in the short reports about these three days in the history of Jesus. One has a tendency to hold fast to the connections, a clear sign that the preceding excerpt had no meaningful connection at all. A large number of textual witnesses, including the Itala mss, read πάλιν after ἔρχονται in 11:15. Wellhausen (*Mark*, 95) obviously did not know about this variant when he wrote: "11:15 is missing its connection to what precedes; πάλιν should be inserted here, as in 11:27." Clearly this *desideratum* had already been recognized and a solution proposed. Similarly, we can perceive a gap before 11:15. In the individual pericope introductions there is much that can be improved, in order to strengthen both the internal coherence of the introduction and its connection forward and backward. The tradition alternates between the plural and the singular: 10:46 = ἔρχονται / ἔρχεται; 11:1 = ὅτε ἐγγίζουσιν / ὅτε ἤγγίζεν; 11:12 = ἐξελθόντων αὐτῶν / ἐξελθόντα αὐτόν; 11:15 = ἔρχονται / εἰσελθών; 11:20 = παραπορευόμενοι / παραπορεύετο; 11:27 = ἔρχονται / ἔρχεται. The main point here is that syr^{sin}, D, and the various Itala mss influenced by D, all consistently replace the plural with the singular. And Codex D consistently tries to smooth out the presentation. 10:46 tips back and forth, at least in its best text: καὶ ἔρχονται εἰς Ἰερειχώ, καὶ ἐκπορευομένου αὐτοῦ ἀπὸ Ἰερειχὼ καὶ τῶν μαθητῶν αὐτοῦ ... At this point D and the Itala mss read: καὶ ἔρχεται εἰς Ἰερειχώ, καὶ ἐκπορευομένου αὐτοῦ ἐκεῖθεν μετὰ τῶν μαθητῶν αὐτοῦ. That the latter text avoids repeating the name of the town, Jericho, is a sign of conscious literary effort. In the introduction to the pericope about the widow's mite we can see a typical effort to smooth out the style, when D reads: καὶ κατέναντι τοῦ γαζοφυλακίου καθεζόμενος δ' Ιησοῦς. The goal of D and its satellites, along with other similar texts, is clear, and in the service of that goal, they replace every plural with a singular. On the other hand we also frequently find the singular, which is in keeping with the standard usage of a pericope, which is obviously not to establish connections with what precedes or follows, but rather to present an individual story about Jesus. Usually the singular is used, followed most of the time by ὁ ις, the infallible sign of a pericope introduction. Certain manuscripts and translations, which ς often follows, may be judged on this basis: thus in 11:11, A ... go arm aeth insert ὁ ις, and again in 11:15 (A Γ ... go), and again in 12:41 (A Γ ... it-Mss vg arm aeth). That this state of affairs owes its existence to the lectionary readings is conclusively demonstrated by certain Gospel lectionaries whose readings were recorded by Tischendorf: 11:1 ὅτε ἤγγιζεν ("here many Gospel lectionaries read ὁ ις"); 11:27 ("in the Gospel lectionaries we read ἔρχεται ὁ ις." The external evidence in these cases is not secure enough for us to conclude that the original readings of the Gospel of Mark lie behind these texts, but the variants in the introductions, which emerged from the use of pericopes, point toward the original texts of the pericopes, as Mark took them up.

How weak the connection to the preceding Markan excerpt really is, how quickly it falls apart into individual stories that are thoroughly independent of each other, we can recognize even more clearly in the treatment it receives from both Matthew and Luke. They make *omissions, insertions, rearrangements, and revisions* to the order in the narrative offered by Mark about the last three days of Jesus, before his arrest.

Omissions

The pericopes about the cursing of the fig tree (Mark 11:12-14) and the conversation about the withered fig tree (Mark 11:20-25) are both missing from Luke. It is precisely these two stories that provide the chronological details for constructing a three-day narrative. Luke's omission makes sense in the light of his presentation of the parable of the fig tree (13:6-9).[1]

It is more difficult to answer the question of why Matthew leaves out the story of the widow's mite (Mark 12:41-44). We can only say that this little narrative would not have fit between the saying against the Pharisees (Matt 23) and those about the parousia (Matthew 24-25), especially because the first saying in Matthew takes the form of a prediction about the future, so as to form the strongest possible through-line in Matthew 23-25. But that does not explain why this narrative is missing from Matthew. We have to reckon with the possibility that this story, which bears the marks of certain Lukan narratives (the widow! praise for the poor!), was originally inserted from Luke into the Gospel of Mark.[2] In any case it could easily drop out of the context within which it now stands in Mark.

Insertions

Just as Matthew and Luke leave certain things out, they also bring other things in. During our consideration of the Lukan Travel Narrative, we discussed Luke's insertion of the Zacchaeus pericope and the parable of the talents (19:1-10, 11-27). After his report about the entry of Jesus into Jerusalem, Luke now introduces a pericope about *Jesus' prophecy of the destruction of Jerusalem* (Luke 19:39-44). As Huck delimits it, the pericope is not coherent. In my opinion it would be better to regard vv. 39-40 as the conclusion of the preceding narrative about Jesus' entry into Jerusalem (Luke 19:28-38): καί τινες τῶν Φαρισαίων ἀπὸ τοῦ ὄχλου εἶπαν πρὸς αὐτόν. Luke is thinking here about Jesus' ongoing arguments with his opponents,

---

1. It is often suggested that this Lukan parable, interpreted allegorically as a reference to the fate of the Jewish people, is the source of the story about the cursing of the fig tree by Jesus; cf. J. Weiss, *Schriften*, 179; Loisy, *Les Évangiles synoptiques*, 2:285ff. Wellhausen, *Mark*, 95, declares: "Whether he (Luke) found both of these pieces (cf. 17:6) and only left them out because of misgivings about their content, they certainly interrupt the train of thought." Spitta (*Die synoptische Grundschrift*, 307), on the other hand, tries to answer the question of why Mark and Matthew inserted these stories.

2. Cf. J. Weiss, *Das älteste Evangelium*, 273; Loisy, *Les Évangiles synoptiques*, 2:391. Wellhausen does not notice the obvious question about composition, but remarks instead: "This little story goes to our hearts more than all the miracle stories that fill up the first half of Mark" (*Mark*, 105).

and so he wants to set up a stark contrast between the enmity of Jesus' opponents and the joy of the people. The setting is a product of the third evangelist's sequencing effort.³ Thus in Jesus' answer he uses a traditional saying, "If they were silent, then these stones would speak," the content of which draws from Matt 21:16, "Out of the mouths of children and infants you have brought praise." The scene in Matt 21:14-16 is in a certain sense a parallel to Luke 19:39-40. After the cleansing of the Temple, the first evangelist has Jesus heal the sick in the Temple, and the children sing hosannas as he enters. But the high priests and the scribes (οἱ ἀρχιερεῖς καὶ οἱ γραμματεῖς) are unwilling on both counts, so Jesus has to cite them chapter and verse. The situation is rather different in Luke, but it is certainly characteristic of the first evangelist to speak as early as possible—after Jesus' first important action in Jerusalem—about opposition to Jesus among those in the circles of authority. There is no parallel passage in Mark, an absence that illustrates just how loose the narrative of Mark actually is. Only Luke sets Jesus' prediction about the destruction of Jerusalem within this controversy. He begins the description anew: καὶ ὡς ἤγγισεν, ἰδὼν τὴν πόλιν ἔκλαυσεν ἐπ' αὐτήν (19:41). What Jesus says here is part of Luke's special material (L), but the content has a parallel in Luke 21 = Mark 13 = Matt 24. In all these places Jesus makes public his deep pain at the fate of the holy city. This is very different from the cry of revenge in Luke 18:7-8 and in 19:27, where Jesus weeps over the punishment of his opponents in Jerusalem. There are two different layers of tradition here, but perhaps also authentic reports about different sayings of Jesus, whose tone of voice with regard to Jerusalem did not have to always be the same.⁴ We cannot identify the reasons for Luke's relocation of the prediction to this place. Again we have here a piece of tradition that prepares for the subsequent saying of Jesus about Jerusalem's fate. In a similar way, as he approaches the walls of the city, Jesus knows about his relationship with the city, and about its eventual fate. The resulting contrast between the joy of the people, which Jesus (unlike the Pharisees) condones, and his own pain over the holy city, is psychologically striking. Luke understands it as having psychological implications.⁵ For this reason, I tend to suspect that external

3. Wellhausen recognizes this when he says: "The phrase τῶν Φαρισαίων (19:39), which is impossible here, is missing from the Syriac" (*Luke*, 109). It seems to me that even syr^sin misunderstood Luke's intention.

4. Wellhausen (*Luke*, 109) observes this tension correctly, but judges it too harshly when he says that the inconsistency comes from the differences in attitude during the times before and after the catastrophe (i.e., the destruction of Jerusalem).

5. Thus I would like to disagree with Spitta (*Die synoptische Grundschrift*, 305), who says: "The contrast . . . is so simple and natural, that we simply cannot entertain the idea that it was introduced retroactively into the text." Merx (*Markus und Lukas*, 375) takes us in a completely different direction, referring to "a lyrical effusion by Luke." He

influences have been involved in the insertion of this material here. In an earlier saying (19:40) the subject is stones that could become witnesses for Jesus. The mention of these stones may have reminded Luke of Jesus' saying about the eventual fate of Jerusalem, to the effect that not one stone would remain upon another.

Matthew's Gospel is especially rich in interventions into the Markan outline. Matthew reports on a large number of controversy scenes in Mark, but he also inserts various selections of his own through speeches and parables. In 21:28–32 he includes *the parable of the two sons*, which comes from his special tradition. As in Matt 18:12, the transition is achieved with the question, "What do you think?" On the one hand, this parable is connected with the one that follows it (the parable of the vineyard and the tenants), because in both cases the subject is a vineyard. On the other hand, this parable also expands upon the parable that precedes it, about authority. For the end of that parable mentions John the Baptist, as is also the case in v. 32 of our parable. The tradition had already established this connection, i.e., the attitude of the Jews toward John the Baptist, and thereby bound the two parables together. But is this connection original? Luke 7:29–30 shows that the saying about the relationship between John and the Jews was also handed down in another context, namely, in a complex of Jesus' sayings about the Baptist.

Matthew attached *the parable of the wedding feast* (22:1–14) to the parable of the vineyard and the tenants, with this introduction: καὶ ἀποκριθεὶς ὁ Ἰησοῦς πάλιν εἶπεν ἐν παραβολαῖς αὐτοῖς λέγων. This piece serves to illustrate the decline in Jesus' relationship with the Jews. The first part (v. 1–10) has a parallel in Luke 14:15–24. The address to which Jesus directs his words is different: in Matthew they are addressed to the high priests, the scribes, and the elders of Jerusalem (Matt 21:23), while in Luke they are directed toward guests in a Pharisee's house, into which Jesus has been invited during his trip to Jerusalem (Luke 14:1).

To his great speech *against the Pharisees* in chapter 23 Matthew has added a short excerpt from Mark 12:38–40, making use of Q and expanding upon other material from the Sermon on the Mount. In Mark 12:38ff the words are addressed to the people; in Matt 23:1, the disciples are also

---

asks whether we should not consider that the saying stands directly in the tradition of a triumphant entry of the messianic king. The difference between these two judgments shows how little unity will ever come from disputes about matters of taste. The psychological feelings of the ancients were not entirely identical with ours, as is demonstrated by the interesting fact that the orthodox in the ancient church, on the basis of the divine nature of Christ, erased from this text the part about Jesus' weeping. Others, by contrast, built precisely upon that very point (cf. Tischendorf's note on Luke 19:41).

included (cf. vv. 8-12), and the total picture is introduced by the typical Matthean adverb τότε. The most important section, v. 13ff consists of a series of seven woes over the Pharisees and scribes. This material is also found in Luke 11:39-52. It is not easy to identify the addressees of the speech. Certainly the individual woes are pronounced over the γραμματεῖς καὶ Φαρισαῖοι ὑποκριταί, although in v. 26 only one Pharisee is mentioned (Φαρισαῖε). There follows immediately and without any transition a prophecy about Jerusalem (Matt 23:37-39), which we have already become acquainted with in the discussion of Luke 13:34-35.

Finally, there are insertions and expansions in the great *discourse about the Parousia* in Matthew 24-25, which basically follows the line of Mark 13. From Q there is a saying about the Son of Man (Matt 24:26-28), which appears in Luke in the context of a large complex about the final judgment. In this latter connection there are further sayings about the Parousia in Luke 17:26-27, which also appear in Matt 24:37-41. There follows the parable of the waking householder (Matt 24:42-44), which Luke places in the context of saying about wakefulness and faithfulness. Sayings about the true and wise servant, as well as his opposite number (Matt 24:45-51), Luke places into a similar context (Luke 12:42-46). The parable of the ten virgins (Matt 25:1-13) belongs to a special tradition, as does the parable of world judgment (Matt 25:31-46). Between these last two we find the parable of the talents, which comes from Q (Matt 25:14-30; Luke 19:12-27). There are no introductions, conclusions, or framing pieces. They all come in a series, saying after saying and statement after statement, without transitions. All is arranged to support a single idea: how will it be in the future, and how should we prepare ourselves for this future?

These insertions and expansions make clear that the outline of the Gospel of Mark is very loose, and not only in the sense that Mark leaves many gaps here and there, but also that he follows no chronological thread. There is not even a relative connection, and the whole thing falls apart into individual stories. We could picture it this way: Mark's presentation is not a loose string of pearls, between which one can now and then insert others here and there; it is instead a heap of pearls in no sequence at all, even if here and there some of them have stuck together. In Matthew 21, some new pieces were inserted into Mark's narrative, just as Mark had earlier inserted the parable of the vineyard and the tenants in 12:1-12. Was this parable spoken by Jesus during the last stage of his life, or does it belong to a collection of traditions about his last days? The answers to these questions are just as uncertain as the answer to the question of whether the parables of the prodigal son and the wedding feast originally belonged to this complex of stories.

Rearrangements

In our investigation we have been following the fact that certain stories were rearranged. We have found that some forms of rearrangement already existed within the Matthean-Lukan tradition, but the stories in Mark also have to be brought into consideration here. An especially vivid case is the pericope about *the greatest commandment* (Mark 12:28-34), which has a close relationship with the preceding story about the Sadducees who come to Jesus with a question. Mark 12:28 reads as follows: καὶ προσελθὼν εἷς τῶν γραμματέων, ἀκούσας αὐτῶν συνζητουμένων, ἰδὼν ὅτι καλῶς ἀπεκρίθη αὐτοῖς, ἐπηρώτησεν αὐτόν. A scribe had heard Jesus give good answers to the Sadducees, as well as the Pharisees and Herodians, so now he poses a question from his own point of view. The question is obviously sincere and not hostile, in contrast to the conduct of the scribes (vv. 32-34). Mark's train of thought is as follows: the Pharisees and Sadducees are prepared to go toe to toe, but a simple rabbi finds himself standing by Jesus on a foundational principle of Judaism. Matthew (22:34-40) basically preserves this course of events, with one significant alteration, when it says: οἱ δὲ Φαρισαῖοι ἀκούσαντες ὅτι ἐφίμωσεν τοῖς Σαδδουκαίους, συνήχθησαν ἐπὶ τὸ αὐτό· καὶ ἐπηρώτησεν εἷς ἐξ αὐτῶν νομικὸς πειράζων αὐτόν. Somehow the *Vorlage* of Mark's version of the story shines through here, as a simple rabbi, encouraged by Jesus' ability to fight back, poses an honest question to him. Matthew leaves that out, thereby creating a text that is not entirely coherent. But the practical sense of it appears to be that the Pharisees instigate the scribes to test Jesus. Unlike the Gospel of Mark, however, in Matthew things never come to a full and open argument. The rabbi asks his question, and Jesus, as expected, gives him a clear answer. The conclusion to Mark's version (12:32-34), in which the rabbi and Jesus show respect to each other, is missing from Matthew. Clearly the first evangelist stumbles over the idea that Jesus and a Jewish teacher of the Law might come to any kind of agreement. Luke follows a similar strategy (10:25-28), but in a slightly different way. He too takes his starting point from the fact that the teacher of the Law wanted to test Jesus (10:25 = ἐκπειράζων), but he drops Mark's conclusion. A strong hint of approbation still shimmers in the closing remark of Luke's report (10:28): "you have answered correctly; do this and you will live." From Luke's point of view, this was not really a controversy story. In his adaptation of the story of Jesus, the opposition between Jesus and his people, which began with his entry into the city (Luke 19:39-40), reaches its apex here. Beyond this point a story about a half-friendly rabbi is no longer possible. That is why this story was re-situated into the middle of the Travel Narrative (10:25-28). But Luke did not totally destroy the historical connection between this pericope and the reports about questions from the Pharisees and Sadducees. Mark 12:28 is an introduction, which did not originally belong to the pericope, which for a time was handed down as an individual story. The phrase ἰδὼν ὅτι καλῶς ἀπεκρίθη αὐτοῖς comes from the description that follows in v. 32 (διδάσκαλε ἐπ᾽ ἀληθείας εἶπες), and the opening words ἀκούσας αὐτῶν συνζητουμένων form a direct link with what precedes. The original pericope would have begun with the words: καὶ προσελθὼν εἷς τῶν γραμματέων, ἐπηρώτησεν αὐτόν. We cannot determine when and where the story is set. The concluding sentence in v. 34, "and after that no one dared to ask him a question," closes out not only this story, but also the series of all three preceding scenes. It would have functioned better as a conclusion to the story about paying taxes to Caesar.[6]

Matthew undertakes a distinctive rearrangement of the Markan pericope about *the cleansing of the Temple*. In fact it is more of a contraction than a rearrangement. According to Mark 11:11, Jesus comes to Jerusalem, visits the Temple, and goes back to Bethany in the evening. Then in 11:12 it is another morning, and he is on his way to Jerusalem. In 11:14 he curses the fig tree, and right after that in 11:15 he cleanses the Temple, and in the evening he leaves the city again. In 11:20, it is another morning, and Jesus passes by the withered fig tree, and then according to Matt 21:10-16, he again visits the Temple, which he had cleansed on his first visit, after which he goes to Bethany in the evening to spend the night (21:17). On another morning (21:18) he is on his way into the city when he curses a fig tree, which immediately withers (21:20). In this way one of the days in Mark's three-day chronology simply drops out of the picture. The reason for this contraction is readily apparent: Matthew knows better than to begin with the brief remark in Mark 11:11, and for that reason he shapes the first visit into a greater event, causing the two fig-tree episodes to bump up against each other. In our evaluation of Mark's arrangement, only one thing really matters: we can now see that even in the earliest period, the narrative of the Temple cleansing was already being moved around. It could have been set beautifully between two stories about the fig tree, and the original context would not have suffered.

---

6. Wendling (153) justifies his own practice of not paying much attention to individual pericopes and their frameworks, which vary too widely for classification. Instead he focuses on the ongoing narrative. Because he wants to postulate these connections, he regards Mark 12:32-34 as secondary and typical of the evangelist, who takes advantage of the motif of original narration. Wendling is of the view that this motif is present in v. 28. But the situation is exactly the other way around: v. 28 is the framing piece, and the motif of original narration is in vv. 32ff.

Excursus: Remodeling of Mark's Pericope Introductions
by Matthew and Luke

We come now to the form of the transitions in Mark's Gospel, which have been remodeled or supplemented in both of the other Synoptics. We know that the Gospel of Matthew is for the most part more of a pericope-book than Mark. That is why the introductions of the first evangelist are often more concise than in Mark. Most of the time Matthew puts chronological and topographical information into a participial construction, but he outlines these things more clearly than in Mark. In 20:29, for example, he follows Mark, but leaves out the details about the itinerary in Mark 10:46a. Matthew 21:1 is on the whole identical to Mark 11:1. Jesus' first entry into Jerusalem is marked out very clearly: ¹⁰καὶ εἰσελθόντος αὐτοῦ εἰς Ἱεροσόλυμα ἐσείσθε πᾶσα ἡ πόλις λέγουσα . . . ¹¹οἱ δὲ ὄχλοι ἔλεγον· οὗτός ἐστιν ὁ προφήτης Ἰησοῦς (ὁ) ἀπὸ Ναζαρέθ . . . With v. 12 the story of the cleansing of the Temple begins, which is fully independent from this introduction. Matthew obviously wants to put a special sheen on this narrative about Jesus' debut in the holy city. He wants to make clear that the appearance of a prophet from Nazareth was a significant occasion that shook the whole city of Jerusalem. The treatment of this matter has a parallel in Matt 4:12-17, where (in contrast to the other Synoptics) Matthew marks out very clearly, perhaps a little awkwardly and with too much verbosity, Jesus' debut in Galilee. There are reasons to doubt that the framing piece Matt 21:10-11 should be credited to the account of the first evangelist: it could either be an introduction to the following excerpt about the Temple cleansing, or perhaps a reference back to the preceding story about the entry into the city.[7]

At 21:18 Matthew substitutes εἰς τὴν πόλιν for ἀπο βηθανίας (Mark 11:12), even though it makes no real difference. 21:20 is missing, since the cleansing of the Temple is narrated in another place (Mark 11:20). And the close conjunction of the two fig-tree scenes is rendered understandable by παραχρῆμα, "right away." In 21:23 we find a participial introduction, which is more characteristic of a pericope, in place of the details of the itinerary in Mark 11:27. 22:15 reframes Mark 12:13 into an attack on the Pharisees, and the whole thing is introduced with the typical

---

7. Editors, translators, and commentators disagree on this point.

Matthew caesura τότε, and the following scene begins in 22:23 with the indefinite expression ἐν ἐκείνῃ τῇ ἡμέρᾳ, although Mark 12:18 has simply καί. The comparison between 22:34 and Mark 12:38 has already been mentioned. Both the participial introduction in 22:41 (= Mark 12:35) and the τότε in 23:1 (= Mark 12:38) are characteristic of Matthew. On the whole, 24:1 coheres well with Mark 13:1, except that the questions are posed to the Master not by just *one* disciple (εἷς τῶν μαθητῶν) but rather by the disciples in general (οἱ μαθηταὶ αὐτοῦ). The same is true in 24:3, where the names of Peter, James, John and Andrew have dropped out, and only the disciples in general are mentioned. In addition, κατέναντι τοῦ ἱεροῦ (Mark 13:3) is missing. This overview demonstrates that, in ways that are characteristic of him, Matthew made various alterations to the framework of Mark, without substantially changing that framework.

More substantial and more interesting is the treatment of these matters in Luke. With his distinctive style of sequencing, from time to time he fashions connections that look back toward what has preceded. He avoids the caesura terms that Matthew loves. Luke 19:28, for example (Mark 11:1 = Matt 21:1) reads: "After he had said this (i.e., the parable of the talents), he went up to Jerusalem." In Matthew the first visit to the Temple and the cleansing of the Temple become one event. A remark in 19:47 extends the connection: καὶ ἦν διδάσκων τὸ καθ᾿ ἡμέραν ἐν τῷ ἱερῷ. 20:1 (= Mark 11:27 = Matt 21:23) includes a typical Lukan transition: καὶ ἐγένετο ἐν μιᾷ τῶν ἡμερῶν διδάσκοντας αὐτοῦ ... ἐπέστησαν οἱ ἱερεῖς ... Once more Luke uses here the construction ἐγένετο with a *verbum finitum* and the transitional phrase ἐν μιᾷ τῶν ἡμερῶν, which is comparable to 5:12, 17 and 13:10. In 20:9, the parable of the vineyard and the tenants is addressed πρὸς τὸν λαόν, while Mark and Matthew do not specify its addressee, although they do seem to be thinking of Jesus' opponents. 20:20 fully reproduces the transition in Mark.[8] Since the subject in 20:19 is the opponents of Jesus, Luke did not need to

---

8. At this point Wellhausen (*Luke*, 113) makes an instructive remark: "Luke worked freely with the introduction and the conclusion, because he was aware that the transitions did not really belong to the tradition. He did not know 'the Herodians,' so he rewrote it as if they were the Pharisees, without naming them, as in 18:9." But I regard it as doubtful that Luke had that kind of insight into the peculiarity of the tradition. What he really wanted to do was improve the connection, and to that end he had to make changes in the introduction. And some transitions did indeed belong to the tradition, because the individual stories circulated with their framework.

mention them by name again. This simple method strengthened the connection, while the new insertion by Mark and Matthew clearly indicated a new beginning for a thoroughly independent pericope. Typically Lukan is the fact that the spies sent to watch Jesus are clearly characterized from the beginning as pious hypocrites. Luke also treats the conclusion to the narrative much more loosely than Mark. Matthew emphasizes the silence of Jesus' defeated opponents. In Luke 20:27, the subsequent scene with the Sadducees is linked more closely to what precedes than in Mark 12:18 and Matt 22:23: προσελθόντες δέ τινες τῶν Σαδδουκαίων. It is similar with other stories that Luke brings in and yet does not quite clearly situate (20:41), such as Mark 12:35 = Matt 22:41. Luke 20:45 provides a succinct transition, because the attention of the hearers is directed back toward what has preceded, and the addressees are specified (i.e., the disciples, but unlike Matt 23:1, the crowds are not present). We can see Luke's literary distinctiveness in 21:1, the introduction to the story of the widow's mite. In Mark's version the old pericope is still evident, presenting a sharp and clear picture: "Jesus sat opposite the treasury and watched . . ." Luke is more concise: ἀναβλέψας δὲ εἶδεν. With the turn of phrase "he looked up" there is a definite connection with what precedes: Jesus directs his eyes toward the place into which he has just arrived, i.e., the treasury. In spite of parallels in Mark 13:1 and Matt 24:1, Luke 21:5 is not about leaving the Temple, nor about one disciple, or even about the four most intimate disciples. It is about "some" (τινές) disciples. Luke often makes an effort to direct certain teachings to the people, rather than just to the disciples (cf. 20:9). It appears that Luke wanted to create a wider base for the preaching of the pericopes about the disciples, which make up a good bit of the Synoptic tradition. While Mark 13:3 = Matt 24:3 introduces a new scene with its distinctive and thorough details about the location, Luke drops the extra description and connects v. 7 directly to v. 6, covering up the seam that had previously been evident. But the very process of intentional removal shows that the seam is there, and that a new pericope, independent of what precedes, begins with Mark 13:3 = Matt 24:3. Luke has created a more smoothly flowing narrative, but only at the high price of diminishing the beauty of the individual pictures.[9] 21:37-38 provides the best documentation

9. Spitta (*Die synoptische Grundschrift*, 336) remarks on this point: "The impression

for Luke's attempt to smooth out the connections, and thereby to arrange his Gospel in a temporal sequence. Here Luke offers a summary statement about the activity of Jesus in Jerusalem: by day, Jesus taught in the Temple, and in the evening, he went out to the Mount of Olives, to spend the night there. Each morning the people waited for him.[10] This summary statement, which comes from Luke's pen, is a clip that provides an overview of the activities leading up to Jesus' arrest, while also preparing and introducing the setting for the events that will ensue. All these attempts at psychologizing and sequencing are strong indicators of Luke's literary distinctiveness. Indirectly, they also tell us about the composition techniques of the other two Synoptics.

Excursus: The Relationship between Framing
and Content in Markan Pericopes

Let us return to the question of composition technique, insofar as we can see it in the framing of the Markan pericopes and their contents. In our discussion to this point we have already encountered several pericopes that have no location at all. The clearest example of this is the *parable of the vineyard and the tenants* in Mark 12:1–12 (= Matt 21:33–46 = Luke 20:9–19). Certainly this story is well-situated in its narrative context, and the parable is highly allegorical, aimed at the members of the Sandhedrin, who clearly recognize (v. 12) that Jesus is talking about them. But we also have to reckon with the possibility that we have here an allegory that originally had to do with the entire people of Israel, which Mark took up from the tradition and gave a new meaning, applying it only to the leaders of the people. To that end he added a closing verse that makes the presence of those leaders explicit. Certainly the result is a typical scene between Jesus and his opponents in Jerusalem, but there are no internal

---

of artistry in Matt and Mark is reinforced by the absence of any motive for Jesus to go to the Mount of Olives." The depiction is indeed artistic, if we read the report in its context. Luke did that, and that is why he made changes. The artistry of the situation cannot have arisen, as Spitta thinks, retroactively, after the Gospel of Luke had been written. It is only comprehensible in the context of the use of pericopes, with their distinctive, unbalanced introductions.

10. We have no basis upon which to think this is Lukan special tradition; cf. B. Weiss, *Markus und Lukas*, 628. Spitta (*Die synoptische Grundschrift*, 369) does not notice the authorial features in this verse.

connections with the preceding episode about authority, nor with any of the preceding stories further back. The pericope therefore has no specific setting in time and no particular location. We might well put it in the line of the sayings tradition, which also has this character. But here we encounter another layer of the tradition, different from the issue of authority and the question of taxes, which points toward another consideration: in both of those narratives, Jesus conducts himself in a generally reserved way; he is not provocative. But in the parable of the vineyard he is openly polemical. The introduction sounds a distinctive note: "he spoke in parables." Instead of the plural, Mark and Luke have the singular. This plural suggests a context in which Jesus also told other parables, even though at this point only one of them is singled out. Then comes a saying from the Old Testament in v. 10 and 11, which has something parabolic about it, even though at bottom it is not a parable at all. At that point a thoroughly independent saying begins. In Matthew (21:42) the new beginning is made clear by the words λέγει αὐτοῖς ὁ Ἰησοῦς, while Luke (20:17) preserves a strong link to what precedes in ἐμβλέψας αὐτοῖς.

The pericope about *the greatest commandment* (12:28–34), which we have already mentioned, is also timeless and without location. It too received a strong link to what precedes.

Other controversy stories, such as the story about *the Sadducees' question*, seem to point toward Jerusalem in the characters that appear. In 12:18 the Sadducees come onto the stage; there is no link to what precedes. This time the connection lies in the content: after the Pharisees, now the Sadducees give it a try. Mark appears to take it for granted that Sadducees could only have lived in Jerusalem, and in fact the Holy City was the primary center for this group, which came primarily from the priesthood. But Sadducees could also have traveled here and there, and they could have had a conversation with Jesus anywhere in the land. It is noteworthy that in Matt 3:7 they talk with John the Baptist, and Matt 16:1ff mentions them in the course of a summary of Jesus' activity in Galilee. Thus the scene before us is probably not set in any specific place, and it is certainly not set at any specific time.[11]

---

11. It has often been suspected that the pericope of the woman caught in adultery (John 7:53–8:11) originally stood between Luke 12:17 and 12:18 (cf. Klostermann, *Markus*, 104). That space is available, since a seam lies just before 12:18. But it is hard to find positive evidence that would compel us to insert the pericope at that point.

The same lack of clarity is also found in the preceding story about *the Pharisees' question* (12:13–17), in which the Pharisees and Herodians appear. We have already seen this unity between enemies of Rome and friends of Rome, who form an unnatural alliance against Jesus, in the story of the healing of a man with a withered hand (3:1–6).[12] Yet here too we must leave open the question about the location and date of this story. As clients of Herod Antipas, the "Herodians" would have been right at home in his territory of Galilee, but it would not be inconceivable to find them in Jerusalem.[13]

12:38–40 is a fragment containing sayings of Jesus against Pharisaism, which are timeless and without place. Luke (11:43) provides a similar saying in the context of the Travel Narrative.

The introduction to another controversy story clearly locates it in Jerusalem: the pericope about *the Son of David* (12:35–37): καὶ ἀποκριθεὶς ὁ Ἰησοῦς ἔλεγεν διδάσκων ἐν τῷ ἱερῷ. Even without the designation of place, this saying would fit well into the context of the last days of Jesus, when the issue of the Messiah certainly stood at the center of the debate, and everyone was thinking about it. The topographical detail, "in the Temple," does not come from Mark: he found it in the tradition. There was no reason for the evangelist to create this detail himself, since in a previous context (cf. 11:27) it has already mentioned that Jesus was in the Temple. Through this new approach to the narrative, we can see it as a thoroughly independent individual pericope, which Mark placed here as part of the Jerusalem story. At the same time we have to keep in mind that, as we have seen in other cases, here too at some point in the course of the tradition the designation of place may have been introduced into the story, in order to locate this meaningful saying of Jesus in the most meaningful city of all.

A sharply delineated little scene is 13:1–2, about *the destruction of Jerusalem*. As Jesus is leaving the Temple, the impressive buildings of Jerusalem are pointed out to him, and he says: "Not one stone will remain atop another." In this case the saying is deeply anchored in its setting.

---

12. Cf. above, p. 74.

13. Wellhausen (*Mark*, 101) overstates the point when he says: "Herodians would have stood out in Jerusalem. Their place was in Galilee."

The case is similar with the subsequent *discourse about the Parousia* (13:3-37), which is introduced with a topographical designation: καὶ καθημένου αὐτοῦ εἰς τὸ ὄρος τῶν ἐλαιῶν κατέναντι τοῦ ἱεροῦ. A seam lies between v. 2 and v. 3. The narrator has no interest in how Jesus got to the Mount of Olives: all at once he is there, sitting. A grandiose picture is presented to our eyes: Jesus seated on the Mount of Olives in view of the Temple, the doom of which he pronounces. Unfortunately, this picture stands at some remove from rigorous topographic consideration, by which one might be able to think about this situation. Just as was the case with the mountaintop scene in the calling of the young man (3:13-19), and also in the transfiguration scene (9:2-8), we have here a trans-historical depiction.[14] It has long been recognized that the Parousia discourse (Mark 13:5ff = Matt 24-25, Luke 23) is not homogeneous but rather a compilation (in fact we have reason to call it a "synoptic apocalypse"), and that it does not belong to the same layer of tradition as 13:1-2.

The story of *the widow's mite* (12:41-44) is an example of an individual scene set in Jerusalem, the temporal setting of which is unknown. We are not told what or where the "treasury" is. The tradition presumes that we already know that. Apparently it was an offering box, located somewhere in the outer court of

---

14. It is lamentable that the characteristics of this scene are not discussed in the Huck *Synopsis*, which includes it in 13:1-4. Many exegetes do not notice the new starting point in v. 3. To discuss the topography at all is to misunderstand the trans-historical grandiosity of the picture. Thus B. Weiss (*Markus und Lukas*, 197) says: "The image of him seated is related in very evocative ways to another image, when he sat down on the Mount of Olives (13:3), but not at the summit (Matt: ἐπί), rather on the slope, in view of the Temple." Matthew, who only thought about the links between pericopes, has not misunderstood Mark in the slightest. For εἰς in Mark 13:3 is identical with ἐν, since the Koiné used both prepositions promiscuously. Even in one of the most recent commentaries on Mark, Wohlenberg transcribes the idea that he "reclines on the Mount of Olives" (*Markus*, 330), without even looking back at the grammar of the Koine. But if we want to understand this text in its original meaning, we will have to examine catacomb paintings and early Christian mosaics, in which Christ sits atop the Mount of Olives in sublime isolation, surrounded by his twelve disciples, or sometimes by a smaller group of disciples. We might also look at a modern painting which is congenial to the New Testament, such as Wilhelm Steinhausen's "The Sermon on the Mount" (in the auditorium of the Kaiser-Friedrich-Gymnasium in Frankfurt am Main). In that painting Christ is depicted at the summit of a mountain. The words καθημένου αὐτοῦ could be translated as "seated on his throne." In my opinion it is important for literary study of the earliest Jesus tradition to pay attention to such material. Mark does not offer, as many are inclined to think, a description with any topographical contours. He just sets individual pictures one after another.

the Temple.[15] Anyone in that area could have noticed how much each individual put in.[16] An additional indication of the historicity of this episode is found in the fact that in the preceding saying Jesus attacked the Pharisees for taking advantage of widows (12:40). Here we get the other side of the picture.

Another story located in Jerusalem is the narrative of the *cleansing of the Temple* (11:15-19). Previously we have remarked upon the fact that this narrative can easily be removed from its present context: on the one hand, the later tradition tried to strengthen the connection with what precedes, while on the other hand, Matthew relocated the narrative, and the later tradition took it up as a free-standing pericope. For that reason it is especially significant that even though the story of the cleansing of the Temple is found in all four Gospels, it is found in four different places. John 2:13-22 puts it right at the beginning of the public activity of Jesus. This presentation is different from the Synoptics in several ways, and yet it is regarded as certain that each one is a report about the same incident. Which chronological arrangement is correct? That is how the question is often posed. The internal evidence produces utterly contradictory answers. These differences have even found expression in one and the same commentary: *Die Schriften des Neuen Testaments, neu übersetzt und für die Gegenwart erklärt*, 2nd ed., 1907/08. In his commentary on Mark (vol. 1, 180-81), J. Weiss prefers the Johannine order of events: "The mission of Jesus could only be successful if public attention was not focused upon him. As opposition intensified, as it certainly did shortly before the end, right after

---

15. To this point scholars have not been able to clarify what the treasury actually was. Cf. the comments of Wohlenberg, who brings in recent archaeological material; Wohlenberg, *Markus*, 326-27.

16. Most interpreters wax eloquent in praise of the clarity and beauty of this narrative; cf. Wellhausen, *Mark*, 277n.2. But following Wendt (*Die Lehre Jesus*, 1:41) who argued that the parable has been altered, Wendling (154) argues that the incident is not historical, but was constructed out of some poetic teachings of Jesus that were made into a biographical anecdote. But Wendling's critique really displays very little discernment. At one point he remarks, "How could Jesus have seen the woman's coin? She would have had to present it for official inspection." But in fact it might not have been all that difficult, especially if the woman pulled out the coin awkwardly, so that people could see what she was putting in. At another point Wendling asks: "How did Jesus know that the woman was a poor widow?" But wouldn't this fact have been evident in her clothing and her behavior? At this point Catholic exegetes appear to be thinking the Jesus had supernatural knowledge; cf. Pölzl, *Marcus*, 281: "Jesus *revealed* to the disciples what had taken place."

the messianic triumphal entry, the Temple police would gladly have arrested argumentative bystanders. Even from Jesus' standpoint, an action like this at the end of his ministry would have been a strong provocation. But at the beginning of his ministry it would have displayed an as yet un-disappointed, hopeful spirit, which is typical of all beginnings." Heitmüller, on the other hand, draws his sword on behalf of the Synoptic order (*Erklärung des Johannesevangelium*, vol. 2, 739): "In the Synoptics, after Jesus steps forward and experiences some early success, steady progress ensues. The messianic entry constitutes an important development in the catastrophe that will befall Jesus. At the beginning of his activity, however, it is as if he is floating on air, for we must not forget that he was a messianic agent." For my part, I regard both of these interpretations as incorrect, because they weigh the story down with psychological considerations, while the narrative is not the slightest bit interested in imputing such motives to Jesus. These controversy stories are found at the beginning of the public ministry, and in the middle and at the end, because Jesus' entire project was a fight against all of the bad things that had befallen his people. Exegetes have forced these questions about the temporal sequence of events upon the narrative. But this does not advance our understanding, so far as that is possible and necessary. In the gospel tradition these Jerusalem stories were not fixed at any specific time. Within the larger framework of the story of Jesus, they could be made to serve various purposes. Mark knows of only *one* stay in Jerusalem, only a few days long, so he can place this story right before the passion of Jesus, understanding it as the prelude to Jesus' final confrontation with his enemies. The fourth evangelist, by contrast, has more room in his series of several journeys to Jerusalem for various festivals, so he can locate this story right at the beginning, understanding it as the prelude to Jesus' long-running disagreement with his enemies.[17] The conclusion to the narrative about the cleansing of

17. I must confess that I do not see any significant problem with the chronology of the cleansing of the Temple. But the history of exegesis of this story is highly instructive methodologically. One group of exegetes, most Catholic but also some Protestants (Wohlenberg, e.g.), do not see the problem at all, as they think the Temple was cleansed twice. More often, however, the answer to the question gets mixed up rather quickly with the problem of the historicity of the Synoptics in contrast to John. The result is a sharp contrast between John and the Synoptics, in which some (Zahn, et al.) opt for the Johannine chronology, while others (Holtzmann, et al.) advocate for the Synoptic chronology. Very few consider that the question of the time of the Temple cleansing

the Temple leaves us hanging: the high priests and the scribes are seeking to destroy Jesus, the people marvel at his teaching, and he leaves the city that evening. There follows a summary statement, which was also composed by the evangelist. The remark about leaving the city is necessary to set up the following episode, which takes place at the gates of the city.

Jerusalem is the setting for the pericope about *the authority of Jesus* (11:27–33): καὶ ἔρχονται πάλιν εἰς Ἱεροσόλυμα· καὶ ἐν τῷ ἱερῷ περιπατοῦντος αὐτοῦ ἔρχονται πρὸς αὐτὸν οἱ ἀρχιερεῖς καὶ οἱ γραμματεῖς καὶ οἱ πρεσβύτεροι καὶ ἔλεγον αὐτῷ· ἐν ποίᾳ ἐξουσίᾳ ταῦτα ποιεῖς; With the exception of the characteristic Markan καί, it appears that a tradition has been taken up here. The evidence for this fact includes the setting in Jerusalem, the mention of the high priests and elders, who can always be found in the company of those other opponents of Jesus, the scribes, and most of all ταῦτα, which refers to the Temple incident. It is said to have just taken place. It is remarkable that the course of the narrative is interrupted by the cursing of a fig tree. For these reasons the story of the question about authority must have played out on some other day than that of the Temple incident. This temporal setting holds firm, even if we were to somehow separate it from the cursing of the fig tree and link it directly with the Temple incident. 11:15–19 (i.e., 11:15–17 + 11:27–33) is certainly not a smooth or steady report, so we must take it as true that the double designation of place at the beginning (in Jerusalem, in the Temple!) was introduced later, after the story of the fig tree had been brought in by the evangelist. Thus the original continuation of 11:17 now lies in these words from 11:27: καὶ ἔρχονται πρὸς αὐτὸν οἱ ἀρχιερεῖς . . . There is also the possibility, however, that the narrative about authority was presented *with* the introduction as it now stands, as a thoroughly independent story from Jerusalem. The word ταῦτα does not necessarily have to refer to the events in the Temple. Of interest at this point is the way that Matthew and Luke interpret Mark, who writes: καὶ ἔρχονται πρὸς αὐτὸν οἱ ἀρχιερεῖς. He speaks only of Jesus coming into the Temple, but says nothing about his teaching. Yet Matt 21:23 reads αὐτῷ

---

is a problem in its own right, quite apart from the general problem of John and the Synoptics. Cf. J. Weiss, *Das älteste Evangelium*, 268–69; Spitta, *Die synoptische Grundschrift*, 310 (who separates the narrative from the earlier Synoptic document). But on the whole this issue has become a matter of an unjustifiable *either-or*, either John *or* the Synoptics. But there is a third choice.

διδάσκοντι (actually, it syr^sin syr^cur leave this word out), and Luke 20:1 has διδάσκοντας αὐτοῦ τὸν λαὸν καὶ εὐαγγελιζομένου. Perhaps there is no connection with the Temple incident; perhaps the accusation is that he is walking around teaching in the Temple. Of course this interpretation is not certain, as ταῦτα may refer to events that are unknown to us. But there is one moment in the story that is significant for the temporal setting: the authoritative circles of Jerusalem do not dare to let the people know that they did not believe in John the Baptist. Here we can clearly see that the Baptist has ongoing influence, and this observation opens up questions that unfortunately cannot be resolved by history. Could the Baptist still have been alive? Could the masses still have been influenced by a living prophet? If this explanation were true, it would revise the ancient chronology, and the narrative before us would be painted in much brighter colors. We have to note at this point that the movement associated with the Baptist ran into rough seas after John's death. Yet, according to Acts 19:3, twenty years after his death, there were still some Christians in Ephesus who had experienced only the baptism of John (εἰς τὸ βάπτισμα Ἰωάννου).[18] At the end of the day we have here a narrative from Jerusalem, the date of which could be determined more precisely if we had more information about the Baptist.

Another Jerusalem narrative, which also fits into Mark's section about the last days of Jesus before his suffering, is the story about *the entry into Jerusalem* (11:1-11). Questions of location are rather complicated here, since the written tradition swings back and forth, and the three Synoptics do not quite agree with each other:

---

18. Little progress has been made toward resolving the internal chronological problem here. J. Weiss (*Das älteste Evangelium*, 269), followed ten years later by Spitta (*Die synoptische Grundschrift*, 313), confidently declared that this pericope must have taken place while John was still alive, while he was still near the zenith of his fame. Neither Weiss nor Spitta engages with the fact that both Acts 19:3 and the Gospel of John, which appears to have been an anti-Baptist document, were well-established in early Christianity.

Mark 11:1-2	Matt 21:1-2	Luke 19:28-30
¹ καὶ ὅτε ἐγγίζουσιν εἰς Ἱεροσόλυμα καὶ εἰς <u>Βηθανίαν</u> πρὸς τὸ ὄρος τῶν ἐλαιῶν, ἀποστέλλει δύο τῶν μαθητῶν αὐτοῦ, ² καὶ λέγει αὐτοῖς· ὑπάγετε εἰς τὴν κώμην τὴν κατέναντι ὑμῶν.	¹ καὶ ὅτε ἤγγισαν εἰς Ἱεροσόλυμα καὶ ἦλθον εἰς **Βηθφαγὴ** εἰς τὸ ὄρος τῶν ἐλαιῶν, τότε Ἰησοῦς ἀπέστειλεν δύο μαθητὰς ² λέγων αὐτοῖς· πορεύεσθε εἰς τὴν κώμην τὴν κατέναντι ὑμῶν.	²⁸ καὶ εἰπὼν ταῦτα ἐπορεύετο ἔμπροσθεν ἀναβαίνων εἰς Ἱεροσόλυμα, ²⁹ καὶ ἐγένετο, ὡς ἤγγισεν εἰς **Βηθφαγὴ** καὶ <u>Βηθανίαν</u> πρὸς τὸ ὄρος τὸ καλούμενον ἐλαιῶν, ἀπέστειλεν δύο τῶν μαθητῶν ³⁰ εἰπών· ὑπάγετε εἰς τὴν κατέναντι κώμην.

When we ask which of these is the correct reading, the question boils down to the two place names, Bethany and Bethphage. Textual critics come to their decision primarily on the basis of a statement by Origen (cf. Tischendorf on Mark 11:1), to the effect that Mark refers only to Bethany, and Matthew refers only to Bethphage, but Luke represents both Bethphage and Bethany. But Origen's comment applies only to his time period, telling us about what manuscripts he knew, and thus cannot be an absolute ruling, as some have thought. The reading in Mark 11:1, εἰς Ἱεροσόλυμα καὶ εἰς Βηθανίαν, appears in D it and vg. But important witnesses such as ℵ A B C L Γ Δ ... cop go arm syr^sin aeth disagree with Mark and include both place names: εἰς Ἱεροσόλυμα (καὶ) εἰς Βηθφαγὴ (καὶ) (εἰς) Βηθανίαν. Indeed, ℵ and C insert εἰς before Βηθανίαν, while syr^sin drops out both instances of the word καί. The readings from Matthew and Luke overwhelmingly attest to the fact that only a few manuscripts of Matt 21:1 read καὶ Βηθανίαν after Βηθφαγή. Are they conforming to Luke? At this point the three synoptic texts were engaged in a process of mutual exchange, and early on, textual critics in the ancient church (who were the earliest editors) were making efforts to improve the text in various ways. A conclusive decision in this matter is therefore impossible, because those people were not only arbitrary in various ways, but they were also impaired by their ignorance of the geography. Logically speaking, Luke offers the smoothest text: Jesus was leaving Jerusalem, and as he came to Bethphage and Bethany, this and that took place. Matthew is not as smooth: as they neared Jerusalem and arrived at Bethphage, such and such happened. Mark is totally opaque: as they were approaching Jerusalem (and Bethphage) and Bethany. Mark ought to have said that the other way around: as they came to Bethphage and Bethany and Jerusalem. Syr[sin] tried to apply a healing touch, by leaving out the καί and thereby smoothing out (a little) Mark's bizarre itinerary. From the standpoint of topography, however, *all* of these readings are unclear. What kind of path are we supposed to imagine? When both place names are juxtaposed, we can either say, "they came from Jericho by way of Bethphage to Bethany, and from there to Jerusalem"; or we can say, "Bethphage and Bethany lay not far from each other on opposite sides of the road, and they went to both places on their way to Jerusalem. But those who are knowledgeable about the topography of Jerusalem do not offer us any help with this problem; on the contrary, they only increase the level of our confusion. Bethany, which is known today as el-Azarije, lies on the southeastern slope of the Mount of Olives. Bethphage, by contrast, cannot be identified. "Bethphage may have been located on the western slope of the Mount of Olives, or it could have been in the general area of Gethsemane. Both were small estates, of which no ruins survive."[19] It appears that Bethphage marked the boundary of the holy city of Jerusalem, and therefore it must have been closer to the city than Bethany, which was located farther to the east. The texts as we have them—certainly Luke and probably Mark—are at this point basically ruled out of the question. Mark's text makes sense only with regard to Bethany, and Luke's text makes sense only with regard to Bethphage. And if Bethphage really was the sacred boundary of the city, then Matthew's text is nonsensical. We can say that Luke's text, which might be logical, originated on the desk of someone who had no knowledge at all about the topography. The general difficulty only increases with the mention of κατέναντι κώμη in Mark 11:2 (= Matt 21:2 = Luke 19:30). If Bethphage is the place to which Jesus is referring, then Bethany cannot be intended, because it

---

19. Merx, *Markus und Lukas*, 368. This conclusion is based on the role of Bethphage in various texts from the Mishnah. As part of a discussion of the boundaries of the holy city, these texts ask whether the holy bread and the Passover sacrifice can be prepared in Bethphage. Thus Bethphage must have been located within the boundary of the precincts of Jerusalem.

would not have been "ahead of them," but rather behind them and therefore scarcely visible. But Bethphage, in the vicinity of which Jesus could have spoken these words, was apparently not a κώμη. This is in fact not a serious difficulty, since κώμη is an expression that may go back to a clumsy Aramaic cognate. The expression, "the village ahead of you," is easy to visualize, since the place is made clear enough to the disciples, even if not to us as readers. I suspect that in the original tradition only one place name was given. Somewhere along the way another place name was substituted for it, even though the first tradition lived on, until eventually both place names were combined. If that is the case, then which one is original, Bethphage or Bethany? The latter name plays a larger role in the early Christian tradition than the former. According to an old tradition (John 11:1; 12:1), Jesus knew some people in Bethany, namely, Lazarus, Mary, and Martha. The synoptic story about the anointing of Jesus took place in Bethany at the house of Simon the leper (Mark 14:3; Matt 26:6). Finally, the story of the triumphal entry also mentions Bethany. Bethphage, by contrast, had no significance in the synoptic tradition. It is likely, therefore, that "Bethany" replaced the unknown "Bethphage." But even that conclusion is still not fully successful, since the fact remains that both readings were handed down side by side.

The cheers of the people, which are described next, take place as Jesus is leaving the Mount of Olives, i.e., still outside of Jerusalem. Only in 11:11 does he enter the city. Verse 8b makes clear that they are outside of the city: "While others strew bundles of green leafy branches (στιβάδας) ahead of him, which they had cut from the fields (ἐκ τῶν ἀγρῶν)." Matthew, by contrast, speaks of branches from trees (κλάδους ἀπὸ τῶν δένδρων), and John refers to "palm branches" (βαΐα τῶν φοινίκων). Luke does not mention this detail. He is obviously the only one who felt the need to bring the topography into the picture. He says so explicitly: "As he neared the bottom of the Mount of Olives" (ἐγγίζοντος δὲ αὐτοῦ ἤδη πρὸς τῇ καταβάσει τοῦ ὄρους τῶν ἐλαιῶν).[20] Although

---

20. At Luke 19:37, D reads: ἐγγιζόντων . . . αὐτῶν, reflecting the fact that Jesus is still with his disciples. In exegesis, too much fuss is made too often about this point, which represents itself as an explanatory remark by Luke, for which no special geographical knowledge was necessary. Against this view B. Weiss (*Markus und Lukas*, 592) has argued: "This . . . local detail can only result from a different account of the triumphal entry . . . the precise knowledge of the area around Jerusalem points to L" (Luke's special

the other evangelists go on about the ovations from the people, Luke (19:37) speaks about the crowds of disciples (τὸ πλῆθος τῶν μαθητῶν), not mentioning the people ntil 19:39. The distinction here is not all that significant, since Luke does not restrict the expression "disciples" only to the twelve, thinking instead of a larger circle of Jesus' followers.

Matthew 11:11 belongs to the continuation of the pericope in the tradition, as is shown by the rather terse designation of place: εἰς Βηθανίαν.[21] The purpose of the journey to Bethany is clearly marked in Matt 21:17 with the words ηὐλίσθη ἐκεῖ ("he spent the night there"). Luke never mentions Bethany anywhere in his entire account. He apparently thinks that after his entry, Jesus remained in Jerusalem, never leaving the city again. Perhaps Luke did not know that Bethany was located so close to Jerusalem that one cannot really speak of a specific journey there.

Two related stories are linked to the location in Bethany: the narrative about *the cursing of the fig tree* (Mark 11:12-14 = Matt 21:18-19) and *the conversation about the withered fig tree* (Mark 11:20-26 = Matt 21:20-22). Both of these scenes can easily be lifted out of their contexts, and both are missing from Luke. Mark gives the following introduction to the first scene: ¹²καὶ τὸ ἐπαύριον ἐξελθόντων αὐτῶν ἀπὸ Βηθανίας ἐπείνασεν· ¹³καὶ ἰδὼν συκῆν . . . The way Mark reports the story is quite remarkable: Jesus curses a tree in the season during which, according to the nature of things, it cannot produce any fruit. He is looking to satisfy his hunger in a way that is impossible. Thus there is no rational motive for the curse. The episode would take on poignant significance if it were set in the true season for figs, i.e., not at Easter, as the current context requires. In v. 13, the explanatory remark, ὁ γὰρ καιρὸς οὐκ ἦν σύκων, makes us aware of the season and is obviously a gloss. A second fact supports this judgment: Matthew, who certainly knows it is the Easter season, leaves this gloss out. In addition, there is a textual variant in Mark: syr^sin leaves out γάρ. This omission takes the edge off of the statement, which is typical of a gloss. Especially disturbing is the fact that during the springtime there are no ripe figs, but only unripe

---

material). On this basis it might be conceivable that Spitta (*Die synoptische Grundschrift*, 301) has found here his "one geographical fixed point . . . which proves that Luke had local information that was not dependent upon Mark and Matthew."

21. Neither Wendling nor Spitta pays attention to the question of whether this kind of place designation can be attributed back to the evangelist.

ones, called *bikkurim* or *phaggim*, and these could be eaten.²² If Jesus was looking for that kind of tree, then we can locate this story in the Easter season.

On the morning of another day Jesus and his disciples pass by that fig tree again (καὶ παραπορευόμενοι πρωῒ εἶδον τὴν συκῆν), and Jesus then utters a saying about the miraculous power of faith and of prayer, which is not necessarily anchored in this particular situation. The reference to mountains falling into the sea (v. 23) seems to have rather less to do with the Mount of Olives and the Dead Sea, which is rather far away, as it does with the Sea of Galilee and its hilly surroundings. The saying thus has a Galilean color and context.

How did the fig tree story come to rest at this point in the Gospel of Mark? It is possible that the place designation in 11:12, ἀπὸ Βηθανίας, was strongly anchored in the ancient tradition, and that it was linked to the story of the triumphal entry. As a result of that place designation it was eventually positioned here. Since both the survival of the individual traditions and their connections are the work of the evangelist, the following analysis recommends itself: the original story of the fig tree was a self-enclosed narrative made up of v. 12 (*without* ἀπὸ Βηθανίας), v. 13 (with the concluding remark about the season for figs), v. 14, v. 20, and v. 21. Jesus sees a fig tree and curses it, and on a later day the curse was fulfilled. Verses 20–21 are a good conclusion to the narrative, and καὶ τῇ ἐπαύριον ("and on the following day") is a pericope introduction, which was certainly not created by Mark, but rather came along with the narrative as it wandered. Certainly this chronological note looks chronological, and in this case it actually is, but the examples in John 1:29, 34, and 44 show that it is better to regard it as a caesura. Mark is the one who put this story in its current context, because he aimed the story of the cursing of the fig tree at the Jewish people: to him they deserved

---

22. M. Brückner, *Das fünfte Evangelium*, 17. A rather difficult explanation is attempted by B. Weiss (*Markus und Lukas*, 176–77): "The abnormality of the tree was not its defective fruit, but rather its leafy outgrowth, which had caused Jess to expect fruit. This anomaly was deceptive, raising expectations it could not fulfill." Even if we relieve the difficulty of the text in this way, something enigmatic still remains. Is this an original parable, which was misunderstood and then refashioned over time? Schwartz ("Der verfluchte Feigenbaum") thinks it may be an etiological narrative: in Jerusalem there was a well-known withered fig tree, which Christian stories said had been cursed by Jesus. But just before the *parousia* it would produce fruit again. For additional interpretations, cf. Klostermann, *Markus*, 96–97.

this warning of impending catastrophe. Since it plays out "on another day," he closes by adding ἀπὸ Βηθανίας in 11:11, where the topic is a visit to Bethany in the evening. He fills the day in between v. 14 and v. 20 with the story of the Temple cleansing, fashioning a rather lonely v. 20 into a new pericope by adding a few appropriate sayings. Matthew moves the Temple cleansing closer to the beginning, and thereby pulls it closer together with the narrative of the fig tree.[23]

Excursus: Literary and Historical Evaluation of Mark 10:46—13:37 and Parallels

The preceding analysis of Mark 10:46—13:37, along with the parallel excerpts in Matthew and Luke, has blown to pieces the chronological outline of the individual traditions in their distinctive character. There is no schema here: three days in Mark, two days in Matthew, and only Luke makes any effort to arrange events along a time-line, as is demonstrated by his characteristic remarks at 19:47; 20:1; and 21:37-38. Various individual pieces have been put together to make this story about the last days of Jesus before his suffering. The process extended over a long time period, perhaps over multiple years in the life of Jesus. Some of the stories go back to Jerusalem, but others to other locations, many of which were located in Galilee. The only episodes that absolutely must have taken place during the last days of Jesus in Jerusalem are the story of the entry and all of his various statements against the city. Everything else comes from Mark the evangelist (whom Matthew and Luke generally follow) in the service of his theme "the last days of Jesus in Jerusalem."[24]

---

23. In this discussion, I put my finger on the framing pieces as they are evident in the tradition, moving with the narratives, unaltered or only slightly so. It is not Mark's style to adorn a narrative with chronological details. It is common for scholars, insofar as they notice this, to criticize Mark for it. Cf. J. Weiss, *Schriften*, 178-79: "In Mark the day-by-day narrative appears to be artfully presented, in that a night is inserted between the entry and the Temple cleansing, and the fig tree story is distributed over two days."

24. This result is similar to what we concluded with regard to the Lukan Travel Narrative, of which only the story of the Good Samaritan had to be attributed to a journey by Jesus to Jerusalem.

Excursus: Perspectives on the Question of the Length
of Jesus' Ministry: Jesus' Earlier Visits to Jerusalem

More than just the chronological and topographical framework of the last days in Jerusalem melts down here. The stories discussed above alter our understanding of the overall framework of the story of Jesus as a whole. As we saw in our early case studies, we are dealing here with an aimless, unselfconscious, and thereby especially valuable tradition of individual stories that overran Mark's best efforts at schematization. The story of blind Bartimaeus (Mark 10:46-52 = Matt 20:29-34 = Luke 18:35-43), whose name Luke did not pass along, and whom Matthew presents as two blind people, suggests that the blind man had previously been in contact with Jesus.[25] How could that have been possible? Had Jesus previously been active in that area? Something of that sort seems to be the necessary conclusion, but in such matters the historian must be very careful. The ancient narrators did not feel that way: on the contrary, to them it was obvious that the blind man simply knew right away, without any particular psychological insight, that it was Jesus who was approaching.

A series of stories tells us that Jesus must have had some contacts in Jerusalem, which can only be explained on the basis of an earlier visit. He had followers in the village into which he sends his disciples (Mark 11:2par). Of course the narrative as it stands does not indicate any such earlier acquaintances; on the contrary, it highlights the miraculous foreknowledge of Jesus. But historians have to arrive at a much different judgment: either certain details will have to be stricken from the narrative, or the supernatural features in the narrative will force us to categorize it as "non-historical." The first option degenerates into a rationalism that destroys the punch, uniqueness, and beauty of New Testament narrative. The second option manages to avoid that mistake, but entails instead an all-too-convenient erasure of complicated questions about the history behind the stories. This problem is evident in the story of the preparation for the Passover meal, when Jesus (Mark 14:13-14 = Matt 26:18 = Luke 22:10-11) describes the man who will provide the disciples with a room. This man is a follower whom Jesus could not have met

---

25. The form in which Luke (18:36-37) depicts the encounter between Jesus and the blind man, in contrast with that of Mark and Matthew, is an especially interesting example of Luke's psychological method.

during his last few days of activity in Jerusalem, at least as they are recorded in the Synoptics.

Still more pointed are two acquaintances of Jesus who are specifically named: Simon the leper in Bethany (Mark 14:3 = Matt 26:6) and Joseph of Arimathea (Mark 15:43 = Matt 27:57 = Luke 23:50-51). Perhaps these people could have gotten to know Jesus in his hometown or somewhere else, but the more likely possibility is that Jesus had made earlier visits to Jerusalem. In this way some general impressions start to become clear. In our earlier discussion of the lament over Jerusalem (Matt 23:37-39), we have dealt with the saying in Luke 13:34. As it was handed down in Luke 19:44 it runs this way: "No stone will left atop another, because you did not recognize the time of God's visitation." Long and repeated activity of Jesus in Jerusalem by Jesus is presupposed here. Finally, there is Mark 14:49 (= Matt 26:55 = Luke 22:53): "Every day I was with you in the Temple." These statements are not supported by the fact that Jesus spends a few days in Jerusalem in the Synoptics. And a passage like Mark 11:11: "he went into the Temple and looked around" is no answer at all. This expression *can* be an indication of the newness of things and Jesus' unfamiliarity with the place, but it does not *have* to. Once again we find ourselves looking at things we have long relied upon, and finding that now they are greatly changed.[26]

26 It is illustrative that, after repeated efforts to present the Markan outline as historical, Wellhausen has said: "Lk 2:41 says that from his early years Jesus' parents traveled every year to the Passover in Jerusalem, and took him with them. But as he looks at everything in the Temple here, he cannot have been there often" (Wellhausen, *Mark*, 95).

9

Jesus' Suffering and Death

Mark 14–15 (= Matt 26–27 = Luke 22–23)

The General Character of the Passion Narrative: The Logical Topography and Chronology

THE CONCLUSION OF THIS story, i.e., the suffering and death of Jesus, stands at some remove from our investigation to this point. For the construction of the reports on Jesus' public activity have shown themselves to have no interest in chronology or topography. Individual stories, or small collections of stories, lie before us in great abundance, in no particular chronological sequence, with an arrangement that is only a framework. Each individual narrative is a separate pericope, which may be either framed or unframed. True, there was a rich framework of chronological and topographical indicators, into which the individual narratives were wrapped. The stories wandered in the tradition in their frame, sometimes exchanging one framework for another. That is why some historically valuable tradition does survive, preserved in the pericope introductions and conclusions. Yet even in the best cases these framing pieces present only the barest scraps of an itinerary for the history of the activity of Jesus.

The Passion Narrative, by contrast, calls for a very different literary perspective. It is the only section of the Gospels that offers information about places and times, indeed, about days and hours. Clearly we have here a continuous narrative. As soon as we read the first words, we know that the story is going to end in disaster, as one event leads to another with pressing logic and necessity.

The small and self-enclosed reports about specific actions and sayings of Jesus did play a role in the collections that the early Christian community put together for use in worship, and in the collections that missionaries used to win new converts. For that reason, these two kinds of stories cannot be sharply differentiated from each other. The collections were not totally separate, and whenever interested outsiders heard them, the stories were serving their missionary purpose. Thus the stories about Jesus played yet another role quite apart from their use in worship and evangelism, for the early Christians also enjoyed the narratives as such, without regard to their liturgical or missionary purposes. In these matters, what part did the Passion Narrative play? The telling of that story did not please the narrators, the liturgists, or the apologists.[1] From their perspective, certain aspects of this story did not make the right point: Judas' betrayal, for example, or the preparation for the Passover meal, or the trial before Pilate. Obviously they would have been more approving of the institution of the Lord's Supper and the crucifixion of Jesus. Still more revealing is the use of the individual stories with regard to worship and missionary efforts. Some of the stories in the Passion Narrative have neither cultic nor apologetic force. This is especially noticeable in contexts where one piece necessarily prepares for another. In Christian groups far and wide, the Passion Narrative would have been read aloud in the worship as a *lectio continua*. Only when read in its entirety could the Passion Narrative answer a question that came up frequently in the early mission of the church: how could Jesus have been sent to the cross by the very people who had seen his signs and wonders?

In these various ways the Passion Narrative played its special role. It is the oldest and most distinguished document in the circle of the early Christian martyr-acts, the literary outlook of which cannot be captured in a word, but that certainly served the story about the martyrdom of Christ. Just as the Passion Narrative was separated from the narratives of Jesus' words and deeds, so this martyr-act was differentiated from the legends of other martyrs, which collected individual stories about their words and deeds. We should not underestimate the desire of the community to get out front with a story about the suffering and death of their leader, a story that could be admired. Most of the martyr-acts were written down soon after the death of the witness, and for that reason they stand much closer to historical reality than legends that were written down only much later, and that introduce

---

1. M. Dibelius, "Herodes und Pilatus," 113ff, understands the distinctiveness of the Passion Narrative so well, although he favors one side of the argument when he says: "Stories about Jesus' words and deeds held only paradigmatic significance for missionary preaching, which sought not to tell stories, but to proclaim salvation. Yet the Passion Narrative was probably used very early for apologetics." It seems to me that in this sense there is no difference between the Passion Narrative and the other stories. The literary distinctiveness of the Passion Narrative did not grant it sole custody over early Christian apologetics. In my view the parallels with the genre of martyrology show that there are other ways to look at the Passion Narrative. But Dibelius may be right that it served the goals of apologetics better than other narratives, for it was fixed rather early, and that would have given it a certain clarity.

material of an historically questionable nature. The same applies to the Passion Narrative of Jesus in its relation to the larger report of his activity. In the latter we often find ourselves on shaky ground: a tradition with many layers, born out of various interests, splintered into a pile of little pieces that we have to try to put back together. The content and arrangement of the material fell out in various ways. It appears that the Passion Narrative was fixed rather early, which resulted in the considerable unanimity of the three Synoptics, and even into the fourth gospel, which was formed so much differently. The report on the suffering and death of Jesus was already fixed before the tradition had time to smooth things out. Even though Jesus at times carried on long disagreements with his opponents, in the Passion Narrative he is almost completely silent. At a later time, for purposes of edification and apologetics, words would be put into the mouth of Jesus, including whole speeches to the high council, Pilate, and Herod.[2] But before then the report would have long since taken on fixed form, so that it could no longer be substantially changed without doing harm to the community. For the earliest community, which laid down the story about Jesus' martyrdom shortly after his death, "the story as it happened was apologetic in itself."[3] The remarkably high and immediate historical value of the Passion Narrative is clear in the sayings.

Some Seams and Gaps in the Passion Narrative

The Passion Narrative can be evaluated as religion, history, and literature, and while its overall character remains undamaged, it does contain some seams and gaps. From the very beginning the earliest tradition was never free of gaps. In certain scenes eyewitness testimony comes into view, i.e., the Lord's Supper, the arrest, denial by Peter, the crucifixion. In others, by contrast, such as Jesus' arraignment before the high council, the reports hold up only conditionally. And some, such as the Gethsemane scene, certainly cannot be regarded as eyewitness accounts.

Where gaps are present, new material can be inserted. That is especially true of Luke, who enriched *the Lord's Supper* with new material, and

2. It is striking that Jesus has so little to say in the Passion Narrative. There are early Christian martyr-acts in which the martyrs conduct themselves in this way. In other acts, by contrast, the eloquence of the one condemned to death is especially great. We can set it up as a general rule, that a report of a martyr who has rather little to say is of greater historical value than one with a lot of words. U. Wilcken has made the same observation about pagan martry-acts: cf. his essay, *Zum alexandrinischen Antisemitismus*.

3. Jordan, *Geschichte der altchristlichen Literatur*, 84. His words apply with equal force to the Passion Narrative of Jesus.

rearranged what Matthew and Mark had offered. The result was a Last Supper that unfolds in two acts: first Jesus institutes the Lord's Supper, which comes from Mark, and then Jesus speaks various words of farewell to his disciples, of which Mark and Matthew placed some earlier, others later. In the narrative about *Jesus before the Council*, Luke's effort to rearrange the material is even more obvious. At 22:56 he attaches the denial of Peter directly to the report of the arrest. Then he narrates the abuse of Jesus by the guards (22:63-65), putting it right next to the hearing before the Council, so that these scenes lead directly into the scene before Pilate. In Mark and Matthew, by contrast, Peter's denial does not take place until after the trial and abuse of Jesus, interrupting the course of events. In contrast to the other Synoptics, Luke alone narrates the scene of *Jesus before Herod*, which he could easily insert, since the connection with the trial scene with Pilate is very loose. On the other hand, Matthew offers a narrative that is found in neither of the other Synoptics, i.e., the story of *the death of Judas*. He fits this episode in ahead of the Roman trial before Pilate. Finally, Mark and Matthew have something that is missing in Luke: at Mark 14:3-9 (= Matt 26:6-13) stands *the anointing in Bethany*, a scene that can be dropped out with no damage to the context. It is a well-formed separate story with an introduction strongly characteristic of a pericope: καὶ ὄντος αὐτοῦ ἐν Βηθανίᾳ . . . (similar in Matthew). The insertion of this scene at this point destroys the continuity of the narrative. Luke, who has already told a similar story (7:36-50), leaves it out. Luke also does not report the mocking of Jesus by the Roman soldiers (Mark 15:16-20 = Matt 27:27-31), but that says nothing against the originality of that episode in its present context. At this point for some reason Luke left out a piece of real history.[4] Except for that particular scene, the differences in the ways that the three Synoptics handle their shared material indicate that there were gaps in the Passion Narrative of Jesus.

Certainly the context leaves something to be desired, as is also evident in the fact that Matthew, and even more so Luke, has made a number of improvements in the course of the narrative, along with an effort to strengthen the connections. In this way they sought to put a finer finish on the Passion Narrative, an effort that they had also undertaken with the words and deeds of Jesus. Matthew generally follows Mark's account as much as possible, but Luke follows his own schedule when it comes to the material given to him by the second evangelist. Particularly illustrative in this regard is his refashioning

---

4. J. Weiss, *Schriften*, 519, says: "Perhaps Luke wanted to avoid doubling up on the mockery of the soldiers. But it is probably that he wanted to let the trial by the Romans appear in the worst possible light." But cf. Wellhausen, *Luke*, 133: "For reasons we cannot figure out, Luke leaves out the mocking adoration of the Roman soldiers."

of the report about Jesus' trial before Pilate.[5] What happened there on a grand scale is evident in small alterations to the connections. The remark in Luke 22:3, to the effect that Satan had entered into Judas, is an elaboration based on religious reflection. In 22:15, the remark, "I have eagerly desired to eat this Passover meal with you before I suffer," was put into the mouth of Jesus in order to set up a sequence in the course of events. κατὰ τὸ ἔθος (22:39) is clearly a Lukan insertion; he then goes to the Mount of Olives, as was his custom.[6] Here the evangelist was trying, after the fact, to smooth out the flow of the narrative with details that sound realistic.

But we can now follow this literary work further back into the Markan outline. What Luke did to Mark, Mark had already done to the tradition he had before him. We have already found a practical detail in Mark 3:9, where πλοιάριον is mentioned. These small summary statements, along with the somewhat larger collected reports, belong here. Within the Passion Narrative, the little scene in Mark 14:10-11, *the betrayal of Judas* must be thoroughly assessed. At the beginning of the account of the arrest of Jesus (14:43), Ἰούδας ὁ Ἰσκαριώτης εἷς τῶν δώδεκα is mentioned by name, as if we had never heard of him before, even though Judas has already been described exactly the same way in 14:10. It appears to me that these statements, 14:10 and 14:43, were not originally recorded in a continuous narrative. On the contrary, as part of his account of the arrest of Jesus, Mark developed this little scene about the betrayal of Judas, which is not especially vivid and is not anchored in any clear setting. The same can be said about the brief report of *the authorities' death sentence upon Jesus* (Mark 14:1-2 = Luke 22:1-2), for it too has none of the right colors. It need not be attributed to any special tradition, even less to Matthew's rearrangement of the Markan text (Matt 26:1-5), which strongly emphasizes this important moment at the beginning of the Passion Narrative. Matthew had already handled in a similar way both the opening of Jesus' public activity (4:12ff) and the first appearance of Jesus in Jerusalem (21:10-11).

The phenomena discussed above change nothing about the overall character of the Passion Narrative as a continuous chronological report. There are gaps, and the connections are not always correctly fastened, but on the whole we cannot rearrange the individual scenes, nor can we trace our way back to separate layers of tradition.

---

5. Cf. in this regard the instructive treatment by Dibelius, "Herodes und Pilatus."
6. Cf. Luke 4:16; Acts 17:2: κατὰ τὸ εἰωθός αὐτῷ; κατὰ τὸ εἰωθός τῷ Παύλῳ.

10

The Pre-Histories

THE SO-CALLED "PRE-HISTORIES" THAT Matthew and Luke have added to Mark are of a completely different character. Here there is no unified story of the childhood of Jesus, but various traditions that have been united with each other. The form of this unification is characteristically different in Matthew and in Luke.

The Matthean Pre-History

After the announcement of Jesus' genealogy in Matt 1:1-17, the birth story is narrated in 1:18-25. It does not offer a genuine biographical narrative, since Jesus is depicted as far too self-aware and self-conscious. Thus the pericope about the *wise men from the East* (2:1-12) ends with the following remark: τοῦ δὲ Ἰησοῦ γεννηθέντος ἐν Βηθλεὲμ τῆς Ἰουδαίας ἐν ἡμέραις Ἡρῴδου τοῦ βασιλέως, ἰδοὺ μάγοι ἀπὸ ἀνατολῶν παρεγένοντο εἰς Ἱεροσόλυμα. It is characteristic that the first indications of the time and place of Jesus' birth appear in the introduction to this narrative. We would expect something different from a running narrative about Jesus' beginnings: such matters belong not in a side comment within the introduction, but rather in the birth narrative itself. This state of affairs throws a clear light upon the origins of the content of Matthew's report. The evangelist found the story of the wise men from the east in the tradition, and arranged it here with no changes, in order to present a better chronological and topographical connection. The subsequent narrative about *the flight and return of the family of Jesus* (2:3-23) appears to belong with the preceding tradition. Verse 13 locates the story within a clear and sequential chronological train of thought. The conclusion is thoroughly biographical: εἰς τὰ μέρη τῆς Γαλιλαίας, καὶ ἐλθὼν κατῴκησεν εἰς πόλιν λεγομένην Ναζαρέθ. We are now properly introduced to the town of Nazareth. Matthew does not use this kind of style elsewhere in his Gospel. We stand here on the ground of the tradition.

The Lukan Pre-History

In his narrative of the childhood of Jesus, Luke presents an abundance of material from his special tradition, which he knew how to bring together into a coherent account. After the prologue (1:1–4), he sets the story of the prediction of John the Baptist's birth (1:5–25) within a chronological introduction of almost epic style: ἐγένετο ἐν ταῖς ἡμέραις Ἡρῴδου βασιλέως τῆς Ἰουδαίας ἱερεύς τις ὀνόματι Ζαχαρίας . . . καὶ γυνή . . . At the beginning of Mark's Gospel we do not find this kind of temporal specification, and in Matthew (2:1) it is set very much in the background, in a participial construction. We are then introduced to the character and voice of John's parents. To a certain extent, vv. 5–7 contain an exposition of what is to come. The narrative itself takes much for granted, with a characteristically Lukan style that is reminiscent of Old Testament narrative: (v. 8) ἐγένετο δὲ ἐν τῷ περατεύειν . . . ἔλαχε τοῦ θυμιᾶσαι. The reader is not told that in their service, the priestly classes took turns, and in v. 23 we learn for the first time that Zacharias did not live in Jerusalem. Everything about the narrative indicates that it is right at home in Jewish circles. Luke took it up and reconfigured it into an authorial introduction. In the original narrative Zacharias and his wife Elizabeth appeared as characters already known to hearers and readers, as was their place of residence and all the rest. The author Luke did not watch closely enough when he moved these esoteric characters to the side. For our purposes these kinds of unevenness are important: we can see how tradition and authorial work stand out from each other.

The next narrative, about *the promise of Jesus' birth* (1:26–38) opens with an exact determination of time: ἐν δὲ τῷ μηνὶ ἕκτῳ (tradition? or insertion by the evangelist?). The place designation in v. 26, εἰς πόλιν τῆς Γαλιλαίας ᾗ ὄνομα Ναζαρέθ, is reminiscent of 1:5 in its almost ponderous detail, just like the precise identification of Joseph and Mary in v. 27. This form of introduction scarcely fits with the original narrative, which took for granted that such things were already known. It has to be credited to the account of the evangelist, who at this point is thinking of Greek readers, to whom he wants to introduce some new and unfamiliar matters. On the whole, he made few changes to a narrative that is consistently tender and poetic, a masterpiece of its kind.

A general designation of time, ἐν ταῖς ἡμέραις ἐκείναις (which certainly comes from Luke) leads into the narrative of *Mary's visit to Elizabeth*

(1:39-56), but the identification of the place, εἰς τὴν ὀρεινήν ... εἰς πόλιν Ἰούδα is somewhat difficult. Where is Mary going in the mountains? Somewhere out of Nazareth? This form of expression strikes us as forced, as if it meant to say: Mary went to the mountains, i.e., southward from Nazareth to the hills around Jerusalem. Then we also have to ponder the expression πόλις Ἰούδα. The topography in 1:39 gives us the idea that Mary is not in Nazareth but in Judea, somewhere in the area of Jerusalem. There is an old tradition, handed down in the *Protevangelium of James*, that the parents of Jesus made their home in Jerusalem. This tradition appears to shimmer over v. 39, especially because the later narrative of the circumcision in the Temple in Jerusalem (2:21-40) appears to designate Jerusalem as the residence of Jesus' parents.[1] Obviously Luke has not looked into the geographical context very thoroughly. The resulting narrative is not Galilean, but a Judean tradition. The designation Ἰούδα is noticeable, bringing to mind the mountains of Judah. But one would rather expect εἰς πόλιν τῆς Ἰουδαίας (cf. 1:26, εἰς πόλιν τῆς Γαλιλαίας), as some Latin manuscripts *Judeae* or *Judaeae*. Perhaps behind the name Ἰούδα there stands a place name that was known to Luke.[2] If the tradition had included anything definite, certainly Luke would have fixed the location more precisely. But picking a detail out of thin air is not his style.[3] After the blessing of Mary by Elizabeth (v. 45), there follows in vv. 46-55 the so-called "Magnificat of Mary" (μεγαλύνει = *magnificat*). Most of the textual witnesses read καὶ εἶπεν Μαριάμ. On the other hand, some Latin manuscripts have *et ait Elisabet*. Whether we attribute the song of praise, which has the character of a Jewish psalm, to Mary or Elizabeth, vv. 46-55 drop easily out of their immediate context, so perhaps they did not belong to the original version of the pericope.[4] Verse 56 is a transitional verse, by which Luke sequences the events: ἔμεινεν δὲ Μαριὰμ σὺν αὐτῇ μῆνας τρεῖς καὶ ὑπέστρεψεν ες τὸν οἶκον αὐτῆς. Quite apart from its content, the use of the verb ὑποστρέφειν speaks for the Lukan

---

1. As far as I can tell, exegetes have not noticed the topographical difficulty here. An exception is Brückner, *Das fünfte Evangelium*, 26: "If someone in Nazareth wants to go to the mountains, they go north, not south into Judea."

2. B. Weiss (*Markus und Lukas*, 282) recalls Josh. 21:16, where the priestly city of Jutta (יטה) is mentioned. Other exegetes suggest Jerusalem or Hebron.

3. In that regard, Luke is more careful than many recent interpreters, who want to determine the reason for Mary's visit to Elizabeth. Cf. B. Weiss, *Markus und Lukas*, 282; also Pölzl, *Lukas*, 48; Loisy, *Les Évangiles synoptiques*, 1:296.

4. Cf. the thorough text-critical note from Tischendorf on Luke 1:46. On the question of who spoke the psalm and its character, there is a fairly extensive disagreement in the literature on Catholic and Protestant sides. Cf. esp. Harnack, "Das Magnificat der Elisabet." He regards only καὶ εἶπεν in v. 46 as original, Μαριάμ as false, and Ἐλεισάβετ as a gloss. On the other side, cf. Spitta, "Das Magnificat."

character of the verse, since in the New Testament that verb appears only once in the Pauline letters, the book of Hebrews, 2 Peter, the Gospel of Mark, and the Gospel of Matthew. But in Luke's historical books it appears thirty-three times (twenty-two in the Gospel, eleven in Acts). It is not clear whether the story about Mary anticipates the birth of the Baptist.

The narrative of the birth and circumcision of John the Baptist follows immediately (1:57–80): τῇ δὲ Ἐλεισάβετ ἐπλήσθη ὁ χρόνος τοῦ τεκεῖν. As in the preceding story, Zacharias' song of praise, the so-called "Benedictus" (εὐλογητός = benedictus), in vv. 67–79 can easily be lifted out, so that the report ends in v. 80 with the following remark: τὸ δὲ παιδίον ηὔξανεν καὶ ἐκραταιοῦτο πνεύματι καὶ ἦν ἐν ταῖς ἐρήμοις ἕως ἡμέρας ἀναδείξεως πρὸς τὸν Ἰσραήλ. We have here a transitional verse, as in 1:56, which Luke inserted in order to create a kind of chronological outline, and most of all to build a connection to the continuing story of the Baptist.

While the content of the poem is generally restrained (growth and strength in spirit), the positive statements—a) "in seclusion" and b) "until his appearance" are taken from traditional material (3:1ff).

The narrative of the birth of Jesus (2:1–20) begins, like 1:39, with a general indication of the time, ἐν ταῖς ἡμέραις ἐκείναις, but then fixes the date more precisely. Verses 1–5 form an introduction, the artistry of which rises well above even the smooth narration in v. 6ff. This introduction as it currently stands was produced by Luke, who wanted to link the birth of Jesus with the history of the Empire, to create something like synchronicity, as he did even more thoroughly in 3:1–2. When it comes to the two leading moments in the chronology, i.e., Davidic descent and the imperial tax assessment, the latter of which has long been recognized as a chronological and legal impossibility,[5] we can no longer tell how much of this is older tradition and how much has been shaped by Luke. But in v. 6 we stand at last on the secure footing of ancient tradition: ἐγένετο δὲ ἐν τῷ εἶναι αὐτοὺς ἐκεῖ ἐπλήσθησαν αἱ ἡμέραι τοῦ τεκεῖν αὐτήν. Totally unexpectedly, the manger comes into the story, although it is not stated that the birth takes place in a stable. It is also important to take note here (as in 1:5ff) of the difference between a proper literary report (2:4) and a naive folk-report, the prerequisite for which is the activity of those who hear it. The inconsistency that results may generally have its foundation in the fact that the manger narrative is deeply connected with the story of the shepherds, which only gradually grew into the birth story. Thus a seam appears to lie between v. 7 and v. 8.

---

5. Cf. J. Weiss, *Schriften*, 423ff, for a thorough excursus on the tax assessment by Quirinius.

Next comes 2:21, a brief report about *the circumcision of Jesus*: καὶ ὅτε ἐπλήσθησαν αἱ ἡμέραι ὀκτὼ τοῦ περιτεμεῖν αὐτόν, καὶ ἐκλήθη τὸ ὄνομα αὐτοῦ Ἰησοῦς, τὸ κληθὲν ὑπὸ τοῦ ἀγγέλου πρὸ τοῦ συλλημφθῆναι αὐτὸν ἐν τῇ κοιλίᾳ. These words are a fragmentary insertion, and we can doubt whether it connects with 2:1–20 or 2:22–39. It was characteristic to avoid saying that Jesus was circumcised; only syr^sin has the text: "he was circumcised and given his name." The bestowing of his name usually appears in place of the circumcision. We should reckon with the possibility that Luke himself created this transition. He does not typically introduce new material, and this brief report does not have the right color. It was in his authorial interest to get further information about Jesus' childhood. A story about the circumcision of a Jewish boy arose almost on its own.

The next story, about *the presentation of Jesus in the Temple* (2:22–38) begins with a detail that would be essential to a reader who knew the Law: καὶ ὅτε ἐπλήσθησαν αἱ ἡμέραι τοῦ καθαρισμοῦ αὐτῶν. It is remarkable here, however, only because both parents participate in the ritual purification, which according to the Law was required only of Mary. It appears that Luke was not correctly informed about such matters. The two following narratives about Simeon (v. 23–35) and Hannah (v. 36–38) stand together in parataxis, so we cannot be certain that they originally belonged together. The remark in 2:39 about the journey to Nazareth is, along with 1:56 and 1:80, another sequencing insertion by the evangelist: καὶ ὡς ἐτέλεσαν πάντα τὰ κατὰ τὸν νόμον τοῦ κυρίου, ἐπεστρέψαν (so ℵ* B; but ϛ ℵ^c A D L Γ Δ Λ read ὑπεστρέψαν, which is more frequent in Luke) εἰς τὴν Γαλιλαίαν εἰς πόλιν ἑαυτῶν Ναζαρέθ. The remark about Jesus' growth (2:40) is also a literary embellishment: τὸ δὲ παιδίον ηὔξανεν καὶ ἐκραταιοῦτο πληρούμενον σοφίας, καὶ χάρις θεοῦ ἦν ἐπ' αὐτό. This verse is supposed to fill in the gap of his first twelve years. On that basis it is doubtful that Luke's use of the word necessarily connects with what precedes or follows. Transitional remarks of this sort can serve as both conclusions and introductions.[6]

Next comes the only narrative from the childhood of Jesus, the story of *twelve-year old Jesus in the Temple* (2:41–51). Perhaps it originally began with v. 42, which is a fairly good example of a pericope introduction. Verse 41 offers nothing new, but only adds to the story a certain amount of narrative breadth. It was inserted by Luke. The return to Nazareth (2:51) generally repeats 2:39. The statements that Jesus was subject to his parents, and that Mary kept every word her son spoke in her heart, have no specific content

---

6. It makes no sense to burden Luke 2:40 with detailed explications and remarks on the question of the development of Jesus. For this verse is not an old tradition, but simply a transitional remark on the part of the author, who paid less attention to its content than to that fact that it built a bridge over those twelve years.

and, more than likely than not, contain no actual tradition. Their purpose is to say as little as possible about the youth of Jesus, about which there was no other tradition. That goes as well for the remark that concludes the story of Jesus' childhood in Luke 2:52 and for the other reference to Jesus' growth in 2:41. They differ in only a few details.[7]

Summary: Matthew 1–2 and Luke 1–2

When we summarize the designations of place and time in Luke's history of Jesus' childhood, two observations become clear: 1) Luke created a smooth and continuous narrative; and 2) the way in which the childhood history of Jesus is interwoven with that of the Baptist shows the authorial touch of the evangelist:

a) announcement;

   aa) of the Baptist;

   bb) of Jesus;

b) the meeting of the mothers;

c) birth and circumcision;

   aa) of the Baptist;

   bb) of Jesus;

d) twelve-year-old Jesus in the Temple.

The meeting of their mothers is the essential link in the entire structure. This observation evacuates the force of all the chronological details in the narrative. They are basically nothing but clamps inserted at the appropriate places to hold a structure together. What is original here are the individual narratives, as they were narrated in certain Jewish-Christian circles. No value was placed upon their chronology and topography. When locations were named, knowledge of them was taken for granted. Later, an author arranged these individual pericopes into a series, changing the introductions of the pericopes in various ways and inserting whole verses in between them.

---

7. Also here an authorial statement from Luke's pen can be interrogated with regard to its content. Orthodox Christians both ancient and modern have felt it necessary to try to answer the difficult question of how Jesus could have "increased in wisdom." Cf. the critique of B. Weiss, *Markus und Lukas*, 319. There is material here that is of great interest to the history of dogma; cf. Pölzl, *Lukas*, 90. The fathers of the ancient church and modern Catholic dogmaticians are going to have to reinterpret the concept of σοφία.

Most of all, it is evident that nothing holds the overall chronology together, and we could never create it ourselves out of the individual narratives. The single datum point is that the story played out during the reign of Herod the Great (cf. 1:5). We find that the only specific temporal indicator within the entire story is the six (6) months that separate the two announcements of the births of the Baptist and Jesus (cf. 1:26, 56). It is not for us to decide who put the narratives into this chronology, which has become so important to the Christian calendar (mid-summer and Christmas). We are looking at a religious and sacred arrangement in time, according to which John was born at the summer solstice (the light turns out), and Jesus was born at the winter solstice (the light turns on). It is even possible that the original narratives were interpreted this way. The ones who arranged these stories may have found them and used them to put events into a sequence. On the other hand, the schematic chronology may have been created. The first two chapters of Luke appear to be more chronological than they actually are. Certainly what Luke has accomplished as an author shows both foresight and prudence: he did not put a final seal on things, but deftly presented what could be recovered from the stories themselves.

Matthew, by contrast, refused to write a biographical narrative. Each evangelist had their own respective literary interests. To be more precise, Matthew had no literary interest at all, since he obviously was more concerned with how individual stories could be used in worship. Luke had much more in mind. It was precisely in the childhood stories of Jesus, where he was not working with a Markan predecessor, that Luke could let his literary personality work to its full effect. But that is also the case in the later parts of the Gospel as well.

The Prologue: Luke 1:1–4

The entire Gospel of Luke betrays its author's effort to arrange an assortment of experiences into a better series, and to develop the psychology of those experiences more clearly. The words ἔδοξε καμοί in the prologue show that this evangelist is possessed of an author's consciousness. He tells us the direction in which he wants to proceed: παρηκολουθηκότι ἄνωθεν πᾶσιν ἀκριβῶς καθεξῆς γράψαι, "to follow everything closely from the beginning and to record the sequence of events." It sounds as if Luke has produced a profound work of scholarship. Based on what we know of this accomplishment, however, that possibility cannot even come up for discussion. Luke speaks here in the dedication of the work to his aristocratic friend Theophilus, who is, in my judgment, quite inflated and exaggerated. When we get a look at what he has actually written, it does not (with the exception of the special source that Matthew also used) even approach a sketch of the story of Jesus, more valuable than the Gospel of Mark. In the prologue it seems as if the author is offering us something special with his precise arrangement of events. But now that we have been checked his work step by step, he has not been able, on the basis of any special tradition that is better than Mark, to introduce any new chronological or topographical facts into the story of Jesus. His effort to construct a better context, to change Mark's outline, relied on psychology and logic. No profound scholarly ability was required, just a certain sort of educated literary taste. Luke was not a scholar or researcher, studying remote and unknown Gospel sources; he was just a smooth writer who, in the absence of real sources about the Synoptic material, confined himself to what was already known and presented it carefully grouped and arranged.[8]

---

8. In my judgment, the widely-held positive view of the quality of Luke's work and research requires thorough revision and correction.

Conclusion
The Framework of the Story of Jesus in Mark, Matthew, and Luke

The oldest outline of the story of Jesus is the one in the Gospel of Mark. The unevenness of the tradition available to him shows us what the earliest Jesus tradition looked like: not a running narrative, but an abundance of individual stories, arranged basically on the basis of content. These stories were not always readily clear, for they were tied into the history of early Christianity, with all of its various religious, apologetic, and missionary interests. Luke initiated the process, as he is the only evangelist who had any literary aspirations, but he misjudged the peculiarity of the gospel tradition, which rounded off the pericopes, shaping them above all for use in worship. Certainly the early church selected the Gospel of Matthew as its favorite, because that Gospel (moreso than Mark) groups the individual stories together, discarding much of the superfluous framework. In Mark, where the separate pericopes are basically just lined up one after another, the stories still include too many unproductive details, but within the introductions to the pericopes lie the ruins and rubble of an itinerary. Luke was mindful of such things and tried to revive them, sometimes by reduction, sometimes by expansion. Matthew, by contrast, regarded all of that as secondary. Thus the actual itinerary of Jesus, in which the Christian community at its beginning had no interest, is now irretrievably lost and gone. If we want to arrange the stories of Jesus, we will have to engage with Matthew, who usually clings too closely to Mark, and in fact we will have to outdo him. The stories of Jesus all lie, for the most part, on the same level. Only here and there will we be able, on the basis of the internal characteristics of a story, to determine somewhat precisely its time and place. On the whole, however, there is no life of Jesus in the sense of an unfolding life story, nor is there any chronological outline for the story of Jesus. There are only individual stories and pericopes that have been set into a framework.

Bibliography

Bauer, Walter. *Die Evangelien. II, Johannes.* HNT 2/2. Tübingen: Mohr/Siebeck, 1912.
Bebber, Johann van. *Zur Chronologie des Lebens Jesu: Eine exegetische Studie.* Münster: Schöningh, 1898.
———. "Zur Frage nach der Dauer des öffentlichen Lehramts Jesu." *Katholik* 1 (1989) 205–22.
———. "Zur neuesten Datierung des Karfreitags." *BZ* 2 (1904) 67–77.
———. "Zur Berechnung der 70 Wochen Daniels." *BZ* 4 (1906) 119–41.
Belser, Johannes Evang. *Abriss des Lebens Jesu: Von der Taufe bis zum Tod.* Freiburg: Herder, 1916.
——— "Zur Hypothese von der einjährigen Wirksamkeit Jesu." *BZ* 1 (1903) 55–63; 160–74.
——— "Der Prolog des Johannesevangeliums." *ThQ* 85 (1903) 485–519.
——— "Zu Lukas 4,23." *ThQ* 89 (1907) 365–73.
——— "Das Johannesevangelium und seine neueste Beurteilung." *ThQ* 93 (1911) 404–49; 569–614.
———. "Zur Evangelienfrage." *ThQ* 95 (1913) 323–76.
——— "Zur Abfolge der evangelischen Geschichte." *ThQ* 96 (1914) 1–49.
——— "Zu Markus 3,20-21." *ThQ* 98 (1916) 401–18.
———. Review of J. M. Pfättisch, *Die Dauer der Lehrtätigkeit Jesu nach dem Evangelium des hl. Johannes. ThQ* 93 (1911) 623–25.
Bernoulli, Carl Albrecht. "Nachlass." In Franz Overbeck, *Das Johannesevangelium: Studien zur Kritik seiner Erforschung,* 527ff. Tübingen: Mohr/Siebeck, 1911.
Beyschlag, Willibald. *Das Leben Jesu.* 2 vols. Halle: Strien, 1893.
Blass, Friedrich. *Grammatik des neutestamentlichen Griechisch.* 2nd ed. Göttingen: Vandenhoeck & Ruprecht, 1902.
———. "Textkritische Bemerkungen zu Markus." *Beiträge zur Förderung christlicher Theologie* 3 (1899) 50–93.
Boehmer, Julius. "Die chronologische und geographische Rahmen des Lebenganges Jesu." *ZWT* 52 (1910) 121–47.
Brückner, Martin. *Das fünfte Evangelium (Das Heilige Land).* Religionsgeschichtliche Volksbücher für die deutsche christliche Gegenwart 1/21. Tübingen: Mohr/Siebeck, 1910.
Christ, Hermann. "Nochmals die Lilie der Bibel." *ZDPV* 22 (1899) 65–80.

Chwolson, Daniel A. *Das letzte Passahmahl Christi und der Tag seines Todes nach den in Uebereinstimmung gebrachten Berichten der Synoptiker und des Evangelium Johannis*. St. Petersburg: Eggers, 1908.

Dausch, Petrus. "Bedenken gegen die Hypothese von der bloss einjährigen öffentliche Wirksamkeit Jesu." *BZ* 4 (1906) 49–60.

———. "Neue Studien über die Dauer der öffentlichen Wirksamkeit Jesu." *BZ* 12 (1914) 158–67.

Deissmann, Adolf. *Paulus: Eine Kultur und religionsgeschichtliche Skizze*. Tübingen: Mohr/Siebeck, 1906.

———. *St. Paul: A Study in Social and Religious History*. 1912. Reprint, Eugene, OR: Wipf & Stock, 2004.

Dibelius, Martin. "Herodes und Pilatus." *ZNW* 16 (1915) 113–26.

———. *Die urchristliche Überlieferung von Johannes dem Täufer*. FRLANT 15. Göttingen: Vandenhoeck & Ruprecht, 1911.

Dobschütz, Ernst von. *Das Kerygma Petri kritisch untersucht*. TUGAL 11/1. Leipzig: Hinrichs, 1893.

Drews, Arthur. *Die Christusmythe*. 2 vols. Jena: Diederichs, 1909, 1911.

Eissfeldt, Otto. *Der Maschal im Alten Testament: eine wortgeschichtliche Untersuchung nebst einer literargeschichtlichen Untersuchung der mashal genannten Gattungen "Volkssprichwort" und "Spottlied."* BZAW 24. Giessen: Töpelmann, 1913.

Fendt, Leonhard. *Die Dauer der öffentlichen Wirksamkeit Jesu*. Veröffentlichungen aus dem Kirchenhistorischen Seminar München 2/9. Munich: Lentner, 1906.

Furrer, Konrad. "Nochmals Gerasa am See Genezareth." *ZDPV* 22 (1899) 184–85.

Harnack, Adolf. *The Acts of the Apostle*. Translated by J. R. Wilkinson. 1909. Reprint, Eugene, OR: Wipf & Stock, 2000.

———. *Die Apostelgeschichte*. Beiträge zur Einleitung in das Neue Testament 3. Leipzig: Hinrichs, 1908.

———. "Das Magnificat der Elisabet (Luc. 1,46–55) nebst einigen Bemerkungen zu Luc. 1 and 2." *Sitzungsberichte der Berliner Akademie der Wissenschaften* 27 (1900) 538–56.

———. *The Mission and Expansion of the Church in the First Three Centuries*. Translated by James Moffatt. 1972. Reprint, Eugene, OR: Wipf & Stock, 1997.

———. *Die Mission und Ausbreitung des Christentums in den ersten drei Jahrhunderten*. 2nd ed. Leipzig: Hinrichs, 1906.

———. *Sprüche und Reden Jesu: Die Zweite Quelle des Matthäus und Lukas*. Beiträge zur Einleitung in das Neue Testament 2. Leipzig: Hinrichs, 1907.

Hartmann, G. "Mark 3, 20f." *BZ* 11 (1913) 249–79.

Haupt, Walther. *Wörte Jesu und Gemeindeüberlieferung: Eine Untersuchungen zur Quellensgeschichte der Synopse*. Untersuchungen zum Neuen Testament 3. Leipzig: Hinrichs, 1913.

Heinisch, Paul. "Clement von Alexandria und die einjährige Lehrtätigkeit des Herrn." *BZ* 4 (1906) 402–7.

Heitmüller, Wilhelm. *Jesus*. Tübingen: Mohr/Siebeck, 1913.

Hennecke, Edgar. *Neutestamentliche Apokryphen*. 1st ed. Tübingen: Mohr/Siebeck, 1904.

Hoffmann, Richard Adolf. *Das Marcusevangelium und seine Quellen: Ein Beitrag zur Lösung der Urmarcusfrage*. Königsberg: Thomas & Oppermann, 1904.

Holtzmann, Heinrich Julius. *Die synoptischen Evangelien: Ihr Ursprung und geschichtlicher Charakter*. Leipzig: Engelmann, 1863.

———. *Die Synoptiker. Die Apostelgeschichte*. HNT 1. 2nd ed. Freiburg: Mohr/Siebeck, 1892.

Homanner, Wilhelm. *Die Dauer der öffentlichen Wirksamkeit Jesu: Eine patristisch-exegetische Studie*. BibSt 13/3. Frieburg: Herder, 1908.

Huck, Albert. *Huck's Synopsis of the First Three Gospels*. Edited by Ross L. Finney. Cincinnati: Jennings & Graham, 1907.

Jordan, Hermann. *Geschichte der altchristlichen Literatur*. Leipzig: Quelle & Meyer, 1911.

Keim, Theodor. *Die Geschichte Jesu von Nazara in ihrer Verkettung mit dem Gesammtleben seines Volkes, frei untersucht und ausführlich erzählt*. 3 vols. Zurich: Orell, Füssli, 1867–1872.

Klostermann, Erich. *Die Evangelien. 2: Markus*. 1st ed. HNT 3. Tübingen: Mohr/Siebeck, 1907.

———. *Die Evangelien. 1: Matthäus*. 1st ed. HNT 2. Tübingen: Mohr/Siebeck, 1906.

Klug, Hubert. "Die Dauer der öffentlichen Wirksamkeit Jesu nach Daniel und Lukas." *BZ* 3 (1905) 263–68.

———. "Das Osterfest nach Jo 6, 4." *BZ* 3 (1906) 152–63.

Lagrange, Marie-Joseph. *Évangile selon Saint Marc*. Etudes bibliques. Paris: Lecoffre, 1911.

Lietzmann, Hans. *Die Vier Hauptbriefe*. HNT. Tübingen: Mohr/Siebeck, 1910.

Loofs, Friedrich. *Wer war Jesus Christus? Für Theologen und den weiteren Kreis gebildeter Christen*. Halle: Niemeyer, 1916.

———. *What Is the Truth about Jesus Christ? Problems of Christology Discussed in Six Haskell Lectures*. New York: Scribner, 1913.

Loisy, Alfred. *L'evangile selon Marc*. Paris: Nourry, 1912.

———. *Les Évangiles synoptiques*. Vol. 1. Ceffonds: Loisy, 1907.

Loofs, Friedrich. *Wer war Jesus Christus? Für Theologen und den weiteren Kreis gebildeter Christen*. Halle: Niemeyer, 1916.

Meinertz, Max. "Methodisches und Sachliches über die Dauer der öffentlichen Wirksam-keit Jesu." *BZ* 14 (1916) 119–39.

———. "Methodisches und Sachliches über die Dauer der öffentlichen Wirksamkeit Jesu." *BZ* 14 (1917) 236–49.

Merx, Adalbert. *Erläuterung: Matthäus*. Die vier kanonischen Evangelien nach ihrem ältesten bekannten Texte II/1. Berlin: Reimer, 1902.

———. *Die Evangelien des Markus und Lukas nach der Syrischen im Sinaikloster gefundenen Palimpsesthandschrift*. Die vier kanonischen Evangelien nach ihrem ältesten bekannten Texte II/2. Berlin: Reimer, 1905.

Meyer, Paul M. *Griechische Texte aus Ägypten*. Berlin: Weidmann, 1916.

Mommert, Carl. *Zur Chronologie des Lebens Jesu*. Leipzig: Haberland, 1909.

Mommsen, Theodor. *Die Römische Chronologie bis auf Cäsar*. 2nd ed. Berlin: Weidmann, 1859.

Moulton, J. H. *Einleitung in die Sprache des Neuen Testaments*. Heidelberg: Winter, 1911. A translation of *Introduction to the Study of New Testament Greek*. London: Culley, 1909.

Nagl, Erasmus. "Die Dauer der öffentlichen Wirksamkeit Jesu." *Katholik* (1900) 200–221; 318–35; 417–26; 481–95.

———. "Zur Dauer der öffentlichen Wirksamkeit Jesu." *BZ* 2 (1904) 373–76.
Nestle, Eberhard. "Chorazin, Bethsaida." *ZNW* 7 (1906) 185.
Nisius, Johann B. "Zur Kontroverse über die Dauer der öffentlichen Wirksamkeit Jesu." *ZKT* 37 (1913) 457–503.
Overbeck, Franz. *Das Johannesevangelium: Studien zur Kritik seiner Erforschung*. Tübingen: Mohr/Siebeck, 1911.
Pesch, Christian. "Über Evangelienharmonien." *ZKT* 10 (1886) 225–44.
Pfättisch, Ioannes Maria. *Die Dauer der Lehrtätigkeit Jesu nach dem Evangelium des hl. Johannes*. BibSt. Freiburg: Herder, 1911.
Plath, Margarete. "Die neutestamentlichen Weherufe über Jerusalem." *Theologische Studien und Kritiken* 78 (1095) 455–56.
Pölzl, Franz X. *Kurzgefasster Commentar zum Evangelium des heligen Marcus: Mit Ausschluss der Leidensgeschichte*. Kurzgefasster Commentar zu den vier heiligen Evangelien 2. Graz: Styria, 1893.
———. *Kurzgefasster Commentar zum Evangelium des heligen Lukas*. Kurzgefasster Commentar zu den vier heiligen Evangelien 3. 2nd ed. Graz: Styria, 1912.
Prat, F. "La date de la passion et de la durée de la vie publique de Jésus Christ." *Recherches de sciences religieuses* 3 (1912) 82–92.
Preuschen, Erwin. *Antilegomena: Die Reste der ausserkanonischen Evangelien und urchristlichen Überlieferungen*. 2nd ed. Giessen: Töpelmann, 1905.
Rauch, Christoph. "Bemerkungen zum Markustexte." *ZNW* 3 (1902) 300–314.
Resch, Alfred. *Agrapha: Aussercanonische Evangelienfragmente*. TUGAL 30. Leipzig: Hinrichs, 1889.
Schlatter, Adolf. *Die Evangelien des Markus und Lukas: Ausgelegt für Bibelleser*. Erläuterungen zum Neuen Testament 7. Stuttgart: Vereinsbuchhandlung, 1900.
Schmiedel, Otto B. *Hauptprobleme der Leben-Jesu-Forshung*. 2nd ed. Tübingen: Mohr/Siebeck, 1906.
Schmidt, Carl. *Gnostische Schriften in koptischer Sprache aus dem Codex Brucianus*. TUGAL 8. Leipzig: Hinrichs, 1892.
Schmidt, Karl Ludwig. "Contributions and Comments." *Expository Times* 20 (1909) 230, 428.
Schubert, Franz. "Das Jahr der Taufe Jesu bei Tertullian." *BZ* 3 (1905) 177–79.
———. "Das Zeugnis des Irenaeus über die öffentliche Tätigkeit Jesu." *BZ* 4 (1906) 39–48.
Schürer, Emil. *Geschichte des jüdische Volkes im Zeitalter Jesus Christi*. 3rd ed. Leipzig: Hinrichs, 1898.
———. *History of the Jewish People in the Time of Jesus Christ*. Translated by John Macpherson et al. Clark's Foreign Theological Library 25. Edinburgh: T. & T. Clark, 1898–1910.
———. "Die siebentägige Woche im Gebrauche der christlichen Kirche der ersten Jahrhundert." *ZNW* 6 (1905) 1–66.
Schwartz, Eduard. "Der verfluchte Feigenbaum." *ZNW* 5 (1904) 80–84.
Smith, William Benjamin. *Der vorchristliche Jesus: Nebst weiteren Vorstudien zur Entstehungsgeschichte des Urchristentums*. Giessen: Töpelmann, 1906.

Soden, Hermann von. "Das Interesse des apostolischen Zeitalters an der evangelischen Geschichte." In *Theologische Abhandlungen: Carl von Weizsäcker zu seinem siebzigsten Geburtstage, 11. December 1892*, edited by Adolf Harnack, 111–69. Freiburg: Mohr/Siebeck, 1892.
Spitta, Friedrich. *Jesus und die Heidenmission*. Giessen: Töpelmann, 1909.
———. "Das Magnificat: Ein Psalm der Maria und nicht der Elisabeth." *Theologische Abhandlungen: Eine Festgabe zum 17. Mai 1902 für Heinrich Julius Holtzmann (17 Mai 1902) für Heinrich Julius Holtzmann*, edited by W. Nowack et al., 63–94. Tübingen: Mohr/Siebeck, 1902.
———. *Die synoptische Grundschrift in ihrer Überlieferung durch das Lukasevangelium*. Untersuchungen zum Neuen Testament 1. Leipzig: Hinrichs, 1912.
Strack, Hermann L. "Briefliche Mitteilung an J. Belser." *BZ* 1 (1903) 59.
Strauss, David Friedrich. *Das Leben Jesu*. 2 vols. 3rd ed. Tübingen: Osiander, 1838–1839.
———. *The Life of Jesus, Critically Examined*. Edited by Peter Hodgson. Translated by George Eliot. Lives of Jesus Series. Philadelphia: Fortress, 1972.
Swete, Henry Barclay. *The Gospel according to St. Mark*. 1st ed. London: Macmillan, 1898.
———. *The Old Testament in Greek according to the Septuagint*. Vol. 3. Cambridge: Cambridge University Press, 1905.
Tischendorf, C., ed. *Novum Testamentum Graece. Editio Octava Critica Maior*. Leipzig: Giesecke & Devrient, 1869.
Vogels, Heinrich Joseph. *St Augustins Schrift De Consensu Evangelistarum*. BibSt 13/5. Freiburg: Herder, 1908.
Warneck, Johannes. *Die Lebenskräfte des Evangeliums: Missionserfahrungen innerhalb des animistischen Heidentums*. 2nd ed. 1906. Reprint, Veröffentlichungen der Freien Hochschule für Mission der Arbeitsgemeinschaft Evangelikaler Missionen D/1. Bad Liebenzeller: Verlag der Liebenzeller Mission, 1986.
Weiss, Bernhard. *Jesus von Nazaret: Ein Lebensbild*. Berlin: Curius, 1913.
———. *Kritisch-exegetisches Handbuch über die Evangelien des Markus und Lukas*. Kritisch-exegetischer Kommentar uber das Neue Testament. Göttingen: Vandenhoeck & Ruprecht, 1901.
Weiss, Johannes. *Das älteste Evangelium: Ein Beitrag zum Verstandnis des Markus-Evangeliums und der Ältesten Evangelischen Überlieferung*. Göttingen: Vandenhoeck & Ruprecht, 1903.
———. *Die Schriften des Neuen Testaments*. 2 vols. 2nd ed. Göttingen: Vandenhoeck & Ruprecht, 1907–1908.
———. "Synoptische Evangelien." *ThRu* 16 (1913) 183–96.
Wellhausen, Julius. *Einleitung in die drei ersten Evangelien*. Berlin: Reimer, 1905.
———. *Das Evangelium Marci*. Berlin: Reimer, 1903.
———. *Das Evangelium Matthäi*. Berlin: Reimer, 1904.
———. *Das Evangelium Lucae*. Berlin: Reimer, 1904.
Wendling, Emil. *Die Entstehung des Marcusevangelium: Philologische Untersuchungen*. Tübingen: Mohr/Siebeck, 1908.
———. *Ur-Marcus: Versuch einer Wiederherstellung der ältesten Mitteilungen über das Leben Jesu*. Tübingen: Mohr/Siebeck, 1905.
Wendt, Hans Hinrich. *Die Lehre Jesu*. Göttingen: Vandenhoeck & Ruprecht, 1890.

Wernle, Paul. *Die Quellen des Lebens Jesu.* Religionsgeschichtliche Volksbücher für die deutsche christliche Gegenwart 1/1. Tübingen: Mohr/Siebeck, 1906.

———. *The Sources of Our Knowledge of the Life of Jesus.* Translated by Edward Lummis. Boston: American Unitarian Association, 1907.

Westberg, Friedrich. *Die biblische Chronologie nach Flavius Josephus und das Todesjahr Jesu.* Leipzig: Deichert/Böhme, 1900.

Wilcken, Ulrich. *Zum alexandrinsichen Antisemitismus.* Abhandlungen der Königlichen Sächsischen Gesellschaft der Wissenschaften, Phil.-hist. Kl. 23. Leipzig: Teubner, 1909.

Windisch, Hans. "Die Dauer der öffentliche Wirksamkeit Jesu nach den vier Evangelisten." *ZNW* 12 (1911) 141–75.

———. "Lehre und Leben Jesu." *ThRu* 12 (1909) 145–62; 171–83.

Wohlenberg, G. *Das Evangelium des Markus.* 2nd ed. KNT 2. Leipzig: Deichert, 1910.

Wrede, William. *Messiasgeheimnis in den Evangelien: Zugleich ein Beitrag zum Verständnis des Markusevangeliums.* Göttingen: Vandenhoeck & Ruprecht, 1901.

———. *The Messianic Secret.* Translated by J. C. Grieg. Library of Theological Translations. Cambridge: James Clarke, 1971.

Zahn, Theodor. "Brüder und Vettern Jesu." In *Forschungen zur Geschichte des neutestamentlichen Kanons und der altkirchlichen Literatur,* 6:225–26. Erlangen: Deichert, 1900.

———. *Einleitung in das Neue Testament.* 2 vols. 3rd ed. Leipzig: Deichert, 1906–1907.

———. *Das Evangelium des Lucas ausgelegt.* KNT 3. Leipzig: Deichert, 1913.

———. *Das Evangelium Matthäus.* KNT 1. 2nd ed. Leipzig: Deichert, 1905.

———. *Geschichte des neutestamentlichen Kanons.* Vol. 2/2. Erlangen: Deichert, 1892.

———. "Das Land der Gadarener, Gerasener, Gergasener." *Neue kirchliche Zeitschrift* 13 (1902) 923–45.

Zellinger, Johannes. *Die Dauer der öffentlichen Wirksamkeit Jesu.* Münster: Aschendorff, 1907.

Zorell, Franz. "Zu Mark 3, 20, 21." *ZKT* 37 (1913) 695–97.

Authors Index

Augustine, 3, 7–9, 53n31, 168n18

Baur, Ferdinand C., 252n27
Bebber, Johann von, 3–5
Belser, Johannes, xxv, 4–5, 11, 72n9, 75n14, 84n28, 84n30, 88n38, 91n40, 180n44, 251n26
Bernoulli, Carl Albrecht, 162n8
Blass, Friedrich, 73n11, 84n29, 148n86
Boehmer, Julius, 10
Brückner, Martin, 35, 129n50, 277n22, 288n1

Christ, Hermann, 61n47
Chwolson, Daniel A., 84n28

Dausch, Petrus, 4, 84n28
Deissmann, Adolf, xxiii, xiv, 86n34, 106n19, 237n1
Dibelius, Martin, xv, xix, 14n30, 162n8, 282n1, 285n5
Dobschütz, Ernst von, 1n1, 85n33
Drews, Arthur, 144n75, 196n69

Eissfeldt, Otto, xxv, 121
Epiphanius, 18, 37
Eusebius, 2, 168

Fendt, Leonhard, 4–5, 7, 84n28
Furrer, Konrad, 129n50

Gerson, Johannes, 8–9

Harnack, Adolf, 53n31, 153n97, 252, 288n4, 296
Hartmann, G., 110n24
Haupt, Walther, 13n26
Heinisch, Paul, 5
Heitmüller, Wilhelm, 12, 270
Hennecke, Edgar, 141n71, 224n37
Hoffmann, Richard Adolf, 198n71, 207n9
Holtzmann, Heinrich J., 11–12, 78n19, 251n27, 252, 270n17
Homanner, Wilhelm, 4–5, 59n44, 105n15, 176n32
Huck, Albert, 145n79, 147n83, 147n84, 235, 237, 256, 268n14

Irenaeus, 1–2, 48

Jerome, 2, 8, 53, 71, 168–169, 218
Josephus, 10, 18, 89, 96n2, 107, 110, 144, 161, 169, 214, 244n16

Keim, Theodor, 12, 252n27
Klostermann, Erich, 13, 45n16, 88n38, 89n39, 97n4, 111n26, 120n33, 129n49, 130n53, 135n59, 140n69, 142n72, 150n93, 155n99, 161n5, 162n9, 170n21, 172n25, 180n42, 188n57, 207n9, 210n18, 215n26, 218n29, 251n26, 251n27, 266n11, 277n22
Klug, Hubert, 4–5

Lagrange, Marie-Joseph, 54n35, 70n3
Lietzmann, Hans, 252n27
Loisy, Alfred, 13, 39n2, 46n17, 55n37,
    64n51, 65n52, 70n3, 71n6,
    73n10, 76n17, 81n26, 87n35,
    97n4, 99n10, 101n13, 111n26,
    139n66, 140n69, 145n79,
    149n88, 161n7, 175n30, 188n57,
    220n31, 245n17, 247n19,
    256n1,2; 288n3
Loofs, Friedrich, 12n23, 14n29
Luther, Martin, xiv, 70n3, 79, 98, 133

Merx, Adalbert, xxiii, 35, 39–40, 44–45,
    47n19, 52n27, 53n33, 72n8, 78,
    103, 105n17, 120n32, 127n47,
    128n48, 129n50, 134n58,
    139n67, 142n72, 144n77,
    147n82, 148, 158, 162n9,
    168n19, 172, 173n26, 193n64,
    210n17, 214, 221n32, 237n1,
    238n2, 252, 257n5, 274n19
Meyer, H. A. W., 98n7
Meyer, Paul M., 25n1, 39n1, 214n24
Mommert, Carl, 4–5
Mommsen, Theodor, 207n10
Moulton, James H., 80n23, 85n32,
    237n1, 240n8

Nagl, Erasmus, 4, 6
Nestle, Eberhart, 52, 84, 103n14, 109,
    129n50, 145n79, 147n83,
    147n84, 195, 196n70
Nisius, Johann B., 4

Origen, 2–3, 5, 129, 189, 213, 224, 273
Overbeck, Franz, 162n8

Pesch, Christian, 9
Pfättisch, Joannes Maria, 4–5
Plath, Margarete, 252n27
Pölzl, Franz X., 35, 105n15, 110n24,
    129n50, 141n71, 142n72,
    145n79, 146n81, 161n6, 168n17,
    208n13, 242n13, 244n16,
    250n25, 251n26, 269n16, 288n3,
    291n7
Prat, F., 4

Preuschen, Erwin, 85n33, 218n29,
    224n37

Rauch, Christoph, 51n26
Reuch, Alfred, 1n2

Schlatter, Adolf, 84n30
Schmidt, Carl, 1n2
Schmidt, Karl Ludwig, xiii–xx, 85n32
Schmiedel, Otto B., 29n51
Schubert, Franz, 4
Schürer, Emil, 50n23, 96n2, 207n10,
    214n24
Schwartz, Eduard, 277n22
Smith, William Benjamin, 144n76
Soden, Hermann von, 32, 52, 84, 109,
    145n79, 147n83, 178n39, 210
Spitta, Friedrich, 13, 14, 40, 45, 46n18,
    48n20, 49n21, 50n25, 52n27,
    52n28, 53n30, 53n31 53n32,
    53n33, 55n37, 58n43, 61n46,
    65n53, 68, 72n8, 79n22, 84n30,
    85n31, 92n41, 101n11, 105n17,
    106n19, 110n24, 114n27,
    118n29, 119n31, 123n42,
    124n43, 130n53, 131n54,
    135n60, 136n61, 139n67,
    143n73, 145n78–79, 150n92,
    177n37, 183n48, 198n71, 201n3,
    206n8, 208n12, 210n16, 213n23,
    222n34, 224n38–39, 249n24,
    256n1, 257n5, 264n9, 265n10,
    271n17, 272n18, 276n20,
    276n21, 288n4
Strack, Hermann L., 84n30
Swete, Henry Barclay, 98n7, 110n22

Tischendorf, Constantin von, 32, 43n10,
    46, 52, 74, 84, 86n34, 109, 113,
    128, 132, 145n79, 147n83,
    168n17&18, 212–13, 237n1,
    255, 258n5, 273, 288n4

Vogels, Heinrich Joseph, 8

Warneck, Johannes, 129n51
Weiss, Bernhard, 39, 41, 47, 48n20,
    50n24, 52, 54n34, 57n42, 69n1,

73n11, 74n12, 75n15, 76n17,
77n18, 78n19, 78n20, 84,
88n38, 98n7, 101n11, 133n56,
145n79, 152n95&96, 159n1,
161n7, 172n25, 178n38, 183n46,
198n71, 199n1, 210n18, 237n1,
242n13, 249n24, 265n10,
268n14, 275n20, 277n22, 288n2,
291n7

Weiss, Johannes, xxiv, 12–14, 29, 36,
42n9, 43n11, 43n13, 51n26,
54n35, 57n41, 58n43, 70n4,
73n11, 78n21, 99n8, 99n10,
111n26, 125n45, 129n50,
130n52, 137n62, 146n80,
147n83, 149n88, 159n3, 162n9,
163n12, 172n25, 175n30,
176n34, 179n40, 180n43,
184n50, 186n53, 188n57,
192n63, 198n71, 199n1, 200n2,
204n5, 205n7, 251n27, 256n2,
269, 272n18, 278n23, 284n4,
289n5

Wellhausen, Julius, xxii, 13–14, 52n27,
54n35, 55n38, 57n42, 60n45, 63,
64n51, 70n3, 71n5, 71n7, 72n8,
73n10, 76n17, 78n21, 80n24,
84n30, 97n4, 99n8, 99n10,
106n18, 111n26, 116, 120n32,
125n45, 126n46, 130n52,
140n69, 143n73, 145n79,
149n90, 150n91, 155n99, 159n2,
160n4, 162n9,10, 172n25,
174n29, 176n33, 176n34,
178n39, 180n42, 185n51,
188n57, 192n63, 194n65,
198n71, 210n18, 220n31,
223n35, 243n14, 245n17,
251n27, 254, 256n1, 256n2,
257n3, 257n4, 268n8, 267n13,
269n16, 280n26, 284n4

Wendling, Emil, xxii, xxiv, 13, 14,
42n9, 51n29, 57n41, 74, 75n16,
78n21, 95n1, 97n4, 99n8,
99n10, 111n25, 111n26, 120n36,
121n39, 137n62, 138n63,
143n73, 144n76, 145n79,
149n88, 159n2, 159n3, 172n24,
173n28, 175n53, 176n34,
177n36, 178n39, 179n41,
180n43, 180n45, 183n49,
188n56, 188n57, 190n58,
192n63, 203n4, 204n5, 205n6,
205n7, 208n12, 208n14, 209n15,
211n19, 213n22, 217n28,
219n30, 220n31, 222n33,
223n36, 226n40, 261n6, 269n16,
276n21

Wendt, Hans Hinrich, 120n35, 269n16
Wernle, Paul, 12n25
Westberg, Friedrich, 10, 86n33
Wilcken, Ulrich, 283n2
Windisch, Hans, 10, 11, 41, 58n44,
66n54, 78n21, 80n25, 88n38,
110n21, 139n65, 176n32,
176n33, 214n25, 226n41,
243n15, 247n19

Wohlenberg, Gustav, 41, 42, 43n13,
47n19, 50n22, 50n24, 54n34,
55n36, 56n39, 57n42, 58n44,
69n1, 73n11, 74n12, 76n17,
77n18, 82n27, 84n30, 88n38,
98n7, 110n21, 116n28, 121n37,
125n44, 128n48, 129n50,
129n51, 133n56, 138n63,
140n68, 142n72, 145n79,
146n51, 148n85, 149n87,
149n88, 156n100, 159n1,
163n11, 170n21, 170n22,
174n29, 183n46, 187n54,
191n61, 210n18, 212n20,
220n31, 222n34, 268n14,
269n15, 270n17

Wrede, William, xxii, xxiii, 57n41, 95n1,
99n8, 121, 183n49, 188n57,
203n4, 208n14, 211n19, 213n22

Zahn, Theodor, 3n10, 25, 47, 47n19,
52n27, 67n52, 66n54, 81n26,
84n30, 89n39, 114, 129n50,
142n72, 170n21, 270n17
Zellinger, Johannes, 4–5, 7, 84n28
Zorell, Franz, 110n24

Subject Index

allegory, 195, 252n, 265
anecdote, 80–81, 92, 95, 269n16
Antipas (Herod), 30, 63, 89–90, 92,
    118, 155, 158–65, 174, 187,
    192, 194n65, 200, 244–46, 267,
    283–84
aphorism, 111
Archelaus, 30, 244

baptism, 16, 29, 107, 272 (*see also* Jesus,
    baptism)

caesura, 17, 19, 24–25, 28, 69, 152, 160,
    177, 177n36, 178, 225, 263, 277
calendar, 175–76, 207, 292
chronology, xxiii, xxiv, xxvi, 1–4, 6–7,
    9–11, 13, 18, 19, 25n1, 29,
    34–35, 37, 42, 44, 48, 55, 57–58,
    65–67, 71, 76, 79–82, 104,
    125n45, 126–27, 138–39, 146,
    161, 163, 165–166, 176–77, 192,
    206, 208, 214, 218, 224, 244,
    251n27, 253–254, 261, 270n17,
    272, 281, 289, 291–92
controversy story, 109–16, 182, 191,
    219–20, 260, 266–67, 270

doublet, 63, 108, 153, 159, 176, 178n39,
    183n49, 186n52, 188n57,
    192n63, 197–98, 213n22, 224

elders, 154, 201, 258, 271

Easter, 10, 80, 80n24, 82, 84, 84n28,
    84–85n30, 214, 246, 276–77

feasts and festivals, 1–3, 6, 10, 72n9,
    78n19, 82, 84n28, 84n30, 85,
    105n15, 108n20, 233, 249n24,
    258–59, 270
    New Year, 84n30
    Passover, 1, 3, 12, 80–82, 81n26,
        84n30, 176, 180n44, 214,
        249n24, 274n19, 279, 280n26,
        282, 285
    Pentecost, 10, 84, 84n30, 105n15
    Tabernacles, 6, 249
framework, 2, 7, 10–11, 14, 35–36, 42–
    43, 45–47, 52, 59, 62, 66–68, 77–
    78, 81, 83, 88, 93, 95, 102, 112,
    119, 123, 125, 125n45, 126, 130,
    132, 139, 142, 166, 176, 181,
    184, 192, 196, 200, 203, 213–15,
    217–19, 219n30, 220n31, 222,
    223n36, 229, 237n31, 238, 244,
    250, 251n27, 253–54, 263, 270,
    279, 281, 294

geography, 46, 131–32, 166, 172, 183,
    186, 189, 192, 199n1, 208,
    220n31, 228, 242n13, 249, 273

Gospel of John, xiv, xxii–xxiii, 1–3, 6–7,
    9–14, 19, 29, 68, 72, 81–82,
    90, 161, 161n6, 175, 181, 248,
    270–71n17, 272n18, 275

SUBJECT INDEX

Gospel of Nicodemus, 134
Gospel of the Ebionites, 18–19, 24–25, 37
Gospel of the Hebrews, 25–26, 218, 224
Gospel of Thomas, 141

harmonization, 6, 11, 68, 72, 81, 91n40, 172n25, 224
Herod, *see* Antipas (Herod)
Herod the Great, 30, 52, 292
Herodians, 89–92, 89n39, 96, 163, 244, 244n16, 254, 260, 263n8, 267, 267n13
Herodias, 23, 161n7, 244
high priest, 2, 257–58, 271 (*see also* priest)
historicity, xxiv, 88, 99, 121, 139, 149, 153, 161, 201, 204n4, 212n20, 218, 269, 270n17

itinerary, xxiv, xxvi, 30, 38, 71, 117, 130–31, 133, 137, 156, 166–68, 184, 192, 219–20, 226, 245, 245n17, 247, 253, 262, 274, 281, 294

Jesus
  birth, xix, 10, 25, 286–92
  baptism, 3, 18, 23–26, 29–31, 39, 96 (*see also* baptism)
  death/crucifixion, xix, 10, 25, 61, 81, 81n26, 92, 99, 118, 149, 201, 212n20, 241, 246, 251, 281–85
  exaltation, 246
  parousia, xxiii, 244, 251, 256, 259, 268, 277n22
  relatives, 23, 110–12, 110n24, 114, 121n39, 141–42,
  resurrection, 202, 241, 246, 254
  suffering, xix, 201–4, 226, 228–29, 241, 246, 272, 278, 281–83
  Temple cleansing, 257, 261–63, 269–72, 278
  temptation, 26–27, 29
  transfiguration, 205–15, 218, 268
John the Baptist, xix, 16–25, 28–31, 36, 77–78, 78n19, 102, 105–7, 136, 147, 159, 161–65, 189, 217, 217n28, 248n23, 258, 266, 272, 287, 289

literary criticism, xxiii–xxiv, 6, 11, 34, 67

legend, 35, 134, 183n47, 195, 215, 282

localization, 21, 34, 49, 55, 64–65, 117

Markan Hypothesis, xxii–xxiii, 12, 14, 40, 45, 66–67, 138, 220n31

New Year festival, *see* feasts and festivals, New Year

oral tradition, 17, 24, 34–35, 116, 118, 192, 210

parable, 107, 109, 114, 116–25, 127, 139, 144, 156, 166, 182, 218, 225, 230–37, 243–44, 250, 252, 254, 256, 258–59, 263, 265–66, 269, 277
participles, 17, 91, 114, 117, 130, 201
Passion Narrative, xix, xxi, 27, 80, 89, 189, 204–5, 226, 251, 281–85
Passover, *see* feasts and festivals, Passover
Pentecost, *see* feasts and festivals, Pentecost
pericope
  introduction(s), 181, 185, 238, 240–41, 243, 255, 262, 277, 281, 318
  use of, 237, 237n1, 255, 265n9
Pharisees, 21–22, 72n8, 77–79, 78n21, 82, 82n27, 89–90, 92, 96–97, 108, 111, 115–16, 166–67, 171, 179, 180n45, 181, 186–88, 191, 197, 209, 217–18, 221, 221n32, 230–31, 233–34, 239–41, 245–46, 250, 254, 256–62, 263n8, 266–67, 269
psychology, xxvi, 12, 101, 174n29, 180n43, 204n4, 292–93
priests, 55–56, 87, 243, 266, 287, 288n2 (*see also* high priest)

Q, *see* Sayings Source Q

report, xxvi, 6–7, 9, 11, 14, 16, 18, 21–22, 24–26, 29, 32, 36–39, 42, 45, 48–49, 50n25, 56, 57n41, 58–60, 62, 66n54, 75, 77–78, 89, 92, 95–97, 108, 110n21, 112, 118, 128, 131, 136, 142, 145, 148, 150–151, 154, 156, 159–161, 164, 179–180, 185, 194, 213, 223, 248–249, 251, 253–54, 256–58, 260–61, 265, 269, 271, 276, 281, 283–86, 289–90

resurrection, 136, 202, 241, 246, 254

Sadducees, 21–22, 89, 89n39, 187, 233, 254, 260–61, 264, 266

Sayings Source Q, 12, 60, 62, 107, 149, 193, 204n5

scribes, 72, 72n8, 74–75, 82, 89, 92, 101, 110n23, 111–12, 115, 166, 179–81, 209, 218, 257–60, 271

Tabernacles, *see* feasts and festivals, Tabernacles

Temple, Jerusalem, 1, 243, 249n24, 253–54, 257, 261–65, 267–72, 278, 280, 288, 290–91

Temple tax, 214–15

text criticism, 15, 50n23, 52, 83, 84, 141, 170, 191, 213, 237n1, 288n4

Two-Source theory, 12–14, 66–67

Ur-Mark, xxiii, 12, 13, 68, 99n10, 120, 122n39, 138n63, 163n12, 175n31, 180n43, 203n4, 223n36

www.ingramcontent.com/pod-product-compliance
Lightning Source LLC
Chambersburg PA
CBHW030434300426
44112CB00009B/992